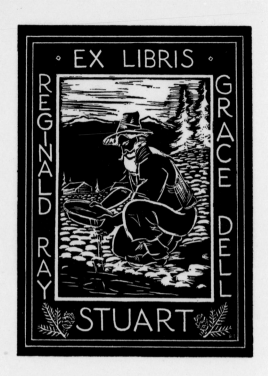

THE FOURTH CORNER

Highlights from the Early Northwest

by

LELAH JACKSON EDSON

MAP INSIDE FRONT AND BACK COVERS DRAWN BY THE AUTHOR

Copyright, 1951, by
LELAH JACKSON EDSON

THIS COPY IS NUMBER

1207

PRINTED IN THE UNITED STATES OF AMERICA
COX BROTHERS, INC., BELLINGHAM, WASHINGTON

ii

DEDICATED

to

EDWARD EDSON

a Pioneer Himself,

Whose Long Life,

Exemplifying the Ideals

of Citizenship, was Devoted

to the Upbuilding and Conservation

of the Resources, Beauties, and Grandeur

of the Northwest He loved so Well,

and to the Preservation

of the History

of the New Land.

CONTENTS

ILLUSTRATIONS

ILLUSTRATIONS

FOREWORD

One volume at best can give no more than a few highlights of Pioneer History. Thousands of citizens who have played important parts in the development of the land and its institution, deserve mention. Hundreds of incidents merit tabulation. Available space limits this recording.

The events described, the individuals portrayed herein, have been selected because they are typical of the life, the times, and the country along the Northwest Border. It is hoped the included "highlights" will give the reader flashes from a picture-roll that starts with the primitive and runs through the hectic years of railroad building and final union of the four towns around Bellingham Bay in 1904. Nothing more is intended.

Because the immigrant's first, and often his most important, contact was with the Indian, a brief sketch of Puget Sound tribes has been given space in this book.

This work represents years of careful research. Some of the matter herein, when presented before pioneer and other societies, has created a lively interest, manifested by numerous requests for copies of such addresses. It is believed that these chapters will supply such need.

Finally, the author wishes to mention the encouragement received from her brother, H. C. Jackson, in the preparation of this history; also his aid in revising and editing the manuscript.

LELAH JACKSON EDSON

Chapter I.

AS IT WAS IN THE BEGINNING

BELLINGHAM BAY

INDENTING THE SHORE of Washington's northwest county, close to a sister Nation's friendly soil, is Bellingham Bay; screened by neighboring islands, and offering shelter to weary storm tossed travelers. For many placid centuries it remained, serene, undisturbed; girt with magnificent forests; its shores and waters alive with furry, feathered, and finny denizens; while traversed only by the simple Redman, who took from Nature's bounty what he needed for his own use;—that, and no more. Then the White Man came.

The fur traders were not the first Whites to visit Bellingham Bay. Nor the Russian or British explorers. Earlier yet were the Spanish who established a post at Hermosa, the little inlet around which Fairhaven was later built. For years the outlines of the old fortifications were plainly visible, as were burial mounds from which many skeletons were later exhumed, and proven by experts to be the remains of Spanish Cavaliers. These explorers in turn were followed by Spanish raiders, who in a roaring three day fight, went down to bloody defeat at the hands of the assembled Indian Tribes.

THE BELLINGHAM HERALD of February 9, 1936 recounts the struggle as follows:

"There is an old story handed down from generation to generation by Indians to early settlers of Whatcom County which told of a terrific fight staged at what is now South Bellingham, near where the Pacific American Fisheries now stand. According to the tale it was where Padden Creek empties into Harris Bay, which is part of Bellingham Bay. The battle was between several hundred Spanish pirates and a horde of Western and Northern Indians. (Opposite page 278).

"The early settlers were told that the Spaniards, on a prolonged marauding expedition, anchored in Bellingham Bay, years before Vancouver's flagship poked its nose through the waters of the North Pacific. Their frequent incursions into the lands of the Redmen, then at the height of their power, aroused the Indians and plans were quickly laid for the Spaniards' destruction. The Spaniards were about 400 in number and occupied two galleons.

1

"As the fleet sailed slowly along the coast after a number of depredations, runners sent out by the various tribes, watched them from the hilltops and reported to their chiefs. When it was seen that the pirates were heading for Bellingham Bay, word was sent to the tribes which had previously agreed to their annihilation, and soon warriors from all over the Sound and from farther North gathered along the shores of the harbor.

"The Indians were arranged under the command of Ractamoos, a renowned Chief of the Nisqually Tribe. Ractamoos, with remarkable foresight stationed his force, numbering about a thousand warriors, in the thick wood that later on was called 'Deadman's Point.' The galleons did not enter the Bay until late one afternoon, and high noon next day had passed before they cast anchor opposite the point where the foe waited.

"After the ships were secure, the Spaniards set out for the shore in small boats. The Indians allowed the entire force of heavily armed adventurers to proceed some distance up Padden Creek, when, with the fury of demons, they began their attack. The outlaws were taken by surprise and rushed for their boats, several of which had been smashed by the Indians.

"The fight continued for three days and nights and hundreds from both sides were killed. The Spaniards lost their leader and attempted to reach the vessels. About 150 of them out of 400 got away, only to suffer death, when the ships reached the Straits and encountered a heavy gale.

"The spot is peaceful enough now, almost deserted, except for the shadows of the cannery, but when the haughty Spaniards and the bloodthirsty Redmen met, blood ran in streams for three days and nights. The conflict ended in the routing of the pirates, according to the Indian tradition, and ultimately their galleons were wrecked and all hands lost in a furious storm which swept over the Strait of Juan de Fuca.

"Historians have said that this is the only instance of an inter-tribal agreement among the Indians of Puget Sound and the North. Later quarrels arose and the tribes became bitter enemies."

The forests which the Spaniards saw, and in which they fought and died, stretched unbrokenly the length and breadth of Puget Sound—as magnificent a body of timber as the World has seen in the present Geological Age.

Seeded four hundred years earlier, its Douglas Firs*, the principal stand, were young vigorous spires, taller than a great ship's masts when Columbus discovered America. Germinated under favorable conditions they crowded the soil so thickly at first that only a squirrel might crawl

---

*Named for David Douglas, London Horticultural Society, 1825.

between the seedling trunks. Fighting their fellows for space, they raced upward toward the sun, the weaklings perishing by the hundreds, while the branches of the others withered and died for lack of light. It was an ideal situation for producing perfect knot-free lumber.

At last the vigorous young survivors crowned out, a hundred feet to the first limb, and thereafter shot their spires higher and higher, rubbing heads and shoulders so closely with their fellows that only a stray bar of sunshine ever reached the moss covered floor so far below.

Yet despite this lusty struggle, the Douglas Fir always was a friendly tree. On moist and richer land the cedar wrestled with him mightily, while on tidal areas the Sitka Spruce gained mastery. Other firs, cedar, hemlocks, larch and yew, accepted the challenge and proved their worth. Unlike his relative, the pine, the Douglas Fir did not cover the forest floor with an inhospitable needle blanket. His short needles disintegrated rapidly. Hence his cousins of the deciduous family crept in and found haven. The result, a forest so dense no horseman could penetrate it. Years afterward when man had done his worst—when the farmer had cleared the logs from his land, he discovered that the stumps, five to ten feet in diameter, were so closely spaced that he could not drive his wagon through his pasture.

These were silent woods mostly. Living creatures seemed awed by the majesty of the cathedral arches overhead, by the dim lights, by the columnar trunks reaching skyward. (Opposite page 7).

A tiny bird might utter an unexpected cheep, then go into uneasy silence, startled by his brashness. Only the blue jay would be brazen enough to raise his raucous charge of "Thief" at the bear, quietly digging skunk cabbage roots. Briskly a little tree squirrel would shrill his "Chickare-e-e" as he fed on the cone seeds far aloft.

Far off the woods might be startled by the sudden drum of the giant woodpecker on a hollow trunk—then his long drawn challenge shrilling from those distant tops, like an Alpine trumpet call rocketing from the crags. Yes, a brave cry, that of this great bird, brave as his flashing red crest; withal filled with sadness as if this symbol of the primitive woods sensed his own doom in the edict of Nature that he must vanish from the face of the Earth with the passing of the virgin forest.

A deer slipped silently through the sword ferns, around a fallen trunk, through a salal patch, then into a vine-maple thicket. Back of him trailed an Indian, just as silent——much more patient——All this——as it was in the beginning.

Then the Rape of the Woods by the White Man, by his fires. A blackened landscape——Stark jagged snags of all heights, great defoliated and charred tree trunks tumbled like jack straws, often crossed fifteen feet above the ground. An area where travel is possible only along the fallen giants——150 feet this way, a drop to another trunk and 100 feet at another angle, zigzagging perhaps 200 or 300 feet to gain 100 feet in a desired direction——all the hideous indescribable chaos left by a great forest fire ——Nature's work for half a millennium wiped out by the White Man—— woods, soil, wild things——gone irretrievably from dwellers of the Modern World.

BELLINGHAM BAY AND PUGET SOUND NAMED

Bellingham Bay was so named in 1792 by Captain George Vancouver, while on his famous expedition up the West Coast and into the inland seas. Presumably it was named for Sir William Bellingham, controller of the British Navy storekeeper's accounts, who personally checked Vancouver's supplies before he sailed from England, April, 1791. The inland sea was named "Puget Sound" for Lieutenant Peter Puget, who served under Captain Vancouver, and who on May 19, 1792, while Vancouver was anchored at Restoration Point opposite the site of Seattle, explored the westward passage. Captain Vancouver and Lieutenant Joseph Baker explored the eastern passage a week later, and discovered the large island which they named Vashon Island in honor of Captain James Vashon of the British Navy.

When Captain George Vancouver sailed down the Strait of Juan de Fuca his third lieutenant, Joseph Baker, saw and reported a large mountain on April 30, 1792. Vancouver promptly named it, Mount Baker, in honor of the vigilant lieutenant.

Vancouver's chart shows that the name of Puget Sound applies to the bays and inlets south of the present Tacoma and Narrows. Later the term was modified over the decades to include other waters northward. At Bellingham Bay, May 1, 1913, Judge Ralston of the Superior Court of Clallam County rendered a decision holding that for the purposes of the fishing laws, the Strait of Juan de Fuca is part of "Puget Sound."

Chapter II.

INDIANS OF THE NORTHWEST

HISTORIANS AGREE that the clash of the Indian's Stone Age culture with the White Man's Way of Life through territorial days was as inevitable as the movement of the tides. The two could not exist together.

The massacres, raids, battles in Washington Territory were but part of the Redman's uncomprehending struggle to save his hunting grounds, his way of life, his freedom. Such names as Whitman Massacre, 1847; White River Massacre, 1855; Battle of Seattle, 1856; Battle of Steptoe Butte, 1858; in the Indian's struggle for liberty, are as significant, perhaps to him, as Lexington, Valley Forge, The Alamo, are to the Whites. The difference —the Indian fought on the losing side.

The cruelty, the savagery of the Indian appalls the mind of civilized man, who forgets that less than 400 years ago his own ancestors were inflicting every refinement of cruelty on captured foes or religious dissenters, the Rules of Land Warfare ("Civilized") being then unknown. To the thoughtful observer the slashing, desperate forays of the Indians remind one of the slashing jaws and terrified eyes of the hopelessly trapped wild animal.

Personal effects only were property to the Indian. Land, territory, were communal holdings useful for hunting and fishing grounds. The arrival of the first white settlers did not disturb him. The traders of the Hudson's Bay Company had not changed his way of life nor usurped his hunting grounds. There was land enough for these few palefaces.

Then the avalanche of settlers startled him. Unfair treaties dispossessing him of his lands made him realize his liberties were threatened. His proud spirit, his sense of being wronged, his fear, made him take the warpath in defense of his rights and liberties. This determination perhaps was hastened by the attitude of some whites, that the only good Indian was a dead Indian; by some Southerners who treated the natives as they would negro slaves; by the downright cruelty of some citizens; by white tricksters.

To many in authority at the time, the territorial wars were insignificant, were even ignored. History passes the struggle casually. Yet the Indian Wars in Washington Territory were more inclusive, covered more territory, caused more families to abandon their homes and property while seeking

5

safety in the blockhouses, than any like struggle since colonial days. The Territorial muster rolls show that practically every male over fifteen years, was called to military service—proof of the seriousness of the struggle.

That the early settlers were not exterminated is due perhaps: First, to the fact that the Puget Sound tribes had broken up into small independent bands, (Governor Isaac I. Stevens had to appoint chiefs in one case so he would have some one in authority with whom to negotiate a treaty.) (The white man's diseases, also had thinned many tribes.) Second, to the raids of the warlike Northern Indians who reduced once powerful tribes to small fractions of their early strength. The report of Edmund C. Fitzhugh, Special Indian Agent in 1857, for Whatcom County, shows to what numbers the local northern tribes had declined:

The report: "The total number of all—men, women and children— estimated at 1,250, divided as follows: Neuk-sacks, 450; Lummis, 510; Samish, 150; and the Sticks, or Neukwers, and Sia-man-nas, about 200."

*Racially the Indians of Puget Sound mostly belonged to the Flathead family, so called because of the habit of binding and flattening the heads of infants. Morally and intellectually they were similar to other Indians of the Continent.

Physically these canoe-using Indians were more squat and shorter limbed than the plain Indians. Some observers attributed this to their way of life. Certainly they had an easier existence than Eastern tribesmen. A mild climate, an abundance of fuel and water, a plentitude of food in forests, streams, bays, and on the tide-flats; all this perhaps induced laziness.

Culturally, according to Judge G. Swan, the women occupied a higher place in family and tribal life than with most Eastern Indians. Some writers have attributed this to the fact that to the woman fell so large a part of the work of securing and preparing food and clothing.

Their social and religious system, Totemism, was symbolized by their totem poles which on the British North Coast, reached a height in color ornamentation, complexity and size, unknown elsewhere. Judge G. Swan says: "In the Indian mind there has always been a close relationship between the Indian race and the wild animals. If the bear became his totem, he looked upon that animal as a friend and partner in all his undertakings.

---

*Data from the following authorities:

Official report of Edmund Clare Fitzhugh, Special Indian Agent of the Bellingham Bay Agency, to the Secretary of Interior, June 18, 1857.

"INDIAN HISTORY AND TRADITIONS" by Eva Charroin Lambert, from Roth's "HISTORY OF WHATCOM COUNTY, WASHINGTON."

Judge James G. Swan's notations on the Indians, from "HISTORY OF THE PUGET SOUND COUNTRY" by Colonel W. F. Prosser.

"INDIANS OF THE PACIFIC NORTHWEST" by Ruth Underhill, Ph. D.

AEROVIEW
OF
WHATCOM COUNTY
WASHINGTON

GEORGIA STRAIT

BRITISH COLUMBIA

TO VANCOUVER

BLAINE

BIRCH BAY

LUMMI BAY

FERRY

LUMMI

BELLINGHAM BAY

BELLINGHAM

PACIFIC HWY.

MT. BAKER

LAKE WHATCOM ELEV. 311' LENGTH 12 MI.

LYNDEN

MT. BAKER HWY.

SOUTH FORK

NORTH FORK

MT. BAKER LODGE

MT. SHUKSAN 9 038'

MT. BAKER ELEV. 10 827'

It became his totem to be carved upon a pillar to be placed in front of his home or on the door-post. A number of totems representing the different families of the tribe might be carved on one pillar, the totem of the chief, placed at the top.

"All the men having the bear . . . for their totem, were supposed to belong to one clan or band, and the social relation between them was in some respects a sacred one, fully as strong as any blood relationship."

The local Indians carved pictographs symbolic of their patron saints or se-ow-en, on the pillars and door-posts of their lodges and "potlatch" houses. The ever-present totem stick marked the ancient burial places of the Lummis, where their dead were put away on the Reservation, and along the River, and the shores of Lake Whatcom. For many years there were well preserved relics of their carvings on the Reservation, and near what were later the towns of Ferndale and Lynden. Now they are gone, having been destroyed by the forest fires. Petroglyphs may be seen today carved on the rocks at Lake Whatcom. (See opposite page).

Each of the early tribes had its own language, and while the tribes of the Coast had some general word roots in common, the language of the Indians east of the mountains was foreign to the western ones. The canoe Indians accustomed to travel a great deal, became familiar with many of the languages; but the interior Indians knew only one tongue. So the Hudson's Bay Company which traded with them all, invented a sort of language which they called "Chinook," containing words of all the different tribes—the French patois of the early voyageurs, the Latin of the missionary priests, and the English and slang of both the colonies, and the United States. The Indians readily learned this jargon and could talk to the white men.

TRIBES

While Puget Sound Indians in general, belonged to the Salishan, or Flathead family, they were divided into many tribes. The most important were the Semiahmoo near the British Boundary line, and the ones on the eastern shores of Puget Sound, which were the Nooksacks, Lummis, Skagits, Samish, Snoqualmies, Duwamish, Puyallups, Nisquallies and the Chehalis. On the west shores were the Skokomish or Twanas, Chinook, Chemakum and Clallam tribes, while lesser bands among all of them, were the Sumas, Suquamps, Swinomish, Stillacooms, Squaxons, Sammamish and Satsops.

The Nuh-Lummis comprised the Lummis, Samish, Semiahmoo and Nooksack bands. The land surrounding Bellingham Bay belonged to them.

UPPER—A hemlock, a Douglas fir, a spruce and a cedar.

LOWER—An Indian petroglyph carved on a rock at Lake Whatcom, Washington.—Photo by the author, 1948.

The Samish tribe lived in what is Skagit County today, giving its name to the Samish River, Samish Island and Samish Bay. The word "Samish" is said to be derived from the Skagit word "samens," a hunter. They were more of a wandering class than many of the other tribes, and fished among the islands and in the channels, claiming several of the islands as their own. They were governed by one chief. In the 1840's, they were one of the largest tribes of the Sound, numbering over 2,000, but were nearly annihilated by hordes of Haidas and Tsimshian Indians, who came down from the North. (The Haidas were from Queen Charlotte Island and the Tsimshians from the central part of the west coast of Canada.) They came for the purpose of taking slaves, and killing all they could not carry off. One Flathead slave was worth more than two Roundheads. In 1856, they had over 2,000 slaves, and had traded some off with those living farther north. These Northern Indians were supplied at an early day with more firearms than the Sound Indians, therefore had a decided advantage over them.

Neuk-Sacks or Noot-saak, or Nooksacks gave their name to the river on which they lived. Their largest village was near what later was called "Nooksack Crossing" close to the present town of Everson. Nooksack meant "fern-eating people," for "Noot" means "people," and "sa-ak" means "fern or bracken roots." The Nooksack Indians ate fern roots as a regular diet. They were divided into three bands, under three heads, but all under one chief.

The Sem-mi-an-mas or Semiahmoos, a tribe of that name which lived in the northwestern part of what became Whatcom County. They too were a powerful tribe at one time, but had suffered at the hands of the same Northern Indians. They had a large prairie country back from the coast for safety's sake; but they would rather live on the bay, and would go there to get shell-fish and vegetables. They inter-married with the north band of the Lummis, Cowegans and Quantlums and moved backward and forward with those tribes for protection.

The Semiahmoos have a legend that over a hundred years ago, Chief Semiahmoo and his people were living peacefully on the Spit, when suddenly the Northern Canadian Indians descended upon them. The Spit Indians were driven to Point Roberts. Chief Semiahmoo was one of the few to get away. Some of them swam. A few took boats, setting fire behind them. Most of the tribe were brutally slaughtered, and the few Indians who survived the massacre moved over on the Canadian side.

The Neuk-wers and Sia-man-nas that the settlers called "Stick Indians" lived back in the woods on some of the lakes in the interior.

The Lummis are believed to have been an island tribe originally for they formerly lived upon and controlled Lopez, Shaw, Orcas, San Juan and Lummi Islands. "Lummi Island" was charted under that name by the United States Coast Survey of 1853, "because inhabited by that tribe." The ancient Lummi name of the island was Skallaham. The Lummis were a very powerful tribe at one time, but the islands were so open to attack from the Northern Indians, that their numbers were greatly reduced and they were driven to the mainland. They in turn drove the Nooksacks and Sakuanch tribes back from Bellingham Bay, up the Nooksack River, while the fishing grounds at the mouth of the river and at Whatcom Creek were taken over by the Lummis.

The custom known as "potlach," from the Nooksack word "Patshal," meaning a gift, was common to the Puget Sound Indians and unknown south of the Columbia or east of the Cascades.

This was like a magnified Christmas sharing of gifts, with this difference, the giver of the potlatch beggered himself in his gift distribution, all of which redounded to his credit and honor.

It was the ambition of every Indian to give a potlatch, and for this purpose he collected gifts for years—such things as calico, knives, canoes, and Indian shell money. Sometimes two or more families gave a potlatch. Roth's History of Whatcom County tells of such a potlatch given by the Samish Indians on Guemes Island about 1875, that lasted two or three weeks and to which friends from many other Sound tribes were invited.

One of the entertaining families would distribute their belongings one day, another the next. This continued until there was nothing left to give. For their part, the guests or visiting tribesmen brought special food delicacies such as cranberries, roasted camas root, fern root, blue berries, sun dried sockeyes, etc.

Besides the gift distibution and feasting, the potlatch included games, contests, and dramatic entertainment. Most of the activity took place in the great tribal potlatch house, made of split cedar lumber and capable of holding hundreds of celebrants.

Roth's History reports that Old Chief Chow-its-hoot (Cha-wit-zit), head of the Nuh-Lummis at the time of the Treaty,* gave seven potlatches in the course of his life and was considered a great man indeed. It is said he waxed wealthy through his success in gambling, but beggered himself in the end with his potlatches.

INDIAN MASSACRES

Legends of the Lummi tribes recount the tale of many raids and battles through the decades as tribal strength was reduced to a pitiful remnant,

---

*Mukilteo Treaty, January 22, 1855, Signed by Cha-wit-zit.

by the forays of the war-like slave hunting Indians of Canada and Alaska.

Tale of one such massacre, engraved on Indian minds because the Lummi tribe never recovered from the blow, is repeated in the WHATCOM EVENING BLADE—1901. According to the oldsters—the Lummi warriors had gone to the mountains to hunt. Women, children, and old men had set up a summer camp on Eliza Island. Thence they made daily excursions to Lummi Island to gather berries for winter use. Northern raiders were not expected until later in the season.

One evening as the fires were dying, the sound of paddles was heard off shore. Young boys thinking their men folks were returning, ran shouting to the water's edge. A minute later their shouts turned to shrieks of pain and terror, as a horde of Yakutat warriors in war paint, shrilling their war cries, swept through the camp. knifing and tomahawking all, young and old alike; then firing the camp and tossing victims' bodies into the flames.

Two of the Lummis only, escaped from the south side of the island where they found a hidden canoe. They made their way to Lummi Island under cover of darkness. Corpses of between three and four hundred Lummis —mostly women and children were left on the camp site. Others were carried into captivity.

A year or so later the Lummi braves had revenge on the Yakutat warriors. Again it was summer. The Lummis learned of the approach of the Northerners. All warriors were summoned to the potlatch house. There the best canoemen were selected and sent out into Hale's Pass to lure the invaders toward the Portage where the armed Lummis waited in ambush.

The Yakutats swallowed the bait, pursued the Lummis to the shore; and into the woods. Suddenly every stump and bush sprouted a Lummi Brave. Surrounded, under a hail of arrows, the Yakutats rallied and fought desperately for more than two hours until the last was killed. No one remained to carry North the message of defeat. The dead—more than two hundred. What the Lummi losses were is unknown. According to Indian customs they boasted they lost not a single warrior.

LUMMI RESERVATION

Chief Cha-wit-zit, or Tsawitsoot signed the memorable Mukilteo Treaty, January 22, 1855.

The original Lummi Reservation was about twice the size it is now, (1951), and upon it were settled not only the Lummi people, but the Nooksack, the Samish and the Semiahmoo tribes also. After a few years it became evident that all these tribes could not live together in peace, so the Nooksacks were permitted to acquire land the same as the white settlers did, by living upon it, but they could not dispose of it as the whites did. The

Samish were given another reservation and the Semiahmoos moved north of the Boundary line. The Lummi Reservation which originally included Ferndale, was contracted to its present proportions.

INDIAN CANOES

In no line did the art and artisans of the Northwest Indians reach a higher plane than in their great carved cedar canoes. Hewed from a single log, capable perhaps of holding fifty warriors or more, with high ornamented prow, these graceful vessels skimmed the waves like living things. In fact America owes a debt to these lowly native craftsmen, since it was from the Indian canoe that the shipbuilders of the Atlantic took the lines of the famous Baltimore Clipper that made it possible, at one time, for the United States to rule the waves as a maritime nation.

No one whoever has witnessed an intertribal race nearing the finish line, each with eleven paddles flashing in the rays of the setting sun, can forget the stirring picture.

The marvel of it all is that the primitive canoe maker was able to produce such an efficient and beautiful vessel with the tools at hand— charring fires; hot water; wedges of sharp rock, bone, elk's horn, wood; stone adzes, and shell scrapers.

"INDIANS OF THE PACIFIC NORTHWEST" by Ruth Underhill, Ph. D., contains the following on canoe making:

"Not every man could make a canoe . . . Perhaps they had spirit helpers and perhaps they observed special taboos while working. Hardly anyone could make the big sea going canoe except the Makah and Quinault or most skillful of all, the Nootka on Vancouver Island. A man might save furs for years in order to visit that land of specially big cedars and order the craft he wanted.

"The canoe maker had to choose a log which was the right length and of even thickness all the way, without branches. For the big seagoing canoes, this meant a giant tree. The canoe was made from one half the log split lengthways, or perhaps a little more than half a log. It was roughly shaped and hollowed out by splitting out slabs with the wedges. The fine work was done by patient charring with fire and hacking off the charcoal with an adze. Good Nootka canoes show rows of adze marks like beading across the canoe bottom.

"The canoe maker worked on the beach where he could get sheets of the big sea lettuce for dampening. He measured entirely by eye until the dugout was nearly in final shape. Then he bored holes through the sides at intervals and thrust a stick through to measure their thickness. Later he plugged these holes with pieces of wood.

"His log had not only to be hollowed out but to be shaped and curved. For this, the canoe maker used cooking methods. He poured the canoe almost full of water and then put hot stones into it. Also he built a little fire under it, and between the two, the wood was steamed until it was soft and pliable. Meantime the workers cut stout pieces of yew wood, just the width the canoe was to have at various points along its length. At the center, it would be considerably wider than the original log, while it would taper at both ends. He wedged these sticks between the gunwales, like thwarts, so that they kept the sides bulging. Then he dipped out the water and allowed the canoe to dry in its curved shape. Finally, the thwarts were fastened tightly to the sides of the canoe, by cedar withes, passed through holes in thwart and gunwale . . .

"The inside of the canoe was usually colored red. The Indians made a sort of oil paint by mixing red ochre with fish or seal oil as modern paint is mixed with linseed oil. The outside, after being smoothed with shark skin was charred lightly with a cedar bark torch. This singed off the roughnesses and left it black. When it became rough from use it was charred again.

. . .

"In Washington, the canoe got the name of Chinook from the Whites, perhaps because it was seen first among the Columbia River people. Every inch of the Chinook was planned for efficiency in the rough sea, and White sailors have reported that it ships less water in a storm than any craft in the world. Meriwether Lewis wrote: 'I have seen the natives near the coast riding waves with safety, and apparently without concern, where I should have thought it impossible for any craft to live a minute.'

"One secret of the construction was the extra, curved projections at bow and stern, carved from a separate piece of cedar and attached with pegs . . . These 'sitting pieces' gave the canoe the effect of a living creature. Indians said it was like a salmon, flat and wide in the middle, tapering and curving up at both ends. The bow end projected most since this must spread the oncoming seas. In landing, when the breakers caught the canoe from behind, it was turned around and brought in stern fore-most.

". . . Paddles were made from yew or maple wood and polished smooth with sharkskin. Some were pointed at the end, so that they could be dug into the beach to hold the canoe. Others were notched, so as to fit over a rope when the canoe was being towed." The usual shape was rounded. (Published by the Education Division of the United States Office of Indian Affairs. United States Department of the Interior.)

The outward bending of this soaked, steamed, wood-shell, to the proper position, and not the carving of the canoe to the desired shape, insured parallel unbroken grain in the sides; not cross grain that would split easily across or break.

The smaller, blunt nosed canoes were used mostly on the rivers, and were called "shovel-nose." The hull usually was flat in the middle with the ends shaped like a shovel or tray, for sliding over sand bars, and for ease in poling or paddling up shallow streams.

The big canoes used on the salt water were called "salt chuck" canoes, and were of great help to the early settlers when used by the Indians in moving the settlers' goods and families across the bays. If a journey continued up a river, the load was transferred from the "salt chuck" to the "shovel-nose" to make the ascent.

Chapter III.

THE WHITE MAN COMES TO BELLINGHAM BAY

FOLLOWING THE EXPLORERS into the Northwest came the furtraders, mostly dominated by the Hudson's Bay Company, whose chiefs, when the fur trade diminished, turned more and more to agriculture. In 1838, the Puget Sound Agricultural Company, a subsidiary of the Hudson's Bay Company, was organized with a capital of £200,000.

At the time the ownership of the Oregon country was a burning political question—one of international dispute. Possession seemed dependent upon colonization. Accordingly Doctor McLoughlin, as manager of the Agricultural Company, in 1841, brought thirteen families from the Red River of the North to Nisqually, the first of a hoped-for British migration. These settlers became dissatisfied with the treatment received, and mostly moved elsewhere or returned to Canada.

When Doctor Elijah White led his little party of Americans into Fort Vancouver in 1842, Doctor McLoughlin recognized it as the beginning of the end so far as concerned British domination north of the Columbia. The great migration of the '40's was under way, and while company officials discouraged settlement north of the river and tried to turn the immigrants into the Willamette valley, an increasing number turned toward Puget Sound.

Tumwater was settled in 1845, but because the Oregon question was unsettled the recent arrivals were in mental turmoil as shown by the following extracts from letters written by Samuel B. Crockett* to his mother, Mrs. Mary Crockett, of Putnam County, Missouri. After describing the country in his first letter, written from Linton, Quality County, Oregon Territory, February 16, 1845, he says:

"Much has been said and heard about the Hudson's Bay Company in the United States, that I do assure you is totally false for if it were not for the many favors that they have bestowed on the settlers of his country, that they would have suffered greatly. The Hudson's Bay Company imports large quantities of store goods, groceries and tools of every description

*These letters are owned by Mrs. Mabel Donovan Bacon of Bellingham, Washington, and were written by her grandfather, who came West in the Michael Simmon's party.

which they sell at Fort Vancouver and their various posts in Oregon."

He then told about the weather and how he had put in his time in boating and making rails and shingles, getting one dollar per hundred rails and five dollars a thousand for cedar shingles. His second letter was from the Puget Sound District, July 4, 1846:

"The Hudson's Bay Company has a trading post and farm about 25 miles north of us where we get our store goods and some of our provisions.

"I cannot tell you whether I will come to Missouri or not, it depends a good deal on how the boundary line of this county is settled, if England gets this part of Oregon I think I will return, but if the United States gets it, it is very doubtful. You may tell my brothers that they should not be anxious about coming to this country until they know who this country belongs to; no earthly event would give me more happiness than to see all settled in this country, but I cannot advise any of you to come while the country is in its present condition.

"I was over to the Willamette a few weeks ago when I saw a good many of the emigrants, some of them are very much dissatisfied, some are talking of going to California and others to the States and all are extremely anxious that the United States may take possession of Oregon.

"A British man-of-war arrived a few weeks ago in Pugits sound, it came from Mexico and brought papers from the United States since Jan. last. They contained President Polk's message and some other news from Congress. The President's message has been published in the Oregon Spectator and read by the citizens of Oregon. It has given great satisfaction and encouragement to the American people here, and I think if the leading men of the United States are of the same spirit and opinions as President Polk, that Oregon will belong to the United States."

S. B. Crockett.

Oregon Territory	Lewis County
Newmarket	Pugits Sound

(This was at Tumwater)

It was weeks afterward, before the settlers learned that the treaty between Great Britain and the United States, fixing the boundary at the Forty-ninth parallel and placing what is now Oregon, Washington, Idaho, and parts of Wyoming and Montana under the American flag, had been signed June 15, 1846 and duly ratified two weeks later. Thereupon the Willamette Valley people, according to the Oregon Spectator of September 3, 1846, celebrated by mounting their only cannon on the rocks of the river bank and firing a salute of twenty-one guns.

And thereafter by trail and canoe, the American tide slowly flowed north toward the new boundary line.

WILLIAM ROBERT (BLANKET BILL) JARMAN
April 3, 1820 — June 11, 1912
1848

Woven through the chronicle of Puget Sound and the Northwest, from Hudson Bay times to recent years, is the colorful story of "Blanket Bill" Jarman, who apparently savored each drop of his ninety-two-year-long-life to a degree granted few men. (Opposite page 22).

Sailor, deserter, trader, hunter and fisherman, fur dealer, Indian slave, tribesman, squawman, homesteader, ship master, telegraph linesman, army courier and mail carrier, interpreter, bar tender, accused murderer, gold digger; there was little he did not find interesting and zestful. The first known white man to visit Bellingham Bay shores (1848), except for the early Spaniards and Hudson's Bay trappers, Jarman retained his vigor until near the end. His niece, Mrs. William Manning of Ferndale with whom he lived until his death, June 11, 1912, reported that every morning, summer or winter, the aged man would run from his cabin on the banks of the Nooksack, plunge into the icy waters of the glacial stream, swim across, climb the bank, turn, dive and make the return swim.

Friends have described Jarman as a fine looking man of upright athletic build, that gave hint of his powers of endurance. A pleasant smile frequently lighted his face above a flowing black beard and grenadier mustachios. In his eyes was something that seemed to affect both red and white maidens alike, as attested by many affairs, marriages, and quasi-marriages. Even in old age, traces of Blanket Bill's good looks remained, although the once luxuriant black beard had shrunken to a broad white goatee, while his heavy white mustache drooped like that of Buffalo Bill.

William Robert Jarman was born at Gravesend, England, April 3, 1820, according to an interview he gave Frank C. Teck, a Whatcom and Fairhaven newspaper man in the year 1897. Coming from a seafaring family, he was early apprenticed to a relative, Captain Henry Jarman.

After some years, Jarman's ship touched at the port of Oberton, Tasmania, in 1844. There the crew deserted. However, Jarman a l o n e escaped, the other deserters being captured and returned to the ship. From Oberton, Jarman walked barefoot to Lanceton, a distance of 122 miles.

He next crossed to King Island, Australia, and signed with Captain Richard Hardy of the trading brig, *Playtpus*, engaged in picking up furseal, platypus and kangaroo skins. Two years later the brig was in the North Pacific. Jarman possessed a number of fur seals, platypus and other skins which he hoped to unload eventually on the China Market for an estimated one thousand dollars. Failing to find the mouth of the Columbia, the *Platypus* continued to Nootka Sound, Vancouver Island, where a number of beaver and sea-otter skins were secured.

At Nootka Sound, the brig anchored to take on water. Captain Hardy and Jarman went ashore with the water casks, which they hired the Indians to fill. The vessel's crew numbered but nine men exclusive of Jarman. Because of his low strength, and the reputation of the Nootkas for treachery, Captain Hardy had taken the precaution of putting out boarding nets on the *Platypus*. At noon the Captain went aboard with a boatload of casks, leaving Jarman ashore. Almost immediately a flotilla of canoes swarmed around the little vessel, the Nootkas attacking with spears, bows and arrows, and two or three Hudson's Bay flint-locks, while the more agile braves tried to climb over the netting. The crew fought desperately, and with the aid of the netting, checked the attack until they could slip their moorings, hoist sail, and stand out in the channel. Incidentally Jarman never heard again of the *Platypus*.

He was captured and immediately became a pawn between the Nootka Chief and the Chief's brother, who had led the attack. The Chief wanted the distinction of possessing a white slave. The Chief's brother wanted to kill the white man in revenge for the killing or wounding of his warriors during the fight. Several attempts were made on Jarman's life but later he knew safety, when the Chief bought off his brother with gifts of blue beads and other trinkets.

The white slave seems to have fitted into the Indian way of life, and to have achieved some standing with them during the next two years. He reported he had two Indian wives while with the Nootkas, neither of whom he liked, but that the Indians wanted it that way. This was in 1846.

In the summer of 1848, Governor James Douglas, head of the Hudson's Bay Company at Victoria, heard of the white man's plight and negotiated for his release. Jarman was placed in a canoe, taken to Victoria, and there ransomed for thirty-two blankets, a pile equal to his height. Thereafter, he was known as "Blanket Bill" to the whites, and "Paseesie" to the Indians, that being their word for blanket.

Jarman remained in Victoria a month or two, acting as messenger from the Governor's office to the Fort. A steady job and civilized regulations irked him after the free and easy life with the Indians, so in 1848, he seized a canoe one night and crossed the Strait of Juan de Fuca to Wilson Point, near the present site of Port Townsend. There he moved into the Clallam Village under their Chief King George and easily slipped back to the Indian way of life. In fact he took an Indian wife, Alice. With her he crossed to the East shore of the Sound and pre-empted 160 acres, southeast of Lake Samish, which was called "Jarman's Prairie." He proved up on this tract but later lost it on a mortgage. While on this claim, he hunted around the site of what later was Whatcom. This was in 1848.

About 1853, Jarman filed on a double donation claim of 640 acres near the present site of Edison on Samish Flats, but failed to prove up. He named the adjacent inlet, "Alice Bay," in honor of his Clallam wife. This body of water later was called "Squaw Bay." Bill's daughter, Alice, was born on this claim when Jarman was Post Mail Messenger.

During the year Blanket Bill was with the Clallams, he became acquainted with the Chemakum Indians, who lived near the present Port Townsend. The customs and language of these people, according to Jarman, were entirely different from those of the Clallams.

In 1848, the Chemakums, under their chief, General Gaines, had been reduced to 200 souls, while the Clallams numbered 2,000. The downfall of the Chemakums dated from the year 1842-'43, when their village was raided by Skagit and Snohomish Indians from across the Sound. At that time the Chemakum village was defended by wooden fortifications or palisades, consisting of timbers driven into the ground. The enemy fired these palisades and as the Chemakums fled to escape the fire, the hostiles killed a large portion of them with spears, knives or arrows, which were made of bone, stone, or wood.

The California gold strike fired the imagination of the few white men in the Northwest, and Blanket Bill became one of these, joining the rush in 1849. He reported that he spent the summer mining on Long Bar on the North Fork of the Yuba River, twenty miles northwest of Marysville, California, but he contracted malaria ("chills and fever" he called it), and so returned to Port Townsend.

Potatoes were grown extensively by the Indians of the Sound. These were a white, rough-skinned variety of Irish potatoes, originally introduced by the Hudson's Bay Company. All supplies were in great demand in California, so Bill traded beads and blankets with the Indians for a cargo of potatoes, purchased at the rate of ten cents a bushel, cranberries at six cents a bushel and feathers at four or five cents a pound. Port wine and London Dock brandy were selling in Victoria at fifteen dollars per gallon at the time and Jarman's limited capital would not permit his including these popular liquors in his cargo. In San Francisco he sold his potatoes at seven dollars and a half per bushel, cranberries at a dollar and a half per gallon, and feathers at one dollar per pound.

The trip to San Francisco in 1850, was made in the 150 ton Brig *North Bend* which carried a load of piling. Other vessels in which he visited California (the ports of San Pedro and San Francisco), Chile and the Sandwich Islands, included the Brig *George Emory* and the Brigantine *Jane*.

During the Indian troubles in the south, including the attack on Seattle, Jarman was on the *U. S. Decatur,* acting as interpreter under Captain Webster, the pilot. He spoke Clallam, a little Snohomish, as well as Kanaka, Bengali, Spanish, and of course the Chinook jargon.

In 1856, one Cooper was given the government contract at several thousand dollars, according to Jarman, for carrying messages, mail and express to and from the government posts at Fort Steilacoom, Fort Townsend and Fort Bellingham. On the first trip up from Steilacoom, Cooper lost his way in Swinomish Slough. Bill and wife piloted Cooper to Fort Bellingham, where Jarman hired out to Cooper as one of the carriers at $120 per month.

For this new job as express carrier and government messenger, Blanket Bill used a large canoe and nine husky Indian paddlers. Each Indian would give almost anything for a red shirt or blanket. Often by the time the crew reached Fort Bellingham from Fort Steilacoom they would have gambled themselves naked.

To Bill's disgust, his employer, Cooper, toward the end of the contract year, suddenly skipped out, owing nearly every one. Jarman, on his part owed his crew $200. Accordingly he went to work at Fort Bellingham at seventy-five dollars a month, splitting rails until he had earned enough to pay off his crew.

Up to this time, mail had been carried from Port Townsend to Penn's Cove, where Charles Phillips of Whidbey Island, picked it up, and, using canoe and Indian paddlers, brought it to Whatcom once a week.

While Jarman was working at Fort Bellingham in 1857, Captain Pickett one day asked him to pilot the Fort's whale boat to Victoria, with Pickett, Lieutenant Davis and Orderly Sergeant McDonald aboard. At Victoria all members of the party bought five gallons each of Port and London Dock brandy. When bidding Governor Douglas good-bye, Pickett said to Sergeant McDonald: "Call Jarman and get the whale boat ready."

Governor Douglas pricked up his ears, asked to see Jarman, and scolded him for his escape. The governor then told Pickett about the blanket episode and how Bill wore nothing when ransomed but a blanket of juniper cedar bark, woven with swan's down, feathers, and Russian (Alaskan) dog's hair. Blanket Bill had to explain that the Nootka Indians had taken all of his clothing, the women or klootchmen making ear rings of his brass buttons, while the red lining of his coat went into a pair of moccasins for Chief Skaas.

On one of his island trips as a messenger, Bill had a close brush with Haidas or Stikens. He had camped for the night on Whidbey Island, moving back in the woods to sleep. Two canoes carrying thirty warriors each, found his canoe and searched for his tracks. He, however, had taken the precaution of wading through the water along the beach before moving up in the forest. The Indians smashed his canoe and stole his provisions. Bill had to walk to Penn's Cove where he bought a small canoe from Snekellum.

In the '60's, Jarman was employed for a time as telegraph linesman by the California State Telegraph Company, whose wires reached Sehome, March 16, 1865. Long stretches of the line followed the coast, hence much of it could be serviced by canoe.

When not employed otherwise, he used his sloop, "Alice" to fish on the Sound, or hunt in surrounding forests. Even then he contrasted the number of waterfowl with the great flocks of swan and brant that had covered the tide flats at the mouth of Whatcom Creek when he first hunted there.

In 1872, Blanket Bill Jarman was tried for first degree murder following the fatal shooting of James Farmer. At the time the former was employed by the coal company at Sehome where he was acting as bar tender in the company's saloon. One account of the affray is that he shot Farmer during a fight which started when the latter made slurring remarks about Jarman's sister, Mrs. Pitchford.

According to Bill, the brawl actually had its start two nights earlier when he had a fight with, and whipped, a six footer named Fred Wilde. On the fatal night, Wilde, Foley, and James Farmer, returned to the saloon and started carousing. All lights were knocked out except the cigar lighter on the bar. Farmer swept this to the floor, and when Bill stooped to pick it up, Farmer attacked. Both struggled for the Colt gun on the back bar, which Jarman finally grasped. Dimly in the darkened room, Jarman saw Farmer seize an iron rod used as a poker and start for him; he fired. Farmer died instantly from the bullet hole in his side. That same night, Blanket Bill gave himself up to Sheriff Cootes and was placed in solitary confinement in the brick jail where he remained three weeks. Public sentiment was strong against Jarman as Farmer was intoxicated at the time of his death.

The trial was at Port Townsend, Washington Territory. Charles M. Bradshaw was prosecuting attorney while Jarman was defended by Attorney Clarke of Olympia. The hearing consumed less than one day. At 4:00 P. M. the case was given to the jury who were out only fifteen minutes before returning a verdict of "justifiable homicide." This, although the coroner's jury in Whatcom had pronounced it a case of first degree murder. One point in Bill's favor made during the trial was that he never took more than two glasses of liquor at a time, himself; and was never intoxicated.

Late in life, Jarman visited his old home in England. Returning he brought his niece, Miss Minnie Vine, who later became Mrs. William

Manning, of Ferndale, Washington, with whom he lived during his closing days.

To the end this first white man on Bellingham Bay clung to pioneer methods, preferring, for example, to walk from Ferndale to Bellingham, rather than to ride in a horse drawn vehicle, an auto, or on the train.

Never one for more hard work than absolutely necessary, he lived a rather easy life in his later years. Occasionally Jarman visited his old friends, the Indians, and spent much time among them, hunting and fishing. Known to be honest, rough, but kindly, he had many friends throughout the Northwest.

WILLIAM R. PATTLE

William R. Pattle, discoverer of coal on Bellingham Bay—the second white man to reach these northerly shores, and the first to take up land (file on a donation claim), might well be called, "Pattle, the Unknown," there being such meager record of his appearance, age, family, antecedents, or final destiny, although Frank C. Teck, Bellingham Bay newspaper man writing in 1903, reported he had died in San Francisco, some years earlier.

During the California boom days, prior to 1852, Pattle suddenly appears in the annals of the Northwest, being engaged in cutting and carrying spars to San Francisco from the San Juan Island group—this under permit from Governor Douglas of Vancouver Island—the islands being claimed at that time by the British.

Pattle had been told by the Indians that "black fire dirt,"—coal— existed on Bellingham Bay. At that time coal was selling for fantastic prices on the San Francisco market. He investigated and found coal out-croppings, October, 1852, on the shore at what later became Unionville— still later Bellingham, between the towns of Sehome and Fairhaven. (In that year, the extreme Northwest was part of Island County, Oregon Terri-tory.) Donation claims of the territory included mineral rights. Pattle left at once to get others to locate donation claims with him, covering the coal outcroppings.

On this trip presumably late in 1852, he met Captain Henry Roeder and Russell V. Peabody at Port Townsend while they were searching for a mill site. With a trader's eye for a quick dollar, Pattle, according to Roeder, told them of a possible falls and mill site on Bellingham Bay and offered to guide them for a thousand dollars. Captain Roeder understood that Pattle was an English subject and an employe of the Hudson's Bay Com-pany, an Indian trader, and familiar with the Northwest.

Pattle did succeed in interesting associates of his in the coal project. These were James Morrison and John Thomas. They returned to Bellingham

Bay to learn that Roeder and Peabody had landed there at the foot of the falls, December 15, 1852, without Pattle's aid, to become bona fide settlers.

Donation claims were staked by Pattle and his associates on the coal outcroppings in January, 1853. The priority of Pattle's coal discovery is proven by the second entry in "Book A" of the records of Whatcom County, which refers to an unrecorded lease of the Puget Sound Coal Mine Association, given April 11, 1853, by William R. Pattle, John Thomas and James Morrison, lessors, to F. Rogers Loomis. The lease was amended May 25, 1854, reiterating that the document was not a sale of the property, but merely a lease giving the right to dig and mine coal. The lease provided for $75 per month per claim, plus a per ton royalty.

According to Captain Eldridge, "A party under the superintendency of Captain Howard, United States Revenue Marine, arrived in the fall of 1853, to open and work the mines, but—there were too many officers to privates employed. But little coal was mined and within a year the enterprise was abandoned."

It was during this period that occurred the first shipment of coal to San Francisco. This was carried by the colorful Puget Sound Mariner, Captain Thomas Coupe, in the bark, *Success*. Movement of coal within the mine, and from mine to boat, was by means of wheelbarrows.

The Pattle coal mine operated intermittently for a number of years, but never at a profit. On June 10, 1855, Pattle sold one-sixteenth interest "in coal that may be found on the Pattle claim," to James Houston.

Later Pattle seems to have become so discouraged by the adventure, that he abandoned his donation claim, since on July 27, 1859, Doctor F. Newsome and S. Doty filed a pre-emption* claim on what "is known as the Pattle coal claim, bounded by the Vail, Lysle, and Morrison claims, and Bellingham Bay."

---

*Pre-emption—The act of September 4, 1841, provided a general system of pre-emption. It granted the right to persons who settled upon, cultivated and improved portions of the public lands, to have the first opportunity of purchasing the land when it became subject to sale. This right was not a title, but was merely a right of occupancy for the time being, with the privilege of purchasing in preference to any one else.—26 AM. & ENG. ENCY. 241.

The purpose of the act was to protect actual settlers who had made improvements.— JOHNSON & TOUSLEY, 13 WALL. 72.

The pre-emption privilege was extended to lands in Oregon and Washington Territories by the act of July 17, 1854. The pre-emption act was repealed in 1891, but all existing rights were expressly saved and preserved.

UPPER LEFT—Captain Henry Roeder.—Picture courtesy Mrs. Edna Roth Abbott.

UPPER RIGHT—"Blanket Bill" Jarman.—Picture courtesy Bellingham Herald.

LOWER LEFT—Edward Eldridge.—Picture courtesy Mrs. Maud Edens Henderson.

LOWER RIGHT—Russell A. Peabody.—Picture courtesy Bellingham Herald.

Pattle appears to have assumed his share of civic duties in the budding community. In July, 1854, the Commissioner's Court appointed him a Road Viewer together with Henry Roeder, and Ellis Barnes to locate a road from Poe's Point to Lummi River. Records also show that on September, 1854, he served as election judge at the Ma-Mo-Sea precinct.

The 1854 session of the legislature, which created Whatcom County out of the present Whatcom, Skagit and San Juan Counties, also provided for a county wreck master. Pattle was appointed to the position, although there seem to have been no duties, no wrecks to seize and administer. This is the last Whatcom County record of the man.

"Pattle's Point," (a short distance south of the present gas works), a name now seldom heard, is the only present day reminder of this pioneer, although the coal mine site once was called "Pattle's Fort." Blanket Bill Jarman so termed it as did Captain Roeder. It is probable that the main building was nothing more than a large log cabin, but it was the rallying point during at least one Indian Foray.

Early settlers, according to A. W. Thornton, pioneer doctor, found comfort in repeating tales to the effect that Captain Pattle had surrounded his fort with covered ways from which he could observe movements of hostiles, and that he had prepared mines of gunpowder and broken glass to be exploded among attacking Indians. This was a case of wishful thinking on the part of the settlers; the pits, ditches and tunnels undoubtedly being part of the surface exploration of the coal seams.

UPPER LEFT—Mrs. Charles Roberts Tuck and her daughter, Lizetta (Lizzie) Roberts Tuck-Frank, first white girl born at Bellingham Bay, 1856.—Mrs. Tuck's picture courtesy of her granddaughter, Mrs. Willa Frank Farmer.

UPPER RIGHT—Mrs. Edward Eldridge, the "Mother" of Whatcom.

LOWER—The first cabin built at Whatcom—1853—the Eldridge home on the west bank of Whatcom Creek.—Photo taken in 1889, courtesy E. A. Hegg.

Chapter IV.

EARLY SETTLERS

HENRY ROEDER

(1824 — 1902)

|T IS PROBABLE that no man in Territorial history has exercised greater influence on the development and destiny of his particular section and community, than did Henry Roeder, one of the two first white settlers in Whatcom county. (The other was Roeder's associate, Russell V. Peabody.) Few indeed have been granted his privilege of living to see his prophesies verified, and his plans so nearly realized.

Sailer, shipmaster, ship-builder, pioneer, trader, miner and mine owner, lumberman, townsite developer, farmer, civic leader—Roeder's activities through a long life, covered the width of a continent—while his destiny and fortune were affected by three great gold rushes—California, Fraser River, and Klondike. (Opposite page 22).

"A short barrel of a man," thus described by one of his granddaughters, who, when a girl, knew him as a gray bearded, bald old man, whose bruskness frightened her and other children.

"A lover of fine raiment"; was one characterization given by his daughter who explained that she inherited this trait from her father.

His bruskness, perhaps, was inherent in his German ancestry, strengthened by years on the quarter deck and in command of men in other projects, and was not the true measure of the inner man. This is indicated by the experience of William Henry Fouts, pioneer school teacher, who, with his family, arrived in Whatcom in September, 1873. Out house-hunting, the afternoon of arrival, Fouts in following the woods trail along the bluff near the point where it joined the old Military Road, encountered a short, aggressive appearing individual about fifty years old, who walked with a mincing gait, evidently, to protect the high luster of his boots from the mud and roots of the trail. The boots, according to Fouts, were of light brown calfskin, expertly sewn by some master craftsman. They were sharp-pointed and very small, not more than size four or five.

Fouts' questions concerning a rentable house, met with a growl. He was told to come out to the Roeder farm if he wished to talk business. Young Fouts knew at once that this stranger was Captain Roeder, who, even then, twenty years after setting up his saw mill, had become something of a legendary figure. A man whose brilliant mind and caustic comments had created bitter enemies and staunch admirers throughout the Puget Sound Country.

Roeder's English was precise and studied, Schoolmaster Fouts noted, although under stress showing a German accent. Later, speaking of hardships of early days, Roeder, sometimes boasted to Fouts, " . . . I am a German and we are a hearty race, raised on thin food and hard work." Fouts tells how Roeder finally relaxed enough to indicate that he might secure for the newcomer the Captain Pickett house recently vacated by Mrs. Pitchford, the sister of Blanket Bill Jarman.

William Bausman, owner of the paper, NORTHERN LIGHT, published briefly during the Fraser River gold rush of 1858, when writing in 1890 said: "Mr. Roeder was kind enough to present us with several lots. He was one of the proprietors of the town and a noble hearted gentleman."

Similar gifts of lots for public purposes, unadvertised aid and bounties to needy persons, seem to have characterized Whatcom's first citizen through his long life.

An interesting item concerning this colorful figure of a man, may be found in Charles I. Roth's account of the Fourth of July celebration in 1883. Three hundred or more local Indian braves and their families were camped on the beach below the bluff when an ancient cannon exploded, killing one Indian instantly and mortally wounding another. At once the encampment was in angry uproar. The Indians started beating tomtoms and threatening war on the community. Captain Roeder, known, respected, and feared by all the tribesmen, young and old, appeared at the first demonstration. He shouldered his way into the milling braves, cuffed two or three on the ears, kicked a couple more in the pants, according to Roth, and won the war single handed—and just that quickly. Such was Captain Roeder in action in his fifty-ninth year.

Captain Henry Roeder was born at Herstadt, Germany, July 4, 1824, the son of John Roeder, who had been one of Blucher's soldiers at the battle of Waterloo. Some observers have held it significant that this fiercely individualistic empire builder should have seen the light for the first time on the natal day of his adopted country.

In 1830, the family moved to Vermillion, Ohio, part of a movement extending over three decades, as so many freedom-loving Germans fled to escape military impressment and tyranny. That these same immigrants should be found in the '60's, from private to general, all wearing the uniforms of free men, and shedding their blood on so many Civil War battlefields, is not a paradox at all.

Life was hard for the Roeders in the new country. Henry went to work at an early age. At sixteen he was a sailor on the Great Lakes. Before he was twenty, he was master of a schooner and junior member of the firm of Pelton and Roeder. It was at this period that he met Edward Eldridge, also a sailor, whose life was to be so closely interwoven with his.

News of the California gold strike fired young Roeder's imagination. Bidding goodbye to his family and to his sweetheart, Elizabeth Austin, who later became his wife, he joined an overland train, at St. Joseph, Missouri, eventually reaching Sacramento, August 14, 1850.

Roeder mined at Ophir or Auburn Gulch; then moved to Poorman's Creek on the upper Feather River, where he ran a store. Here he formed a partnership with Russell V. Peabody. The store was not a success so Roeder next acquired control of the Sacramento Fishing Company which he operated successfully, employing Peabody as his clerk. A fire destroyed Sacramento and the fishing company quarters; fishing was stopped by legislative enactment; so, accompanied by Peabody, he moved north to try the same business on the Columbia River. He reached Portland in 1852, to learn that San Francisco had been wiped out by fire and that lumber was in demand at from $400 to $1,000 per thousand feet in the California market. Immediately his plans changed and he and Peabody began searching for a waterfall and sawmill location in the great timbered Northwest. Tumwater Falls near Olympia was reported as an ideal site. Accordingly, by canoe and afoot they proceeded to Olympia, only to learn that a mill was being erected at Tumwater Falls.

At each possible location, thereafter, they found the same situation, someone had preceded them. Discouraged they reached Port Townsend, where for $1,000, Captain Pattle offered to guide them to a waterfall on Bellingham Bay.

Refusing this offer, Roeder and Peabody returned to Olympia and there encountered Chief Cha-wit-zit, of the Lummi Tribe, together with the boy, Kwina, later a chieftain, who told of the incident in after years. Cha-wit-zit was questioned by Roeder as to where there was, "any water falling down from a high hill." The Chief replied that he knew of none, only "at Whatcom, noise all time." Accordingly, the two white men hired Indian guides, and headed north. Days later, on December 15, 1852, the weary paddlers drove their loaded canoe into Bellingham Bay and toward the northeastern shores. Solid walls of virgin timber surrounded the waters. Two breaks only existed in the green forest line, so the Indians assured them, where streams entered the Bay. One, they called "Nu-Qual-le-hum," meaning "water containing dog salmon," which the settlers later called Squalicum Creek; and one the Indians termed "What-coom" meaning "noisy rumbling water." Into the quiet inlet, where the "noisy rumbling water" of Whatcom Falls tumbled down to tidewater, the Indian guides steered their canoe. Roeder and Peabody stepped ashore to inspect this new empire.

In all the wilderness, no site could have surpassed the Whatcom Falls location. Here was a clear tumbling stream with sufficient drop and volume to turn a mill wheel. Salt water transportation touched the mill site. Serried rows of fir and cedar marched away from the tide line as far as the eye could see—magnificent timber, with many giant columns leaping upward one hundred feet before branching.

Roeder and Peabody first erected temporary shelter at the Falls; next sought Chief Cha-wit-zit of the Lummis to secure permission to erect and operate the saw mill. The two white men found Cha-wit-zit newly returned from Olympia, camped at the Portage on the Lummi Reservation, a long boot-shaped cape that divided Puget Sound waters from the Gulf of Georgia. Cha-wit-zit greeted the white men cordially, as did his people, many of whom rushed into the water to meet them.

Not only did the Chief give Roeder and Peabody the Falls and surrounding timber, but he promised to send help to erect the mill. This promise was faithfully kept as were others. In fact this chieftain remained friendly to the settlers throughout his life, although his friendship was sorely tried at times by unscrupulous whites.

Before securing men and machinery for the mill, Roeder and Peabody, with the use of Indian help, erected the shell of a mill-building on the east bank of the Creek. Roof and sides were covered with split cedar shakes.* Next—through boisterous winter weather, they made the long journey to Olympia, chief trading center of the Territory—(the others, Steilacoom and Port Townsend).

Supplies and a few workmen were secured, and Roeder and Peabody turned their canoe northward. The new hands were not sailors. Stormy seas and tide rips threatened the frail overloaded craft. So terrified were the battered and seasick men that they refused to go farther than Port Townsend.

Moving on to Dungeness, Roeder chartered the sloop of Captain McCalman. This vessel traveled during daylight hours only. Under advance winds and tides the party made Guemes Island the first day. During the night a pack of wild dogs with which the island was infested, raided the camp and ate or destroyed all edible supplies. For some time thereafter the island was known as Dog Island. Arriving at Whatcom Creek without provisions,

---

*Shakes, like home-made shingles, are split from cedar blocks. They are longer and thicker than shingles and may or may not be smoothed by a drawshave. Shingles are shaved to an edge. See opposite page 166 for frow and mallet used in splitting shakes and shingles, also for picture of shaving horse used in shaving shingles.

the party was forced to live off the country, or on clams, fish, and venison secured from the Indians.

Roeder left at once for Victoria to buy supplies from the Hudson's Bay Company's store. The Company did not welcome American enterprises in these Northern waters, but reluctantly sold the necessary rations.

Leaving Peabody in charge of preliminary work at the mill-site, Roeder again took canoe for Olympia enroute to San Francisco, where he intended to secure machinery, mechanics and millwrights. Luckily, at Budd's Inlet, close to Olympia, he secured passage on the Barque, *Mary Melville*, loading piles for San Francisco.

Roeder's capital was seriously depleted by prices he had to pay on the California market. Mill castings and forgings cost twenty-five cents per pound. Next, he employed an experienced millwright, William Utter; also located and hired William Brown and Henry Hewitt, two men with whom he had crossed the plains. As he was about to leave, he encountered his old friend of Lake Erie days, Edward Eldridge, destined like Roeder to become one of the leading citizens of the Northwest. Roeder's eloquence concerning the north country decided Eldridge to cancel passage to Australia and to bring wife and babe to Bellingham Bay.

EDWARD ELDRIDGE
(1828 — 1892)

Edward Eldridge, who so definitely influenced the trend of state and local history, like Captain Roeder, had been a sailor, school teacher, town-site developer, County Commissioner, Auditor, Treasurer, Deputy Collector of Customs, and later was president of transportation, financial and public service companies; legislator, exponent of Women's Rights; Speaker of the House; member of the Territorial Convention, and of the State Constitutional Convention. (Opposite page 22).

The man has been described by one of his granddaughters as a person of medium height and weight, calm and somewhat slow spoken, with the kindliest of brown eyes. He was prematurely gray, white haired in fact, at twenty-five years of age.

This pioneer was a self-educated, well-read man, who, over the years, acquired a large library that was destroyed when the house burned shortly after his death. His granddaughter has related that he seemed impressed by educated people, by artists, and the like, and was prone to forgive acts in these persons that he would not have tolerated in others; also that he might enter into deals with these same people, when such deals sometimes were to his disadvantage.

Edward Eldridge desired the best of education for his children and grandchildren. Often he would press a forefinger against a small child's brow, explaining solemnly that this was to give the youngster a high and intelligent forehead. Associates seem to have set high store by his judgment and decisions in matter of business; and by his memory of details in the various companies he headed. Fellow legislators have stated that he might have gone high politically had his Scotch integrity permitted him to compromise on matters of principle.

Edward Eldridge was born December 7, 1828 at Saint Andrews, Scotland. Orphaned at an early age, he, together with brothers and sisters, was reared by his grandparents. At eleven years, he ran away to sea. For nearly a dozen years he was a sailor, this period including service in the British Navy.

In 1846, young Eldridge came to America, and shortly afterward was sailing the Great Lakes. There he met Captain Roeder. Again he returned to salt water, and was on the *Tonquin,* when she sailed into San Francisco, October, 1849, at the height of the gold excitement. With others he joined the gold rush to newly opened diggings on Yuba River. After twelve months of mining on the Feather River, he returned to the sea as second mate on the Pacific Mail Steamship *Tennessee* plying between Panama and San Francisco. On one of these trips in 1851, he met Teresa Lapin, whom he married in February, 1852.

TERESA LAPIN ELDRIDGE
(1832 — 1911)

Teresa Lapin Eldridge, known as the "Mother of Whatcom," has been described by her granddaughter, as a good looking young woman, above average height, inclined to be stout, "a typical Irish girl with raven black hair and blue eyes—twinkly they were. She was quick tempered and outspoken, just the opposite, in many respects, of her studious husband." The pioneer scene into which she soon was to be projected at Whatcom Creek, gave her no time for the improvement of her mind, what with rearing her family, feeding and mothering the homeless men at the mill site, and later running the boarding house at Sehome. (Opposite page 23).

Teresa Lapin was born in County Armagh, Ireland, June 24, 1832. With a sister she came to America in 1850, and there took service with a Long Island family, which joined the California rush the next year. After her marriage to Edward Eldridge the young couple moved to Northern California, where the husband mined unsuccessfully in the Yreka camp. There their daughter, Isabelle, was born. Discouraged, they were in San Francisco, preparing for a trip to Australia, when Eldridge met Captain Roeder.

To transport his machinery and supplies, and the company of twelve souls, Captain Roeder chartered the schooner, *William Allen,* Captain Mc-Lain, master. The tedious voyage ended in May, 1853, when the little vessel dropped anchor in the estuary just below the Whatcom Creek Falls.

Her infant daughter in her arms, her voluminous skirts and petticoats wrapped about her, Mrs. Eldridge was carried ashore, to become the first, and at that moment, the only white woman in the far northwest corner of the United States. Her arrival, in fact the setting up of the first home, marked the beginning of the town of Whatcom, later to be part of the City of Bellingham. Years afterward, Mrs. Eldridge reported the enthusiasm of her husband at sight of the Bay and the selected townsite. She has left no word of her own reaction. An irrepressible Irish spirit no doubt overrode a housewife's heart-sickness at sight of the untenanted shores and the dark, somber, conniferous forests.

With a woman and child needing shelter, the mill hands hurriedly constructed a cabin of logs, split cedar boards, and shakes. (Opposite page 23). This was where Clinton Street later crossed Division Street. Bunk and mess houses were erected even as the machinery was being installed. Hungry men had to be fed. Thus naturally, the young wife became cook for the crew. In the meantime, there were homemade bunks, benches, tables, cupboards required to make the Eldridge cabin livable. In after years, when questioned about her beautiful home and belongings, Mrs. Eldridge said she was prouder of her first table cloth, made of four flour sacks and used in this cabin, than of any later possessions.

Burdened with the task of providing three hot meals per day for the hungry mill hands, Mrs. Eldridge could spare little time for the mothering of her small daughter, Isabelle. The Indians, who had shown stolid indifference at the arrival of the whites, soon became interested in the little girl and brought gifts of food—a great aid to a meager larder. The crews in the woods and at the mill increased in time, and the pioneer woman became more occupied. Satisfied that the Indians were entirely friendly, she allowed the women to take care of Isabelle. They would call for the little girl early each morning, and take her with them while they fished or picked berries. Soon the child was talking the Indian language, not the Chinook jargon; rather the ancient dialect, known only to the older tribesmen, and now a lost language. Isabelle, Mrs. Eldridge was wont to declare, could talk the Indian tongue, before she could speak English, while she, herself, who had to know Chinook, could not understand a word her baby said.

While working at the Roeder mill, Eldridge and wife, in 1854, staked two donation claims totalling 320 acres, and including the mouth of Squalicum Creek. Since the law required residence on the property, he constructed a cabin on the beach to which he moved his family. On the bluff above was a bit of open land or prairie—very poor soil. First efforts at raising a crop were a failure.

The Eldridge family was increased in 1855 by the arrival of Edward Eldridge, Junior,* the first white child born at Whatcom.

Money was scarce around the Bay. A reported gold strike near Fort Colville in the Okanogan country lured the ex-prospector east of the mountains. In his absence, he was elected to the Territorial House of Representatives, the first representative from Whatcom County. Indian outbreaks drove Eldridge south. Traveling afoot, and mostly at night to avoid the hostiles, he made the journey of several hundred miles to Olympia. There, according to Roth, he learned that he had been elected, reported killed, and that a special election was about to be called to fill the vacancy. He decided to fill the vacancy himself and remained in Olympia for the second session of the legislature, meantime notifying his wife that reports of his death had been "grossly exaggerated."

In an interview given the AMERICAN REVEILLE, June 14, 1908, Mrs. Eldridge stated: "We depended almost entirely on the Lummi Indians for food . . . They brought us clams, fish, and many different sorts of birds', ducks', gulls', and divers' eggs. They were nearly always friendly, although I was twice badly scared by them." The first time, she reported, was when Chief Cha-wit-zit, in a drunken rage declared: "The Bostons all will have to go. They are stealing my coal. All the coal and all the land is mine."

The second incident occurred a few years later when the Indians broke down the door of the Eldridge's cabin, captured a Kanaka slave girl,** who was hiding under the bed, and dragged her away by the hair to a waiting canoe. No violence was offered Mrs. Eldridge, who had tried to save the fugitive.

When Eldridge realized he could not make a living by farming, he moved across the Bay and went to work at the Sehome Coal Mine, running the engine. His wife opened a boarding house for the miners. This was so successful that it grew into the Keystone Hotel, corner of State and Laurel streets. Here their fourth child, Hugh, was born in 1860. The third child, Alice, had been born in Sehome about two years previously.

In 1862, the family erected a fine house on the bluff at the Squalicum Creek farm, and began the development of the place. This home became the center of hospitality for the district. Dignitaries, officials, scientists, and plain travelers made it a point to arrive about meal time or to stay over

---

*Edward Eldridge, Jr. Accidentally shot and killed, 1868, age thirteen, while in a boat on the Whatcom waterfront.

**In the early '50's, the Hudson's Bay Company brought a shipload of natives from the Sandwich Islands. This slave was evidently one of these Hawaiian girls.

night. Mrs. Eldridge later told how, on some Sundays, she set her table five times.

Edward Eldridge served as delegate to the Territorial Constitutional Convention held at Walla Walla in 1878. He also helped launch the new state of Washington by serving as delegate to the State Constitutional Convention convened in 1889 at Olympia.

The Eldridge residence burned in 1878. In 1891, one of the largest and finest mansions in the west was erected on the bluff nearer to the Creek. When the 1894 forest fire threatened the town, the street car company of which Hugh Eldridge was a heavy stock holder sent hundreds of fire fighters out to the farm. Despite several days' exhausting struggle, the flames from the forest consumed the mansion.

Meantime Edward Eldridge had died in 1892. Mrs. Teresa Eldridge followed her husband in 1911.

SAWMILL DIFFICULTIES

The sawmill machinery was installed and the Roeder-Peabody-Page mill was ready to operate by the middle of the summer of 1853. But the year had been exceptionally dry, and Whatcom Creek was too low to turn the water-wheel that provided power. By the time the fall rains remedied this, there were so many saw mills in the Northwest, that the price of lumber on the San Francisco market had dropped from $1,000 to $20 per thousand.

The Whatcom Creek sawmill, which had a capacity of 10,000 feet in twenty-four hours, made use of two upright or "muley" saws. One was operated by Captain Roeder and the other by William Utter.

With the California market closed, Roeder turned to Victoria, where he later established lumber yards. The first two schooner loads were shipped to Governor Douglas in vessels furnished by the latter. Lumber for the First Church of England buildings at Victoria, for the barracks at Esquimault, erected to house British wounded after the Crimean War, came from the Whatcom mill. Early settlers on the American side also began to use mill-cut lumber as this was easier than cutting and fitting logs, or in splitting cedar boards and timbers.

Shortly after the mill began operating, in the fall of 1853, Brown and Hewitt were logging on the Sehome side of the Bay, between State Street and the shore line. There the upturned roots of a fallen cedar disclosed a coal deposit. This, when developed, became the Sehome Coal Mine (covered elsewhere in this history), which was to operate for years as the Bellingham Bay Coal Company, with Edmund C. Fitzhugh as resident agent. Thus the growth of the Bay area, even at this early period was developing from three focal points.

As stated, the saw mill was not profitable, because of low water, falling markets, transportation, and other difficulties. The owners became indebted for more than $2,000 in about two years. One mortgage for $731 carried an interest rate of three per cent per month. Later A. C. Latson purchased a one-third interest in the mill and leased the property from the owners. Shortly thereafter, he was sued by R. V. Peabody for recovery of rent.

CAPTAIN ROEDER RETURNS TO THE SEA

Captain Roeder, who had come to Bellingham Bay to run a sawmill soon turned back to the sea, which was his first love. To cut market costs, in 1854, he built the schooner-rigged scow, *H. C. Page.** This boat, named for his friend and sawmill partner, was the first launched on Bellingham Bay, and the third in Puget Sound registry.

Roeder was skipper of the *Page*. Associated with him were William Utter and James Taylor. For several years the little craft afforded the North Sound ports the only dependable means of communication with the outside world. However the vessel was no money-maker. Records show that Captain Roeder on September 17, 1855, gave a mortgage to E. C. Fitzhugh for $551.78 at four per cent per month, said mortgage being secured by Roeder's two-thirds interest in the *Page*. In June 1858, Roeder sold the little boat to Selucious Garfielde of Thurston County for $1,000, and began building the 100-ton schooner-rigged scow, *General Harney,* which was to appear in the San Juan episode.

Roeder continued his maritime activities, until the channels and shores of the Sound were as familiar as his own back yard; the while he became the messenger, friend and counselor of the settlers over a wide area. With the years his interest grew to include land on Whidbey, Vendovi and other islands; a store and hotel in the Cariboo country, British Columbia; larger shipping activities; as well as valuable holdings in Whatcom County. He passed away in 1902.

---

*H. C. Page—42 tons registry, 70 feet overall length.

Chapter V

PIONEER WOMEN OF THE FOURTH CORNER

MARIA WILHELMINA ROBERTS

(1828 — 1891)

1854

MARIA WILHELMINA ROBERTS, second w h i t e woman resident of Bellingham Bay; closely identified with the history of Fort Bellingham, and with the long struggle to regain her property from the hands of the military, was born in 1828 at Hanover, Germany. (Opposite page 23).

A large, courageous, motherly woman of dark complexion, characterized by Mrs. Charley Roth as "one of the indispensible, never-to-be-forgotten women of the early days," Mrs. Roberts came to America when she was eighteen years old. She made the long hard trip around the Horn to San Francisco, and there met and married Charles Roberts. The groom, an employee of the Hudson's Bay Company, took his bride to Whatcom in 1854. There, on September 10, 1854, they filed on their Donation Claim, the land chosen being more than three miles northwest of Whatcom Creek, beyond the Eldridge and Compton Claims, and not far from the present town of Marietta. This was the site on which Fort Bellingham was built.

The Roberts' land, called "The Prairie" or "The Plateau," was nearly level and required little clearing. Thus they became the first to grow vegetables, a boon they generously shared with the others.

Before Mrs. Roberts' arrival, Mrs. Eldridge,* first permanent woman resident, had reigned alone and supreme over the wistful and homesick men of the colony. She therefore welcomed another woman enthusiastically. The Irish immigrant and the one from Germany, became lifelong friends.

Like Mrs. Eldridge, Mrs. Roberts became the nurse, comforter, and steadfast friend of the entire community. She, it is recorded, kept up the courage of the women huddled in the little blockhouse above the Creek, when Indian raids threatened. She it was, who frequently walked three miles through the dense woods from her home, revolver in her pocket, to

---

*Before Mrs. Eldridge's arrival, a laborer by the name of Dickenson, engaged to work on the mill structure, appeared briefly with his wife, then moved on without taking root.

stay with Mrs. Roeder and children when the Captain was away on one of his freighting or trading missions.

To the Roberts there was born on October 2, 1856, Elizabeth Lizette Roberts, the first white girl on Bellingham Bay.*

When Captain Pickett and his men reached Bellingham Bay in 1856, to build a fort, they did so at a site selected a year earlier. This was on the Roberts' claim, the only open ground available in the entire district. Roberts and his wife were asked to leave. This they refused to do. Under plea of "military necessity," the soldiers removed the roof from the Roberts' house, and the couple perforce moved to the beach, where they erected a cabin. There Mrs. Roberts and family lived until time to go to Olympia and prove up on their claim. Later Roberts was lost in the Cariboo country and declared officially dead.

Bitterly Mrs. Roberts carried on the fight for her property over which the government maintained a guard for twelve years. The territorial legislature took notice of her claims against the United States. Lawyers, who handled the case, in the end took one-third of the property as a fee. After the Civil War, Major General Halleck, on a tour of inspection decided that the site was no longer needed for military purposes, and the claim of Mrs. Roberts, then Mrs. Tuck, was surrendered to her, in 1868. For the twelve years occupancy by the government, she received no compensation.

MARY FRANCES LYSLE
January 21, 1833 — December 26, 1910
1854

According to the worn and tattered pages of the family diary, Mary Frances Lysle, wife of John Wilson Lysle, arrived at Bellingham Bay, September 24, 1854, to become the third white woman to take up her residence on the Bay, and the first in the town of Sehome. (Opposite page 38).

Pioneer friends have described Frances Lysle as a joyous, helpful person—withal a very pretty girl with long red curls. She created quite a sensation among the Indians on the overland trip. One of the savages offered Lysle several blankets in exchange for his wife. Refused, the Indian next tried to trade horses for the young woman, and it took some diplomatic talking on the part of the husband to keep peace with the thwarted brave.

Mary Frances Lysle was born in New York State, January 21, 1833. At eighteen she married John Wilson Lysle, who was born in Pennsylvania, August 20, 1826.

---

*Mrs. Eldridge has stated, that the first white children born on the Bay, earlier even than the birth of her son, Edward, Jr., 1855, were the twin boys of William Cullen and wife, born in 1853. The Cullens lived at Chuckanut, but early moved to California.

Shortly after the wedding, the couple made their way to St. Louis, leaving in the spring of 1852, for the Oregon Country. Six months were consumed in the soul-trying journey from St. Louis to The Dalles, Oregon. In fact, the hardships were such that Mrs. Lysle became sick and lost her first baby en route. The frantic husband took horse and rode the backward trail as far as time permitted, unsuccessfully looking for a doctor. Later he learned that had he ridden back one wagon train farther, he would have found the doctor who was to treat the sick woman on arrival at The Dalles.

When Mrs. Lysle was able to travel again the couple proceeded to Olympia, where Lysle taught school at Chamber's Prairie. In 1853, they took up a small farm on Whidbey Island. While there, Lysle, who had come from the Pennsylvania coal country, heard of the coal discovery at Sehome. Accordingly they decided to move to Bellingham Bay and take up a homestead near the strike. In the meantime another child was born to the couple.

For the movement to the mainland, two canoes were secured and lashed together. Space was left in one end of the canoes, among the household goods, for Mrs. Lysle and her baby to sit. Their effects included a keg of dried apples and a keg of candles.

When rounding one of the islands, storm waves threatened to swamp the overloaded canoe. Lysle snatched up a keg and heaved it overboard to lighten the load. This proved to be the keg holding the family supply of candles. Consequently in the long months to follow, the Lysle's Sehome cabin was lighted only by the flames from the fireplace. Mrs. Lysle afterward said that she was sorry that the keg of dried apples had not been jettisoned instead, although the contents of the second keg materially helped, since the Indians were ever ready to trade fish or a pheasant (grouse) for a handful of dried apples.

En route from Whidbey Island, the Lysles camped at Swinomish, sleeping under their drop leaf table for protection from the rain. The next night they stayed with the William Cullens near Chuckanut; then on to the A. M. Poe's cabin at Poe's Point where they remained until their cabin on Sehome Hill was completed.

This cabin was on the three hundred and twenty acre Donation Claim on which the Lysles had filed, and where part of the Western Washington College buildings were erected decades later.

At the time, forests covered the slopes from the beach to the hilltop, the woods being so dense that neither the Bay nor the heights above were visible from the cabin site. All of this was most depressing to the young wife whose hope it was that no water could be found on their property and that, therefore, the family would have to take up residence nearer the other whites.

One day her husband, who was digging the well, blasted her hopes by reporting a nice flow of water had been encountered, and she resigned herself to her little hillside home, although the Lysles did move to the beach for protection during the Indian troubles.

When the cabin was completed, Indians were hired to move the household goods up the slope. But the hill was too steep, the work too hard; the same Indians could not be hired to make a second trip.

Five years after their arrival, during which period Mrs. Lysle had helped her women friends institute the first social life on Bellingham Bay, the Lysles returned to Olympia, then later to Pennsylvania, where they had interests in coal properties.

In 1884, then a widow, Mrs. Lysle returned to Whatcom where she spent her last days.

MRS. HENRY ROEDER

February 11, 1826 — February 12, 1897

1855

When Captain Henry Roeder joined the gold rush in 1850, he left in Ohio his childhood sweetheart, Mary Elizabeth Austin. Four years later she had the opportunity to join her lover, "Out West." (Opposite page 38).

The Holden Judsons, who were friends of hers, had crossed the plains in a covered wagon in 1853. After journeying for seven months, they reached the home of Mrs. Holden (Phoebe) Judson's father and mother, the J. H. Goodells, living at Grand Mound, about twenty miles south of Olympia. The Goodells had crossed the plains in 1851.

A year later, Charles Judson, father of Holden Judson, decided to follow his son. The company was composed of Charles Judson and wife, their daughter, Lucretia, (she became Mrs. George W. Corliss); Mrs. Phoebe Judson's brother, William Goodell with his wife and child; the father, mother and brother of Ezra Meeker; Elizabeth Austin; Jacob and Winfield Ebey, the father and brother of Colonel I. N. Ebey; also his mother and two sisters, and a few others. This was known as the "Ebey Train."

The migration of the settlers in the '40's to the West, was as nothing compared to the '50's, when 300,000 people swept in a vast tidal wave of humanity from the Middle West to the Pacific Ocean. Many miles of trail were worn so deep, that centuries later the trail will remain. In places the iron wheels of the wagon and the myriad feet of the cattle and of the pioneers, cut a pathway six to ten feet in depth, and from fifty to one hundred and fifty in width; the fine dust, ground out by the traffic, being blown away by the fierce winds of the plains. In some sections the tracks cut the very rocks, where, at times, the axles would drag on the solid stone, necessitating new trails.

Mary Elizabeth Austin was born in Vermillion, Ohio, February 11, 1826. Her parents were pioneers in the Ohio country, then almost as new as was the West Coast when she arrived in Washington Territory in 1854. The worn, scuffed pages of Elizabeth Austin's diary present a moving picture of her overland journey.

The first entry: "Left home April 18, 1854, for Sandusky, Ohio."

A month later she was with a wagon train in the Indian Country of the Platte River. There another train joined them, making a larger caravan; this for safety's sake. The diary tells of the chilly nights in their wagons, of how they waded through streams, trudged beside and pushed schooners up rocky mountain sides, battled storms of lightning, thunder, and rain, fought whirlwind prairie fires, met charges of buffalo herds, or buried comrades who cracked under the journey's strain.

"One yoke of oxen went off the bridge. Several articles were lost in the wagon. Obliged to attach ropes to the wagons to guide them," thus reads one entry.

June 2, 1854, found the caravan in the buffalo country, where strict watch was necessary lest the pioneers be trapped in a buffalo stampede.

Death first came to a member of their company, June 9. "His name was James Wood. He died with no relatives near him. Was buried about one hour after he died, without a coffin."

On June 19 she wrote: "Mrs. Meeker (mother of Ezra Meeker) died this morning, Fort Laramie."

In places where the roads were bad, they would make only fifteen miles or so a day. Occasionally the wagons had to be floated across the streams, while the cattle were made to swim. Sometimes this took an entire day.

"Thursday, August 22, 1854. This morning we noticed four wagons approaching our encampment, and we waited for them to come up before resuming our journey. This sorrowful company imparted to us the distressing information that, 'they had been attacked by the Indians, and two of their number killed and wounded, and five of their horses stolen.' They traveled along in our company, and the next night the wounded man died.

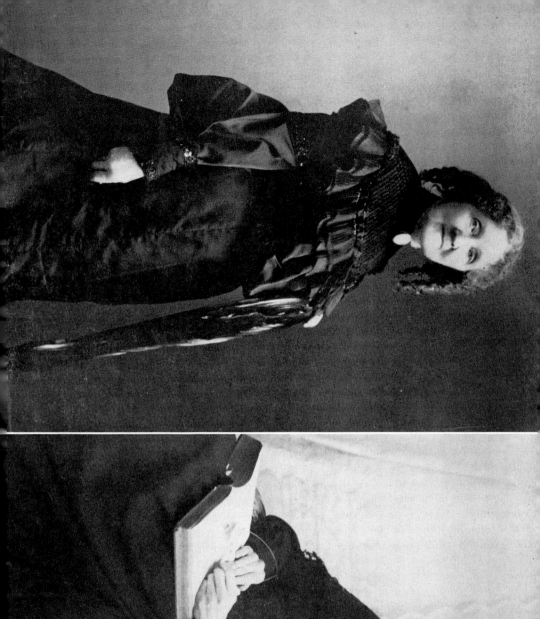
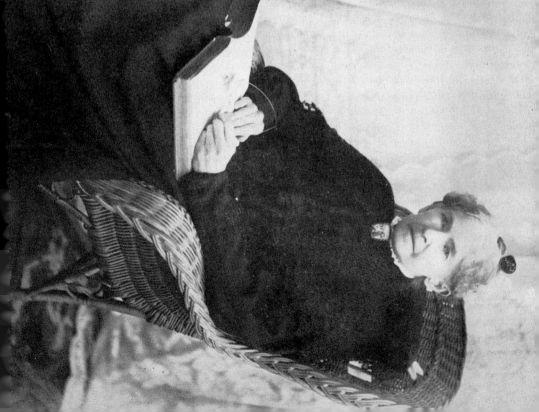

"August 23—This afternoon an Indian brought us a message from Captain Grant, informing us of the horrible massacre of the whole of Captain Ward's train by the savages. We kept the friendly Indian, who brought us the message, in our camp through the night. Only three miles travel the next morning brought us to the scene of the awful tragedy. Ten men, eight women, and all the children killed, with the exception of one boy, who, although wounded, made his escape. We sadly asssisted in performing the last mournful rites for our murdered fellow beings."

"August 31, 1854. No wood or water near. Burned buffalo chips. Many mountains to cross. We wade the streams."

"September 2—Two Indians seen after dark and fired upon."

"September 11—We crossed Walla Walla river four times today before we got to the Fort."

The next day the caravan ferried across the Columbia River, paying eight dollars per wagon and a dollar a head for cattle.

Another item showed the Natches River was crossed eleven times in one day.

This entry on September 27: "Judson's wagon turned over coming down a very bad hill." The train at this time paid $2 a bushel for potatoes and $15 a hundred pounds for flour.

On the ninth of October, 1854, they came to the end of the trail, the Holden Judson's home at Grand Mound near Olympia.

The future Mrs. Roeder was not a robust woman and must have seemed out of place on the overland trek, but she surprised her companions by her courage, patience, and endurance; by an inner strength that no hardships, suffering or poverty would ever break. It is of record that her kindliness and cheerfulness, cheered and strengthened many of the heartsick and homesick on the weary trail.

When word reached Captain Roeder that his promised bride, Elizabeth Austin, had arrived at the Judson ranch near Olympia, he hurriedly erected a home close to the Eldridge cabin and the Falls. Then he sailed for Olympia in his sloop, the *H. C. Page*. The last lap of the journey was made with the Captain aboard a cayuse—or Indian pony.

The marriage of the pioneer couple was performed by Chief Justice Edward Lander of the Territorial Supreme Court, February 10, 1855, in the

UPPER—The Roeder and Peabody mill house and Post Office, in 1853, built with the first lumber from the mill. Picture taken in 1903.

LOWER—Captain Roeder's second home, begun in 1858. It stood on Elm street.—Taken in 1903.

parlor of the old hotel at Olympia. On the marriage certificate appear the signatures of George Corliss and McLancthon Goodell, the two witnesses. Immediately after the ceremony, the couple sailed for Whatcom aboard the Captain's sloop.

While Roeder was absent, the three young wives on the Bay scurried about, dividing their scanty belongings, and doing what they might to make the new cabin seem homelike to the bride. These three were watching excitedly when the sails of the *H. C. Page* appeared, beating up past Lummi Island, and were ready to greet her when Captain Roeder carried his wife to the beach at Whatcom Creek—the fourth white woman to touch the shores of Bellingham Bay.

The first of these pioneer women was Mrs. Eldridge, 1853, who had been living in a small cabin on the west bank of the Creek; the second, Mrs. Roberts, 1854, who resided three miles west, at the later site of Fort Bellingham; the third, Mrs. Lysle, who arrived in September, 1854, and whose home was on Sehome Hill.

While these women were not far apart in terms of miles, the difficulties, danger, and time consumed in visiting each other were considerable. Mrs. Lysle had to walk through a steep forest trail, from Sehome Hill to the beach, thence along the beach to the Creek, where she either rowed across to her friends, or climbed a sandstone ridge east of the Creek and crossed on a footbridge at the mill. Mrs. Roberts had to walk three miles through woods, or row a boat that distance from her homesite to the mouth of the Creek.

THE FIFTH WHITE WOMAN ON BELLINGHAM BAY, 1856

McKinney Tawes and his wife, Mary Bird Tawes, the fifth white woman in the settlement, arrived on Bellingham Bay in 1856. Tawes, a sailor and Chesapeake Bay oysterman, moved from Baltimore to San Francisco in 1852. There he met and married Mary Bird from Dublin, Ireland, via New York.

Hired to transport machinery for the Sehome Coal Mine, Tawes, with his bride of seventeen, boarded a northbound sailing vessel, in 1856. Mary Tawes stopped at Port Townsend, while her husband continued to Sehome where he installed and operated the first steam driven coal hoist. Later, his wife, traveled to the Bay on the Roeder sloop, the *H. C. Page*. There the couple took up residence in one of the two-room cabins built for the miners along the bluff near the mine, and situated close to the future site of Sehome School—erected in 1861. In the picture (opposite page 183) one of the small houses to the right of the whitewashed school building, left center, doubtless is the Tawes' cabin.

Early years were hard for the young wife, who lost her first baby through lack of care. The next child born to the Tawes in the Sehome cabin was Anna, 1859. She was Mrs. Anna Tawes Ray, deceased 1949.

For several years until politics obtruded, Tawes worked for the Bellingham Bay Coal Company as an engineer. Then the employers handed out little tickets telling the men how to vote at the coming election. Tawes expressed himself freely, and indignantly quit the mine.

Next, Tawes homesteaded 160 acres on the Nooksack River below the present town of Ferndale, and here the family made their permanent home in May, 1862. At that time wolves and cougars were so numerous and threatening that the settlers had to shut up their pigs and cattle at night.

During these years, it is recorded that Anna Tawes, who with her sister, Emily, were hunting pheasants, foolishly fired her muzzle-loading shotgun at a cougar lying on a tree limb above the girls' path. A post mortem revealed that a lone shot pellet had penetrated the eye and reached the brain of the snarling animal.

A COUGAR LOOKS ON

Captain Roeder erected three different residences in Whatcom, of which the first was the cabin near the saw mill. The second, in order to comply with the residence requirements of the land laws, was constructed on the common line between Roeder's donation claim and his preemption claim. The sleeping and living rooms were over the preemption claim, while the kitchen and dining room were over the other. In later years, the Roeder mansion was constructed at Monroe and Elm streets, just south of the second home.

The NORTHERN LIGHT on July 24, 1858, stated: "Mr. Roeder has an office under way in the vicinity of the NORTHERN LIGHT office, and a dwelling house partially completed on the upland a short distance above."

Foundations of the two-story, six room house were cedar blocks. Interior finishing was of California redwood. James H. Taylor, the shipwright, fashioned an ornamental scroll for the exterior decoration.

Hard times which followed the collapse of the Fraser River gold rush, affected Roeder's finances. The new house was not finished on the interior; nevertheless, the family occupied the place. (Opposite page 39).

The forests hid all view of the Bay. To Mrs. Roeder, alone in the woodland clearing much of the time while Captain Roeder was away on his trips, the "short distance" mentioned by the NORTHERN LIGHT seemed a very long way. Nor was she worried without reason. The tide of humanity following the Fraser stampede had vanished so quickly that it had not disturbed the wild animals. Repeating firearms were undeveloped. As yet instinctive fear of the white man had not been bred in the wild beasts.

Shortly after the Roeders had moved into their uncompleted house in 1859, Mrs. Roeder with her small son called on Mrs. Mary Tawes, who was living near the Sehome Coal Mine. Mrs. Tawes accompanied her visitor on the return, to see how the new house was progressing. The women had no more than turned from the Military Road into the Roeder trail, when a cougar barred their way. The great cat slid into the dense foliage and the women hurried forward. A few minutes later he was in the path behind them. Again they froze in their tracks. When he vanished in the undergrowth, they scuttled forward once more. Again he appeared ahead, seeming to keep his unwinking gaze on the small boy huddled between them. When the cougar sauntered off the trail, Mrs. Roeder began calling at the top of her voice hoping to arouse her dog. The latter came bounding down the trail barking and growling. The cougar, which once more appeared behind the women, glared at the dog briefly, then vanished.

Mrs. Tawes later was escorted to her Sehome cabin by an armed man and a dog. Next morning when the Roeders glanced through their window they saw the body of their dog, its jugular vein slashed by the cougar.

In this second house there were born Henry Junior, Lottie, and Victor Roeder. The eldest son, John, was born at the Ebey home, Whidbey Island, in August, 1856, while the Roeders were living near the mill site. When Mrs. Roeder and her infant son, John, were being returned from Whidbey Island, a storm forced them to beach their canoe and take refuge in an Indian Potlatch House for the night.

John Roeder died in 1886 from injuries caused by the fall of his horse on floating corduroy of the Telegraph Road.

Like the Eldridge home, the Roeder residence for many years was a center of hospitality for the Northwest. Friends of the Captain, State and Federal officials, soldiers, judges, financiers from far and near gathered under the Roeder roof or assembled around the table. The imposing Roeder mansion on Monroe and Elm streets was not completed until 1896. At the time of Mrs. Roeder's death, February 12, 1897, it was as yet unfurnished and unoccupied. Elizabeth street and Elizabeth Park in Bellingham were named for Elizabeth Roeder.

LUMMI INDIANS TAKE REVENGE

Despite their fear and suspicions of the Whites, the Indians too rarely united against the invaders. Worse, they continued their age-old tribal wars and hatreds. Thus the fierce Northern tribes raided Whites and Puget

Sound Indians alike; while the latter tribes, such as the Lummis, remembering the horrible massacres they had suffered in the past, lost no opportunity
to be revenged on their ancient foes. All of which left the few settlers clustered
around the mouth of Whatcom Creek, very nervous indeed.

During the war scare of 1855-'56, the Lysles for greater security moved
their home from the dense woods on Sehome Hill to a cabin at the foot of
the present F Street. At night they, like the others, crowded into the blockhouse on Peabody Hill, while the men stood guard.

By day all went about their business, to the peaceful sound of the upright saws fussily slashing through the logs. Thus Mrs. Lysle, playing on the
beach with her children, was frozen and speechless the day she looked up
to see a group of Lummi warriors silently moving past in single file, each
armed, each in war bonnet, each hideously painted. Ignoring the woman,
they pressed on toward the sawmill, while she fled to the cabin and bolted
the door.

Captain Roeder was away. Mrs. Roeder was alone with her baby; the
mill crew was unsuspecting, unarmed. An hour passed. Then the Lummis
filed past the Lysle cabin again and launched their canoe. Carrying one child
and leading the other, Mrs. Lysle hurried toward the Roeder cabin. In the
mill pond floated the body of a bright little Northern Indian boy, whom
Mrs. Roeder was training in various tasks. On the cabin floor lay the bleeding, bullet pierced body of a large Northern Indian. Mrs. Roeder was kneel-
ing at her infant's crib in the rear room, giving thanks for their delivery.
Her story—the Indian had come to the cabin in evident excitement. Not
understanding the language, she did not realize he was asking for protection from the Lummis. Just then James Taylor dashed in, shoved the
crib and Mrs. Roeder into the rear room, and closed the door in the face of
the Indian. A moment later the Lummis reached the cabin entrance and
fired a volley into the body of their Northern enemy, as he strained against
the inner door. Mrs. Roeder at this time was crouching over the crib protecting her child with her body—a fortunate thing as one of the bullets
that pierced the flimsy door might have killed her had she been standing.
Not offering to injure Taylor or Mrs. Roeder, the raiders departed. The
incident—just another case of intertribal bloodshedding. Unable to hire the
Lummis to work in the sawmill, the management had employed some Northern Indians. Their presence was just too tempting an opportunity for the
Lummis to strike in revenge for other killings.

Chapter VI

WHATCOM COUNTY

THE BEGINNING

IN A LITTLE OVER A YEAR after the arrival of
the first settlers on Bellingham Bay, the Territorial Legislature on March 9,
1854, established the County of Whatcom, fixed the boundaries therefor,
named a temporary set of county officers, provided that election of permanent officers take place in September, 1854, and designated the residence of
R. V. Peabody, near the mouth of Whatcom Creek as the county seat.

The legislature further stipulated that the Whatcom County Courthouse shall remain permanently in Whatcom and on the Peabody Donation
Claim, the south boundary of which is Champion Street; and may not be
removed unless three-fifths of the electors in the County, so approve.

Minutes of the first meeting of the newly appointed county commissioners were as follows:

"Commissioners' Court, Whatcom County,
Regular Term, July, 1854.

"Present: R. V. Peabody and H. C. Page, commissioners; A. M. Poe,
auditor; his deputy, E. C. Fitzhugh; and Ellis Barnes, sheriff.

"On motion it was ordered that all that portion of Whatcom County
north of a line running from the northern end of Lummi Island in an easterly
direction by Pattle's Point, be and is hereby made an election precinct to be
called Whatcom precinct. And all that portion of Whatcom County lying
south of said line, be and the same is hereby made an election precinct to
be called Ma-Mo-Sea precinct.

"Ordered that election for Whatcom precincts be held in the house of
R. V. Peabody, and that the elections for Ma-Mo-Sea precinct be held in
the house of A. M. Poe.

"Ordered that W. R. Pattle, H. Roeder and Ellis Barnes be and they
are hereby appointed road viewers to view out and locate a county road on
the nearest and best road from Poe's Point to the Lummi River. (This was
from the point near the P. A. F. Cannery of today—1951—to the western
branch of the Nooksack River emptying into Lummi Bay.)

"Ordered that B. F. Lewis be and is hereby appointed assessor in and
for the county of Whatcom to hold his office until the general election.

"Ordered that the county seat shall be located at the residence of R. V.
Peabody, at Whatcom, (his cabin was on the west bank of Whatcom Creek

and next door to Captain Roeder's), for the purpose of holding district and county court until otherwise ordered.

"Ordered that Charles C. Vail be and is hereby appointed constable in and for the precinct of Whatcom.

Ordered that the court adjourn.

Signed: R. V. Peabody

H. C. Page."

Further arrangements were made for the general election, which was called for September 1, 1854, and W. R. Pattle, Joel Clayton and Marcus Brown were appointed judges for Ma-Mo-Sea precinct, while Henry Roeder, William Utter and Edward Eldridge were to act in the Whatcom district.

The first regularly elected officers of Whatcom County were as follows:

Auditor, Edmund C. Fitzhugh; sheriff, Ellis Barnes; treasurer, William Utter; assessor, B. F. Lewis; coroner, W. A. Carpenter; Justices, R. V. Peabody and William Cullen; Commissioners (the length of the terms being decided by lot), William Cullen, three years, chairman; R. V. Peabody, two years; H. C. Page, one.

John W. Lysle, who arrived September, 1854, was appointed constable of Ma-Mo-Sea precinct in December of the same year. In the regular election of 1856, he was made auditor. The first survey of the town of Sehome was recorded by him. (Opposite page 102).

BOUNDARY OF WHATCOM COUNTY ESTABLISHED
IN 1854

The original boundaries of Whatcom County, as described in the law establishing it, March 9, 1854, were as follows:

"All of Island County from the north point of Perry's (Fidalgo) Island, due east to the summit of the Cascades; north along the summit to the boundary of British Columbia; west on the boundary to the Canal de Arrow; through the middle of the Canal de Arrow to the Straits of Juan de Fuca; through the straits to the mouth of Ringgolds Channel; across the mouth of Ringgolds Channel to the point of beginning."

On January 31, 1859, these rather confusing boundaries were amended to read (following the words "west on the boundary to"), "the point dividing the American and British possessions in the Gulf of Georgia, thence through the middle of the Canal de Arrow, to the Straits of Juan de Fuca; thence easterly to the place of beginning." This amendment was evidently to clarify and strengthen the American claim on the San Juan Islands.

A second boundary amendment was made in 1877, fixing the line between Island and Whatcom counties as the "center of the deepest channel at the west entrance of Deception Pass, until it intersects the northwest or west boundary of Snohomish County."

Officers of Whatcom County were provided for by the legislature of 1854. In 1855, the office of wreckmaster was created; the office of county surveyor the same year. The session of 1856, passed the first law relative to fisheries, enacting that "county commissioners may appoint an Inspector of Salmon, to examine all salmon for export, cured or put up at any fishery and destroy it if unfit," but no inspector was appointed for Whatcom County. In 1857, Whatcom County was allowed one member of the house of representatives, and districted with Island, Clallam, and Jefferson for the Council. A year later, the territorial militia was established. The office of probate judge was created in 1859, and the office of county superintendent in 1860.

Commenting on the County Status, Roth says:

"Thus in the six years following 1854, Whatcom County was firmly established with a name and an identity of its own, due representation in the territorial legislature, the machinery of courts, the nucleus for a school system, a county seat, a court house and a full set of county officers."

Boundaries of Whatcom County were undisturbed until October 31, 1873, when San Juan became a separate county, with Friday Harbor its county seat. Again, November 28, 1883, the county was divided, the southern portion being set off as Skagit County, with the county seat fixed first at LaConner, and later, by election, at Mt. Vernon. (Opposite page 6).

Since this last date, boundaries have remained unchanged, with Whatcom, now a part of the City of Bellingham, continuing as the County Seat.

DONATION CLAIMS

The Oregon Land Bill, commonly called the Donation Law, was signed by President Fillmore, September 27, 1850. This provided that any citizen above twenty-one years of age, who would journey to Oregon after December 1, 1850, might take up a half section of land (320 acres), and receive therefor without any payment whatsoever, as the free gift of the nation, provided he lived upon and cultivated the land for a period of four years. If accompanied by his wife, he might thus acquire 640 acres. The law was effective until December 1, 1853. Before the expiration date, however, the act was extended two years, but the amount of land that might be taken, either by a single or a married man was reduced one-half. The law further provided that any white man, half breeds included, who had been a resident of Oregon Territory prior to 1850 might file on double this amount of land as a donation claim.

Pioneers were not eager to accept land as a gift from the government, being more interested in coal and timber than in agriculture. Many that took up donation claims later sold them for a trifle, although those who retained their claims profited in later years. Present titles to Bellingham real estate practically all rest on these donation claims.

The first filing under this law at Bellingham Bay, was made by Captain William R. Pattle in January, 1853. Immediately thereafter like claims were filed on by James Morrison and John Thomas, both associates of Pattle, working for the Hudson's Bay Company. Thomas died in 1854 and Dan Harris who had been living with him perfected and succeeded to the claim in 1860, getting patent thereto, August 27, 1871. Thomas, who was buried on his claim, was the first white man to die on Bellingham Bay.

Other donation claims in order of their priority were those of R. V. Peabody, Roeder, Hedge, Vail, Fauntleroy (sold to Fitzhugh), Eldridge, Compton, Roberts, Poe, Page, Utter, Lysle and Jones. All of these were 160 acre claims, except those of Eldridge, Roberts, Lysle, and Jones, who with their wives took 320 acres; also that of A. M. Poe, who took advantage of the provision giving 320 acres to persons resident in the Territory prior to 1850.

Nineteen donation claims were filed upon in Whatcom County. The two farthest to the west were taken by John and Ellis Barnes, but were canceled later when found to be on the Indian Reservation. List of claims follows:

J. D. Hedges—claim—west of the present Marietta.

C. E. Roberts (and wife)—claim filed September 19, 1854. This was the land on which Fort Bellingham was located, later called the "Tuck Farm."

Enoch Compton—claim—later purchased by John Bennett. (Cement Plant stands on property today.) Located northwest of Squalicum Creek.

Edward Eldridge (and wife). Her claim of 160 acres was all west of Squalicum Creek. Part of his claim of 160 acres was east of the Creek and extended to West Street.

The Roeder Claim—extending from West Street to about G Street, or to the Roth Block. (When Captain Roeder first filed on land, he chose shore line land, on what later was the Sehome site; then released this and took the claim from West to G Street, because of the fine stand of timber.)

Russell V. Peabody—Claim—from G Street across Whatcom Creek to Champion Street, east to Unity Street, and north to about H Street.

E. C. Fitzhugh—Claim—from Champion Street to Army, to a point near Berry Street, and extending easterly to the York Addition. This would include most of the business section of Sehome, and took in the coal mine. This claim had been filed on by Captain W. H. Fauntleroy, Commander of the steamer, *Massachusetts*. On January 10, 1854, a quit claim deed was recorded as given by Fauntleroy to E. C. Fitzhugh, by which, in consideration of 500 shares in the Bellingham Bay Coal Company, Fauntleroy transferred his claim on Bellingham Bay to the Company. On May 5, 1854, Fitzhugh in consideration of stock, gave the Coal Company the right to mine on his claim.

Charles C. Vail—Claim—from Berry Street to a p o i n t near St. Joseph's Hospital, near Beech Street. In 1855, he sold his claim, bounded on the north by the Fitzhugh Claim, and on the south by the Pattle Claim, to Fitzhugh, agent, for $500.

William R. Pattle—Claim—from the hospital near Beech Street, to a little south of the gas works of today, (1951), near Twelfth and South State Streets.

James Morrison—Claim—from Twelfth and South State Streets to Douglas Street.

John Thomas—Claim—later known as the Dan Harris Claim—from Douglas Street to near the Fairhaven Junior High School on Cowgill Street.

A. M. Poe—Claim—including Dead Man's Point—originally called "Poe's Point," and extending south about a quarter of a mile.

Maurice O'Conner—Claim—this included the property on the hill at South Bellingham. The north line was Douglas Street, the south, Harris, the west, Twelfth, and the east, Lenora. (Approximately)

John W. Lysle (and wife)—Claim—lying back from the waterfront, occupied in part today by the Western Washington College.

Thomas Jones (and wife)—Claim—later became the Eldridge and Bartlett Addition, between Sehome and Fairhaven.

Henry C. Page—Claim—was part of the Bellingham Bay Company's first addition near the Darigold Plant of today on Ellis Street.

William Utter—Claim—contained the major part of the York Addition. The north line was Fraser Street.

Out of the hundreds of acres in Donation Claims around Bellingham Bay, parts of the Eldridge and Lysle claims, and a few Roeder lots, are held by the original families.

Chapter VII.

PIONEER MEN OF THE NORTHWEST

and

INDIAN TROUBLE

MANY ADVENTUROUS MEN helped write the history of this Fourth Corner and deserve mention, but space forbids the recording of more than a few.

ALONZO M. POE

Alonzo M. Poe was born in Wisconsin, May, 1826. He journeyed to the Coast in 1845, and became one of the founders of Olympia, Washington, also a delegate to the first Territorial Legislature from Thurston County. Poe moved to Bellingham Bay in 1853. The following year he was one of the county officials. By profession a civil engineer, he platted Whatcom in 1858, and surveyed the first trail to the Fraser River during the Gold Rush Days of 1858. The piece of property on the present South Bellingham, known as Poe's Point—Commercial Point—was on his claim. Later this was called "Dead Man's Point." Poe next returned to Olympia, where he remained until 1862; then moved to Napa City, California, where he spent his last years.

RUSSELL V. PEABODY

Russell V. Peabody, Captain Roeder's associate during the California Gold Rush days, and partner in the mill enterprise, left a permanent impress on the community. He was prominent during the Fraser River Gold Rush boom, being particularly active in real estate. As captain of the Whatcom County Volunteers, he moved his company south to guard Snoqualmie Pass during the Indian outbreaks. Peabody served as County Commissioner, also as member of the Boundary Commission. (Opposite page 22).

Like so many whites of the day, Peabody took an Indian wife, who bore him three children—Frank, Kate and Minnie. The three led brief tragic lives and are remembered chiefly because they complicated settlement of the Peabody estate.

Russell V. Peabody died in California in 1868, but the claims of the Peabody heirs, retarded the growth of the community, and still had citizens at swords' points almost two decades later.

EDMUND CLARE FITZHUGH

Edmund Clare Fitzhugh, as head of the coal mine and company store, was at that time the largest employer of labor in the Northwest, and at once the most important man in the settlement. He has been described as a fearless, high strung Virginia gentleman, generous, hospitable, impulsive, self indulgent, imperious and self-willed; a born fighter, and quick to take offense—something of a roisterer.

Fitzhugh had early joined the rush to California, where in 1849, he formed a law partnership with Edmund Randolph and A. P. Critterden. He became Whatcom County auditor; also Indian commissioner; and, under President Buchanan, he served four years as United States District Judge. His official reports on Indians and Indian affairs of the district afford invaluable data to the historian and to the student of the aborigines.

While on the Bay, Fitzhugh married a daughter of Chief Sehome.* Three children were born to this union. Like Pickett, Fitzhugh gave his allegiance to the State of Virginia. He joined the Confederate forces, rising to the rank of major. After the Civil War, he served four terms in the Virginia legislature. Again he married. Later he moved to Iowa. In 1879, he left his wife and family and returned to San Francisco, where, the victim of poverty and dissipation, he died of apoplexy in the WhatCheer Hotel, November 24, 1883.

CAPTAIN WILLIAM UTTER

Captain William Utter was born in Genessee County, New York, June 18, 1810. A master shipwright, he built many of the largest and best vessels on the Great Lakes. In 1852, he moved to the Pacific Coast and joined Captain Roeder. Arriving at Whatcom in May, 1853, he carried on for Roeder and Peabody as master mechanic of the new saw mill. At one time Utter leased and ran the mill under his own name. Between the years 1859 and 1873, when the mill burned, he was in charge almost continuously, operating on behalf of the owners who were engaged in other affairs. Like his employers he took up a donation claim.

In later years, when his friends affectionately called him "Captain Billy," Utter served Whatcom County as treasurer and also as County Commissioner.

---

*Roth's History of Whatcom states:

"Sehome was a sub-chief of the Clallam tribe of Indians, married to a Samish princess, so that some of the whites considered him a chief of the Samish. He lived in the Samish Village on Samish Island until his death, about 1860, according to Thomas Jefferson of Lummi, Sehome's grandnephew."

JAMES H. TAYLOR

James H. Taylor, reportedly one of the best ship carpenters ever to land in the Northwest, was another pioneer who had an important part in settlement of the district. During the gold rush to California, he made three trips around the Horn. As ship carpenter of the Clipper *Eclipse,* he landed in San Francisco, two weeks before the fire. In July, 1854, he reached Bellingham Bay on the lumber bark *Success,* Captain Coupe, and became associated with Roeder and Utter in the building and operation of the *H. C. Page.* Taylor next built the *General Harney* for Roeder, this being the first vessel launched on Puget Sound that was large enough to transport cattle. He figured prominently in the community during the Indian troubles. For a time he lived in a little cabin near the Fort. Later he moved to a homestead at Brennan five miles northwest from Whatcom, where he lived with his Indian wife, who was the widow of John G. Hyatt, deceased merchant. Together they reared her son, John G. Hyatt, Junior.

INDIAN TROUBLES

In 1854, Louis G. Loscher, a blacksmith, arrived in Whatcom with his Northern Indian wife. Previously, a cousin of hers, a chief, had been hired by a settler in Olympia, to clear land, being promised his pay at the completion of the job. When the time came for settlement, the white man refused to pay the Indian, declaring the work was not satisfactory. A quarrel followed and the chief was killed.

Loscher's wife warned the settlers around Bellingham Bay, that her people would have their revenge, and that without regard to the guilty person, they probably would strike at the nearest settlement which was Whatcom.

When Governor Douglas heard of this murder, after the Indians had returned to Victoria from Olympia, he tried to appease them by paying a certain number of blankets. Nothing would satisfy them but the murderer's head, or that of some other "Boston." Immediately the Governor sent word to the settlements, warning them of the danger, and offering to furnish arms if needed, provided some responsible person would give security for their return.

Seventy-five of the raiding Northern Indians killed a settler on Vancouver Island by the name of Bagley. With British efficiency, Governor Douglas soon had his troops in pursuit, but the Indians were lost among the many coves of the San Juan Islands. Having escaped so easily, they carried on boldly.

On May 24, 1854, two of the canoes landed on the shores of Bellingham Bay, opposite Joel Clayton's cabin below Chuckanut. At first he thought they were friendly; then becoming suspicious he returned to his cabin on the pretense of getting money to buy blankets which they offered for sale. He then fled to the woods, with the Indians in pursuit, and managed to reach the log house of William Pattle. (South of the present gas works.) Friendly Lummis had notified the settlers of the danger, and seven of the whites had gathered in the Pattle house to resist the anticipated attack. Captain Pattle, meantime, sent out two English miners, Melville and Brown, in a boat, to patrol the Bay and to give the alarm if the Indians should appear.

In the cabin, one of the men, Dick Williams, had tried all afternoon to dislodge a charge that had stuck in his flintlock musket. That evening he took a red hot wire, went to the front door, and rammed the wire down the firing vent into the barrel. The loud report was heard by the approaching Indians, and was answered by a war-whoop and a volley of shots from two Northern canoes. The settlers fled to the woods and two of the Lummis kept up an incessant firing all night.

In an interview Blanket Bill Jarman gave to Frank Teck in 1897, he was quoted as saying: "Dick Williams came out of Fort Pattle and fired off his musket just as the Indians were passing on the beach. They were surprised but returned the fire. The flashes from their guns lighted up the recesses of shelf rock, and they saw the two miners asleep in their canoe. The Indians captured and beheaded them."

Before the Northern Indians left the Bay, they destroyed Clayton's cabin and fired into the home of Alonzo M. Poe on Poe's Point. (Near the P. A. F. site.) The headless bodies of Melville and Brown, found in the canoe the next morning, told the story of their fate.

These Indians next raided Whidbey Island, and destroyed the homes of several settlers. It was this raid which thoroughly alarmed the legislature, and caused the enlistment of a company of volunteers, under Colonel Ebey, which did effective work, chiefly in Snohomish County.

In March, 1853, the northern part of Oregon Territory was set aside as Washington Territory, with the seat of government at Olympia, and with Isaac I. Stevens as the first Territorial Governor. Next, the settlers in the Northwest, asked the governor to establish a military post at Bellingham Bay. This request was granted and a commission in 1855, selected a site, on the Roberts' claim, at a spot called "The Plateau." The following Memorial to the Federal government by the territorial legislature, December 21, 1855, undoubtedly hastened the building of the Fort:

"In 1854 a descent was made by the Northern Indians upon our settlers on Bellingham Bay, murdering our citizens and destroying their property to a large amount. The settlement is on the extreme verge of our Northwestern frontier, isolated from the other settlements and liable to be cut off before any assistance could reach them. A petition was forwarded to the proper authorities praying for the establishment of a military post. That committee has since visited and selected a site, but no further action has been taken. If action is not promptly taken, settlers will be obliged to abandon that neighborhood.

Signed: A. A. Denny, Speaker of the House.

Seth Catlin, President of the Council."

A second resolution asked that a military road be built from Fort Steilacoom to Bellingham Bay, pointing out the proposed fort presently could be reached only by water, which might delay sending needed reenforcements, "on account of long calms in the summer and the storms in the winter."

A third Memorial stated: "An Indian war is raging with unparalleled violence in our midst, rendering the navigation of the Sound by small crafts extremely dangerous, consequently all that portion of our territory lying north of Pierce County, in which is included King, Jefferson, Clallam, Island and Whatcom Counties are destitute of any mail service, although they contain the custom house and some of the most important commercial towns on Puget Sound."

A joint memorial also asked that men-of-war be stationed on the Northwest Coast, "on account of the Northern Indians, and also as to the disputed boundary, the coast being frequently visited by British men-of-war."

Three naval vessels were assigned to the Puget Sound Patrol. Of these the *Decatur*, the *Active*, and later the *Massachusetts*, all helped make history.

While waiting for the federal government to act, Governor Stevens recommended that the settlers at Bellingham Bay build a blockhouse for their protection. The site chosen, was the highest ground above Whatcom Creek to the west, on Peabody Hill. (On what is now D Street between Bancroft and Clinton Streets.)

The blockhouse was built by James Taylor, Charles E. Roberts, Captain Roeder, William Utter and R. V. Peabody. Taylor, who was most active in its operation, has left this description: "It was built on Peabody Hill, in the winter of 1855-'56. The lower story of the blockhouse was 22 by 22 feet, with an upper story projecting over all sides. The stockade was 60 by 60 feet, and there were two bastions built of eight inch timbers, one on the southeast and one on the northwest corner."

These projecting bastions were their loopholes, affording sentries unobstructed views of the outside walls of the stockade. The government furnished flintlock rifles, but the Indians were so provided also, through the Hudson's Bay Company's traders.

In regard to the Indian situation in 1855-'56, Edward Eldridge wrote at one time: "Our own local Indians have always been true friends to the whites, but we could not tell how far we could rely on them, and whenever rumors of Indian troubles reached us from other points, they caused a feeling of apprehension on our part. Our greatest danger was from the Northern Indians, who came to the Sound in the spring in large canoes, from fifty to one hundred in a canoe, and returned to their homes in the fall. These canoes could land in any of the isolated settlements, plunder and kill, and before any neighbor could know of it, be beyond the reach of pursuit.

"When the Indian war broke out in 1855-'56, it was confined to the Indians east of the mountains, and few tribes in the upper part of the Sound, but the great mass of the tribes remained friendly to the whites, although efforts were made by the hostile tribes to get all the Indians to join them, and exterminate the whites.

"To prevent this, and believing it cheaper and better to feed, than to fight the Indians, the Governor, who was then Superintendent of Indian Affairs also, placed all friendly Indians on reservations under proper officers, and issued rations to them regularly, and had a government express established that visited every reservation once a week which afforded the settlers an improved system of obtaining their mail.

"General Wool, who commanded the Military Department of the Pacific at that time, would not acknowledge the magnitude of the Indian uprising and would not furnish the assistance Governor Stevens required, but Governor Stevens, being thoroughly posted on the feeling, strength and resources of the various tribes, having been making treaties with them during the previous months, and having just been recalled from the Blackfoot nation by an express from acting Governor Mason, and knowing the great danger from the isolated position unless prompt and energetic measures were taken at once, he determined to act upon his own judgment and assume control of affairs, notwithstanding the opinion of General Wool, and to this bold and timely course the inhabitants of both Washington and Oregon almost unanimously concede the averting of a great calamity. Governors Palmer of Oregon and Stevens of Washington, both called for volunteers which calls were promptly responded to."

After Governor Stevens arrived at Olympia, he found that General Wool, had ordered the regular army officers not to supply the volunteer forces with arms and ammunition; consequently Stevens appealed to Governor Douglas of Vancouver Island.

UPPER—Fort Bellingham Block House. Built in 1856. F. F. Handschy at the side.

LOWER—Fort Bellingham, U. S. Military Post, July 16, 1857. From an original drawing by Lieutenant Alden aboard the survey steamer "Active."—Photo courtesy of J. S. Whiting.

Kent and Hunter in WASHINGTON WEST OF THE CASCADES sum up the great assistance Governor Douglas rendered to Governor Stevens and the Americans across the border, in the following: "Douglas gave his personal order on the Hudson's Bay Company for $5,000 worth of supplies; the steamers *Beaver* and *Otter* were, at different times, employed by the territorial officials; Douglas took measures to prevent the Northern Indians from coming into Sound waters, and the Victoria and Nisqually posts of the two British companies furnished arms and ammunition and other supplies to the value of more than $25,000."

The moral effect of this action was enormous. The Indians saw that the white people made common cause against them. In December, 1855, Legislative Assembly of Washington Territory, formally expressed the thanks of the people to Governor Douglas for this assistance. (December 18, 1855, Laws of Washington, 1855, p. 31.)

Edward Eldridge continues: "There were no settlers in Eastern Washington then, but nearly every able bodied man in Western Washington was enrolled and took to the field, leaving small detachments at various points to protect the families who were collected in the towns in log forts built for the purpose. Every man was enrolled in Whatcom County, except those working in the coal mine; this in order that coal could be had for the war steamers on the Sound.

"The Whatcom Company, under Captain Peabody, together with a company formed on Whidbey Island, and another formed at Port Townsend, constituted the northern battalion under Major Van Bokelyn, all of whom went up the Snoqualmie, except a detachment of twelve men from the Whatcom Company, who were left under Lieutenant Eldridge to guard the settlement and coal mine. The families were collected within a stockade built on the hill at Whatcom, near the site of what was later the home in turn of three county auditors, Kellogg, Smith and C. Donovan."

The following is the list of the Whatcom County Volunteers as given in Roth's History; all of whom enlisted in Company H, Second Regiment, Washington Volunteers, in February, 1856, of which Company, Russell V. Peabody was Captain, Charles C. Vail, First Lieutenant, and Edward Eldridge, Second Lieutenant:

"R. V. Peabody, George Richardson, H. C. Page, William R. Stuart, _____ Tamboree, George Stanhope, Samuel Brown, Charles C. Vail, R. Williams, Henry Roeder, Andrew Wilson, Henry Deland, S. D. Howe, Edward Eldridge, James H. Taylor, William Roberts, Francis Cootz, William Utter, Ank Stout, David Snorer, Frank Mahoney, James Fraser, Edward

---

UPPER—Pickett House—Ceremony transferring the deed of the property to the Washington State Historical Society—1936.

LOWER—Old Pickett Bridge on the Military Road, completed in 1858. Taken by the author in November, 1900, while standing on a wooden bridge, at Seventeenth street (Dupont).

Chandler, John Clark, William Hughs, Joseph Snubb, _____ Williams, Enoch Compton, James E. Jewett, James G. Hedges, Peter Cogley, James Grant, John Short, Bob Johnson, Charles E. Roberts, Lewis Loscher, Maurice O'Connor, John Whitebread, Charles Folsanbee, John Long, Jack Spencer, Dick Wilson."

This list of forty-two men embraces nearly all who lived on Bellingham Bay in 1856. The names of many who were doubtless employed at the mine or mill, appear in no other place in Whatcom County history, but it should not be forgotten, that while they saw no fighting, they were ready to go to defend their homes and the people of Washington Territory regardless of the dangers which might have confronted them."

The petitions and memorials to Congress resulted in the final establishment of Fort Bellingham, and the location and partial construction of the Military Road; but before this time, the women and children of the settlement had spent many an anxious, weary night in the stockade on Peabody Hill, while the men stood guard.

When Congress finally authorized the establishment of a fort at Bellingham Bay, General W. S. Harney, Commander of the Department of Oregon, ordered Colonel Casey of the Ninth Infantry to move Captain George E. Pickett and Company D, north from Fort Steilacoom, prepared to construct and occupy the proposed post.

Chapter VIII.

FORT BELLINGHAM

CAPTAIN GEORGE E. PICKETT with sixty-eight men of Company D, Ninth Infantry arrived at Bellingham Bay from Fort Steilacoom, August 26, 1856, preparatory to erecting Fort Bellingham on a site previously selected. This was on the Charles E. Roberts Donation Claim, situated about three miles northwest from the mouth of Whatcom Creek.

Officers assigned to this one company post included First Lieutenant Robert H. Davis,* nephew of Jefferson Davis, Second Lieutenant Flemming, Second Lieutenant J. W. Forsythe, Surgeon George Suckley, and Assistant Surgeon Craig.

In a recently published book, FORTS OF THE STATE OF WASHINGTON, J. S. Whiting, the author writes:

"Fort Bellingham, a U. S. Military Post.

"Fort Bellingham was situated on the bluff overlooking the Bay at a point 3.6 miles westerly from the mouth of Whatcom Creek. The general plan of Fort Bellingham consisted of a wharf at the foot of the bluff quite directly in front and below the Fort. Above the bluff was a palisaded inclosure measuring 215 feet square. The Northeast corner and the Southwest corner of the palisade was completed by the inclusion of a typical blockhouse in each of those corners. The ground dimensions of the blockhouses were 22 feet square. The palisade posts were from mill cut timbers 8 feet in thickness and random widths up to 18 inches. The posts were dug into trenches and were dowelled together near the top. The flag mast was located near the south wall about midway east and west. A drill ground was directly to the east, and a gate was in the east wall line. Also a gate in the north line near the Northeast corner."

Second story loopholes or firing slits in the blockhouses commanded all walls. Headquarters building, barracks, officers' mess and other structures, also the sutler's store over which E. D. Warbass presided; all were constructed of lumber from the Roeder mill. Later, walks of Chuckanut stone connected the principal buildings. Water and fuel were convenient to the Post. Illumination was provided by candles, or dip-wick lamps, mostly tin, fed by dog-fish oil. (Opposite page 54).

---

*Davis had trouble with Edmund C. Fitzhugh over a card game and challenged the latter to a duel. This Fitzhugh declined. After differences with Captain Pickett, Davis resigned the service and became a deer hunter. At the outbreak of the Civil War, he joined the Confederate forces, leaving behind an Indian wife, Princess Tol Stola and son, Samuel Davis, the latter killed when the Steamer *Josephine* exploded January 17, 1883, off Suzan Bay.

Stables for the Post animals were constructed in a sheltered nearby gulley. With the first death, a graveyard was started to the Northwest of the stockade. Of the five persons buried there, one was a civilian named Grant, who was killed by the explosion of a musket, July 4, 1858.

The Fort Bellingham Reservation was a mile square, including the Roberts' Claim of 325.04 acres, which had been seized under "Military Necessity" as affording the only open land in the area. When the Roberts refused to vacate their claim, Captain Pickett had the family forcibly ejected.

During the San Juan incident the blockhouse at the southwest corner of the stockade was torn down, and with other lumber and supplies, was moved to the trouble zone and there reconstructed.

The Post was vacated April 28, 1860. For years the Army maintained a guard at the Fort. On recommendation of Major General Halleck, who visited the Coast in 1868, it was abandoned finally.

With the closing of the Fort, business and mail service suffered. The district lost prestige; while the settlers' sense of security against Indian raids, vanished.

The remaining blockhouse at the northeast corner of the stockade burned August 27, 1897. David Tuck, living on the Tuck Farm, believed the fire to be of incendiary origin. Some thought it had been started by tramps sleeping in the blockhouse. Others were of the opinion that it had spread from the fire of smelt fishermen, picnicking on the beach.

Three stepping-stones, now at the Harry Smith home on the Tuck Farm, once were part of the walks at Fort Bellingham. These, together with two large timbers from the stockade, a section of the flag pole, and a heavy iron lock, now reposing in the Bellingham Public Museum, with a few stray shingles, comprise the only relics of Fort Bellingham.

THE PICKETT HOUSE

The oldest house in Bellingham, the Pickett House, dubbed the "Head House" by early settlers, stands on Peabody Hill—Bancroft Street, between E and F Streets. This was constructed by Captain George E. Pickett, Company D, Ninth Infantry, the year his command erected Fort Bellingham.

Pickett's force reached Whatcom, August 26, 1856, to find that the settlers, fearful of Indian raids, were crowding each night into the stockade and blockhouse on Peabody Hill. Tension was relieved by the presence of the soldiers who themselves occupied the stockade during preliminary construction work at the Fort.

Immediately, Captain Pickett ordered land cleared for a home, and, on what afterward became Bancroft Street, he erected a two story frame house.

This he occupied as his residence while at Fort Bellingham, conducting much official business from the front room. To this home, the Army man brought his Indian bride, daughter of a Northern chieftain. And in this house the couple's son, James Tilton Pickett, was born December 31, 1857. In the front hall of this building, there are visible today some of the wide undressed boards, exactly as they were cut by the Roeder-Peabody mill.

Few changes have been made in the structure. A winding stairway leads upward from the front hall, replacing the ladder that originally provided the only access to the two second story rooms. The fireplace with its stick and mud chimney is gone from the west wall of the leanto. The addition of a small kitchen and a glassed-in front porch and a window comprise other alterations. (Opposite page 55).

A pear tree, oldest in the Northwest, stands in the back yard where it was planted by Captain Pickett. A cherry tree that rubbed branches with the pear until recent years, has been removed because its roots were undermining the house, while its scraggly limbs raked off shingles with each wind storm. At the rear of the lot is an old shack, the remains of the Pickett stable.

Through the years the Pickett House has been owned and occupied by many persons. Owners include John E. Peabody (brother of R. V. Peabody), John G. Parker, General M. A. McPherson, Estella Harris, Wesley Lawrence, C. O. Rapelje, Hattie Strothers, and the Washington State Historical Society.

At one time, Mrs. Pitchford, sister of Blanket Bill Jarman, rented the "Head House." In 1873, when W. H. Fouts taught at Marietta, his family occupied the property. That winter was cold; the snow deep; the fire never allowed to die in the fireplace. A pair of cougars was attracted by the warmth, and, according to their tracks, spent nearly every night on the leanto roof close to the chimney, where their movements were plainly audible to the terrified woman and children below. Fearful that the weight of the animals might crush the roof, or that they might come down the chimney, Mrs. Fouts and her young ones habitually closed the leanto door and spent the night in some unheated room.

General M. A. McPherson, promoter of the Kansas (Washington) Colony purchased the property in December, 1882. Judge W. H. Harris, who, with his family landed at Sehome in 1883, bought the Pickett House in November, 1884. In an article written years later while living in California, Judge Harris thus described some of his experiences:

"We were living in an old time place known as the McPherson House, said to have been built by General Pickett when stationed at Fort Bellingham in the '50's. Its location was on 15th Street, near E. These streets were

unimproved and unused, being thickly covered with brush, logs, and standing timber, at the top of a high abrupt hill, reached only by long steep
stairs, made of two inch planks with platforms about four feet square and
about 30 feet apart, used as resting places, that you might recover your
breath to reach the next platform above.

"There were hand rails on these stairs that you might help yourself
up with your hands, also to keep you from falling off and rolling down the
hill. They had a further and quite important use. In case the men who
used these stairs in getting to their homes, should linger during the evening
at Pardon O'Brion's talking politics, or at Mohrmann & Johnson's listening
to Albert Mohrmann pull music from his accordian until a late hour, they
could get up those stairs between the rails. In fact when they got started
they couldn't go anywhere else. There were three or more separate stair
systems. One going up C Street to the Reveille Office, (corner of C and Dupont), one to the neighborhood of the Charley Donovan house, (near Clinton
and D Streets), and another to my neighborhood. Family supplies for all the
residents along the brow of the hill, from Whatcom Creek to the foot of
E Street, for some time were carried up those stairs. One might expect pre-
mature death from heart failure from such unusual efforts."

Hattie Strother became owner of the Pickett House, September 5, 1889,
her father having purchased the premises on arrival from the South. After
the death of her parents, Miss Strothers continued her residence in the old
home together with Aunt Mary, a free born negress who had accompanied
the family to the Coast.

Finally Hattie Strother transferred the Pickett property to the Washington State Historical Society, January 25, 1936. With appropriate ceremonies the deed was presented to W. P. Bonney, secretary of the Society,
April 29, 1936. Under terms of the transfer Miss Strothers was privileged
to live in the historic home as long as she desired. At the age of seventy-six
she passed away after fifty years of occupancy.

MILITARY ROAD

Complying with territorial memorials, Congress in 1856 appropriated
$10,000 to build a military road between Fort Steilacoom (south of Tacoma)
and Bellingham Bay—this for the movement of troops and supplies in case
of Indian raids.

After Fort Bellingham was established, work began at that end of the
line, a road being slashed through the woods along the shoreline to Squalicum Creek, which was bridged. The second bridge was on Fourteenth
Street (Astor) over the great gulch between F and G Streets, variously
called "Chinook Ravine" or "Little Squalicum." This was the most elabo-

rate of the three bridges, but was destroyed by the great forest fire of 1868. From Chinook Ravine, the Military Road turned uphill on F Street; thence angling along the bluff to approximately the vicinity of Eighteenth (Ellsworth) where it crossed Whatcom Creek about a block above the present Dupont street bridge. This last known as the "Military Bridge" or the "Pickett Bridge." The building of these structures was reported by the pioneer newspaper, the NORTHERN LIGHT, as follows:

"July 24, 1858—A substantial bridge is being erected across 'Chinook Ravine' on Fourteenth Street, one block above our office, and grading approaches on either side, to make it easy of access."

"July 31, 1858—ANOTHER BRIDGE—A substantial bridge is almost complete on the Military Road over Whatcom Creek, a short distance up above the mill at the falls. (Opposite page 55).

From the Pickett Bridge the road plowed easterly through the timber past the site of the present city hall, thence in a southerly direction. Laboriously giant trees were felled, huge logs cut and burned, great stumps excavated along the meandering right-of-way, past the present corner of Elk (State) and Holly Streets, until at last a narrow, muddy, rutted thoroughfare emerged from the forest at the mine on the Sehome shoreline.

Funds were exhausted by this time and although the Territorial Legislature bombarded Congress with petitions, no further appropriations were made, and the Military Road was uncompleted. Most travel was by foot; horses and mules were scarce; wagons practically non-existent. During the goldrush days and for years afterward, trails in the out-land were generally wide enough for the passage of pack-stock only. Nevertheless, the Bellingham Bay communities profited by, and achieved no little prestige through, the possession of the only passable wagon road in the northwest. However, footpads or hold-up men became most disturbing after gold rush days, and the citizens avoiding the road through the woods, generally followed the shoreline trails from Whatcom to Sehome, crossing Whatcom Creek on the foot bridge at the Roeder mill.

The Military Road eventually was taken over by the county and maintained as such for many years although much of the work had to be done through private contributions of labor and money. Roth's History lists a group of citizens who, in 1875 contributed their labors to the repair of the Whatcom Creek bridge and trail, then almost impassable. As late as 1884, it is recorded that: "The Cornwall Company improved the road along Eighteenth Street on the old Military Road to the Nooksack Road, but waited in vain for Whatcom to make connections between Thirteenth and Holly Streets, so wagons might pass between Old Whatcom and New Whatcom."

FORT BELLINGHAM FLAGPOLE

The first flagpole at Fort Bellingham was a clear straight fir, 100 feet tall and eighteen inches in diameter at the base. This was placed near the south wall of the stockade by William Utter, ship carpenter. Unfortunately no proper foundation was provided, and the staff soon blew down. Thereupon another carpenter, by the name of Young, erected a seventy foot pole, which he set securly in a square timber foundation.

The Fort was abandoned in 1860. Finally the pole rotted at the base and fell, while the one remaining blockhouse burned in 1897. At the time, David Tuck was living at the site of the Fort—the Roberts' Donation Claim, then known as the Tuck Farm. Next, the property was sold to the Smith Brothers in 1902 for use as a truck farm. Prostrate amidst bushes and blackberry vines, the Smiths found the historic shaft, much of it still sound and useful, and this was presented to the City of Whatcom, which turned it over to the Ladies' Co-Operative Society. That organization then arranged a semi-centennial celebration by the cities of Whatcom and Fairhaven during which the upper portion of the pole, appropriately marked, was reerected in Elizabeth Park, Whatcom.

After standing for many years the flag pole was lowered because of old age. A section thereof is preserved in the Bellingham Public Museum. This is encircled by an iron band, which bears the inscription:

"Erected at Fort Bellingham, October, 1856, by Captain George Pickett. Reerected by the Ladies' Co-Operative Society, April 30, 1903."

The Honorable Clarence B. Bagley, Washington Territory pioneer from Seattle, and Mrs. Charles Magee, secretary of the Ladies' Co-Operative Society, in their speeches contrasted the changes wrought by nearly half a century—the 1903 flag with its forty-six stars floating over a peaceful, victorious country—that other banner of 1856 bravely flaunting its thirty-one stars on a lonely shore over the Nation's last outpost, amidst raids and threats of wars.

The Junior Order of American Mechanics erected the old flag pole, after which the flag itself, one obtained from Dewey's flagship, the *Olympia,* was hoisted to the peak of the historic staff. And this ceremony tied the old to the new by an additional touch. At the first flag raising, the soldier managing the hoist had dropped one end of the halyard, which fouled in the block. Accordingly Blanket Bill Jarman, who in his youth, before he deserted, had been captain of a fore-top on a British man-of-war, was sent aloft by Captain Pickett to clear the rope. In the ceremony in 1903, Blanket Bill, then eighty-three, handled the halyards.

Chapter IX.

NORTHERN RAIDERS

and

COLONEL ISAAC N. EBEY

Colonel ISAAC N. EBEY, former Collector of Customs for the Puget Sound District, on the night of August 11, 1857, at Whidbey Island, was shot and beheaded, by vengeful Northern Indians. This coup by painted warriors, striking in the dark from their great high prowed canoes, preyed on the imaginations and upset and terrified the settlers of the Northern Sound Country more than any other incident during early days; more than previous raids; more even then the Indian wars fought a few years earlier in the south central part of the territory. Yet the blow could have been predicted—its cause being obvious.

The cause—the massacre of Indians at Port Gamble in November, 1856, when a Chieftain and many of his tribesmen fell under the fire of the United States Naval Steamer *Massachusetts*. None of the dead, of course, under the Redman's belief, could rest easily until revenged.

Colonel Ebey kept a diary. Under date of November 25, 1856, he listed the incidents leading up to the Port Gamble battle, (and parenthetically to his own death); how certain Indians after committing robbery fled north to take refuge with their tribesmen who were working peacefully at Port Gamble; and how a third or more of their number fell under the naval guns when they refused to surrender the accused raiders.

It was but one more example of the bungling of Indian relations by the Americans—of the understandable reaction by the perplexed savage to the laws, rules, and often unreasonable demands of the "Boston men"—all in contrast to the fair dealing and peaceful methods generally prevailing across the Border under the British and the Hudson's Bay Company. Bancroft, the historian, in later years, after interviewing numerous settlers of the Northwest, and the makers of history, said that he was almost sickened at times by the casual admission of injustice and deliberate physical cruelty toward the Indians on the part of the Americans, as contrasted to the peace and justice generally prevailing across the Border.

Colonel Ebey was first identified with Whatcom County history at an early stage of the International Boundary dispute. This was in 1854, when, as Collector of Customs, he went to the San Juan Island in a futile attempt to collect import duties on a flock of sheep imported by the Hudson's Bay Company. The present counties of Whatcom, Skagit and San Juan, also Whidbey Island and the San Juan Archipelago were included in Island County, created by the Oregon Legislature in 1852.

The name of Isaac N. Ebey also appears in Northwest history, when, as Oregon Territorial assemblyman from Thurston County, 1852-'53, he drafted a memorial to Congress, asking that the portion of Oregon, north of the Columbia River, be organized as the Territory of Columbia. In 1853, President Pierce appointed him as Inspector of Revenues and Collector of Customs for Puget Sound, a position he held until 1856. During the Indian hostilities in 1855-'56, he served as Captain of Company I, First Regiment, Washington Territorial Volunteers. On July 13, 1857, a month before his death, he was elected as prosecuting attorney for the Third Judicial District of Washington Territory.

In the meantime, while Collector of Customs, Ebey had succeeded in having the Customs office established at Port Townsend and had developed a farm across the channel on Whidbey Island, a farm he had filed upon in October, 1850. This he called "The Cabins."

The entry in the diary of Colonel Ebey* for November 25, 1856, covering the bombardment of the Indians at Port Gamble by the U. S. S. *Massachusetts,* Commander Swartout commanding,—an event directly connected with Ebey's death, reads as follows:

"Tuesday, November 25, 1856.

"Morning clear and pleasant. Been employed today in hauling timber up the hill. I think three fugitive Northern Indians passed here today. I think they must have been some of the party that escaped from the fight at Port Gamble—which I neglected to mention yesterday. It appears that a party of Northern Indians had been up the Sound and had been committing depredations as usual, robbing homes, etc. When about returning to Vancover Island they were pursued by the U. S. Steamer *Massachusetts,* and overtaken at Port Gamble, where Captain I. Ellis had a number of the same tribe at work, who, as these people arrived, joined them, making the party near one hundred strong. The Captain of the steamer sent word to the Indians that they must deliver up the Indians who had been concerned in the depredations above.

"This they refused to do, and sent word to the Captain that if he wished to fight, they would fight him and immediately hoisted a red flag.

*From an article on Colonel Isaac N. Ebey in the Pacific Northwest Quarterly of July, 1942, by Professor L. A. Kibbe, then of Western Washington College of Education.

This was in the evening. At daylight the next morning the Captain had two parties on shore—one with a brass howitzer, and had the little steamer, *Trawler* up in shore and had a mortar on her. These dispositions were all made before the Indians were awake. This completed, the Captain sent Dr. Bigelow as an Interpreter, to demand the surrender of the Indians who were guilty. To this the Indians returned a defiant answer, hoisted a red flag, and commenced firing on the parties. The steamer *Massachusetts* then let off a broadside. The parties on the shore made a charge and waited. The enemy took refuge in the timber near by. The Captain would not suffer his men to follow them into the timber. The firing was then kept up all day, the steamer, *Massachusetts* throwing her heavy metal in the timber where the Indians had taken refuge, and the mortar on this little steamer throwing shells made dreadful havoc. Some two thousand dollars worth of property belonging to the Indians was destroyed, among which were three hundred new blankets. The next morning the Indians hoisted a white flag. Twenty-seven were found dead—seventeen in one place. Ten were missing. Those who were killed were dreadfully cut up. Some had been killed from splinters from the trees. One woman was killed. She and another woman had come from the timber to the camp to carry off the chief who was wounded (both legs were broken). They were called to come to the marines. One of them started to them, the other started to run off. She was fired upon and killed, six balls having taken effect in her body. The Captain of the steamer, then dictated his term to them, which were that all who were there should come aboard the steamer, and he would take them over to Victoria. This the Indians did not wish to do, but rather wished to purchase some canoes from the natives and go to Victoria by themselves. This was not suffered. One marine was killed by a slug of iron taking effect in his head. Two others were saved from wound and death by the ball of the enemy striking the handle of a large knife, and the other the butt of a pistol.

"A vessel is at anchor tonight at the landing. I believe it is t h e *H. C. Page*, from Bellingham."

If the settlers thought that the proud Northern tribes would take the massacre at Port Gamble with no thought of reprisal, they were quickly disabused. Rumors soon were afloat through the Sound that various tribes, making common cause, were planning raids to weaken the white man's prestige.

Less than a month after the Port Gamble battle, a war party of fifty or sixty Stikens landed on San Juan Island, avowedly to kill Oscar Olney, United States Customs Inspector, and for the purpose of obtaining and taking back with them five additional "Boston" heads. Warned in time, Olney fled the island.

A jittery territorial legislature adopted a law prohibiting trade with the

Northern Indians; and forbidding their employment. The legislature also passed a resolution requesting Commander Swartout of the U. S. Steamer *Massachusetts* to continue cruising the Sound as a measure of protection.

With the arrival of the spring weather the tension increased. The first of April, 1857, a party of Northern Indians descended on Whatcom in the night, but they did little besides threatening Louis G. Loscher and ransacking his cabin on the outskirts of town. To him they boasted they were scouting the military strength at Fort Bellingham and would return in force to destroy the garrison and to take the heads of Captain Pickett, E. C. Fitzhugh*, and Russell V. Peabody. (Captain Roeder reported in his manuscripts that: "Several times the Indians reconnoitered the Fort, but withdrew without attacking. These acts were retaliatory of the injury suffered in 1856.") Immediately the worried settlers at Whatcom organized a militia company under Peabody to do guard duty.

Threats by the Whatcom raiders quickly were accepted at face value when Governor Douglas of Vancouver Island advised that 300 Northern Indians had arrived at Victoria, while a like number had appeared at Nanaimo. Warned by the Governor of this force, Oscar Olney again judiciously quitted his post as Customs Inspector at San Juan Island.

In the face of this situation tension mounted everywhere when it was learned that the U. S. Steamer *Massachusetts* had sailed for San Francisco, leaving Puget Sound without adequate naval protection.

Alarmist stories were augmented toward the end of April, when the Schooner *Phantom*, out of Victoria, was boarded and looted by Northern Indians; also by the report of Captain Roeder of Whatcom, that his vessel the *H. C. Page* enroute to Olympia was pursued half the distance from Port Townsend to Volcano Point by a large canoe carrying sixty warriors.

By the first of May some of the elder settlers and women had moved or were preparing to move, from Whidbey Island to the safer port of Olympia.

Colonel Ebey and his brother, Winfield, seemed to consider the fear of Indian raids as groundless. Nor were they worried when on May 25, twelve large canoes, carrying 154 persons (half of them women or men dressed as women), put in to the landing for water. The flotilla then continued up Sound, professedly for employment.

Nevertheless the Ebeys sent word to the Revenue Cutter, *Jefferson Davis* at Port Townsend concerning this movement of Indians. Next day

---

*Edmund Clare Fitzhugh was superintendent of the coal mine at Sehome, the largest employer of labor in the Northwest. He also managed the Company's store. In addition he became county auditor, Indian Commissioner, and under President Buchanan was appointed United States District Judge, a position he filled for four years.

that vessel with a detachment of Company I, of Fourth Infantry, under Major Haller, proceeded up Sound for the purpose of enforcing the law against the employment of Northern Indians.

The *Jefferson Davis* failed to locate the Northerners. However on July 14, 1857, according to the log of the cutter, the vessel, cruising in the lower Sound, sighted a party of Indians, believed to be Stikens. The *Jefferson Davis,* crowding on all sail, swung in pursuit. But the Indian warriors, with the aid of their banks of flashing paddles, easily outdistanced the government vessel and were lost in the maze of island channels. As a gesture of derision this party of tribesmen swung aside to raid a village of the Clallam Indians, where they shot and wounded three of the tribe.

Their search continued for a white Tyee, whose head they must have, to revenge the death of their chief killed at Port Gamble. They finally chose Doctor J. C. Kellogg—a "Medicine Man"—of Whidbey Island as their victim. His high black hat and long coat made him an important man in their eyes. The Indians stopped at the Kellogg home and asked for the Doctor. He was away, so they moved on up the Island.

The session of the Third District Court, Judge Chenowith presiding, opened August 3, 1857 at Coveland, Whidbey Island. Colonel Ebey newly elected prosecuting attorney for the district, was present for the session. Present also were United States Marshal George W. Corliss and Mrs. Corliss, who were guests of the Ebeys.

Court adjourned August 11. Lodging at the Ebey residence that night were seven persons, adults and children.

During the afternoon of August 11, a party of Northern Indians came to the Ebey Landing and tried to buy provisions. The Colonel, obedient to the law against trading with these people, sent them away. As they departed they questioned Thomas Hastie, a young man who was cradling oats for Ebey. Particularly they inquired as to the number of persons at the farm house, and as to whether Ebey was a real chief or Tyee. Young Hastie assured them that he was a Hyas Tyee (Great Chief) and thought nothing of the incident. Nor was Colonel Ebey himself alarmed at the presence of the Indians.

The same afternoon Blanket Bill Jarman had observed these Northern Indians on the beach engaged in gambling. He warned Ebey to be on guard against them, but the Colonel replied that they were good Indians—this according to an interview given by Jarman to Frank C. Teck in 1897.

Of those in the Eby home that night, Mrs. Corliss, wife of the marshal, a rather delicate woman, seems to have been the only one worried by the Indians. She had noted them on the beach, faces smeared with war paint.

Near midnight of August 11, 1857, the Ebey dog aroused the household with furious barking. Thinking that a crew member of the cutter had arrived, preparatory to taking some of the officials to Port Townsend in the morning, Coloney Ebey, in his night shirt, opened the door and stepped outside. Almost instantly a ragged burst of musketry greeted him. His body thudded to the porch floor, while the Indians raised their war whoop.

At the crash of the muskets, Marshal Corliss leaped to the door and bolted it. At the same time he shouted to Mrs. Corliss, Mrs. Ebey and the others to escape through the rear window. Mrs. Corliss, barefooted and in night dress, crawled through the window, only to be fired upon by an Indian guard. She tumbled across the nearby picket fence and pitched into the tall grass. The Indian, thinking perhaps he had killed the woman, left his post and raced around to the front of the house where his companions were busied chopping at the front door.

Picking herself up, Mrs. Corliss ran barefooted to a bachelor's cabin, three-quarters of a mile away, occupied by four men, and sounded the alarm. Marshal Corliss, meantime herded his charges through the rear window. He ripped pickets from the fence and all scuttled through the tall grass and hid in the woods.

At the bachelor's cabin, the occupants sent messages by friendly Indians to other settlers. With freshly loaded guns, the residents finally closed through the night, on the Ebey residence. But the Indians had been given ample time to wreck and plunder the interior of the house and make their escape. From over the water as they slowly paddled away through the dark, came the rise and fall of their exultant war chant.

The headless body of Colonel Ebey, with a bullet hole through his breast and one through his hand, lay on the porch where he had fallen. In beheading him the Indians had used an ax freshly sharpened only a few hours earlier by the victim.

The murder and decapitation of Colonel Ebey caused much hue and cry up and down the territory. Reportedly the raiders were led by a brother of an Indian killed in the battle at Port Gamble.

After displaying their trophy* at several places, the Indians scalped

---

*From the book, THE LUMMI INDIANS OF NORTHWEST WASHINGTON by Bernhard Joseph Stern, the method of bringing home the head as a trophy is described:

"The warriors behead the victims and bring home the heads as trophies. The heads are pierced through the neck on sharp poles, called tcanegan which are placed in front of the houses for this purpose when they are built and to which the side boards of the house are fastened. Although the number of trophies on the pole determines to some extent the reputation of the warrior who lives in the house, it is not so much the number of heads as the persons they represent that brings prestige. Warriors at the beginning of their careers, display as many heads as possible, even of women and children, to gain recognition, but after one attains distinction, the standing of the victims determines the importance of his victory. While the trophies are on display, each warrior participating in the battle gives his victory dance as a sign of defiance to anyone to challenge his right to the victory. After the dances, the heads are kept on display for a brief time and then removed."

the head and buried it at Smith's Island, whence it was eventually recovered and interred with the Colonel's body.* The search for the scalp continued.

Chief Trader Dodd of the Hudson's Bay Company, a friend of Colonel Ebey, finally traced the scalp to a village of the Kaka tribe, 750 miles north of Victoria.

Dodd's first attempt to recover this relic brought on such a warlike show of force by canoe borne tribesmen, that the trader's vessel had to be cleared for action and the shotted guns run out the portholes. Later Dodd was more successful; by persuasion and purchase he was able to secure the scalp of Colonel Ebey.

The British Columbia historian, Bruce A. McKelvie, copied the following from the Trading Log of the *s s Labrouchere* in the Archives at Victoria:

"Shortly after Midnight a canoe with 3 young men came off to the Steamer with the scalp of Col. I. Ebey (The unfortunate gentleman who was shot by the Indians at Whitby Island) to sell to Capt. Dodd after repeated applications by him and a disturbance last year endangering the safety of the Steamer they have succumbed to their characteristic love of property and parted with their highly prized Trophy for the undermentioned articles,

Six blankets   1 Cotton Hdkcf.   1 fthm (fathom) Cotton
3 pipes   6 Heads of Tobacco.

they left us on very friendly terms Capt. Dodd impressing on their memory that the American people would be very glad to obtain the scalp and feel less angry at what they had done."

"Winfield Scott Ebey Diary** No. 6, p. 282.

"Thursday, April 5, 1860 . . . Captain Coupe got over today from Port Townsend brin(g)ing My Friend A M Poe Esqu. Mr P brings My Brothers Scalp which was recovered from the Northern Indians by Capt. Dodd. At last this memento is rec(eiv)ed. At last a portion of the mutilated remains of my Dear Brother is returned. Near Three Years have Elapsed Since his

---

*Commenting on the Colonel Ebey murder, Mrs. Nellie S. Coupe, pioneer school teacher of Whidbey Island writing from California in 1926 to Miss Edith Carhart of Bellingham said:

"In reading Mrs. Judson's account of the murder of Colonel Ebey, which his son, Eason, very graphically related to me, she did not add this fact which Eason told me. Our government entered into negotiations with the government of B. C. for the recovery of Colonel Ebey's head. It was finally sent back to the family and interred in the Colonel's grave. By the time I reached the Sound in January '66, all fear of the Northern Indians had passed."

**PACIFIC NORTHWEST QUARTERLY for July 1942.

murder & now his poor head (or portion of it) returns to his home . . . The Hair looks quite Natural It is a sad memento of the past . . ."

GOVERNOR JAMES DOUGLAS
("BLOOD IS THICKER THAN WATER")

"Blood is thicker than water"; thus Commodore Josiah Tattnall, United States Navy, justified his action in breaking neutrality during the Battle of Pei-Ho River, China, 1857, and going to the rescue of a stricken English ship. He could not know that at almost the same time, half a world away, a Britisher, the dour Scotsman, James Douglas, Hudson's Bay head, and Governor of Vancouver Island, had been exemplifying the same sentiment by providing a ship and arms—these last purchased with his private fortune, to aid the Washington settlers during the Indian wars. And this help was supplied in spite of the irritations caused by boundary disputes. That the people of the territory were grateful; that the legislature thanked him, was thin fare for Douglas, who waited three years to be repaid the cold cash the good deed cost him.

Bancroft has declared: "The life of James Douglas is in truth the history of British Columbia from its beginning through all its early changes down to 1875." With Doctor John McLoughlin, Douglas scouted the southern end of Vancouver Island in 1842, sighting Esquimalt and Camosun Bay, site of modern Victoria. Rights to Vancouver Island were granted to the Hudson's Bay Company in 1849. The following year Richard Blanchard became governor. On his resignation in 1851, James Douglas, chief factor of the Hudson's Bay Company, was named chief executive.

Gold discoveries in the Queen Charlotte islands and the arrival of ships and prospectors alarmed Douglas, who asked the British Government to exclude foreigners from the islands. This was refused, but Douglas was named Lieutenant Governor of the Queen Charlotte Islands with authority to regulate prospectors and mining.

Further gold discoveries along the Fraser River caused the stampede of 1858 with its horde of American citizens. The international situation was handled, not without some friction, but law and order generally prevailed, traffic routes and trails were constructed, through the efforts of the Governor, and when British Columbia was created in 1858, the province was on a substantial foundation. Douglas served as Governor until 1862. Meantime, when the second five year grant of Vancouver Island to the Hudson's Bay Company was not renewed in 1859, Douglas sold all his interests in the Company. That year he received his knighthood.

James Douglas was born in the West Indies, in 1803; his mother was a Creole, his father a descendant of the Earl of Angus, the Black Douglas of

Scottish history. He inherited the comeliness of his mother's race and the iron strength, will and reserve of his Scottish father.

At seventeen he became apprenticed clerk of the Northwest Company. His first post was Fort Williams on Lake Superior. Thereafter he served at many posts, in many positions, under varied conditions, as he learned the Company business. At twenty-one, he married the beautiful half-breed Nellie Connolly, fifteen year old daughter of Chief-Factor Connolly. During the early years of service he was rigid in the matter of respect and obedience to his superiors. When he arose to authority he expected the same from his inferiors. Years of meager supplies and equipment in the frontier posts had caused him to adopt the motto: "Great ends from small means." Thus plows and harrows of oak wood were made to serve on post farms; although in some instances the moldboards would be bordered with metal strips made from iron barrel hoops.

Douglas' weather-beaten countenance was severe, unbending. Bancroft has written that Doctor McLoughlin "would flatter you a little, Douglas never."

Although Victoria was no larger than an English village, Douglas carried himself as if attempting to make the position of governor seem grand and august. His tall frame, over six feet, was habitually clothed in a semimilitary uniform; while in office or on street, he was attended by an armed and uniformed orderly. Agnes C. Laut has written that "James Douglas died at Victoria, full of honors, in 1877."

The history of the Bellingham Bay and North Sound settlements is closely interwoven with that of Victoria and Governor Douglas. Concerning the munitions provided for the settlers, B. A. McKelvie, historian and author of Victoria, has supplied some very illuminating official correspondence. Mr. McKelvie writes:

"In March 1856 Captain Robinson came to Victoria on behalf of the Territorial Government in an effort to purchase, with unsecured territorial script, arms and munitions with which to outfit the volunteers for the defence of such places as Seattle, Bellingham Bay and Port Townsend. The traders of Victoria could not take the chance of selling upon such a basis as proposed. In desperation Captain Robinson went to Governor Douglas.

"I quote from a letter written by Douglas to Governor Stevens, March 7, 1856:

" 'I have purchased a quantity of sugar, coffee, the number of blankets wanted for the troops, with a supply of gunpower and lead with my own private funds for Captain Robinson, with the view of meeting your present necessities, leaving the payment for your settlement in any manner that will secure me from loss.'

"Let me further quote from a letter written by Governor Douglas to the Colonial office, under date of May 19, 1856:

" 'Since the date of my dispatch of the 10th of April last, another pressing appeal has been made to me by Governor Stevens, through Commissary Robinson for assistance, and I once more advanced funds out of my own private fortune for the purchase of supplies, to the amount of $3535 dollars, making with the former advance the sum of $7,000 for which I hold Governor Stevens' acknowledgement.

" 'This is a serious drain on my resources, but in the circumstances I could not with propriety deny the assistance so pressingly claimed, and I confess that it was not motives of humanity alone that induced me to lend such aid, as I could command; as other reasons of sound policy were not wanting strongly urging to that course, such as the conviction on my mind that the triumph of the Native Tribes would certainly endanger the position of this colony, which in that case could not be maintained without a vast increase of expense for military defences. It is therefore clearly to our interest that the American cause should triumph, and the natives be made to feel that they cannot successfully contend against the power and resources of the whites.' "

As reported by McKelvie and other historians there were other occasions when aid was given by Governor Douglas. Also the Hudson's Bay Company's steamer, *Otter,* was used to cruise off the settlement, to show the Indians that the Company was friendly to the Americans. Further, this steamer was employed to discipline and intercept Northern raiders.

Governor Douglas made request through official channels for reimbursement. Congress had made no appropriation for such territorial expenditure. The matter dragged. On December 28, 1858, Douglas wrote the Colonial Secretary, Sir Edward Lytton as follows:

"I have to acknowledge receipt of correspondence from the Foreign Office of the United States in reference to money forwarded for supplies to Governor Stevens of Washington in 1856.

"I regret to observe that the United States Government have not repaid the money due to me on that account, a want of good faith which, I confess, has called forth in my mind a feeling of pain and surprise. This is, however, not the first instance in which I have suffered in consequence of relieving the distress of the United States citizens who have applied to me for assistance, and I therefore trust that such instances may not occur often hereafter during my tenure of office."

When Lord Lyons became Minister to Washington, he presumably made a direct appeal to President Buchanan that brought results. Douglas' letter of July 26, 1859 to Lord Lyons follows:

"My Lord:—I have the honor to acknowledge the receipt of Your Lordship's dispatch of the 21st of April, forwarding me a copy of a letter from the United States Secretary of State and its enclosure respecting my claims upon the Government of the United States and requesting certain details in connection therewith.

"I regret that it is not in my power to furnish the Gov't of U. S. with a detailed statement of the articles supplied with the precise dates as requested by the Sec. of War, as I hold no other evidence of the debt than six bonds for $7,000 which I now herewith forward in order that they may be surrendered to the Scy. of War.

"I have also had the honor of receiving yr subsequent dispatch of the 4th of May last, and with reference thereto, I beg acquaint Y. L. that by the same mail I received under cover from Y. L., in a sealed packet a draft from the Treasurer of the U. S. for the sum of $8,306.66.

"There is a trifling discrepency between the amount received by me and the amount I forwarded to Lord Napier in June; but as the difference is not in my favor and is not of large amount, I have no objection to offer to the present settlement, or to regard it as otherwise than satisfactory and final.

(Signed) James Douglas."

Chapter X

FRASER RIVER STAMPEDE

"GOLD!" THE ELECTRIC WORD flashed the length of the Pacific Coast in 1858.

"Gold on the Fraser River!" and the greatest stampede in history was under way—greatest, when measured by the brief period it ran and by the number joining the rush. It was a flash flood reaching a sudden crest, then as suddenly subsiding.

Men and women—tens of thousands of them, left California shores, in almost anything that would float; or toiled overland from the Columbia through a forbidding land teeming with hostile Indians. All states and territories of the Union, as well as most of the foreign lands, were represented in this flood; while back of this tide, the world over, a hundred thousand other wild-eyed argonauts were preparing to join the migration when the end came.

Clinton A. Snowden, historian, estimates that between 75,000 to 100,000 persons came into British Columbia and Washington in the summer of 1858.

From time to time the residents of the sleepy little villages on Bellingham Bay, had listened to stories of gold finds in the back country. Such rumors excited no one. The settlers did not know that maps showed Whatcom to be astride a short-cut from tidewater to the Fraser strike. Thus they rubbed their eyes in surprise when a steamer, her decks black with excited gold seekers, dropped anchor in the quiet harbor. Other ships followed. The stampeders descended on the Bay like a cloud of locusts—10,000 or more of them finally, cluttering the shores at one time—more people than in all the remainder of the Territory.

They came—the bearded young miner in wool hat, red shirt, wool trousers tucked into high leather boots—bearing camp supplies, fire arms, picks and shovels, metal and canvas for rocker and sluice boxes.

They came—the eager merchant in skin tight trousers and flaring coat, shepherding his stock of goods; the diamond bedecked saloon keeper in flashy raiment, guarding his casks, bottles, and glassware; the gambler in frock coat and high hat, cold of eye, slim fingered, a derringer in his vest pocket.

They came—the perfumed and painted ladies of the night—in brocaded

74

silk and velvet, saucy plumes above finger-length curls, aglint with tinsel finery; shrill voiced; with calculating eyes alert for the miner and his gold.

And gold there was aplenty—the California miners carried it north. News of the Fraser River strike found California in the doldrums. The lush days of the Mother Lode country were gone; the rich shallow placers worked out. The miners wanted some excuse to stream off to another promised El Dorado.

Many towns on the Mother Lode were almost depopulated after word of the Fraser River strike was received. Business houses were locked up or abandoned, buildings vacated, property worthless. At San Francisco, such was the exodus, that real estate dropped to a mere fraction of its actual value.

In San Francisco harbor, there lay the hulks of many ships rotting since the California gold rush. These were resurrected. Leaky hulls were caulked; rotting timbers braced, cracked and defective machinery was puttied and painted. Loaded to the guards, some with a thousand or more passengers these fugitives from Davy Jones' Locker, sailed North.

Some of the vessels anchored at Victoria. Many discharged at Bellingham Bay. Edward Eldridge, writing of the stampede, has reported that at one time he saw seven ocean steamers and thirteen square rigged ships anchored in the Bay, all heavily loaded with passengers and merchandise.

There were no clearings for the accommodation of these people, so they pitched their tents on the beach—a line of camps extending from Chuckanut Bay to Squalicum Creek. Into the narrow opening near the saw-mill site, which was the embryo town of Whatcom, they poured as from a funnel and milled about like the individuals in a disturbed ant hill. William Munks, Fidalgo Island pioneer, one of the gold seekers of the day, has stated that later in the summer after building had begun and clearings were extended, it took him one half hour to fight his way through the milling throng on Division Street, from the Terminus Hotel to the brick building on E Street, a distance of about two blocks.

The Fraser River gold strike was not the first on British soil. A rich strike on Moresby Island in 1851 drew American adventurers. Hostile Indians resisted their inroads, attacked various parties. One vessel was wrecked, one captured. James Douglas, governor of Vancouver Island and chief factor for the Hudson's Bay Company, was appointed Lieutenant Governor for Queen Charlotte Islands and at once issued regulations governing mining and miners. Indians made other gold discoveries in the interior where one Hudson's Bay Post, it is said, traded them an ounce of lead for each ounce of gold. Reports of gold discoveries on river bars reached headquarters through the years 1853-'56. Governor Douglas noted in his diary, "Gold was first found on Thompson River by an Indian, a quarter of a mile below Nicomen. The Indian was taking a drink out of the river and having no vessel he was quaffing from the stream, when he perceived a shining pebble, which he picked up, and it proved to be gold."

In 1857, Americans from the Columbia River made their way into the territory and despite Indian interference found gold prospects widely distributed over the Thompson River watershed.

Governor Douglas in December 1857 wrote: "The reputed wealth of the Couteau mines (within the Thompson and Fraser River Districts) is causing much excitement amongst the population of the United States Territories of Washington and Oregon, and I have no doubt a great number of people from these territories will be attracted thither in the spring." In March, California was touched by the gold fever when the Hudson's Bay Company shipped 800 ounces of gold to the San Francisco mint.

First published reference to the Fraser River strike is found in the following extract from a news story appearing in the PIONEER AND DEMOCRAT of Olympia, March 5, 1858:

"* * * According to representations, they (the gold strikes) are located between Fort Hope and Thompson River, and not to exceed four or five days' journey removed from the mouth of the Fraser River. It is represented that persons with canoes can approach within ten or twelve miles of the diggings, although, in so doing, some pretty strong rapids will have to be encountered. Report has it that miners are getting out from $25 to $50 per day each, and that Indian women are panning out $10 or $12 each. Nearly all the French and half-breeds on the Island had either started for this new El Dorado or were proposing to start. Fort Langley is sure to be entirely deserted—the chief factor being gone to the diggings with provisions, merchandise, etc., leaving but one clerk and a few Kanakas in charge. The company's blacksmith at Victoria is employed day and night in manufacturing picks, and shovels, etc., for the mines. It may not be amiss in this place to correct an error into which some of our citizens have fallen, concerning the license required by the British Authorities, as per proclamation of Governor Douglas, for the privilege of working in gold diggings. 'The same license (21 s. a month) is demanded of British as well as American subjects, or of any other government; no distinction whatever is made regards nationality or color.' British subjects and American citizens stand on terms of equality as to the privilege of working the mines."

In April, 1858, three San Francisco ships carried 455 gold seekers; in May three ships bore 1,262; through June 21, ships passed the Golden Gate with 7,149 stampeders; in July a total of 6,274 sailed north. The largest crowd to leave on any one day, 1,732, sailed from San Francisco on July 3.

The fare by steamer was: First Class, $65; steerage, $32.50, while rates on sailing vessels varied from $25 to $60 according to speed and seaworthiness of the craft.

Portland was the destination of a number of the steamers in the early days of the excitement, since it was advertised as the easiest way to the diggings via Wallula, Okanogan, and the Kamloops. Joel Palmer, the first man to reach the Thompson River with wagons, has stated that in the summer of 1858, companies of 400 and 500 men with pack animals, over-took his wagons on the way. These traveled in quasi-military organizations as protection against Indians.

Whatcom Creek meanders westerly across a low plateau to pitch down a sandstone escarpment into the most easterly curve of Bellingham Bay. From the estuary below the falls, commonly known as "The Basin," the waters of the Creek, at low tide, flow southwesterly across wide tideflats. At high tide it was possible to float log booms into the basin at the site of the Roeder saw-mill; possible also during the gold rush days to land passengers or freight at the Terminus hotel or other buildings erected on the western shore and over the adjacent tide-flats.

On the east bank of the Basin, below the Falls, in the spring of 1858, there stood the Roeder mill, the mill house in which the post office was located, the bunk house, and the mess shack over which Mrs. Eldridge had presided. Along the western shore of the Basin on the only level land be-tween high tide and the sandstone bluff were the cabins of Roeder, of Peabody, and the one built for Mrs. Eldridge. These were on Division Street* —a forty foot alley platted that year and lying between C and D Streets, and extending from Astor to Dupont Streets. One-half a block to the north-west on the crest of the bluff on D Street was the blockhouse erected by the settlers in 1855. One block and a half to the northwest stood the Captain Pickett house built in 1856. Three miles farther west was Fort Bellingham, also constructed the same year. (Opposite page 39).

The gold seekers aboard the first steamer to push into the Bay in April 1858, must have strained their eyes eagerly for signs of habitation, for methods of accommodation and transportation. They must have been dis-couraged, many of them, by the wide sweep of the dark green forests.

Sharp eyed argonauts may have noted plumes of smoke rising through the trees from the cabin or two at the site of Pattle's coal mine—between what was later Fairhaven and Sehome. The little clearings and scattered cabins at the Sehome coal mine must have been visible to most eyes. So also no doubt, were the few shacks on the shoreline near the Whatcom Creek

---

*Division Street is in the gully where the fill is today (1951), and near the gar-bage dump.

sawmill, as well as the blockhouse and the Pickett house in clearings just above. A mariner's telescope would have disclosed the Fort Bellingham stockade three miles west with the Stars and Stripes snapping briskly from its tall staff; would have revealed also, perhaps, the Fort's whaleboat and an Indian canoe or two pulled up on the beach.

This was Bellingham Bay in the spring of 1858. There was the tang of the tideflats in the air, the movement and cries of circling gulls. Otherwise the scene must have appeared lifeless, or somberly portentous to the gold seekers who had sold all, to join the mad rush into this forest-green wilderness.

Miners, as well as all camp followers of the great stampede, poured into Whatcom, expecting to find a road or trail from the town to the Fraser River. This, if in existence, would be thirty or thirty-five miles long and would strike the Fraser at the nearest bend, cutting off one hundred and twenty miles of water route. Unfortunately this trail extended no farther than the Nooksack River.

In September 1857, the County Board of Supervisors adopted the following order:

"Supervisor of District Number One, is ordered to proceed forthwith on the Noot-sack Road, and cut said road suitable for a pack trail not to be less than six feet in width, and not to cut fallen timber less than eight feet in width." This trail was completed to the Nooksack, May 18, 1858, even as the stampeders were overwhelming the little settlements.

A. M. Poe, first surveyor and engineer to locate in the Northwest, (he had surveyed the Whatcom townsite), was immediately employed to locate and open the trail through to Fort Hope on the Fraser River. Money was needed and this was secured chiefly through subscriptions of miners, who were marking time in their beach camps, until the trail might be usable. A large force of men was employed at once to push the slashing and grading; the wage being three dollars a day, or two dollars and board. As finally constructed, the trail proceeded via Nooksack Crossing (below Everson today), thence northerly and easterly to Sumas Prairie, thence northeasterly through the Chilliwack Valley to a point on the Fraser about twenty miles below Fort Hope. (See map inside front or back cover).

The Whatcom-Hope trail even when completed, was no answer to the Miners' problems, since it left them stranded on the river below the Cascade Mountain range, remote from the diggings. Steamboat navigation to Fort Hope did the same thing.

Accordingly a meeting was called in Whatcom at which it was decided to build a trail by-passing the Fraser river canyons and the Cascade mountain range, so the mines could be reached at any stage of the river. Every settlement on the Sound offered financial aid. Under Captain W. W. DeLacy an expedition was organized and outfitted to explore and open the proposed route.

Paralleling the Fraser River canyons thirty miles to the east, the Hudson's Bay Company in 1849, had used a route known as the Brigade Trail. This was the path sought by the Whatcom boosters. The new line as laid out by DeLacy, left the earlier Whatcom-Fraser River trail at the Chilliwack Lake, thence apparently up Depot Creek, and Maselpanikm to Klesilkwa River watershed, all on the British side of the Boundary; then northeast up the Skagit River watershed and Snass Creek, and past the Punch Bowl at the source of the Tulameen River to Blackeye's Trail, thence to intersect Brigade Trail on the Tulameen River. This route was alto-gether too long, and was impassable during winter months because of snow. However, had it been put through during the summer, something might have been saved from the wreckage of the gold rush—Whatcom might have remained a trading and outfitting center. (See map inside front or back cover).

By the time the Whatcom Trail was connected with the Brigade Trail in August, Governor Douglas was moving to provide better year around routes closer to the Fraser. That month, he organized 500 miners, divided into twenty companies, for the building of trails on the portages along the water-way west of the Fraser. The route chosen followed the Harrison River, through Harrison Lake, Lillooet River, Lillooet, Anderson, and Seton Lakes to Lillooet on the Fraser. This was completed the last of September and brought the freight charge down to 18 cents per pound, while the rate from Yale at the mouth of the Thompson (Lytton), only half the distance, re-mained at 46½ cents per pound.

The new route gave no relief to the miners working the rich bars be-tween Yale and Lytton. True the Indians had a highwater trail that fol-lowed shelves along the canyon walls. At times the path was carried across the cliff on a pole swung from ropes of deer skin. The traveler inched along the pole, with arms extended and grasping the rock wall. A misstep, dizzi-ness, a swaying pole and he pitched to his death below. Only the legerdemain of the Indians brought a few goods over the airy way.

In August, Governor Douglas moved to remedy this and called for proposals to cut a mule trail from Yale to Spuzzum, thence thirty-five miles along the river to Lytton at the mouth of the Thompson. When 100 mules, part of a 400 mule train from Walla Walla, Washington Territory, arrived via Okanogan, some hundred miners volunteered for the trail work. The way followed the west bank of the river from Yale via Douglas Portage to Spuzzum, thence up the east side of the stream. The Governor carried on with the improvement. By September 7, it was estimated, 500 mules were moving freight over the route at 46½ cents per pound. The Whatcom Trail seemed remote and of little use.

As fast as the miners disembarked at Whatcom, they squatted on the first available open ground. Merchants, while demanding lots and building material, set up for business under canvas as did saloon keepers, dance hall proprietors, prostitutes, blacksmiths and professional men. In general, the sheriff had to deal with few serious crimes. The situation was analogous to that in the Klondike forty years later. Because of the isolation, the difficulty of leaving, criminals seem to have restrained themselves or speedily quit the territory.

Across the water at Victoria, it was the same. The town of 500 souls, suddenly was surrounded by an encamped army. Lot prices rose from $50 to $75 to $1,500 or as much as $3,000. Rental on desirable lots ranged from $250 to $400 per month.

At Victoria as at Whatcom, the crowd was composed mostly of Californians, who brought with them their habits of thought, interests, hatreds, theories, implements, money, newspapers. The Steamer *Commodore,* sailing from San Francisco April 20, 1858, brought the vanguard of 450 Californians to Victoria. Before their arrival these men had been represented to Governor Douglas as being of the very dregs of society. Their conduct he reported led him to a different conclusion. Despite scarcity of supplies and shelter; despite temptations, there were few committments for rioting, drunkeness, or other offenses. While their attitude was anti-British, the Governor found the miners on the whole to be men of intelligence, well provided with mining tools and capital.

American flags were displayed in plenty by the Californians. Frequently some rowdy would cry through the streets that he was a true American. Governor Douglas took a tolerant attitude toward the ill-directed patriotism so often derived from a bottle.

On the one occasion he had to display official power, he handled this matter as competently and easily as he had managed the Indians. One of the rowdies, whom the police had arrested, was rescued by his friends, who thereupon proposed to hoist the American flag on the Fort. Douglas ordered H. M. S. *Plumper* to the scene. The ring leaders of the riot were arrested, given small fines, and bound over to keep the peace.

From San Francisco, James W. Towne and Company brought a newspaper plant, and on June 25, published the first issue of the VICTORIA GAZETTE. This paper consistently fought British interests and institutions sometimes even criticizing the Governor himself.

Following the GAZETTE, another San Franciscan, William Bausman, brought another printing plant north, and on July 3, 1858, started publication of the NORTHERN LIGHT at Whatcom, thereafter boosting his town and projects enthusiastically, while exhibiting his disproval of the way Governor Douglas was handling matters across the Border.

TOWNSITES PLATTED

Sehome was first of the Bay towns to come up with a platted townsite, this having been surveyed and platted by W. W. DeLacy, and filed of record May 8, 1858, just as the boom was gaining impetus. E. C. Fitzhugh, manager of the coal company which controlled the townsite, did a brisk business in lots. Nearly all sales in Sehome were conditioned upon improvements being made. However, mineral rights were reserved by the company. (Opposite page 102).

The plat of Whatcom, surveyed by A. M. Poe, was not recorded by the owners of the property, Henry Roeder and R. V. Peabody, until July 24, 1858, when the stampede was at its height. Previous to the recording, however, some sales had been made, based on the new survey.

Alarmed by the gold rush, Governor Douglas, who a few weeks earlier had fixed miners' license fees, on May 8, 1858, by proclamation ordered the seizure and condemnation of all boats and goods in British Territory unless covered by a Hudson's Bay Company's license and a sufferance from the Customs officer at Victoria. An exclusive and onerous contract was offered the Pacific Mail Steamship Company covering Fraser River traffic. This was declined. Thereupon sufferance was issued to other American river steamers. First to accept and first to reach Fort Hope, June 6, 1858, was the sidewheeler, *Surprise*. Among other steamers that followed on the Fraser River run were: The *Seabird, Umatilla, Maria,* and *Enterprise*.

On her first memorable run, the *Surprise* left Bellingham Bay at 7:15 A. M., June 5 and entered the Fraser River at 1:30 P. M. She ran thirty miles to Fort Langley in four hours. After reporting to the British Customs, the *Surprise* proceeded sixteen miles above Fort Langley and anchored for the night. At the Fort, she picked up an Indian pilot, named Speel-es, who joined the ship barefooted and in a blanket, but who returned after his successful mission in a pilot-cloth suit, white hat and calfskin boots, the proudest Indian in the valley. He was paid $160 for his services, in eight $20 gold pieces. Henceforth he was known as Captain John.

Governor Douglas' orders and proclamations seem to have been chiefly for the protection of the Hudson's Bay Company's trade, although he doubtless had patriotic motives as well. At the time he was governor of Vancouver Island, not of the mainland.

In May, when writing to the British Secretary of State for the Colonies, Douglas had pointed out the danger of unrestricted immigration without, in the first place, requiring the foreigner to take the oath of allegiance and give surety for good conduct.

On July 1, 1858, Sir Edward Bulwer Lytton repudiated all proposed restrictions except necessary police measures, and enforcement of customs law. Referring to the exclusion policy, applied to Americans and other foreigners, Lytton wrote: "On the contrary, you are distinctly instructed to oppose no obstacle whatever to their resort thither for the purpose of digging in those fields, so long as they submit themselves, in common with subjects of Her Majesty, to the recognition of Her authority, and conform to such rules of police as you may have thought proper to establish."

The attempt of Douglas to advance the interests of the Hudson's Bay Company at the expense of the citizenry created such an unfavorable reaction with the Secretary of State for the Colonies, that the Company's license, which had but a short time to run, was revoked forthwith. The Province of British Columbia was then created and Douglas offered the governorship, a position he accepted.

NORTHERN LIGHT

William Bausman, publisher of the NORTHERN LIGHT, the first newspaper on Bellingham Bay and the third on Puget Sound, had been working on the San Francisco Call when the gold fever struck. He induced his friend, Watson, to join him, bought an old hand press and a few fonts of type, and set sail. Concerning his part in the Fraser River stampede, Bausman, in 1890, three years before his death, wrote as follows:

"The Steamer *Cortes,* which carried us and our printing office into Bellingham Bay, had on board from 1,200 to 1,300 passengers, all bound for the Fraser River and most of them intended to disembark at Victoria. When they heard there was a printing press aboard going to Whatcom, they supposed the owner had inside information and changed their destination. I had $3,000 in gold when I arrived in Whatcom and $275 when I left. Mr. Roeder was kind enough to present us with several lots. He was one of the proprietors of the town and a noble hearted gentleman." Bausman later returned to San Francisco, where he became a prominent newspaper man.

The NORTHERN LIGHT, consisting of two sheets, 12 by 17 inches, was a newsy, well written, four column folio weekly. The first issue appeared July 3, 1858. The price per copy, 25 cents; annual subscriptions, $7; advertising, $5 per inch of twelve lines, three insertions.

Extracts from this paper, which printed eleven issues before the boom cracked, give a more revealing picture of the stampede days than any other sources. Fortunately all regular numbers have been preserved in a bound volume in the possession of the Bellingham Herald, which has allowed the author free access to this invaluable record.*

"Judge" Warbass, later the patriarch of San Juan, who, at the time was sutler at the military post, Fort Bellingham, speaking of the arrival of Bausman said, during an interview in 1890: "The Northern Light people put up a building where the Utter machine shop was." This site was on lots given by Captain Roeder on E Street, across from the brick building of Richard and Hyatt. (Opposite page 86). Describing the tent city Warbass wrote: "There were dozens of saloons, and gambling houses without number. Lots were all on the waterfront. From $500 to $600 was the ordinary price for a building lot. In six months when the gold excitement was over, you could not give a lot away."

The week-by-week life of the Bellingham Bay boom towns, is well covered by the Northern Light. Excerpts from the first issue:

THE NORTHERN LIGHT
Vol. 1.   Whatcom, Whatcom County, W. T., Saturday, July 3, 1858.   No. 1

W. BAUSMAN & CO.
Editors and Proprietors,
Published on Saturdays

"The Northern Light is, we believe, the most truly hyperborean of any newspaper on the American continent. We are in latitude 48 degrees, 42 minutes; longitude 122 degrees, 36 minutes—within eighteen miles by direct line, of the British possessions; and yet with an atmosphere the summer temperature of which is delightful.

"OUR PAPER—Having full faith and confidence in the growing prosperity of Whatcom, we have come among its citizens with a complete job office and newspaper establishment, for the publication of an independent sheet, devoted entirely to the interests of Bellingham Bay. We have in

---

*The complete bound file of the Northern Light was in the possession of the Bellingham Reveille for a number of years. It disappeared about 1906, when the paper was published in the basement of the Daylight Block corner of Elk (State) and Chestnut Streets, but was recovered later.

This same bound file of the Northern Light again mysteriously disappeared in the 1930's, this time from the morgue of the Bellingham Herald.

In 1939, the Bellingham Chamber of Commerce was informed by an individual in San Francisco, whose name is unknown to the Herald, that he or she was in possession of an old Bellingham newspaper, in bound form, and the suggestion was made that it was obtainable for an undisclosed amount of money. The Chamber advised the Herald of receipt of the letter, and Mr. Charles Sefrit, business manager, undertook negotiations through Mr. Patrick E. Healy, former executive secretary of the Bellingham Chamber of Commerce, who then (in 1939) was in charge of the Washington State exhibit at the exposition in San Francisco. Mr. Healy contacted the writer of the letter and was successful in obtaining possession of the file for the sum of $25, which Mr. Sefrit had offered for it. Mr. Healy indicated in subsequent conversations that this person had come into possession of it indirectly, but gave no information concerning his or her identity, the arrangements having been largely on a no-questions-asked basis.

addition invested our capital in the erection of a permanent building, (20 x 45 feet) and we look forward confidently to their liberal support.

"FOR THE DIGGINGS—The Steamer *Surprise* will leave for Fort Hope with a full load of passengers tomorrow morning. A number of small craft will start within a few days for the same point. It is feared that the steamboat will not be able to reach Fort Hope after the next trip.

"A GLANCE AT WHATCOM—Mr. John T. Knox has kindly furnished us with the following glance at Whatcom, embracing a list of business houses, occupations, professions, etc., of the town—viz:

"STORES—Groceries and Provisions—12. Hardware—1. C l o t h i n g, Boots, and Shoes—5. Variety—5. Dry Goods and Groceries—2. Drugs—2. Stationery—1.

"SHOPS—Tin and Copper—3. Blacksmiths—3. Gunsmith—1. Hotels— 3. Restaurants and Eating Houses—8. Butchers—2. Bakers—3. Bars and Saloons—12. Physicians—8. Lawyers—4. Express Offices—3. Real Estate Agencies—2. Drays—3. Cart—1. Wagon—1.

"County offices, Post Office, Printing Office, etc.

"There are eighty houses erected on the flat or beach, and over 130 tents on the table land, overlooking the city.

"SEHOME WHARF—The last or outer crib of this work, was sunk the other day at 15 feet, low water. It will be entirely completed during the coming week.

"DUST FROM FRASER RIVER—On Thursday last, at the store of Wilson & Co., Sehome, we were shown $1,800 worth of Fraser River gold dust, purchased by the firm on Tuesday previous. It was a portion of a large amount brought down from that region by the miner who sold it to Wilson & Co. In addition to this amount, they have, in the last two weeks, purchased and shipped $4,500 worth of Fraser and Thompson river dust."

In the first issue, Bausman warned against the "Misrepresentations" of runners or "paid blowers" who were inducing passengers to land at Victoria, instead of coming to Whatcom for their start to the diggings. He also began his editorial fulminations against "that monster monopoly, the Pacific Mail Steamship Company, which is using every kind of effort to injure the growth of Whatcom and other towns on American territory."

Excerpts from the Second Issue of the NORTHERN LIGHT, Saturday, July 10, 1858:

"ANOTHER ARRIVAL FROM THE GOLD DIGGINGS—EXCITING NEWS—CONFIRMATION OF PREVIOUS REPORT!—MINERS EATING HORSE FLESH!

"Mr. Charles Brown, an Italian, in company with ten others, returned to this place by canoe, from 35 miles above the junction of Fraser and Thompson Rivers, on Thursday afternoon. They were on a prospecting expedition, but exhausted their provisions before doing much. Wherever they took out prospects, they found gold; some places more, some places less. They saw miners who were making $20 to $150 per day, in surface diggings.

"Above the forks of the two rivers the gold is coarse. The Indians exhibited pieces to them as large as pidgeon eggs, and signified to them by signs, that during the diurnal revolution of the sun, they could take out a double handful of it. They are very numerous and insolent, making their appearance in great force, when least expected.

"On their return, they fell in with a Canadian, who was building a fort at or near the forks, where they left two partners. He had been three days without food, and was forced to kill a horse; fifteen pounds of the flesh of which Mr. Brown and party purchased at fifty cents a pound, their own provisions having been exhausted. From this point they suffered severely from hunger; procuring a scant supply from time to time, from those they met, in the best manner they could.

"There are about a thousand miners at Fort Yale, doing nothing, waiting for the river to fall. Provisions are very scarce there also.

"Mr. Brown was a miner in California nine years; but he says he never saw as rich surface diggings there, as on Fraser and Thompson rivers. He intends returning with his party to the diggings, in a few days." ·

"CLEARING OFF—We stood upon the wharf of the Belllingham Bay Coal Company (Sehome) for about ten minutes the other day, during which we counted no less than eleven reverberations, made by the crash of as many falling trees. The owners of town lots there are clearing the forest off rapidly.

"SCARCITY OF WATER—A bucket of bad water costs from two to four bits in Victoria, and is procured with difficulty.

"CELEBRATION OF THE FOURTH—Owing to an imperative necessity which compelled Mr. Wallace to leave for Olympia, on the morning of the 5th, our citizens were prevented from listening to his oration. At sunrise, however, twelve guns were fired, and twelve at noon, which were responded to, gun for gun, by Captain Haley, whose vessel, the *Pacific,* happened to be anchored in the harbor at the time. The twelve sunset guns were responded to by a piece of ordnance in possession of Mr. Fitzhugh, at the coal mine.

"It was inspiring on both occasions, to hear the thundering cannon and the booming reply. The sounds mingled with each other, crashing through the forest, and sending their reverberations far out over the waters of the sea.

"July 10th, 1858: A. A. Green reports that just returning from the Lummi River, Captain Lippels, schooner *Rover,* told him that on Tuesday, while a large number of canoes were pursuing their way into the open sea, toward Point Roberts, and had passed Birch Bay, they were struck by a gale and three canoes were instantly swamped. The captain rescued the occupants of the two canoes, but three men in the third canoe were drowned. The rescued men were taken to Point Roberts on the *Rover;* Captain Lippels thinks other canoes were lost and the inmates drowned—of whose names no record will ever be made."

Advertisements in the second issue—July 10, 1858:

"MINERS' DRUG STORE
Whatcom, W. T.

WHOLESALE AND RETAIL

Paints, Oils, Brushes, Camphene, Burning Fluid, Patent Medicines, Beeswax, Pure Brandy, and Port Wine for the sick, Lampblack, Resin, Borax, Cream Tartar, Tartaric Acid, Muriatic Acid, Sulphuric and Nitric Acids, Hops. Whatcom, July 8, 1858.

NOTICES TO PURCHASERS OF TOWN LOTS

"All persons who have engaged lots on my plat of the town of Whatcom are requested to come and close their contracts and take deeds immediately, or their lots will be resold to other parties.—H. ROEDER. Whatcom, June 30, 1858.

"The Auditor's and Recorder's Office is now permanently located in the New Court House, on the hill, near the Plaza.*—J. W. Lysle, Auditor and Recorder. Whatcom, July 8, 1858."

Northern Light July 10, 1858:

"INSPECTOR OF CUSTOMS APPOINTED—Major Van Bolkelen, Deputy Collector of this District, who arrived by the Revenue Cutter, *Jeff Davis,* informs us that he visits us for the purpose of appointing, and has appointed H. C. Page, Inspector of Customs for this port. Mr. P. is one of the oldest residents of the Bay, and universally esteemed.

"FOR THE TRAIL—On her last trip, the steamer, *Constitution,* brought up twenty horses and mules, designed to be put upon the Whatcom Trail.

"THE ELECTION—The following officers were chosen at the election held in this county on Monday last: Representative to the Territorial Legislature, John A. Tennant; Sheriff, Wm. A. Busey; Auditor, J. W. Lysle; Assessor, Thomas Wynn; Surveyor, A. M. Poe; Treasurer, Wm. Utter; Constables, J. E. Jewett, J. G. Chapman; Commissioners, H. Roeder, Geo. Gallagher; Justices, Nelson Young, H. R. Crosbie; Wreck Master, J. W. Sackett; Supt. Common Schools, R. V. Peabody; Prosecuting Attorney, B. P. Anderson.

"The highest number of votes polled was 73. There were two distinct tickets. The names of several candidates were on both."

---

*According to Poe's survey and Plat, this Plaza was located three blocks above the beach, between E and F streets, and 16th and 17th (Clinton and Dupont), on the Peabody Donation Claim. The Court House built on this public square, was a cheap wooden building, which was finally blown down.

UPPER—The first brick building in Washington Territory, built by T. G. Richards & Co. in 1858 at Whatcom on E street. Picture taken in 1889 by E. A. Hegg.

LOWER—Old Fraser River Gold Trail built in 1858 which later became the Telegraph Trail. Bridge over a branch of the Ten Mile Creek.—Photo by the author in 1948.

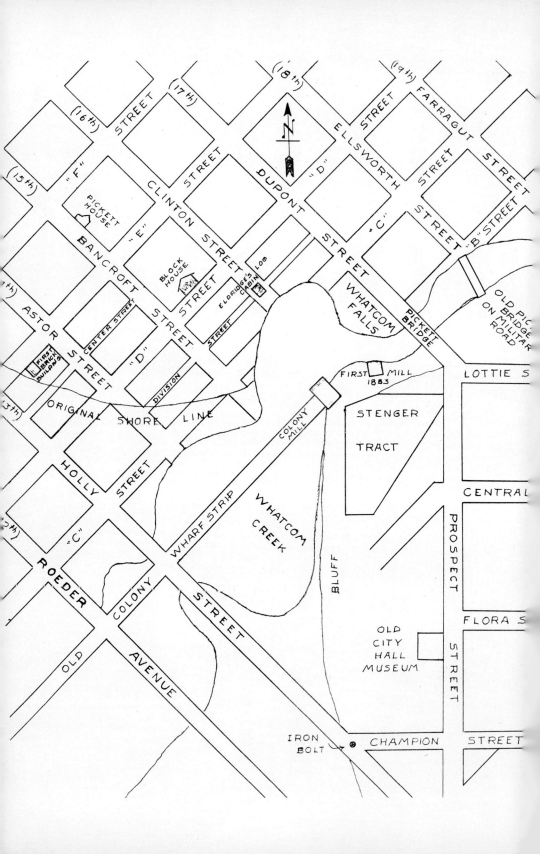

Work on the proposed E street wharf was rushed during the boom. Previously a stock company was formed for the purpose of constructing a 1,500 foot pier, later increased to 2,300 feet. John E. Peabody* donated the right-of-way, May 24, 1858. Winter storms partly destroyed the new wharf, but it was repaired with lumber left by the departing miners after the boom collapsed.

"NORTHERN LIGHT, July 17, 1858: Supposed to be Drowned or Murdered. Matthew C. C. Murphy, U. S. Deputy Surveyor, requests us to state that Dr. D. Hunt, also a U. S. Deputy Surveyor, left his camp near Whidbey's in a canoe on Monday, 5th inst to come to Whatcom. He was seen passing the Indian camp near the north end of Swinomish Pass at noon Tuesday, since that time nothing has been seen or heard of him. His canoe was picked up adrift in that vicinity the following day.

"Mr. Hunt was about forty years of age, and had on a gray pair of satinet pants, a black wool hat and blue overcoat. He had also some money about his person, a silver watch and Colt's revolver. In the canoe was a one gallon blue-painted water-keg and black leather valise. The canoe paddles were marked 'D.H.' The discovery of any of these articles may afford some clue to Mr. Hunt's fate."**

THE NORTHERN LIGHT
Vol. 1.   Whatcom, Whatcom County, W. T., July 24, 1858.   No. 4

"Deputy Postmaster—Mr. J. G. Hyatt has received the appointment from R. V. Peabody, of Deputy Postmaster, and has removed that institution to the new building of T. G. Richards & Co., on Center street, where he has provided a hundred boxes, at private expense, for the accommodation of the public. He assures us that the arrangements of the office are now such as to occasion no delay in the delivery of the mail matter, and as not to be in any manner interfered with by other business transactions of the contiguous room."

(The T. G. Richards and Company building mentioned was a frame structure erected at the edge of the tideflats on Center street a half block southeast of the site then being cleared on E street for the same firm's brick building. Center street, according to the original blueprint, was a forty foot

---

*In December 1856, John E. Peabody bought 85 acres in Whatcom precinct from R. V. Peabody.

**Two Skagit Indians were arrested and hung in Whatcom for the murder of Surveyor Hunt. A pole was placed in the crotches of two trees on the opposite sides of the Military Road near the Pickett Bridge. This served as a gallows. According to James Taylor, Charles Wolfe, deputy sheriff, officiated.

The first sheriff of Whatcom County, "Yankee" Ellis Barnes, was drowned off Fort Bellingham in 1858, while scuffling with some friends on a boat in which he was taking them to his ranch at the mouth of the Lummi River. William Busey, who succeeded him, was sheriff during the gold rush. He formerly had been teamster for Captain Pickett. His deputy, Charles Wolfe of California, was of the western border type, carrying guns and a bowie knife in sight.

OPPOSITE—Diagram of the community around Whatcom Creek.—Drawn by the author.

alley between D and E streets extending from 13th (West Holly) up hill to 15th street (Bancroft). (Opposite page 87).

"VERY UNWOMANLY—It was asserted by one of the Chiefs who spoke at the meeting Saturday, that there was a groggery kept in the heart of the town, by a couple of white women, who supplied the Indians with liquor through the medium of a trap-door, leading under the house. A thorough investigation of the suspected premises, by the civil authorities, should be had, and if the charge is found to be true, even the sex of the guilty occupants should not prevent their being made an example of."

EZRA MEEKER

The NORTHERN LIGHT of August 28, 1858, recites that, "Fifty-three head of fine beef cattle from Olympia, were landed in this harbor from the Barque *Gold Hunter* on Monday."

These were not the first by any means. In June, Ezra Meeker, of Steilacoom, the pioneer historian, having heard that the Whatcom miners were ready to pay one dollar a gallon for milk and any asking price for butter, rounded up a scow load, mostly cows, which were taken in tow alongside the Steamer *Sea Bird*." Narrowly escaping being swamped off Whidbey Island, the scow was set adrift in Bellingham Bay and landed near the mouth of Squalicum Creek, where Meeker, fired with the gold fever, made a deal with Edward Eldridge for an unsurveyed lot. To Meeker's amusement in later years the description of his lot read much like some of the mining claim descriptions recorded during the California gold rush.

Meeker's lot was described as: "Beginning at a stump on the bank of said creek (Squalicum), about twenty feet above the bridge near the mouth of said creek; thence running due west 240 feet; thence due south 60 feet; thence due east 240 feet; thence due north 60 feet to the place of beginning." This deed was recorded June 25, 1858. To Meeker, to Eldridge, as to other settlers of the day, the great stumps of the original forest must have seemed as permanent as the pyramids.

Four steamers with more than 2,000 persons anchored shortly after the arrival of Meeker, who rowed out to one to peddle his milk. The largest was surrounded by an acre or more of small craft trying to take on or discharge passengers and freight.

Meeker wrote that there were a few women in the crowd, although there were more ashore, too many of whom resembled the famed "Old Mother Damnable" of Seattle. Staking of lots on the tide flats was in full swing at the time, with the usual clashes and hot words.

"NORTHERN LIGHT, July 31, 1858: THE FIRST BRICK BUILDING— The two story brick building of T. G. Richards & Co., commenced a week ago, is progressing finely. The walls have gone up some six or eight feet, and have received the joice for the first floor. The iron shutters and doors are on the ground, so that no delay will be occasioned in carrying the ediface forward to speedy completion."

(This building stands today—1951—on E street, just off West Holly. Author.)

Excerpts from the 6th issue of the NORTHERN LIGHT, August 7, 1858:

"The following appointments by President Buchanan, for Washington Territory, were confirmed by the Senate:

"Hon. O. B. McFadden, Associate Justice, to be Chief Justice, and Judge Wm. Strong and Col. E. C. Fitzhugh, to be Associate Justices for this Territory.

"James Tilton, Surveyor General, re-appointed.

"BODY FOUND—DEATH FROM THIRST AND STARVATION— Mr. Henry Hanson who resides at Fort Langley, called upon us Monday, and gave us the following particulars: 'Four men started on the blind trail from Semiahmoo for Fort Langley, and got lost in the woods. While wandering about in the underbrush and among the fallen timber, endeavoring to find their way out, they came upon the body of a dead man, to whose blankets a small piece of paper was pinned, bearing this inscription: "July 6. Three days without food or water. J. R. Dillerson, of Sacramento City".'

"The men who discovered the body, were too near famished themselves to afford it burial. They reached Fort Langley haggard, torn, and almost in a nude conditon. When Mr. Hanson left, they were at his home lying up for recovery."

"GHIRARDELLI & ANDORNETTI,

"Dealers in Wines, Liquors and Provisions, G Street, next to Sneat, Arnold & Co., Whatcom, (Branch of Mr. Ghirardelli, manufactory of Chocolate, Coffee, Syrups, etc.). Just landed by ship, *William* a fine assortment of Cognac Brandy, Port Wine, Maderia, Clarets, Gin, Whiskey, Alcohol, Absynthe, Vermouth, Anisettes, Curacoa, Maraschino, Native California Wine, Ginger Wine, Bitters, Peppermint, Syrups, Coffee, Chocolate, Tea, Mustard, Sardines, Matches, Segars, etc., etc. They will receive by every vessel a constant supply of the best articles from their houses in San Francisco. D. Ghirardelli, T. B. Andornetti, Whatcom."

NORTHERN LIGHT, August 14, 1858.

"DEER ABUNDANT—A hunting party returned from the Islands on Tuesday, with 24 deer, which in addition to numerous other lots of venison on hand and which subsequently arrived, has materially reduced the price of the commodity and reduced it something of a drug on the market."

C. FINKBONNER
"COMMISSION MERCHANT AND GENERAL DEALER IN CALIFORNIA AND OREGON PRODUCE. Next to the NORTHERN LIGHT Office. Whatcom, August 7th, 1858."

Eighth Edition, August 21, 1858.

"THE LAST ENUMERATION—A gentleman of the city, for his own personal gratification, yesterday made an enumeration of the buildings erected in Whatcom. The count stands thus: Frame buildings, 92; Frame tents, 19; Tents, 76; Brick, 1. Whole number, 188."

DELACY TRAIL

Throughout the summer, miners and merchants anxiously awaited a report from Engineer W. W. DeLacy* as to the trail that was to connect with the Hudson's Bay Brigade Trail beyond the Cascade Range. Handicapped by lack of information concerning the country; by snow in the passes, heavy timber, swamps and rivers; by lack of clothing and transport; by rains, sickness, desertion and inefficient help, DeLacy struggled forward doggedly to the more open country beyond the Range; there to connect with the '49 trail to the Thompson River.

On August 19, Bausman received word from DeLacy that the trail was complete. He promptly issued an extra in which he said:

"This news is perfectly reliable . . . It has come at last . . . to cause a thrill of joy in every American bosom. It was the only thing wanted to insure the rapid growth and prosperity of Whatcom and Sehome, and secure to us direct passage over the headwaters of the Thompson and Fraser Rivers without the dangers of ocean and river navigation."

DeLACY'S LETTER

"On the Trail, August 17th, 1858.

Editors NORTHERN LIGHT:

Sirs: Will you please announce in your paper that the Trail from Whatcom to Thompson's River is now finished. It strikes the Fort Hope trail in what is called on Anderson's Map, 'Blackeye's Portage.' I will be in town tomorrow, and will then be able to give you the particulars. Col. Shaw, who went with me to the Brigade Trail, can tell you more about it. Respectfully, W. W. DeLacy, Surveyor of the Trail."

NORTHERN LIGHT, August 21, 1858. "There was wild joy around the Bay over the news and plans were made to go out on the Trail to meet Captain DeLacy but he arrived before this could be carried out. At one-thirty they began firing the cannon (on the hill at the blockhouse), and kept it up intermittently all afternoon. At four o'clock the piece at Sehome answered and fired until sundown. All the people around the Bay celebrated and champagne flowed freely.

---

*Captain Walter W. DeLacy came to Washington Territory in 1854. The next year he surveyed the Yakima-Steilacoom Trail for the U. S. Government. Later he blazed a trail from Steilacoom to Whatcom, via Seattle. DeLacy was wounded twice during the Indian wars. His most difficult accomplishment was the 1858 survey and construction of the Whatcom-Fraser Trail. Later DeLacy was with the Union Pacific and Southern Pacific railroads.

"A mass meeting was called to give Captain DeLacy an appropriate welcome . . . Three or four hundred people gathered in front of Curtin and Pettibone's store in Whatcom where a platform had been erected."

Such was the admiration for DeLacy that the citizenry gave a monster testimonial dinner at which more than twenty speakers toasted him, as well as all other conceivable subjects that might justify draining another glass. After a session running far into the morning, a committee was appointed to prepare a large sized medal and to present same "To the President of the Pacific Mail Steamship Company, for the very especial pains they had uniformly taken to oppose the best interests of Whatcom."

The NORTHERN LIGHT later carried the DeLacy report in full. An editorial in the August 21 issue, paid high tribute to the man.

Bausman, optimistic editor, like his fellow townsmen, refused to admit that the trail had arrived too late; refused to take notice of Governor Douglas's trail building activities along the Fraser.

Ninth issue of the NORTHERN LIGHT—Saturday, August 28, 1858.

"THE LEVIATHAN—Captain Bulger, of the steamer *Leviathan,* took our citizens by surprise on Thursday afternoon, by steaming directly into shore, (up the Creek on high tide), near Division Street, instead of anchoring a half mile out in the harbor, as has been heretofore the custom. Crowds of people were assembled to welcome the little craft, and Captain Bulger received general commendation for the spirit of accommodation manifested in the performance of the feat."

WALKER HOUSE
E Street, Two Doors North of the Brick Building of T. G. Richards & Co.

"The proprietor of this new establishment has the pleasure of announcing to the citizens of Whatcom, miners, and the traveling public, that he has spared no expense in his arrangements to keep a first-class Hotel and nothing shall be wanting in his House to make the public comfortable. The house contains fifty beds. The public are respectfully requested to give him a trial.

Board, per week	$10.00	Meals	75 cents
Board and Lodging	$12.00	Lodging	50 cents

The NORTHERN LIGHT on September 4th, reported that the Trail was something less than a boulevard.

THE TRAIL
"The editor made a journey of thirty-five miles over the Trail and did not pronounce it a 'Good Trail', but felt that it could be made so by a moderate expense.

"But very little chopping of standing trees or grading would be required. Most of the labor to be done is in sawing and removing logs, some of which, are in an advanced state of decay and might be easily disposed of; but others of which are of gigantic proportions are so numerously piled up top of each other, as to demand the combined efforts of saw, axe, fire and oxen to effect their removal.

"The impediments on the Trail are fallen timber. There is perhaps no obstacle which a heavily packed mule cannot surmount. But the constantly recurring necessity for a full exertion of his powers to do so, is more than any humane driver should ask. Not a few of the logs which now lie across the Trail are so high, that an animal is compelled to jump them. This is not only straining, but killing upon the poor brutes, and ought not be forced upon them. The amount of $1,000 ought to be raised to improve the Trail through to the Chilliwack Lake.

"Unless they do so promptly, our voice, at least, shall be silent when an attempt is made to induce packers and others to travel the route. The result of the meeting was, that the amount of money was raised at once. The work will be put under contract on Monday and a sufficient number of men employed to rush it through in a few days."

Vol. I.   Whatcom, Whatcom County, Saturday, Sept. 11, 1858   No. 11

FROM FRASER RIVER

"Mr. Peter Brando arrived here from Fort Hope on Thursday afternoon. He reports Fraser River to have fallen about four feet since Monday.

"He learned from passengers on board the *Wilson G. Hunt,* that the steamer, *Sea Bird,* which was launched last week, and had gone to Victoria and taken on 200 tons of freight, and passengers for a return trip to Fort Langley, caught fire in the Gulf, and was burned to the water's edge. She was run upon the rocks, and all on board thus saved.

"Fraser River has been declared open to reciprocal trade, on the payment of ad valorem duty of ten per cent.*

"Governor Douglas was at Fort Hope, and intended to ascend to Fort Yale.

"Ned McGowan had a difficulty a few days ago, on a bar between Forts Hope and Yale, with a former member of the San Francisco Vigilance Committee, in which he struck his antagonist over the head with a club, doing him great injury. Gov. Douglas was inquiring into the facts, and it was thought would have McGowan arrested. The Indians are quiet."

THE AMERICAN JOINT BOUNDARY COMMISSION

"During our visit to the Semiahmoos, we had the pleasure of spending an agreeable evening at the headquarters of the American Joint Boundary Commission, and of sharing the hospitalities of Mr. Commissioner Campbell, and the officers generally of the expedition.

"The site of these headquarters is on the beach, flanked by a running stream of fresh water, about two miles west of Semiahmoo on the mainland,

---

*This followed the repudiation by the British Government of Governor Douglas's onerous regulations, and the revocation of the Hudson's Bay Company's exclusive license to trade in the territory.

(Blaine today), neatly laid off in military style, with parade-grounds, surrounded by guard houses, and long rows of frame buildings, occupied by the officers, soldiers, attaches, commissary stores, etc., of the Commission. The soldiers which constitute the escort, some 75 in number, are in command of Captain Woodruff, and present an appearance of health, cleanliness, and general efficiency, worthy to be commended."

THE EXODUS

With the shallow bar diggings on the Fraser worked out, and with winter at hand, September brought an end to the rush. Miners and camp followers streamed from the river, a few bringing well filled pokes, but many more carrying less gold than they had taken north. Population in settlements on British and American sides of the line melted away.

To the last the NORTHERN LIGHT of Whatcom remained fighting for the life of the town and paper. Then Bausman stated, "Whatcom has gone in, and the Light has gone out." His final word was an extra, reportedly dated September 18. Bausman and Watson packed up their belongings and headed for San Francisco, where the former worked on the SAN FRANCISCO CALL for many years. The printing plant is believed to have been sold in Whatcom as some relics appeared in later years. Undoubtedly the bulk of the equipment was used later in the publication of the PORT TOWNSEND ARGUS (1861).

In less time than it had taken them to gather, miners, and craftmen, merchants and hotel keepers, saloon men and gamblers, all had vanished.

While many buildings in Whatcom were torn down and removed to Victoria when the boom collapsed, Sehome appears to have been more permanent, as is indicated by the number of structures shown in a sketch of the town, drawn April 10, 1859 by Captain George E. Pickett. The following advertisements, appearing the previous summer in the NORTHERN LIGHT, indicate how the occupants were engaged during the "Rush," (Opposite page 102):

SEHOME HOTEL
Sehome, Bellingham Bay,
Larcombe & Co., Proprietors,
Board and lodging by the day or week
The choicest Liquors at the Bar

FREEMAN & CO'S EXPRESS!
For San Francisco, Fraser River, and the different points on the Sound.
D. F. NEWSOM, AGENT,
Bellingham Bay.

E. H. WILSON & CO.
Sehome, Bellingham Bay
Dealers in Groceries, Provisions, Clothing, Boots, Shoes, and Miners'
Outfits complete, wholesale and retail

MUDGETT, EBBETS & CO.
Sehome
Commission Merchants
and dealers in
Groceries, Provisions, Liquors, and Miners' Outfits.
Agency, Wells, Fargo & Co.

M. LOUISSON
Corner Pickett and Front Streets, Sehome
Groceries — Provisions
Clothing, Boots and Shoes
and
Mining Tools of all Descriptions

WILLIAM STANNAH
Pioneer Bakery, corner of Mason and Main Street, Sehome
Breads, Pies, Cakes and Crackers
Constantly on Hand

He understands that a spurious article of Bread, represented to be from the "Pioneer Bakery," is sold in Sehome. The genuine article can only be produced at the establishment as above.

REMINISCENCES

As in the case of all gold rushes, the stampeders reached Bellingham Bay and Victoria carrying all sorts of possible and impossible clothing, and equipment. In 1895, Captain Verich of Doe Bay, during an interview given the WHATCOM REVEILLE, told the story of a Frenchman who came to the Bay by steamer in 1858, equipped with a carriage, horses and a pet poodle. He did not attempt the trail by carriage, but started for the mines on horseback accompanied by his dog. When he reached the Nooksack and learned that it was not the Fraser, he returned cursing the world at large and the mosquitoes in particular.

John Alexander, member of a general mercantile company, in later years, left an account of how his firm lost $12,000 in one venture. This was near the closing days of the Whatcom boom, when their heavily loaded string of pack animals became snow bound and died in the passes beyond the Chilliwack.

Canadian authorities made some effort against those preying on the gold seekers, with the result that most gamblers early moved from Victoria to Whatcom. In June, when steamboats began the run of the Fraser River, a large percentage of these shifted to Fort Yale, so as to have first chance at the miners' newly washed gold dust. Whatcom, however, continued to support many gentlemen of shady repute according to Colonel G. Godfrey Short, who in June, 1892, gave the WHATCOM REVEILLE the following account of his 1858 experiences:

"In June of 1858, I found myself dead broke in one of the most curious cities, if it might be called a city, in the world. There was a fringe of tents and board shanties hanging to the ragged edge between an impenetrable forest and deep sea.

"Occupying these ephemeral dwellings were ten thousand men of every nationality, and half a dozen women, loose and otherwise. Lawyers, gamblers, bankers, refugees from all parts of the world appeared, al fresco, in their boot legs, with derringers in their belts. The entire population were not so accoutered, but a good sprinkling of the rough element leavened the whole mass, and the future judge was only to be distinguished from the gambler by his conversation.

"I had $800 with me when I landed, but the second day my landlord 'Diggles,' who had taken a great fancy to me (or my money) asked me to loan him $200 'until Saturday night,' when his board bills came due. He charged $15 a week for three meals of bacon, bread and black coffee, with a bunk at night. I was only eighteen years old and I loaned him the money. A well dressed gentleman, who said he was a banker, and who was afterwards hung at White Pine, then persuaded me to become a silent partner in the banking business he proposed to start.

"One morning before I had seen anything of his bank, he informed me that he had opened up and had been unfortunate, and that he had lost all of my money. I found out it was a faro bank he had started."

Mr. Short then tried to get his money back from the landlord, Mr. Diggles, who informed him that he didn't intend to pay it back and if he, Short, made any fuss about it, he would be thrown out of the house. At this, an Irishman, Moriaty, sat up in his bunk having heard the conversation between Short and Diggles, when they thought they were alone in the room. The Irishman made Diggles give the money back to Short and when Diggles left the room, Moriaty helped himself to $50 for collecting the money.

Colonel Short continues: "Next morning I was pulled out of my bunk by the banking gentleman who assured me he had 'busted' the bank, and in token thereof he presented me with fifty double eagles as my share of the investment. Ten days after my arrival in camp, I had increased my capital about $500, had gained experience worth an incalcuable amount, and a friend in Jim Moriaty.

"I left Diggles House and went to board with a Scotch woman who kept a boarding house on Division Street, a kind of gulch alley that ran from the waterfront. Diggles' house was over the water at high tide, and he was liable at any time to push a disagreeable boarder into the sea, pound him on the head with a club, all the while crying for help. He was none too good for this.

"My new landlady's name was Doodle, a bustling Scotch dame with a little inoffensive husband with a red nose. He kept the books, and pottered around, his wife treated him as if he were a son that required close watching. They were 'forty-niners' that followed every rush to new diggings as a matter of habit."

Chief Justice Dennison, who practiced law in Whatcom in 1858, stated in 1889, that while he was fortunate enough to find shelter in the Roeder home, during the rush, there were 5,000 persons in tents or toy houses. Court was held in a log courthouse on Whidbey Island with the bench and bar camping out. Indians served as cooks. A cold stormy winter in '58, brought much snow and ice, and the highest tides known. Logs, escaped from broken booms, filled the Bay and damaged the E Street wharf. Exposed buildings had to be protected from these drifting logs. "It is no wonder," reported the judge, "that with such winter weather and bad reports from the mines, the population of Whatcom rapidly disappeared."

The Fraser River Gold Rush was not without benefits to both the Puget Sound Country as well as to British Columbia. Many who were stranded, settled perforce, and became leading citizens. Others, attracted by the land and its resources deliberately chose the life in this last frontier. Word of mouth advertising no doubt served to bring many settlers west in the near future.

British Columbia, a wilderness, profited even more by the stampede. The great rush brought an end to rule by the Hudson's Bay Company. In one year's time, it was responsible for the creation of the Province of British Columbia. Further, of the great hordes drawn by the lure of the Fraser, many thousands remained to become permanent residents of the country.

The Sehome Coal Mine and the Whatcom Mill were unchanged by the Gold Rush. A few wider clearings, some new shacks, the E Street and Sehome wharves, the Richards and Hyatt's brick building; these were the visible additions left by the stampede.

Again the woods closed in on the settlement, while the primeval silence of that great forest seemed to weigh and depress the minds of the few remaining settlers as never before. All writers speak of the black days that followed.

Chapter XI.

BOUNDARY DISPUTE

SAN JUAN ISLAND

P RESUMABLY the Washington Treaty of June 15, 1846 ended the Northwest boundary dispute between Great Britain and the United States, a dispute that had caused much war talk and brought forth the inflammatory presidential campaign slogan "Fifty-four forty or fight."* Unfortunately the dispute and war talk revived within a few years, owing to the indefinite description of the boundary after it reached tidewater.

In the words of the treaty this line ran along the 49th parallel of latitude "to the middle of the channel which separates the continent from Vancouver's Island, thence southerly through the middle of said channel and of Fuca's Strait to the Pacific Ocean."

British representatives held that Rosaria Strait which would place the San Juan Archipelago in British possession, was the specified "middle of the said channel." Americans claimed that since the boundary had been diverted south, from the 49th parallel for the purpose of placing Vancouver Island under the English crown, the channel intended was the one circling the tip of that island. (See map inside front or back cover).

Anticipating a difference of opinion, George Bancroft, when Secretary of the Navy in Polk's cabinet, had charts of the disputed area prepared. Later as Minister to England, he took pains to indicate that America understood the western channel to be the Boundary line. Similarly diplomatic correspondence between London and Washington affirmed the British views.

In the meantime, or in 1845, Governor Douglas formally claimed San Juan Island for the Hudson's Bay Company. Five years later a salmon-curing plant was opened there, while in 1853 the Company, partly as a defensive measure against American claims, established a post on San Juan and moved a flock of 1,300 sheep to the island.

Colonel Isaac N. Ebey was appointed Collector of Customs and Inspector of Revenues for the Puget Sound district in 1853, and the following year visited San Juan Island to collect duties on the sheep which, he claimed, had been imported to American soil. Arguments with Charles John Griffin,

---

*American claim for a boundary at 54° 40'.

97

the Company's agent, Governor James Douglas and Captain James Sangster, British Collector of Customs were futile. No duties were collected. Thereupon, Ebey appointed Captain James Henry Webber as Deputy Collector of Customs for the island and returned to his Port Townsend headquarters.

THE SHEEP CASE

In March, 1854, the Washington Territorial Legislature created Whatcom County, which included the San Juan Island group as well as the present Skagit and Whatcom counties. Hudson's Bay property was duly assessed and when taxes were unpaid in 1855, "Yankee" Ellis Barnes, the sheriff, was ordered to levy upon and sell the Company's sheep.

No one appeared at Sheriff Barnes' first advertised sale according to an account published in the SUMAS VIDETTE in 1893, so he returned to Whatcom, collected eight prospective bidders and in three rowboats, once more headed for San Juan Island. After rowing the better part of two nights and one day, including a trip to the southern tip of the Island and return, the sheriff's party located forty breeding rams in a corral near the upper end of San Juan. These were knocked down to the Whatcomites at from fifty cents to one dollar per head, and since the sum total did not equal the tax claim, sheep running at large were sold at one and two cents per head.

While members of the sheriff's party were carrying their property to the beach, Agent Griffin charged down the hill accompanied by about twenty Kanakas, who were armed with knives, and ordered that the sheep be cut loose. Dramatically, Sheriff Barnes ordered his men to protect the property "in the name of the United States." Since Barnes' men were armed with revolvers, the Kanakas retired and shortly afterward six of them, in a canoe, started across the channel to Victoria.

Before Barnes could free his beached boats and load all the sheep, some one reported that the *Beaver* was steaming out of Victoria Harbor. Barnes' flotilla fled, and after an all night struggle with wind and waves, reached Bellingham Bay.

Damage claims of the Hudson's Bay Company for thirty-four breeding rams were presented by Great Britian to the United States in July 1855. Meantime there was an exchange of notes between Governor Douglas and Governor Stevens; also between state department heads of the two governments. An understanding was reached whereby both nations were to avoid all acts likely to provoke conflict.

By the year 1859, the arrears of taxes charged to the Hudson's Bay Company by Whatcom County had increased to $935, but no further attempt was made to collect.

At high levels, the Boundary matter and the San Juan claims always were handled amicably. Friction and threat of war over such incidents as the "Pig Episode" arose or were aggravated through action of low level officials; these were due in part to slow communication with their superiors; to jealous fear that they might jeopardize some national right; and to the undue military importance they attached to San Juan Island.

THE BOUNDARY COMMISSION

Ten years after ratification of the Boundary Treaty, or in August, 1856, Congress, their action accelerated possibly by the San Juan situation, authorized the appointment of a commission to determine and mark the International Boundary line west from the Rocky Mountains. Archibald Campbell was named Commissioner, with Lieutenant John G. Parke, chief astronomer. In December, 1856, Captain James C. Prevost, Royal Navy, Captain George Henry Richards, Royal Navy, and Lieutenant Colonel J. S. Hawkins, Royal Engineers, were selected as the British Commissioners.

Campbell and staff arrived at Victoria in June, 1857, and there met Captain Prevost. The American party of about 150 men, including scientists, and topographers, together with a military escort of about seventy men from Company F, Ninth Infantry under Captain Woodruff, established a headquarter's camp near Semiahmoo.*

After a survey of the San Juan Archipelago, Campbell and Prevost tried to solve the controversy of Haro Strait versus the Strait of Rosario. Finally Prevost offered to compromise on the middle channel through the islands which would have given San Juan Island to the British, and the remainder of the Archipelago to American rule. This offer was refused and the Commissioners then turned to the determination of the initial point of the survey at Point Roberts.

When the observations and computations of Prevost and Richards were complete, they were gratified to note that their initial point was only eight feet from that determined by the American Commission.

Lieutenant Colonel Hawkins arrived in 1858, when the British set up their construction and survey camp on Sumas Prairie.

At the initial point of the 49th parallel, the joint commissions erected a large granite obelisk inscribed with the words: "Treaty of Washington, June 15, 1846," the date, "Erected 1861"; the latitude and longitude; and the names of the several commissioners.

---

*When the editor of the NORTHERN LIGHT newspaper visited the American Joint Boundary Commission in 1858, he reported that there were two Semiahmoos. One was the Spit, the other, the village of Semiahmoo on the mainland, (Blaine today), named for Chief Semiahmoo. "The site of these headquarters is on the beach, flanked by a stream of fresh water, about two miles west of Semiahmoo on the mainland."

Between Point Roberts and the Rocky Mountains, a distance of 409½ miles, a total length of 190 miles was cleared and marked by the survey. Clearings were in the vicinity of settlements and for a mile or more at convenient intervals.

On the section from Point Roberts to the DeLacy Trail, forty-three iron markers, each four feet high, were used. The placing of these fell to the British Commissioners. *H. M. S. Hecate* landed twenty-five of the pillars at Semiahmoo (Blaine), while *H. M. S. Grapple* carried the remainder to Sumas River in 1861. The remainder of the Boundary line to the Rockies was marked with about 115 piles of stone, from six to eight feet high, and by earthen mounds covering wooden posts.

THE "PIG EPISODE"

While the Boundary Treaty of 1846 confirmed to British corporations their lands and holdings on American soil, and provided for the purchase of the same by the United States, the document failed to define the boundaries of the land. Delays in the settlement, and indefinite land claims of the Company caused much claim jumping throughout the Territory, with many protests and counter protests.

This was the situation on San Juan Island in the spring of 1859, when stampeders returning from the Fraser River gold rush, drifted across the channel from Victoria and squatted on the island, which was claimed in its entirety by the Hudson's Bay Company. The late arrivals held that the Company had come upon United States territory after the treaty date and hence had no title. When Lyman Cutler, one of the settlers shot a breeding boar owned by the Company after the animal had repeatedly broken into his potato patch, an international incident developed that brought two nations to the verge of war.

Cutler offered to pay for the porker, but Resident Agent, Charles J. Griffin set the damages at $100, and when the former angrily refused such a settlement, the agent said he would send to Victoria for a gunboat and have the offender arrested.

Charles McKay, an early settler, has told how he persuaded Cutler to hide next day when the gunboat arrived and so prevented bloodshed, since the Americans, he said, who were good shots would have stood by their countryman, if an attempt had been made to take him by force.

On July 4, 1859, the fourteen resident Americans, convened near the south end of the island at the cabin of Paul K. Hubbs, Deputy Collector of Customs, erected a flag pole, ran up the national colors, and celebrated by each delivering a patriotic oration, thus further increasing the international tension.

A few days later, Brigadier General William S. Harney, commander of the Department of Oregon, while on an inspection trip, which had included a visit to Governor Douglas, sighted the flag on lower San Juan Island. Eagerly the settlers told the story of the pig and the threatened arrest of Cutler. Harney acted at once.

On July 18, 1859, Captain George E. Pickett with Company D, of the Ninth Infantry, was ordered from Fort Bellingham to San Juan Island to protect the Northern Sound Country from raids by Northern Indians and for the protection of American citizens in their rights as such. He was further directed to inform the authorities at Victoria that they would not be permitted to interfere with American citizens and that redress might be had only under the laws of the United States.

Pickett received the order on the night of July 26. The following morning he and his Company were landed by the Steamer *Massachusetts* on the southern end of San Juan where earthworks were hastily constructed, not far from the cabin of Paul K. Hubbs, Deputy Collector of Customs.

That same morning, July 27, John Fitzroy de Courcy, newly appointed Justice of Peace for San Juan Island arrived aboard the Corvette *Satellite,* prepared to arrest Cutler. Pickett intervened, declaring that: "This being United States Territory, no laws, other than those of the United States, nor courts, except such as are held by virtue of said laws, will be recognized on this Island,"—this despite the fact that under the Treaty of 1846, the ownership was yet to be decided.

Governor Douglas also ignoring the same uncertainty of title, issued a proclamation declaring that the sovereignty had always been in the British crown; and protesting the occupation by any one disputing that sovereignty. To back his proclamation, Douglas ordered a naval blockade of the American position.

Meantime, Agent Griffin wrote Pickett that the latter's force was trespassing on Hudson's Bay property and asked them to vacate. The Captain stated, in reply, that he would vacate only on order of his government. Copies of this correspondence were enclosed with the following letter addressed to his Regimental Commander:

MILITARY CAMP,
San Juan Island, W. T., July 30, 1859.

"My dear Colonel: I have the honor to enclose you some notes which passed this morning between the Hudson's Bay authorities and myself. From the threatening attitude of affairs at present, I deem it my duty to request that the *Massachusetts* may be sent to this point. I do not know that any actual collision will take place, but it is not comfortable to be lying within range of a couple of steamers. *The Tribune,* a thirty-gun frigate, is lying broadside to our camp, and from present indications everything leads me to suppose that they will attempt to prevent me carrying out my instructions.

"If you have any boats to spare, I shall be happy to get one at least. The only whale-boat we had was, most unfortunately, staved on the day of our departure. We will be very much in want of some tools and camp equipage.

G. E. PICKETT,
Captain Ninth Infantry.

Lieutenant Colonel Casey,
Ninth Infantry, Commanding, Fort Steilacoom, W. T."

Captain Geoffrey Phipps Hornby, commanding the *Tribune*, was the first officer dispatched by Douglas to prevent the landing of further armed parties. He was accompanied by George Hunter Cary, Attorney General of British Columbia, who wrote Douglas that the American forces were more powerful than had been reported and that resistance was probable.

Concerning the threatened clash, the PIONEER AND DEMOCRAT, of Olympia, Washington Territory, reported:

"H. B. M. ship, *Tribune*, lies with spring cables and her guns double-shotted broadside to the camp of Captain Pickett; her decks are covered with redcoats, having on board 450 marines and some 180 sappers and miners.

"We thank God we have, in this officer, of the Department of Oregon, a man equal to any and all emergencies in the protection of American citizens in the Northwest Coast."

Governor Douglas as Vice Admiral, had ordered Captain Hornby to land a force to protect the lives and property of British subjects. When Captain Hornby, together with Captains Prevost and Richards of the Boundary Commission called on Captain Pickett, he informed them he would resist such landing to the last man. In face of protest from his naval commanders about starting an armed conflict, Douglas withdrew this order and suggested a joint military occupation. Pickett refused this offer and asked that the respective governments be consulted. Throughout, the conversations seem to have been friendly on both sides.

On arrival at Esquimalt Harbor, Admiral R. L. Baynes, commander of the Pacific Fleet, approved the forbearance of Captain Hornby, and while he did reinforce the blockading fleet, he scoffed at the idea of involving two great nations in war over an insignificant pig.

On his part, General Harney approved the action of Pickett, directed that no joint military occupation or civil jurisdiction be permitted, and

---

UPPER—Sehome, the first platted townsite on Bellingham Bay. Surveyed, May, 1858 by Civil Engineer W. W. DeLacy.

LOWER—Drawing by Captain George E. Pickett, of Sehome, Washington Territory, April 10, 1859.

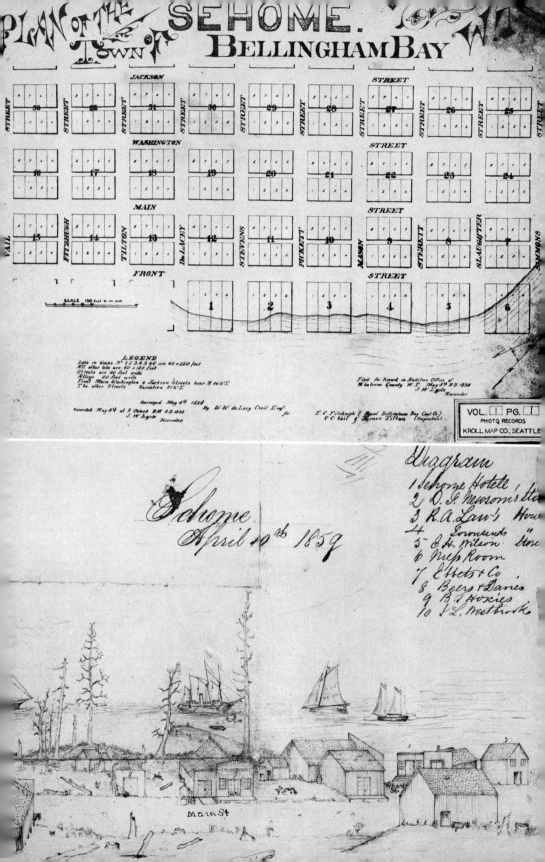

For and on behalf of the United States of North America, I do hereby promise and agree with Capt. Henry Roeder of the scow Genl. Harney; that, in the event of any harm or damage coming to his vessel from the interposition of any of H. B. Majesty's forces in these waters, in consequence of his landing, or attempting to land, certain guns and ammunition from the steamer Massachusetts, to and on the beach of San Juan Island, that the Government of the United States will make good such damage to him.

N. Roberts Scott
Lieutent 4th Infy
A. A. Q. M.

U. S. Steamer Massachusetts.
San Juan Island. W. T.
August 14th 1859

Witness
W. W. Harriman

ordered Lieutenant Colonel Casey to reinforce the Island command.

To do this, Colonel Casey stripped Northern Sound posts of guns and men, transporting them in the Steamers *Julia* and *Massachusetts*. Captain Roeder's 100 ton schooner, the *General Harney*, also was pressed into service. To protect Roeder, a guarantee of indemnity against loss was given by Lieutenant Robert N. Scott of the U. S. Steamer *Massachusetts*. (See opposite page). Nothing was said about loss of life or limb, nor is it likely that such a guarantee issued by a Lieutenant of the Navy would have been honored should Roeder's vessel have been sunk by the British.

The southern end of San Juan Island terminates in a peninsula about one-half mile wide, which extends eastward about two and one-half miles. Pickett's fortifications were on this neck of land. Griffin Bay borders the peninsula on the north. While the British vessels lay opposite the earthworks, the little American flotilla on the morning of August 10, under cover of a dense fog, came down from the northeast through Griffin Bay and landed troops about 7:00 A. M. A march of half a mile brought the soldiers into camp where their cheers apprised the British of the landing. When the fog lifted, the Steamer *Julia*, was observed close inshore unloading supplies.

The American forces finally landed comprised Companies A, C, and I, Fourth Infantry; Companies D, and H, Ninth Infantry; Companies A, B, D, and M, of the Third Artillery; and a detachment of Company A, Engineers, making a total of 461 men. The armament included eight 32 pounders from the U. S. Ship *Massachusetts,* one 6-pounder and five mountain howitzers.

Aboard the five British ships, the *Plumper, Satellite, Pylades, Tribune,* and the Flag Ship, *Ganges,* were 2,140 men and 167 guns.

Major Haller, who arrived with his Company a day later than Colonel Casey, thus further increasing the tension, later stated that he believed his arrival was the critical moment, and a conflict would have been precipitated but for the fact he carried some late newspapers containing accounts of the battle of Solferino in the French-Austrian War. When the British officers read these reports and considered the question of England's possible involvement on the continent, the matter of a controversy over an insignificant island like San Juan must have seemed very small to them, for immediately, Haller said, a marked change in conduct and bearing was noticeable.

At the American encampment an earthwork was thrown up paralleling the waterfront for three hundred and fifty feet, with refused angles at either

UPPER—Guarantee of indemnity against loss of the "General Harney," given to Captain Roeder by Lieutenant Robert N. Scott of the U. S. Steamer "Massachusetts."

LOWER—Monument and gun emplacements, center. Fort San Juan, San Juan Island.—Photo by J. A. McCormick.

end. The north side of the fort was left open. Five gun platforms were constructed inside the redoubt.

Harney's report, when it reached Washington, caused grave concern and led to much diplomatic activity. In his desire to preserve peace and prevent collision between British and American authorities, President Buchanan dispatched Lieutenant General Winfield Scott to the West Coast with the suggestion that it might be desirable to provide for joint occupation of the island until the title question could be settled.

Meantime war fever increased on both sides of the Border. On Vancouver Island, Admiral Baynes was criticized for his non-aggressive attitude. By contrast, in Washington Territory, General Harney authorized a call for volunteers and placed at disposal of the State Troops many thousand rounds of ammunition.

General Scott arrived at Port Townsend early in October, 1859, and on the twenty-eighth of the month, offered to Governor Douglas a proposal for joint occupation of the Island, each government to station thereon not more than one hundred men. This offer was submitted by the Governor to the Home Authorities.

In the end, Captain Hunt's Company C, Fourth Infantry, was left, while Captain Pickett, whom the British considered more bellicose, was ordered to Fort Bellingham. At the same time Admiral Baynes landed a detachment of Royal Marines under Captain George Bazalgette on the northwestern end of San Juan Island—eighty men, one captain, two lieutenants and a surgeon.

Hot heads South of the Border considered the joint occupation a "craven surrender," Scott was called the great "Pacificator," guilty of "almost treacherous concessions."

Friction between General Scott and General Harney, which had its origin during the Mexican War, when Scott relieved the impetuous Harney from his command (only to restore him later on higher orders) continued as to the West Coast situation. In a memorandum* dated February 14, 1860, Scott expressed a doubt "whether it be safe in respect to our foreign relations, or just to the gallant officers and men in the Oregon Department to leave them longer, at so great a distance, subject to the ignorance, passion, and caprice of the present headquarters of that department."

By a departmental order dated April 16, 1860, General Harney relieved Captain Hunt of the post on San Juan and directed Captain Pickett to assume command. When the Secretary of State learned of this, he informed the British Minister that General Harney's orders, being in violation of the

*Ex. Doc. 65, pp 190, 191.

arrangement made by General Scott, "have been read by the President, both with surprise and regret."

As a consequence of this act, Harney was relieved as Commander of the Department of Oregon, while Captain Hunt was returned to command of American troops on San Juan Island and Captain Pickett reassigned to Fort Bellingham, which post the latter held until he resigned to join the Confederate forces.

Harney was mildly reprimanded by the Secretary of War, for his violations of General Scott's orders. Bancroft, in writing of this incident, said: "General Harney was invited to Washington upon a pretense of being needed to testify in the Oregon and Washington Indian-war-debt-claims, in order to pacify the British minister, and Governor Douglas by removing him from proximity to the San Juan Island boundary-war ground."

As for Pickett, the American Congress previously, or on January 11, 1860, had adopted a vote of thanks to him for his "gallant and firm discharge of his duties under most trying circumstances, while he was in command on the Island of San Juan."

Some writers, notably LaSalle Corbell Pickett, the wife of General Pickett, have suggested that perhaps Harney and Pickett were trying to involve the United States in war with Great Britian so as to prevent or delay the Civil War. This theory is not in accord with history or with the character of the two men. The elderly Harney has been described as an extraordinary physical specimen, six feet two or three inches tall, of fine proportions, of sandy complexion, blond hair, small head, and cold of eye. His career is that of a patriotic, capable, if impetuous officer, intolerant of opposition.

Pickett's action also was that of an efficient commander, carrying out his orders with nerve and intelligence that characterized him during the Civil War. Certainly his whole professional bearing and friendly personal relations tended to preserve the peace; whereas a rude or less skillful soldier certainly would have precipitated the conflict.

Fred John Splitstone in his volume ORCAS has done a bit of speculating as to what the situation on San Juan might have been had two actors been removed from the scene; "the fiery Virginian Pickett, and the calm Scotsman, Admiral R. Lamb Baynes." He thinks that but for the belligerent Pickett, the British would have landed forces on the island and so strengthened their claims; while but for the practical Baynes, who believed that war was too high a price to pay for the tops of some submerged mountains, and so declined to land his forces and crush Pickett; war would have been a certainty.

Admiral Baynes deserves a memorial for his acts. Military leaders who have won battles and wars; who have started conflicts that spilled oceans of blood, have been honored by great monuments. The name of the Admiral, whose common sense stopped a war before it started, who prevented a great blood bath by two civilized English speaking nations, should be placed high on the International Peace Arch.

THE BOUNDARY DECISION
1872

First attempts to settle the San Juan boundary dispute languished because of the Civil War. For more than twelve years the garrison lived in amity. The settlers also enjoyed pleasant years free from taxation and customs duty. However, they were irked by the military rule, so much so that Charles McKay, a settler dispatched the first telegraph message from the island, one costing thirty dollars and fifty cents, and addressed to General Halleck, in which he complained of the arbitrary actions of one of the American captains who, even at that moment, had been replaced by another commandant.

The following from the diary of Sheriff James Kavanaugh refers to the absence of civil authority on the island:

"August 1, 1863—I returned from San Juan after an absence of eight days, Friday, July 31. Did not collect any license or poll tax because of the interference of Captain Bissel. Military law is supreme on the Island."

With civil law suspended, smuggling flourished. Unable to prove the settlers guilty of smuggling wool from Vancouver Island, but to satisfy their own curiosity, Federal Customs officials took a census of the San Juan sheep. This census seemed to show that, according to exports from the island, each sheep thereon was growing an annual clip of more than 150 pounds of wool.

An attempt to arbitrate the boundary question in 1869 failed because of a proviso offering an alternate channel between Canal de Haro and Rosario Strait. In May, 1871, the Joint High Commission of the two countries, voted to exclude this alternate passage and submit the question to Emperor William I of Germany solely on the merits of the two outer straits.

Three German experts made exhaustive investigations—Doctor Grimm, vice president of the Supreme Court at Berlin, Doctor Kiepert, a pupil of Carl Ritter, and Doctor Goldschmidt, a member of the Superior Commercial Court at Leipsic. As a result of their report, Emperor William I made his award on October 21, 1872. "Most in accordance with the true interpretation of the treaty concluded on June 15, 1846, between the government of her Britannic Majesty and of the United States of America, is the claim of the Government of the United States that the boundary line between territories of her Britannic Majesty and the United States should be drawn through the Haro Channel." George Bancroft, then minister at Berlin, argued the case for America.

Because the settlement was in favor of the American claims, the Gladstone administration was criticized by the British, as being an exponent of "peace at any price." In their negotiations, the British High Commissioners may have held the view of the British Admiralty that freedom of navigation was what mattered mostly; that, and the retention of Vancouver Island. The whole line had been laid down originally in haphazard manner, the islands and lands being considered of little value and unlikely to be occupied for many years.

Shortly after the decision, the British forces were withdrawn; military authority ended; and civil processes were resumed.* In 1874, President Grant appoined General Hazzard Stevens, son of the first territorial governor to hear and pass on claims** of the British citizens against the United States. He later stated: "It appeared, however, that there were none, all former British subjects having become American citizens and taken their lands under American laws."

On October 21, 1904, the Washington University State Historical Society erected marble monuments on the sites of the British and American camps. (Opposite page 111). Commemorating confirmation of American title to the 172 islands of the Archipelago, the citizens of San Juan Island in October, 1938, celebrated by unveiling at the court house in Friday Harbor, two paintings of actors in the earlier drama.

These were of Emperor William I,*** who had acted as arbiter of the Boundary dispute; and of General George Pickett, as he had appeared when serving on San Juan.

GENERAL WILLIAM SELBY HARNEY
August 22, 1800 — May 9, 1889

General William S. Harney, whose impetuous seizure of San Juan Island, so nearly involved Great Britian and the United States in war, was born at Haysboro, near Nashville, Tennessee, August 22, 1800. Entering the

---

*San Juan County was organized November 17, 1873, under legislative act of October 31, 1873.

**In 1869, President Grant had reported that a Joint Commission (authorized July 1, 1863) of British and American nominees, had awarded the Hudson's Bay Company and the Puget Sound Agricultural Company (a subsidiary) the sum of $650,000 in extinguishment of their rights in Old Oregon. The two companies previously had presented claims totaling $4,970,036.67.

***The former had been obtained through the offices of Kaiser Wilhelm II, then in exile at Doorn, Holland; the latter was brought to the celebration by Lieutenant George Edward Pickett III, grandson of General Pickett.

Army as a second lieutenant in 1818, he served in the Florida Indian campaigns. A lieutenant colonel of the Second Dragoons in 1836, he was brevetted colonel in 1840 for gallant conduct in the Everglades campaign. The rank was permanent in 1846.

When the Mexican War opened, he was senior cavalry officer under General Scott, who distrusted his judgment and impetuosity, and relieved him of his command. Harney acquiesed at first, then resumed command and was court martialed for disobedience. He apologized to Scott as required by the court order, then appealed to Washington authorities. Scott in turn was mildly reprimanded but returned Harney to command of the cavalry. The heroic and brilliant leadership by the latter justified Scott's act. At the battle of Cerro Gordo, Harney led the charge up El Telegrafo Hill at the head of Smith's brigade, winning the victory. He was brevetted brigadier general in April, 1847.

Stationed in the Platte country, he defeated the restless Sioux Indians at the battle of Sand Hill, and presently in 1858 was rewarded with the command of the Department of Oregon with the permanent rank of brigadier general.

Following the San Juan incident, and the second clash with General Scott, he was recalled and placed in command of the Department of the West with headquarters at St. Louis. In May, 1861, he was relieved of his command after he had entered into an agreement with General Sterling Price, Confederate General commanding the Missouri militia, not to molest the state troops so long as they made no hostile move against the Federal Government. Because of this incident perhaps, and because he was suspected of Southern sympathies, he was retired in 1863. Near the close of the war, the government, remembering his long and brilliant services, brevetted him Major General.

General Harney died May 9, 1889, at Orlando, Florida, the scene of his youthful triumphs over the Indians.

Chapter XII.

GENERAL GEORGE E. PICKETT

January 25, 1825 — July 30, 1875

BUT FOR ABRAHAM LINCOLN, the story of the Northwest might have been different, with another actor on the stage, a different script.

But for Abraham Lincoln, history would not have known that soul-stirring spectacle, that bloody, crashing finale at Gettysburg.

In short, but for Abraham Lincoln, George E. Pickett might well have lived and died, an obscure attorney in the State of Illinois.

Against his own inclinations, the young Virginian had been persuaded to enter the law office of his uncle, Andrew Johnston at Quincy, Illinois, where he met Abraham Lincoln, an associate of his uncle. Although they were opposite in temperament, a fast friendship developed, and the grave Lincoln found delight in listening to the happy Virginian's songs and guitar music. In the end, the future president decided that Pickett would not be content as a lawyer, and therefore interceded with Congressman John G. Stuart of the Third Illinois District to secure the appointment of the young man to West Point.

The friendship continued through life, as evidenced by letters during Pickett's cadet days and by a visit the President paid to Mrs. Pickett and child after the fall of Richmond, only a few days before he was assassinated.

George Edward Pickett, son of Colonel Robert and Mary (Johnston) Pickett, was born January 25, 1825, in Richmond, Virginia, where he attended Richmond Academy.

Appointed to the United States Military Academy in 1842, he was graduated July 1, 1846, the last in a class of fifty-nine, just in time for the Mexican campaign. A roster of his young fellow officers in that war, reads like a roll of the future greats in the Civil War, as indeed it was; most of the Civil War leaders having been trained in campaigns of General Taylor and General Scott.

Brevet Second Lieutenant George E. Pickett joined his regiment, the Eighth Infantry, in November, 1846, after the battle of Monterey. Next he was transferred to Scott's Army for the Siege of Vera Cruz, being promoted Second Lieutenant, Second Infantry, March 3, 1847.

The battles of Scott's campaign all are on his service record: Vera Cruz, Cerro Gordo, Contreras, San Antonio, Chapultepec, Mexico City. His first wound was received at Contreras, but does not seem to have kept him very long from the fighting. In August, 1847, he was brevetted First Lieutenant "for gallant and meritorious conduct in the battles of Contreras, and Churubusco"; and again September 13, 1847, was brevetted Captain "for gallant and meritorious conduct" at Chapultepec, where he was first to gain the heights and plant the national flag on the summit of the castle.

Following a tour of garrison duty in Texas, Pickett was promoted to Captain of the Ninth Infantry March 3, 1855, and the next summer sailed with the regiment for Washington Territory where the Indian wars were under way. Six companies were assigned to Fort Vancouver and four to Puget Sound.

Three years before his departure, he met LaSalle Corbell Pickett, his third wife. Then a child, just recovering from whooping cough, she became attached to the kindly young man. He was at that time mourning the loss of his first wife, Sally Minge, of Richmond, whom he had married in January, 1851, and who had died the following November.

Pickett, in command of D Company, Ninth Infantry, was sent to Bellingham Bay in 1856 to erect a fort for the settlers' protection. During this same year he built his house on Bancroft Street. Shortly thereafter he met and married an attractive Haida maiden, who on December 31, 1857, gave birth to a son, James Tilton Pickett. Her death occurred some months later.

At this time George E. Pickett was a vigorous, competent appearing officer, possessed of a head of flowing brown hair, gray eyes, a small mustache, a magnetic smile and a well shaped powerful figure.

The year of 1859 was a critical one for Captain Pickett as well as for the nation and the world. Acting under orders of General Harney, he landed his company on San Juan Island July 27 and defied greatly superior British forces, while leaving Washington and London jittery as war clouds gathered over the northwest.

Until Fort Sumter was fired upon, the Captain remained on duty in Washington Territory, alternating between San Juan Island and Fort Bellingham.

Many years after the Fort had been abandoned, Chief Henry Kwina of the Lummi Tribe, then ninety-two years old, told of his friendship for

UPPER—Old Hudson Bay Camp, San Juan Island.—Photo by J. A. McCormick.
LOWER—Block House, English Camp.—Photo by J. A. McCormick.

General Pickett, while the latter was captain at Fort Bellingham and on San Juan Islands. "Tillicums" they were, he said. Kwina was the runner or messenger for the Captain, habitually carrying mail and dispatches by trail from Whatcom to Gooseberry Point and thence by canoe to San Juan Island.

In the REVEILLE of May 2, 1890, D. E. Warbass, one time sutler at Fort Bellingham, who had played important parts in the history of both San Juan and Whatcom Counties was quoted as follows: "I made a curious trip from San Juan Island to Whatcom in two canoes tied together and planked over. I brought with me a pony which belonged to Captain Pickett, then stationed at Fort Bellingham, afterward General Pickett of the Rebel Army. My crew was four Siwashes. On the trip we were wrecked on little Sucia Island, but rigged up again, and finally landed all safe on the Point Francis sand-spit. The pony enjoyed it."

Pickett's first allegiance seems to have been to his native state. When Virginia passed an ordinance of secession on April 17, 1861, he submitted his resignation as Captain, Ninth Infantry, and started east. Judging by correspondence, he intended traveling overland. However, because resignation might be considered an act of desertion, he changed his plans and made his way down the coast in a sailing vessel, across the Isthmus of Panama, and to Virginia. There he was commissioned a Colonel in the Confederate Army.

David Tuck, later of Whatcom, often called one of Pickett's soldiers although actually never under Pickett's command, was on San Juan Island when the Virginian departed. Tuck's Company was among the reenforcements sent to San Juan in 1859, where he took part in building the earthworks and dragging up the cannon removed from the ship *Massachusetts*.

He stated that Captain Pickett was a great personal friend of Captain English, H Company, Ninth Infantry, to which Tuck belonged. Both Captain and Mrs. English were Southerners, Mrs. English being from near Pickett's home in Virginia. The sympathies of the southern Captains were no secret to the men of their commands. In 1861, it was reported that a legacy had been left to Captain Pickett, and it was while on a visit to Captain and Mrs. English at San Juan, that he left the American Army, supposedly to secure this legacy in Virginia, but in reality to join the Confederate forces. Tuck and two other soldiers were sitting on a log on the beach when he was leaving the island, and he waved to them, saying, "Good

LEFT—American Monument—Fort San Juan. On one side of the stone is carved: "First officer in charge was Captain George E. Pickett of the Ninth U. S. Infantry." On the other side: "As arbitrator William I Emperor of Germany, decided the San Juan case, October 21, 1872."—Photo by J. A. McCormick.

RIGHT—General George Edward Pickett.

bye Boys!" In Tuck's opinion the Captain's friends knew his plans, but no one else did.

George Pickett never returned to the Coast. His ability as a capable and inspired leader brought rapid promotion. On February 14, 1862, he was promoted to brigadier general in command of Cocke's Virginia Infantry Brigade. (Opposite page 111).

At Gaines Mill, the turning point of the Seven Day Battle, on June 27, 1862, Pickett was shot from his horse, when a minnie ball pierced his shoulder. Picking himself up, his arm hanging limp and bloody, his sword in his uninjured hand, with his horse following like a dog, he continued to lead the assault that broke the center of the Union line.

His wound kept Pickett from the field until September, when he rejoined his brigade, although even then unable to wear the sleeve of his coat. On October 10, 1862, he was promoted Major General.

Three months later, Pickett's division was fighting on the flank of Marye's Hill at Fredericksburg, where the serried rows of Confederate guns combed through the flanks of Burnsides' men in the open fields below, as they strove to pass the musket guarded sunken road, and the stone wall.

Pickett contemplating that field with an estimated one thousand Union dead and wounded littering each acre before the stone wall, could have no premonition of that other field, just six months in the future, when he would leave the men of his division strewn across similar open fields before Cemetery Ridge.

Gettysburg! July 3, 1863: The General mounted on his charger, "Old Black"; a soldier's soldier, confident, inspiring; remindful of a knight of old! Behind him the serried ranks of gray, marching as on parade ground, the morning sun aglint on fixed bayonets; the massed guns on Seminary Ridge behind, and on Cemetery Ridge up ahead, silent for the moment, as stupendous drama unfolded. Then the holocaust of flame and metal as the cannon opened; and, a little later, as the musket balls combed the field.

A year afterward, the sad faced President Lincoln was at Gettysburg for the purpose of dedicating the field, during which he delivered his immortal address. As he was walking along the foot of Cemetery Ridge, one of his companions exclaimed, "think of the men who held these heights." Lincoln's reply: "But think of the men who stormed these heights."

In September, 1863, General Pickett was detailed for special duty and was able to reach Petersburg where he married LaSalle Corbell Phillips of Chuckatuck, Virginia. Many of the messages that passed between them during these months of war, were written in Chinook, the Indian jargon he had learned on the Coast.

At Five Forks, the last month of the war, Pickett covered Lee's retreat. Commenting on this in 1898, James Longstreet, Pickett's old corps commander declared: "George E. Pickett's greatest battle really was at Five Forks, April 1, 1865, where his plans and operations were masterful . . . At Five Forks, Pickett lost more men in thirty minutes than we lost, all told, in the recent Spanish-American War from bullets, sickness, or any other casualty, showing the unsurpassed bravery with which Pickett fought, and the tremendous odds and insuperable disadvantages under which and against which, this incomparable soldier so bravely contended."

It was at Sailor's Creek, a tributary of the Appomattox, that Pickett fought his last battle on April 6. Here Pickett's men were faced with Sheridan's cavalry; who, scenting the final victory, were moving like hounds, head high, when the quarry is in sight. Twice the hungry, weary men of Pickett's division, under their leader's urging showed flashes of their old fire, and threw the Blue Coats across the creek; only to be overwhelmed in the end.

Achievements by Pickett's commands, including the Game Cocke Brigade of Virginia, confirms the observation of historians that fighting men can perform the impossible under leaders in whom they have complete confidence. So it has been with the American soldier from Ticonderoga to Bastogne.

This same idea, that soldiers through history have pledged their loyalty to some one leader and have followed him confidently and cheerfully to death, is voiced by Rudyard Kipling as follows: "In War, it is as it is in Love. Whether she be good or bad, one gives one's best but once, to one only. That given, there remains no second, worth giving or taking."

Pickett was paroled like other southern officers. Five days after Appomattox, Abraham Lincoln was assassinated, and the witch hunt was on. Mrs. Pickett writes that General Butler, whom General Pickett "had bottled up," during one of the late peninsular campaigns, and who never had forgiven her husband, charged the Southern General with treason and even made speeches against him in Congress. The Confederate officer had to flee to Canada, followed by his wife.

Later General Grant, Commander of the United States Armies, sent Pickett a kind personal letter, and enclosed a permit which allowed the latter to travel throughout the United States, unmolested.

The end of the war left Pickett poor and broken. The Khedive of Egypt offered him a commission as Brigadier General, but he refused service under a foreign flag. Instead he became general agent of the Washington Life Insurance Company for the State of Virginia, accepting the changed status of a civilian during the bitter reconstruction days, both cheerfully and with high courage, so his wife has written. President Grant offered him the Marshalship of Virginia, a position he declined. "Broken in health," at the age of fifty years, taps sounded for George E. Pickett, July 30, 1875, at Norfolk, Virginia, ten years after Appomattox. His body was placed in a temporary vault, then, on October 25, 1875, with full military honors, he was buried in Hollywood Cemetery, Richmond, Virginia.

Old friends have thought that deprivation of his profession, may have hastened his end. Serving under the Stars and Stripes for nineteen years (counting cadet service) and four years under the Stars and Bars; trained to arms, he must have felt like a pinioned eagle as his thoughts, perforce drifted back to earlier scenes:

"With Pickett leading grandly down,
To rush against the roaring crown
Of that dread height of Destiny."

HIGH TIDE AT GETTYSBURG,
By WILL HENRY THOMPSON.

Chapter XIII.

JAMES TILTON PICKETT

"JIMMIE PICKETT"

MANY PROUD AMERICAN FAMILIES today boast that in their veins there flows the blood of real Americans—the Indians—a state of affairs existing since Pocahontas' time.

When the Army ordered Captain George E. Pickett to duty at the frontier forts, he found that many of the leaders of the Northwest had married Indian women. His first wife had died shortly before. White women were few. He was lonely. A pretty Indian maiden, whom he first saw at Semiahmoo, and later at Fort Bellingham, interested him greatly. So George E. Pickett, West Pointer, wed his "Indian Princess," said to be the daughter* of one of the proud Northern tribes.

At that time no opprobrium attached to such a union. It was only in later years while the native Americans were making their last desperate and despairing stands in the attempt to save their lands from the greedy Whites, that the Redman became "the villian of the piece": that the Indian and the half-breed became criminals per se, as witness the popular thriller of the day—the dime novel, where on almost every page "another redskin bit the dust."

Little is known of the courtship which took place after Captain Pickett assumed command at Fort Bellingham. The area in the vicinity of the Fort was a neutral or meeting ground for warring tribes. And there the glance of the soldier must have been drawn repeatedly to the chieftain's daughter.

---

* (Mrs. Pickett's Indian name.)

The name of George E. Pickett's Indian bride, supposedly of the Haida tribe, is unknown today. When the author was a girl in Whatcom County, many of the actors who played important parts in the Northwest drama, were yet living. They could have revealed the name borne by the young Indian woman. All have long since answered the last curtain call. The query was made too late. There remained only one lead. At the Lummi Reservation there lived an aged man, son, by an Indian mother, of the Doctor with the Boundary Commission. His mother, who had been a friend of Mrs. Pickett's, had told him, that the Picketts first met at Semiahmoo. In his boyhood, he had listened to the story of Pickett's bride many times, had heard her name mentioned frequently. But memory's curtain was so heavy with the weight of ninety years, that it would not lift—would reveal nothing. Other aged Indians recalled that their people had said, that the Captain's wife was always called "Mrs. Pickett"; thus her name was forgotten.

Therefore unless the name of the little Indian mother of Jimmie Pickett is preserved somewhere in a yellowed pioneer letter, it must ever remain a matter of speculation.

The wedding was solemnized both according to tribal ceremonials of the bride's people, and according to the "Boston Way."

For her wedding, under one of the tribal ceremonials, the gloved right hand of the bride was clasped in the gloved right hand of the bridegroom. The two white gloves used in this wedding ritual are preserved in the Jimmie Pickett trunk.

The Picketts took up residence in a house yet standing on Bancroft Street in Bellingham, built in 1856. Here, on December 31, 1857, was born their son, James Tilton Pickett, so named from the Captain's friend, Major James Tilton. The little Indian wife died shortly after the birth, severely jarring George Pickett's world; since he had a real affection for his "princess."

At that time George E. Pickett was 32 years old. Fort Sumter lay little more than three years ahead. No soothsayer was needed to read the portents of the Civil War cloud on the horizon. Pickett must have known, even then, that in the clash he inevitably would join forces with the South.

Moreover, the trouble with the British over the San Juan dispute had become a running sore. And Pickett was aware that hot heads, both North and South were urging war with Great Britain as one way of postponing or avoiding the Civil War.

All in all, Fort Bellingham in 1859 did not seem to be the place or time for rearing a motherless son. Accordingly he turned to Mrs. William Collins, who lived on a farm near the little trading center of Arcadia in Mason County. William Collins and his wife had become acquainted with Captain Pickett while he was stationed at Fort Steilacoom—this during their periodical trips to Olympia for supplies; and he regarded them as high type substantial citizens and capable of properly rearing his son. (Opposite page 118).

Mr. and Mrs. Collins had come west in early days and had taken up land on one of the numerous points extending into southern Puget Sound. This later was called "Collins Point." Having no children of their own, they were glad to take Jimmie Pickett into their home. Major James Tilton,* Pickett's friend, who was stationed at Olympia made arrangements with the Collins for the care of the boy and for the transportation of Jimmie to the Collins home.** This was December 1859. Later when the Civil War divided the officers of the army into two camps, Tilton was delegated to continue the supervision (through the Collins) of the boy's upkeep and care. After the declaration of war, when Pickett was leaving to join the Southern armies, he wrote as follows regarding this arrangement:

* James Tilton was Adjutant General of Volunteer Forces during the Indian Wars, and later was Surveyor General of Washington Territory.

**In the Jimmie Pickett trunk are the old accounts kept by Mrs. Collins for Jimmie's upkeep, which ran from December 12, 1859, to September, 1865.

"Camp Pickett, San Juan Island,
July 2, 1861.

Dear Goldsborough:

Having applied for a leave of absence and being in expectation of leaving this country very shortly, I here-with enclose an order on you to pay the amount of $100 to Major James Tilton. Tilton has been kind enough to look after the welfare of my little boy, and will during my absence continue to take care of him. It is for this purpose that I give him the order.

In haste,

Yours truly,

GEORGE E. PICKETT."

Goldsborough Eng.,
Olympia, W. T.

The Collins couple gave the child the loving care needed during his formative period. However, they leaned heavily upon Major Tilton. And no father could have taken greater pains or shown more interest in the boy's upbringing than did he. One of his letters to Mrs. Collins is full of this interest, as well as containing bits of historical news:

"Olympia, W. T., August 8, 1861.

Mrs. Collins,

My dear Madam:

I received your letter of August 1, and send you one pair of shoes, one-half box pencils, two toy books, four or five yards of nankeen and some thread and buttons.

I cannot find any suitable check or any proper stuff for pants and jacket, but Mr. Philips assures me he will have plenty of both in time for the mail to your place. I will send it soon.

Captain Pickett passed through here a few days since on his way to Virginia, he having resigned his commission in the army. He bid me say good-bye to Mr. Collins, yourself, and the boy. He regrets much that he could not take time to come down, but he was on a 30 day leave and had to reach Washington City in that time, so he went through via St. Louis and Sacramento and Portland, overland.

He hopes some other time to come out here again and promises to write to me as soon as he can. I hope this Civil War will stop soon. He sent his Bible, his commission and his leave of absence for his boy that the youngster might know who his father was, and should Pickett be killed, his aunt in Virginia will look out for him.

I wish also you would let me know when the next half year's salary is due for the keeping of the boy, or to what time or date the last payment came up to.

Yours truly,

JAMES TILTON."

Captain Pickett's original plans were for the overland route, but necessity made him change them. Again the following month Major Tilton wrote:

"Olympia, W. T., September 23.

Mrs. Collins,

My dear Madam:

I send you enclosed $50 for J. T. Pickett. I heard that Capt. Pickett had gotten off safe from San Francisco for New York but have not heard yet of his arrival there.

When I do hear I will write you and let you know. I will write to the Captain about his boy as soon as I hear where he is.

Yours truly,

J. TILTON.

There is no record that General Pickett corresponded with William Collins and wife about his boy. Campaign duties left little time for letter writing, while it was practically impossible for mail to get through the Union lines to the Pacific Coast. Nevertheless funds were forthcoming for the support of the child.

Although the fortunes of war had advanced Captain Pickett to the rank of Major-General, and greatly increased his responsibility, he yet managed to get word through the underground to Major Tilton. Early in 1864 Tilton wrote:

"Olympia, W. T., June 4, 1864.

Mrs. Collins,

Dear Madam:

I received your letter last week, only a few moments before the mail carrier returned from here to Skookum Bay.

. . . I hope J. T. P. got the Christmas gifts my children sent him in time for New Years, as Mrs. Champ left on Christmas morning before I got the package down town.

My old friend, his father, is married, as you will see by the notice I enclose.

I heard lately from Mr. Isaac Smith in Baltimore, who had heard directly from General Pickett, that he was well and very desirous of hearing of his son, J.T.P.

Your friend,

J. TILTON."

UPPER LEFT—Jimmie Pickett about three years old.

UPPER RIGHT—James Tilton Pickett at thirty.

LOWER—Jimmie Pickett's red leather trunk, circled with brass bands and ornamented with rows of brass headed tacks. His Haida mother brought this from Russia-America (Alaska).—Photo by the author in 1941.

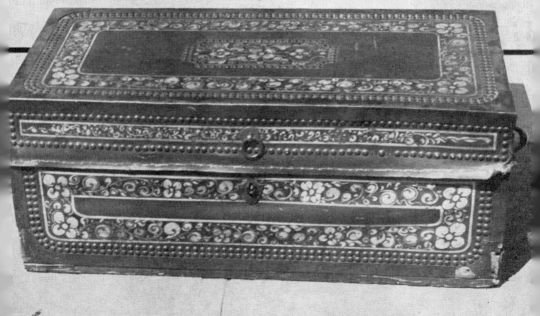

On a claim adjoining the Collins, lived a young settler named, William Walter. When the Civil War started, he boarded up his cabin and left to join the Northern forces. After the war, he returned only to find his friend, William Collins, had died. Mrs. Catherine Collins was continuing to care for Jimmie Pickett. William Walter soon married her, and brought the woman and child to his cabin. There they raised Jimmie Pickett.

In 1904, the author then a teacher in Mason County, became acquainted with the pioneer, William Walter. While she sat in front of his fireplace, he told of the early days and the life of Jimmie:

"One day," he said, "I saw a ship drop anchor in front of Collins' Point. As I watched, a row boat was lowered. Then two men climbed down into it. A box was next let down, then a bundle. One man held the bundle. The other rowed the boat to shore in the Cove by Collins' Point. Later I learned, what appeared to be the bundle, was little Jimmie Pickett, while the box was a red trunk that had accompanied him.

"He was left in care of Mr. and Mrs. Collins, with Major James Tilton assuming the responsibility of the child for his friend, Captain Pickett.

"Mrs. Collins became Mrs. Walter after the war, and we began the training of the little boy. Mrs. Walter admired the General very much, but I didn't like him because he was a Southerner.

"Very early Jimmie showed signs of being an artist. He wanted to draw nearly all the time. In those days there were few pencils and very little paper. So the boy used chunks of charcoal from the burned logs and drew on the side of the barn and on all the smooth split cedar boards he could find. When he wished to color a picture he used the juices from berries and leaves. He had inherited this gift from both his father and mother.

"In time a little school was started in our district and Jimmie went there. After he finished there we sent him to Olympia to the Union Academy. We realized now that this talent of his should be developed, so we worked and skimped and saved and Jimmie was sent to an Art School in California. When he had finished, he had a position as artist on the SEATTLE POST-INTELLIGENCER, then later on the PORTLAND OREGONIAN.

"One day in 1889, a letter finally reached us from Portland, saying our boy was very sick. Mrs. Walter left at once. She was rowed to Olympia, took a boat from there to Seattle, then one to Portland. When she reached the boarding house where Jimmie lived, she found he was gone. He had died from a combination of typhoid fever and tuberculosis.

"When the boarders returned after the funeral, they found that some one had gone through our boy's room and stolen some of his pictures, the letters from his father, General Pickett, and the thing he prized above everything else in the world, the saber his Father had worn in the battle of Gettysburg. We felt bad about this, and now we have only some of his little pictures to show for all the years of his painting. I'm going to have my housekeeper take you upstairs to see the little red trunk that belonged to Jimmie."

The trunk which was covered with red leather, had an elaborate design in white painted on the top and the sides. It was circled with brass bands each ornamented with rows of brass-headed tacks. This had belonged to Jimmie's mother, and had come from Russian America—Alaska. (Opposite page 118).

In it was the little red and white hand-made calico dress worn by Jimmie when he was taken down to Mrs. Collins. The white gloves (no longer white), worn by the General and his bride at their wedding, were there; also school books, copy books, diaries, a drawing of "Sehome, April 9, 1859" by George E. Pickett. Included were thirteen letters from his step-mother, Mrs. George E. Pickett, eighteen letters to his foster-mother, Mrs. Catherine Walter, and many others. There was, also, a large silk handkerchief in purple and yellow.

In the trunk were the Resolutions tendering thanks to Captain Pickett from the United States Congress for his stand on San Juan Islands; also his Commission as Captain of the United States Army, his leave of absence, and some tintype pictures of the Captain and Jimmie.

There was the Bible, bound in brown leather, previously mentioned in one of the Captain's letters. This had been printed in 1832. Inscribed on the fly-leaf, were the words, "May the memory of your Mother, always remain dear. Your Father, George E. Pickett."

On another page he had written, "James Tilton Pickett—born December 31, 1857," and Mrs. Walter had written underneath, "Mr. Pickett's own hand writing." To one of the pages she had sewn a lock of Jimmie's soft brown hair, as it was when he came to her.

Here in this beautiful trunk, was placed everything the Captain thought would prove to his son and to the world, that he had fathered the boy.

Walter said his wife could not have loved this child more, if he had been her very own.

Mrs. Catherine Collins Walter was born June 5, 1828, and died January 15, 1902. William Walter was born April 18, 1825 and died December 24, 1908.

Jimmie Pickett was nearly nineteen years old, when he entered the Union Academy at Olympia in the fall of 1876. He lived at the home of Captain and Mrs. Hale throughout the term. She was a teacher at the Academy and an active worker in church and civic circles. In all probability Jimmie helped pay for his keep by doing chores mornings and nights and on Saturday, in assisting Captain Hale in farming, and land clearing activities.

During school days, Jimmie Pickett enjoyed the companionship of few boys, one Dea Williams, being his only close friend. A serious rather lonely youngster, he preferred to slip away to his sketching or to his studies. Referring to other classmates, his diary contains the entry: "Such boys! They think of nothing but play." The good grades obtained by some of the girl students at the Academy impressed young Pickett. Entries in his diary, frequently mention three of the girls who boarded at the Hales, and indicate a natural interest in them, but their chattering tongues brought his severest condemnation.

Jimmie seems to have been greatly disturbed because he could not achieve perfection in his studies, and his diary shows many entries on this topic. His final grades were Physiology, 98%; Grammar, 100%; English Literature, 93%; Arithmetic, 100%; Philosophy, 99%.

An unusual penman, he was selected to give instructions in penmanship to the younger students of the Academy. In his third term, he also gave drawing lessons to the Primary Department.

During the three terms at the Academy, all his spare time was spent in drawing. He sketched the Academy, his schoolmates, the ships, U. S. Steamers *Shubrick* and *Messenger,* Varneer's Bridge, Tumwater Falls, and many scenes about Olympia. One time he sat for hours sketching Tumwater Falls, not aware of the rising tide that surrounded his vantage point, and so had to wade through the cold water to reach shore.

His painting of the U. S. Steamer *Messenger,* was probably the most successful work finished during his school days. Unlike his feeling of failure at the majority of his attempts, he states that his picture of the *Messenger* was good. "Am elated by my success with my painting of the *Messenger,*" he wrote. "All colors work so much better than I supposed."

As a little child Jimmie Pickett did not show his Indian blood. At twenty, he had a decided Indian cast to features and general appearance.

The young man was evidently aware of this. Quiet, retiring; his sensitive, artistic temperament caused him to withdraw more and more into himself.

During the years that Pickett was growing to manhood, few citizens of the West showed any understanding of the Indian or the half-breed. The general attitude ranged from tolerance, to downright cruelty. It is not of record that Jimmie Pickett "kept company" with any young woman of his age. His foster father, William Walter, mentioned no such girl during the young man's days at Union Academy in Olympia, nor at the Art School in California. Nor did he know of any attachment formed while Pickett was artist on the SEATTLE POST-INTELLIGENCER, or the PORTLAND ORE-GONIAN. Apparently at the last none such mourned his passing.

Pickett was in his late twenties, leading a dreary boarding-house exist-ence in the bustling city of Portland. Being neither red nor white and unable to merge with one race or the other, his refuge seems to have been in his painting. The Redman's deep appreciation and veneration of the forces of Nature was strong within him. This was evidenced in his land-scapes, also in his studies of the great extinct snowclad volcanoes of the Northwest. Also poems from his pen, show a sense of frustration, of melancholy.

The young man's foster mother, Mrs. Catherine Collins Walter, knew nothing of his unhappiness. Perhaps her Anglo-Saxon mind could not comprehend the tumult within him. And for his part he took pains to prevent his beloved foster parent from learning that all was not well with him, as witness the following letter with its forced cheerfulness:

Oakland, Or., April 6, '84.

Dear Mama:

I have forgotten where I was when I wrote to you last. I have been sketching all along the coast. Have had a rough trip. All kinds of traveling, horseback, steamboat, stage, rowboat, car, and on foot, bad weather, and general discomforts.

But we are back into Douglas Co. again which is a lovely country, and the spring weather is fine.

This volume of the History is nearly complete, and we go back to Portland in a couple of weeks. I hate to go back to work in the hot noisy office at Portland just as the pleasant weather comes on, especially after being out in all the winter storms.

Have had good health all the time. I lost lots of things on this trip. Left my knife, pencils, overshoes, papers and gloves, scattered all over the country. Had lots of trouble with our mail. As we had to be moving around all the time and it kept following us up from post office to another without overtaking us and I think a great deal of it got lost. And our washing, we leave it and have it sent after us by express. Am getting tired of so much travel.

Oakland is about the size of Tumwater and is the prettiest little place I have seen in Southern Oregon. We have been here only one day. Will be here a week, then return to Roseburg for a few days. Going to Roseburg is like going home. We thought it was a most contemptible little place when we first came up from Portland. But we have more respect for it everytime that we get back from one of our country trips. And now I am quite satisfied there.

We have been having a very entertaining time in our Lodge. The lodge is drawn up in two sides and at every meeting one side furnishes entertainment for the other in the way of plays, readings, tableaus and the two sides take turns at entertaining each other.

At the end of the quarter the side that has furnished the best entertainment during the past quarter is invited to an oyster supper gotten up at the expense of the other party. My side is getting badly beaten and I guess will have to furnish the supper.

Well if you write soon, write to Roseburg. I will write you as soon as I get to Portland and tell you where to address me. Had a letter not long ago from my step-mother. She is in Washington (D.C.) and has been very sick. Well I must close. So good bye.

Very truly yours,

JAMES PICKETT.

At thirty, young Pickett had changed and looked more the Caucasian than the Redman (Opposite page 118); but he still kept himself aloof from any affairs of the heart, particularly after he had been cruelly hurt by his half brother, George E. Pickett, Jr. This incident he told to the Roeders, when he visited the various old friends of his father around Bellingham Bay in 1888.

Mrs. George E. Pickett (LaSalle Corbell Pickett) in her books has no mention of her predecessor, Captain Pickett's Indian wife. However, she acknowledged Jimmie as her husband's legitimate son, wrote him frequently, and quit-claimed her interest in Whatcom property.

Before Jimmie's Whatcom trip, she with her own son, planned to visit her stepson, then studying in a San Francisco Art School. Sickness prevented her going, so her son, George E. Pickett, Jr., went alone. Young George E. apparently had a Southerner's contempt for a mixed race, and to Jimmie's notion, it seemed, treated the latter accordingly. At least he never recovered from the fancied slight.

In 1888, James Tilton Pickett came to Whatcom to try and realize something on the land that had belonged to his father, General George E. Pickett. The old records show that on May 24, 1858, George E. Pickett purchased land at the corner of F and 17th Streets (Dupont Street today), from John E. Peabody.

Jimmie's step-mother, Mrs. George E. Pickett, from Washington, D. C., gave him a quit-claim deed to this property, where a brick building stands today (1951). The old record states, that on July 23, 1888, LaSalle Pickett transferred this property to James T. Pickett. Hugh Eldridge bought the lots from him. Charles Roth made the legal transfer.

While at Whatcom he was the guest of the Roeders at their farm on Elm Street. Roth refused to take pay for his services, therefore Jimmie painted a picture of Mount Baker and presented it to Mrs. Lottie Roeder Roth.

He visited old Fort Bellingham and sketched the ruins of the stockade, and other buildings, including the one blockhouse left standing.

Pickett also made a drawing of Bellingham Bay, that was correct as of that date, but he added details of a fanciful future as he visioned it. On April 19, 1889, the REVEILLE had a large engraving made from this drawing for a special edition.

The artist's boarding house existence, the irregularity of a newspaper man's life, coupled with his unhappy mental state, left him susceptible to tuberculosis, which he had contracted by the time he last visited Whatcom.

The year of 1889 was his last. First hand observations on Jimmie Pickett and his death are found in the words of E. C. McReavy who roomed in the same Portland boarding house with the young artist:

"Jimmie Pickett painted a number of pictures. One of Mt. St. Helens had a place of honor in the old Portland Art Gallery and was used on the front cover of the Art magazine for which he was an illustrator.

"His painting of the sinking of the S. S. *Alaskan* was Jimmie's most noted painting. He had sketches of the boat before she sailed, and also drawings of the captain and some of the officers. By getting one of the surviving seamen to sit with him, describing the wreck as he saw it, Jimmie produced a painting that was remarkable in detail. It was praised by every sailor who saw it. I remember how some people would go away crying after viewing the picture. It sold for $600. (A mighty big sum of money then. It furnished the funds to pay his board bill and funeral expenses).

"I don't remember who bought the picture, but it was printed in one of the magazines and reproduced by several newspapers. During the time he was working on the picture, Jimmie was so depressed he could hardly eat or sleep, and I am sure this hastened his end. The seaman who worked with him would break down, and I have seen them both crying while Jimmie strove to reproduce some detail. Jimmie was buried in Portland Heights near the point where he would go to draw his sketches of Mount St. Helens, Mount Hood, and the sunsets over Willamette and Columbia. (Opposite page 119).

"Shortly before he died, I took turns with other boarders in sitting up with Jimmie. During one night he asked me to read him a couple of letters from his father, General Pickett, and some others from his step-mother, describing the death of the General and announcing that he was to have his father's saber, worn in the battle of Gettysburg.

"After the funeral, the saber and letters had disappeared, and I never heard what became of them."

As McReavy indicates, the dreary end came to Jimmie Pickett in a Portland boarding house, the boarding house of one Mrs. Jones on the corner of Eighth and Salmon Streets. Death occurred, August 28, 1889.

A week later, on September 7, 1889, a Portland paper carried an "In Memorium" eulogy over the By-Line of David Wetzel. In the customary flowery language of the day, Wetzel dwelt on the sound qualities of the young man; on his ability as a poet; on his proven genius as an artist.

Had Jimmie Pickett been permitted to read this eulogy—three-quarters of a column long, the melancholy of his last days might have lifted; he might even have laughed aloud at the one-sided picture of a man whose blood lines, at that time, set him apart from his fellows.

Chapter XIV.

SCHOONER "GENERAL HARNEY"

1859 — 1885

HER FIRST VOYAGE so typically one of peace—carrying lumber from Utsalady for the construction of the Catholic church at Port Townsend—the sturdy 100 ton schooner *General Harney* sailed into international history on her second charter, when she picked up guns for the proposed earthworks, loaded Captain Pickett's men from Fort Bellingham to man these fortifications, and dared the British fleet in order to land the American force on San Juan Island in 1859.

Two names loom prominently in the twenty-five year history of the *General Harney*—Captain Roeder, for whom she was built, for years the principal owner; and Captain H. H. Lloyd, early skipper, later a half owner, then owner, up to a few months before the historic craft died on the rocks of Goose Island during a raging storm.

Captain Roeder's first boat, the *H. C. Page* had been sold to Selucious Garfielde of Thurston County for $1,000; the same Selucious Garfielde whose craft, the *Flying Mist,* was to become the competitor of the *Harney,* and, with the latter, comprise the shipping fleet of the Sound for several years.

Under the supervision of James H. Taylor, shipwright in charge of construction, the keel of the *General Harney* was laid on Bellingham Bay in January, 1859. Her description: schooner rigged; length, eighty feet; beam, twenty and one-half feet; depth of hold, six feet, three inches; registry, one hundred tons. Douglas fir was used throughout from keel and knees, to deck and spars. And so well constructed was the craft, so durable her lumber, that, twenty-one years later when the Steamer *Yakima* crashed into her side, her timber and planking were found to be quite sound except for inroads of the teredo.

The Roeder schooner was launched in the spring of 1859, being named for General Harney, veteran Indian fighter then commanding the Pacific divison, U. S. Army, with headquarters at Vancouver, Washington Territory.

The *Harney* was the first sailing vessel built on the Sound, large enough

126

to transport cattle and horses.* She could carry these at lower rates than the *Eliza Anderson* and other steamers and hence, over the years, aided materially in the distribution of livestock through the islands.

Northern Indians were active in 1860 when Captain H. H. Lloyd took command of the *Harney.* Masters of sailing vessels were particularly apprehensive. These skippers were aware that, with their small crews, especially when at anchor, or during calms, or in adverse winds, they would have little chance against the great, swift-moving, and heavily manned war canoes.

A few months earlier, in the fall of 1859, Northern Indians had captured the Sloop *Ellen Marie,* slaughtered the crew, plundered and burned the vessel. Early in 1860 Indians captured the *Blue Wing,* killed all hands, scurried off with the boat to Seymour Narrows, where she was sunk.

These tragedies caused all navigators of the narrow Northern waters to increase their vigilance. Thus when Captain Duncan Warren, sailing his sloop through Queen Charlotte Sound, sighted the flashing paddles and high prow of a heavily manned war canoe, he changed course and swung away in flight. Ordering the mate to hold the vessel steady, he opened fire on the pursuing Indians with his Henry repeating rifle. Before the howling savages could close and board, Captain Warren killed sixteen of them and the chase was abandoned. When Warren reported this affair, authorities at Victoria proposed punishing him, but after investigation they dropped the charges.

Captain Lloyd's experience with the savage raiders occurred that same year of 1860. On a dark and stormy night he anchored in Griffin Bay at the south end of San Juan Island. The crew turned in below as the skipper himself took the deck watch. While all was quiet, according to the story Lloyd later told Edmund S. Meany, history professor at the University of Washington, the master heard the wash, as of a log drifting toward the schooner. Through the darkness he soon discerned the outlines of two canoes. Without sound of paddles they came alongside. There one of the raiders tapped gently on the *Harney's* planking to learn if the crew members were asleep. The alert captain made no sound and the Indians withdrew. Then Lloyd quietly aroused and armed his crew ready for an Indian attack. He lighted his lantern, hid it under his great coat and resumed the watch. In a short time the canoes returned, now crowded with

*The first cattle brought to the Nisqually district were from California. These were both wild and wicked. The animals increased rapidly. Several thousand head soon were roaming the prairies, a constant threat to the crops of the settlers. Accordingly officers at Fort Steilacoom began inviting citizens to the plains on wild cattle hunts. Experienced hunters declared it often was as hard to kill an old Spanish bull as a plains' buffalo, and just as dangerous. To relieve further pressure on the farmers, the cattle together with half wild horses and domestic sheep, were rounded up from time to time and shipped to Vancouver and other islands.

more Indians, and again quietly and stealthily crept up to the schooner. This time, as they tapped on the vessel's side, Captain Lloyd flashed his lantern in their faces and demanded to know what they wanted. Although surprised, they promptly offered venison for sale. The captain bought the meat and the canoes made off. Under Lloyd's quiet orders, the crew quickly hoisted anchor, made sail, and swiftly laid a course out of the narrow waters.

The *Harney's* first contract under Captain Lloyd was the freighting of brick and lime from San Juan and stone from Port Orchard for the territorial university at Seattle.

With the freight money thus earned, Captain Roeder, the owner, then purchased the Chuckanut stone quarry, which, over the years, was to provide many cargoes for his schooner.

Stone, brick, lime, lumber, livestock, hay and grain, iron ore, general merchandise—the *Harney* carried all types of cargo for a quarter of a century. In fact it is an even bet that the sandstone appearing in early structures on both sides of the International line was carried by the little schooner.

When Captain Lloyd was lured from the sea to the gold mines, Captain Goodell took command of the *Harney* in 1862. Two years later Goodell retired to become U. S. Customs Inspector at Port Angeles, only to meet his death by drowning shortly afterward, when the Customs House and other buildings were swept into the sea during a cloudburst.

Captain Tucker, the next master, resigned in 1867 to become the Dungeness lighthouse keeper. Captains Oberg, Chris Williams, and Mason Clark followed Tucker, with Captain Roeder filling in during slack periods.

Captain H. H. Lloyd returned from the mines in 1872 and purchased a half interest in the *Harney* from Captain Roeder. The following year the vessel was given the contract for freighting the stone, brick, and lime needed for the construction of the U. S. Penitentiary on McNeil's Island.

In 1875 Captain Lloyd purchased Captain Roeder's remaining half interest in the *Harney,* and, as sole owner, placed the schooner in the lime-carrying trade between the San Juan Islands and Tacoma. A year later the vessel narrowly escaped destruction because of this cargo. While en-route south, a deck leak reached the lime and set it afire. Hastily the skipper beached his craft near Appletree Cove and covered it with mud. This treatment smothered the fire after five days, when it was found that the lime was uninjured but that the barrels were charred to an ash.

The loss from the fire was some 500 barrels of lime, but the *Harney* was found unharmed. This was in line with the good luck that followed the sturdy little craft—a record that caused the Victoria underwriters to insure her cargoes for the lowest of rates.

For nineteen years longer, until 1885, Captain Lloyd operated his lucky schooner, then sold to Captain Mason Clark, one of the *Harney's* earlier skippers. Twenty-three years later when interviewed by Professor Edmund S. Meany, Lloyd was still following the sea with the Pacific Steamship Company on the Alaskan run.

But with the change of owners and masters the luck of the *Harney* seems to have run out. A few months after Captain Clark took over in 1885, in darkness, during a howling gale the little schooner drove ashore on Goose Island in mid-channel between San Juan and Lopez Islands. The *Harney* was dismasted and completely wrecked, although all hands managed to make the shore.

By coincidence, the *General Harney* went to her death only a few miles from the spot where, twenty-five years earlier, through Captain Lloyd's quick action, she escaped the clutches of the fierce Northern Indian raiders.

BARK "GLIMPSE"

Captain Roeder's largest vessel was the Bark *Glimpse,* launched at Newburg, New York, in 1856—a two decker, 135 feet overall; tonnage, 483. She was registered August 9, 1860, and bore the Puget Sound registry Number 6. On an early voyage, the three-master ran aground at Clover Point, Victoria. Next, she was sold at public auction to Captain Roeder, who pulled her from the rocks and spent several months repairing the vessel at Port Ludlow in 1861. The new owner disposed of the vessel after three years. Refitted, the *Glimpse* operated in the coastal trade until 1873, when she was sold for $12,000, and went to New Zealand. Thereafter, the bark sailed under the British flag, until she foundered in 1881, off the Australian coast while on a voyage from Puget Sound to Melborne. The Captain, his son, the second mate and the cook were lost.

LAST INDIAN RAID IN WHATCOM
(1859)

The last Indian raid in Whatcom County was the direct outcome of intertribal warfare that had raged for centuries. It was caused by the attempt of a Nooksack Chieftain to be revenged against a member of one of the powerful Northern tribes that had massacred his people so many times in the past. Had white men not interfered under their laws, the Nooksack Indians would not have felt honor-bound to attack the Whites.

The incident occurred in the late summer of 1859,* when Chief Telliskan-

---

*Captain Pickett and troops from Fort Bellingham had moved, under orders of Major General Harney to San Juan Island on July 27, so there was no military force in Whatcom at the time.

nem and his son, Johnnie, came to Whatcom from their Nooksack Village. As was their habit, they stopped at Captain Roeder's house for dinner. (The old house stood in the block on Elm Street between Monroe and Jefferson Streets.) (Opposite page 39).

At the time, Captain Roeder had working for him a Northern Indian, named Jim. When the noonday meal was announced, the three Indians entered the house and sat down together. Chief Telliskannem recognized Jim as one of the Northern tribesmen and therefore his enemy, but he betrayed no emotion, and he and Jim attacked the food imperturbably.

After the meal, Jim returned to work, while Telliskannem and Johnnie, after some polite talk, ostentatiously took the back trail toward their Nooksack village. As soon as they were out of sight, they quietly circled and stalked their Northern enemy.

Shortly afterward a shot was heard. One of the Roeder family remarked that Jim must have killed a deer. Nothing more was said. But Jim did not appear for supper. A search revealed his bullet pierced body lying in the garden. He was buried where he fell.

Sheriff W. J. Kelly was notified, listened to the story, examined the scene of the killing, then sent his deputy, John Tennant,* to the village of the Nooksack Tribe. He arrested Chief Telliskannem without much trouble and he accompanied Tennant peacefully enough to Whatcom. There he was locked in the old blockhouse** that stood on Peabody Hill, not far from the brick building on E Street.

The Chief was perplexed by this unfriendly act, as were the tribesmen. Throughout the Indian wars of 1855-'56, this tribe had remained friendly with the Whites and therefore expected an understanding attitude from the latter. When the authorities refused to release their Chief, they became incensed, held a war council, and organized a rescue party.

Accordingly, twenty Nooksack braves in full war paint, crowding one of the large war canoes, descended the Nooksack River, and quietly crossed Bellingham Bay. In the early morning they beached the high prowed canoe under the bluff, just west of the settlement. There they deployed, skirmish fashion, and began the stealthy approach toward the blockhouse. The plan, evidently was to rush the blockhouse, stab or silently overpower any guard on duty, and escape with the Chief to the beach.

*David Tuck was the one who stated that John Tennant was sent up the Nooksack River to arrest Chief Telliskannem.

**There is some difference of opinion as to whether Telliskannem was jailed in the blockhouse on D Street, or in the brick building on E Street. Undoubtedly he was incarcerated in the blockhouse, where the jail had been located during the gold rush, according to John Fravel. The brick building at the time, still was a store, full of merchandise, and did not become the courthouse or jail, until in the '60's. The battle is called the "Courthouse Battle," because it was waged around the brick building, which later was the courthouse.

Unfortunately, for them, a hunter, known as "Buckskin" Roesell was astir, and as they closed on their objective, they encountered him near the brick building on E Street. Their presence being discovered, the Indians rushed Roesell hoping to silence him, several knives reaching for his body. Roesell shouted at the top of his voice and fired his rifle, then clubbed his gun and swung at his assailants.

John Fravel, builder of the first telegraph line in the district, heard the shooting and arrived in time to see Roesell drop dead under the thirsty Indian blades. But the clamor had aroused a dozen other citizens, who dashed up, muzzle loaders in hand. Like the Indians themselves, they took cover and opened fire.

Three or four of the Nooksacks were killed almost immediately. The others, discouraged by the unexpected turn of affairs, and by the death of their warriors, forgot their objective—the blockhouse—forgot also about retreating by means of the big canoe on the beach.

In panic the defeated Nooksacks scuttled over the bluff to the Nooksack Trail, and started for home, pursued by the Whites. This trail led past the home of Captain Roeder.

The citizens, pursuing cautiously for fear of ambush, were startled by sudden shrieks up the trail. Thinking Mrs. Roeder and children were being murdered, the whites sprinted forward. They arrived in time to see Captain Roeder twisting the hair of a Nooksack squaw, who under his urging was yelling at the top of her voice, advising the Indians not to touch Mrs. Roeder and children. The advice was not necessary. The braves were vanishing along the trail.

Next day, slaves of the Nooksack tribe arrived in Whatcom and were permitted by authorities to carry away the Indians killed in battle. Meantime the settlers around the Bay were quite nervous and maintained guards for a few days, while effort was made to bring in military authorities.

The U. S. Steamer *Massachusetts* was known to be in the Puget Sound area, being assigned to the duty of removing foreign or hostile Indians, and of assisting and protecting the Boundary Commission. Daniel Harris, owner of a donation claim in present day South Bellingham, started out in his smuggling sloop to intercept the *Massachusetts* which was known to be carrying Major Haller and his company of soldiers.

At the meeting with Haller, Harris advised the officer of the Indian attack on Whatcom, the attempt to release Chief Telliskannem from custody, the death of one white man, and the dangers to the others.

Landing his men, a forced march of twenty-five miles up the Nooksack trail enabled Haller to surround and surprise the Nooksack Indian Village.

This move, coupled with the demand for the surrender of the war party so discouraged all young braves, that there was no further threat to the security of settlers or to that of the Boundary Commission.

Twenty years later, Chief Telliskannem again appears in criminal records of Whatcom County when he attacked and mutilated Sam Moses, another Indian, while on a drunken spree. Moses recovered. At that time the Nooksack Chief was currently known among the whites as a "Bad Indian."

DEATH OF CHA-WIT-ZIT (CHOW-ITS-HOOT)
1861

Published in the Whatcom High School Annual "Echo" in June, 1899. Written by Clyde M. Hadley, class of 1901.

(Facts furnished by Captain Henry Roeder, who witnessed the scene.)
"Once, while Chief Cha-wit-zit was on a visit to Cowitchin, on Vancouver Island, he became involved in a quarrel, conseqently a fight, with the chief of that tribe, and killed him. But during the encounter a Cowitchin had secured a lock of the Lummi Chief's hair. It was a superstition among the Indians that if an enemy should obtain a lock of one's hair, the former might return home and call upon the spirits to destroy his adversary, which it was firmly believed they would do.

"Cha-wit-zit returned home, and nothing happened for some time. One day a band of Cowitchins appeared, and demanded of him, in recompense for the death of their chief, a certain Indian slave. Cha-wit-zit refused; whereupon they paddled away, warning him that, through this lock of his hair, they would cause mesachie tamahnous—evil spirits—to kill him. The chief became very melancholy; because, at a certain time the next day—the hour the Cowitchins would reach home—he said he would be sick, and nothing could dissuade him from this belief. When the appointed time came, he took sick, sure enough; and the tribe gathered at his lodge to save him from death. This lodge was near the place where is now the corner of C and Dupont Streets, Whatcom. (Bellingham.)

(The chief sent for Captain and Mrs. Roeder, and they went to see him, and tried to talk him out of the notion.)
"In the lodge there were many klootchmen, some pounding a sort of tom-tom, some wailing a mournful chant, while others were shrieking and groaning their grief. The noise and racket made it seem as though pandemonium had been turned loose. The Chief was suffering intense agony, moaning, and saying the Cowitchins were drawing his tum-tum—i.e., heart, from his body. Three medicine-men, or doctors hideously painted, were preparing to get the evil spirits out of him. They thrust his hands into a

basin of boiling water; and when he jerked them out they said it was the evil spirits that did it, and straightway proceeded to rid him of these demons.

"One medicine-man began rubbing the chief's body, working the demons down to the toes, where they would be captured. Finally he caught one, supposedly, and held it tight in his hands until an old musket could be loaded with powder. Then he clasped his hand over the muzzle of the gun, pushing the demon inside, while another doctor seized the ramrod and shoved the imp down to the powder, then filled the rest of the barrel with wads of paper to hold him down until they could fire the gun through the smoke hole in the Chief's lodge, thereby destroying that spirit.

"Again they thrust the Chief's hands into the hot water, and again he jerked them away; this was a sign that there were more devils left in him. The next witch-doctor began rubbing his body to capture a spirit, while the others began building a fire. He too caught one and held it on a mat, while the others carefully wrapped it therein, tying the mat with cedar cords. Then they threw it into the fire, and thus disposed of another spirit. A third time they put Cha-wit-zit's hands into the boiling water; but as he again withdrew them, some evil spirit yet remained.

"The third doctor began to work on him, using the same process of rubbing, and finally captured a demon just as it was about to escape. They piled stones on this one, and cast it into the bay, thereby drowning it.

"Once more they subjected the poor Chief's hands to the boiling water; and as he did not draw them out, being too much exhausted, there were no more evil spirits left in him. They began to dance for joy, now, because they thought he would recover. But for three days he continued to suffer intensely, eating nothing meanwhile, and at the end of the third day, although he had been in the prime of life and in the best of health, Chief Cha-wit-zit was dead."

Evidently the Chief was the victim of mental suggestion. Mrs. Roeder later stated that of all the Indians, his daughter, Mrs. John Tennant, seemed to be the only one who did not believe in the charms, and who comforted her father or showed real grief at his death.

Over the years, many versions of the Chief's death have become current, most of them at variance with the Captain Roeder story.

Chapter XV.

DANIEL J. HARRIS — "DIRTY DAN"

FOUNDER OF FAIRHAVEN

1826 — 1890

"DIRTY DAN" HARRIS, rugged founder and zealous promoter of Fairhaven, probably is the central figure in more legends, tales, and accepted historical incidents than append to any other pioneer of the Northern Sound country. For three and one-half decades, from his arrival in 1853, this sailor, trader and rum-runner, this unsophisticated Boniface, this artless Paul Bunyan, claimed the spotlight in many roles.

According to Frank C. Teck, Fairhaven newspaper man, who, in 1903, wrote a series of articles on Dirty Dan Harris, the man regarded himself in all seriousness. He never did understand that his garb, habits, and actions could be the cause of merriment. Therefore for years, he thought all men were against him. Because of this trait of character; perhaps to hide his hurt, or to establish himself as a hail fellow; Dan habitually told stories which featured himself in ridiculous situations. He ended each tale in an uproarious burst of laughter at his predicament.

One of the stories with a "Blanket Bill" Jarman flavor, as recorded by Frank Teck, concerns the capture of Harris and two other whites, off Point Roberts, by Fraser River Indians. A British sea captain finally ransomed the three slaves. The first captive brought five blankets; the second, seven; but when the Indian chief was asked his price for Dirty Dan, he looked at Harris in disgust. "Ugh!" he grunted, "Him delate skookum! You takum —no blanket. Heap eat, no work!"

While it would have been in character for the joke-loving Harris to eat great quantities of food and do no work, thus making a nuisance of himself, Teck regards the tale as fiction.

As a matter of fact Harris was anything but lazy. He performed herculean labors while packing on the Cariboo trail, while clearing land, while on overland treks. Also during his first years on the Bay he tirelessly rowed a large dory to and from Victoria on countless freighting trips.

In the middle and late '50's Harris rigged up a large sloop and thereafter, according to his friend, James H. Taylor, traded through all the inland waterways. Even during the hair-lifting days of the 1855-'56 Indian Wars, he was known and unmolested by the Indians from Puyallup to Nootka Sound. To anyone, regardless of color, who could give the grand hailing sign of the thirsty, and produce one dollar per pint, the sea-going bartender dispensed his particular brand of hootch. This whiskey, admittedly was bad, but one and all agreed that it was too good to throw away.

Only once, so far as recorded, did this booze running have an embarrassing flare-back. This was about 1858 or '59 when Harris was bringing a cargo of "rice, etc.," from Victoria to Whatcom and Sehome. Surprised and boarded by Semiahmoos, Dan, perforce watched his captors tap his barrel. The fun-loving Red Men soon became hilarious, stripped their captive, and set him adrift naked.

Dan later recovered his sloop, doctored a barrel of firewater, and went fishing for Semiahmoos off Point Roberts. The tribesmen bit hard, but after sampling the liquid bait became very sick indeed. Harris was not molested again.

Dirty Dan Harris won his sobriquet because of picturesque and soiled apparel, careless eating habits, and cluttered living quarters. In early days, perhaps because he had been a sailor, he wore no shoes or socks. At that time he sported a shabby, greasy coat, an unbuttoned red flannel undershirt that exposed a massive hairy chest, bedraggled homespun trousers, and a bent and indescribable hat. During the Cariboo stampede, while packing on the trail, he perforce wore shoes. After the collapse of the Jay Cooke, Northern Pacific boom, he spruced up a bit more.

Charles Donovan reported that he first saw Dirty Dan Harris when the latter came to the Bellingham Bay Company store at Rose and Elk Streets, Sehome, about July 4, 1874, and bought a stiff white vest to wear over his red undershirt. At that time, twenty-one years after his arrival, his appearance had changed but slightly. A fairly well-preserved and very dignified plug hat shaded his long unkempt brown hair and shaggy, sandy beard. A faded, old fashioned frock coat covered the red undershirt but did not hide a rent in one trouser leg. His feet were encased in hand-made Indian socks, thrust into unlaced cowhide boots.

Physically Harris was a robust, muscular, board shouldered individual, about five feet eleven inches in height, and weighing 200 pounds. Habitually he was friendly and even-tempered. When aroused he gave a good account of himself in a rough and tumble fight. However, his very prowess created enemies who delighted in his downfall, as evidenced by the following entry in the diary of Sheriff James Kavanaugh:

"Sept. 22, 1867: A grand ball in the engine room of the B. B. Coal

Co. last night. It was a very successful affair. Sam Brown gave Dirty Dan Harris a beating night before last. I treated him for doing it."

Generally Harris was well regarded by the male population of the area. But the women-folk looked askance at this uncouth, unsanitary appearing individual, and failed to invite him to dinner. Little girls likewise avoided him, while little boys, as Hugh Eldridge was wont to relate, delighted to gather around him on the beach, and listen to the stories of his thrilling adventures.

While Teck does not make the definite statement, the inference is plain that this, to him incomprehensible exclusion from the better homes of the Bay, may, perhaps have influenced Dan Harris, and may have caused the rather tragic and pathetic incidents of his last days, spent so far from his beloved Fairhaven and Puget Sound.

Daniel Jefferson Harris was born at Patchogue, Long Island, in 1826, according to statements made by him and his brothers to James H. Taylor. After a quarrel with these same brothers he ran away to Sag Harbor, New York, where he shipped before the mast on an Alaska whaler. It was not until 1852, however, that the ship touched at Honolulu, where Harris and others deserted, reaching Victoria, and thence Bellingham Bay, in 1853.

One of the first friends made by Dan Harris in the new land was John Thomas, who, in January, 1853, had taken up a donation claim covering what was later part of the Fairhaven townsite. Thomas hired Dan to help erect a log cabin on the beach at Padden creek, near the present corner of Seventh and Harris Streets. The two were thus engaged when Thomas sickened, and later died in May, 1854.

Harris, reportedly was so superstitious and fearful in the presence of death that when other settlers told him he would have to shave and dress his dead companion, he fled to the woods and remained in hiding until the funeral. Thomas was buried near the cabin site. Harris thereafter completed the structure and made it his home.

Probate Judge Edward Eldridge appointed William R. Pattle administrator of the Thomas estate. After a mellowing period of seven years in court, the property was sold to Daniel J. Harris, "without publication in order to save expenses to the heirs." This was in 1861. Patent for the land was issued ten years later in 1871.

Having worked up from dory to sloop in his freighting and trading business, Dan Harris was ready for the quick harvest from the Fraser River gold rush, when thousands of stampeders descended, locust like, on Bellingham Bay in the summer of 1858. There were hundreds of these impatient argonauts with their supplies, to be transported from Victoria to Whatcom—the "terminus of the Short Route to the mines," there were scores of gold seekers to be taken to Victoria in order to secure their miners' licenses. And always there were liquid refreshments in demand by Reds and Whites.

After his regular cargo had been landed on the Whatcom and Sehome shore; during the long summer twilight, dimly illuminated by candle flare within tent walls; to the scrape of fiddles, the shrill laughter of women in the canvas dives, or the roar of drunken miners camped near the creek; through the aromatic tang of fresh sawdust or of fir needles and forest moss exposed by the slashers' axes; barefoot Dirty Dan Harris padded softly along the dusty footpaths, making his deliveries of joy-water.

Perhaps the likable Dan entertained some of his customers with a bit of jig-dancing, an art he had acquired as a sailor. The man fancied himself as a dancer and during pioneer days was featured in various exhibitions and contests wherein he reportedly traveled "like a house afire," sometimes winning by sheer energy and speed over contestants with more virtuosity.

Harris also favored exhibitions of "the manly art" and thus his donation claim became the scene of the first prize fight of record on the Bay. This occurred about 1859. (One writer fixes the date at 1860.)

The fight had its origin in an alleged insult to a Presbyterian minister, given by Billy Blimpton, an Irish miner at the Sehome Coal Mine. Tom Sheldon, an Englishman, took up the quarrel. Feelings ran high, reaching, almost, the proportions of a race war.

Citizens, traveling mostly by water, came from all over the Sound to witness the contest which was fought under London Prize Ring Rules. The battle lasted 104 rounds, being won by Billy Blimpton.

In early days smuggling was not regarded as a serious offense, and numerous, otherwise respectable, citizens engaged in the trade. Before the Civil War whiskey sold as low as fifty cents per gallon. Afterward the price was from three to six dollars per gallon.

Harris customarily took a cargo of vegetables to Victoria and returned with rice, and whiskey, and with hats, finery, and gegaws for the Indians. So far as known, he was apprehended but once when Edward Eldridge, customs inspector, seized his cargo of hats and finery, which articles were sold later at public auction in Port Townsend.

On another occasion, when he saw the customs inspector approaching, Harris quickly buoyed a small barrel and dropped it overboard. Inspector Eldridge found the cargo of rice in order and rowed away. Later Dan towed his barrel ashore and cached it in an abandoned tunnel of the Pattle Coal Mine.

Not all of Harris' seafaring activities were extra-legal. His fast sloop carried word to Major Haller at Port Townsend of the attack on the Block

House by Nooksack Indians, an action that enabled the Military to crush the uprising most speedily.

In 1860, lured by the Cariboo gold rush, Dan Harris turned from sea to land and became a packer. By 1861 he had earned enough on the Trail to become a business man. Accordingly he sailed for San Francisco, crossed to Salt Lake, and there bought a flock of 700 sheep which he drove to California. Many animals died from dust and thirst on that hazardous desert-mountain trek.

Poor accommodations and lack of water on the freighter out of San Francisco killed many more. When the ship docked at Sehome wharf, the thirst-crazed animals stampeded into the Bay and filled themselves with salt water with generally fatal results. The few survivors were wintered at Marietta. In the spring of 1862 Dan took the sorry looking flock, now reduced to but twenty-two sheep, into the Cariboo country, where he traded them for cayuses. With these horses he operated a pack train the remainder of the year.

The west boundary of Harris' donation claim is Seventh Street. In 1861, for the sum of $53.75, Dan bought from Americus N. Poe the forty-three acres adjoining him on the west, extending to the waterfront, and including Poe's Point.* This tract later became the principal part of his town. However, the title was defective. Alonzo M. Poe, owner of the Poe donation claim had conveyed this portion of his land to his brother Americus N. Poe early in 1858. Later in the same year, this forty-three acres had been included, through mistake, in the sale of 310 acres by Alonzo M. Poe to A. A. Denny of Seattle. It was not until 1870 that Harris cleared his title to the tract by means of a quit-claim deed from Denny for which he paid an additional $53.75.

Poe's Point also became known as "Graveyard Point" in 1862 when Dan supposedly sold four acres thereon to Whatcom County for cemetery purposes; the price being $150. (See map opposite page 278). It was not until 1888 when the Harris estate was sold to the Nelson Bennett syndicate, that it was found that the description in the deed was erroneous, being for Lot 2, Section 11 instead of Lot 1, Section 2 (Poe's Point). For twenty-six years Whatcom County presumably had owned, and had used Graveyard Point as a cemetery wherein forty bodies had been interred. In 1889 all were removed to Bay View cemetery.

In 1872 Harris undertook to clear the Eldridge farm north of Squalicum creek and along the Eldridge Avenue plateau. Hugh Eldridge stated that

---

*Later, "Dead Man's Point," so called after many settlers had unearthed brass buttons, Spanish arms and skeletons, presumably relics of the legendary battle between the Spaniards and Indians near the mouth of Harris or Padden Creek (Harris avenue and Seventh street).

Dan's pay for this heavy task was a cow and a steer. Characteristically Harris at once drove these animals together with a second steer over the old Fraser River trail and down the Skagit River to the gold camp at Ruby Creek. After a wearing trip, he reached the diggings, only to find the men broke, morose, and hungry. Generously he killed one of the animals for which the gold seekers promised to pay (a promise conveniently forgotten by most of the transients). He then drove the cow and steer back to Bellingham Bay through nearly a hundred miles of rough and trackless forests.

Five years later in 1877 Harris figured in another Paul Bunyan performance. Working alone, and without the aid of Bunyan's blue ox, Babe, Dirty Dan Harris, in one summer, slashed, cleared, grubbed, and sketchily graded the road from Sehome to Lake Whatcom over which were to move the machinery and supplies for the newly opened Blue Canyon coal mine. His camp, which he moved frequently, was merely the space between two fallen trees. He had no tent or table. Charles Donovan who visited Dan several times while he was on this stupendous job, reported that the man wrapped himself into a blanket capsule at night to avoid the clouds of mosquitoes, and remained completely sealed until morning.

Dark days followed the closing of the Sehome Coal mine in 1878, but Harris was one of the faithful who remained on the Bay. The outlook brightened in 1882 with the Washington Colony project and with the arrival of the Kansas settlers, known as the Kansas Colony, all prospective lot and land buyers. Harris thereupon subdivided his land, the plat being filed January 2, 1883.

Angrily refusing to designate his town as a subdivision of Whatcom or Sehome, Dan Harris selected the name of Fairhaven. This, he told E. M. Wilson, came from the Indian name, Seeseelichem or Seeseelichel, meaning a place of safety, or safe port, hence, a fair haven. Hilaire Crockett interprets the Indian name to mean, "a quiet place where something good is always found," probably referring to the flotsam that collected in Harris Bay. Other settlers claimed that Dan named his town after an old Maine whaling port.

In Whatcom, dissension had arisen over riparian rights of waterfront property. Hearing of this, Harris would excitedly urge prospects to come to Fairhaven and buy his lots. "Remember," he would tell them, "my Hungarian rights go with all these waterfront prices."

Other defects in title to some of the Whatcom lots also helped to turn buyers toward Fairhaven. Hence Dan's property was in demand. He sold on fixed prices, and for gold only. Soon he had more cash than any other person on Bellingham Bay. Citizens, with new respect in their eyes were wont to remark as he boarded a Seattle steamer, "There goes Dirty Dan, carrying another wad to the bank." Also, like other pioneers with extra money, Harris often left bags of gold for safe keeping with the county treasurer,* whose office was in the brick building on E Street, purchased as a courthouse in 1863.

Lot sales during his first year (1883) as a townsite promoter brought Harris about $32,000. Of this sum he spent $16,000 in erecting his three-story Northern Hotel at the end of Harris Avenue;** and in the construction of his deepwater wharf, later known as "Ocean Dock."

The parlor of the hotel was fitted luxuriously with marble topped furniture, and with one of the first pianos on the Bay. To Dan, who was very proud of his hotel, the structure doubtless was a symbol of his arrival as a personage of importance. At any rate he made no money on this investment, since he provided no regular hotel service for his patrons.

No political demonstration in the first half century or more of the Northwest settlements, equalled in color or general irresponsibility that which Dan Harris stage-managed to celebrate the inauguration of the first Democratic president since the Civil War.

Dan, an ardent Democrat, had promised during the 1884 campaign that if Grover Cleveland were elected he would fly in front of his hotel the largest flag*** that money could buy. San Francisco flag makers supplied this great banner which measured fifty-four feet in length, weighed fifty pounds, and cost $116.

The flag pole, 125 feet tall, was fashioned by James H. Taylor, ship carpenter and friend of Harris. This was made in two sections so that the upper portion might be either raised or folded down like the blade of a jacknife.

On inauguration day, March 4, 1885, Democrats of the area, traveling afoot or by horse power, but mostly by water, began arriving at the Northern hotel before sunrise. In his storehouse the host had set out great quantities of liquid refreshments. Unfortunately (some said fortunately, since this left more room for whiskey) he had forgotten to supply food. Thoughtfully the celebrators passed the bottles from hand to hand while the toasts to the Democratic party, to the new president, and to the glorious Northwest grew more flowery and involved as the day wore along. Smiling broadly, his

---

*Such practice was common, according to Frank Teck, even after L. G. Phelps of Buxton, and P. E. Dickison of Fargo, North Dakota, established the Pioneer Whatcom County Bank in November, 1883.

**Harris Avenue in Fairhaven was named for Daniel J. Harris.

***The WHATCOM REVEILLE of November 14, 1884, refers to the giant flag that Harris had "unfurled to the Cleveland breeze," a flag "so large it will have to be suspended between two staffs at least 125 feet high . . ." However the elaborate celebration of the Grover Cleveland victory was held on the inaugural date the following March.

shining topper on his graying head, Dirty Dan Harris greeted each arrival, matching toast for toast.

Because of loose sands the digging of the hole for the flag pole proved too much for the merrymaking Democrats. Republican Delaney had to complete the excavation. Finally, about noon, with all hands on the guy ropes the first section was swayed aloft. Through the afternoon the crowd vainly tried to lift the second section. In the end, sailors loading lumber at the Eldridge and Bartlett mill (later the E. K. Wood mill) between Fairhaven and Sehome, came to the aid of the clumsy landsmen and lifted the last section into place about 5 o'clock. An eyewitness has reported that despite twelve hours of liquor consumption, there was plenty of "holler" left in the Democrats when the enormous flag rose slowly to the peak and the evening breeze first moved the colors. No chronicler says anything about accidents due to runaways or drowning on the homeward journeys, nor of any damaging effects from the daylong bout (unfortified by food) with John Barleycorn; all of which attests to the general durability of the pioneer stomach.*

With growing prosperity and prominence Harris carried himself with increasing dignity, although his general aspect was unchanged. But let a boat appear, and he hastily covered his red undershirt with his white vest, donned his plug hat, and smilingly greeted each newcomer. However, having been a sailor, he was unable to resist handling the mooring hawser of the arriving craft, this despite his semi-clerical garb.

Sycophants may have swarmed about him, old cronies presumed on his generosity, but despite his achievements and possessions, of which he was very proud, Harris must have realized that nothing was changed; that in the homes of the old timers and to the man on the street he was still "Dirty Dan" Harris. This doubtless influenced him in his later move to Los Angeles.

In his fifty-ninth year, October, 1885, Dan Harris married Miss Bertha L. Wasmer. The ceremony was performed by the Reverend B. K. McElmon of the Presbyterian church, in the bemarbled parlor of the Northern hotel.

Because of Mrs. Harris' poor health the couple decided to move to Los Angeles. Thereupon Dan sold most of his Fairhaven property to E. M. Wilson, E. L. Cowgill, and Nelson Bennett of Tacoma for $70,000, of which price he received a substantial down payment.

In Los Angeles Harris built a fine residence and made other real estate investments. During this period he carried himself as a reserved, quiet, and

---

*One of the spectators at the flag-raising celebration was a little boy—the first white native son of Fairhaven, John V. Padden, one of the few present day surviving witnesses of the scene.

dignified citizen of wealth. Old friends in fact characterized this new Harris as a Sampson with shorn locks.

Mrs. Harris died in Los Angeles in November, 1888. A few months later he visited Fairhaven and collected the final payment on his $70,000 townsite sale price. Thereafter, in Los Angeles he is said to have reverted to type, cooking his solitary meals on an old box stove.

In his loneliness, and in a strange city where none knew him as "Dirty Dan" Harris, he must have been an easy victim for a clever flatterer. During this period, just prior to his death which occurred in his Los Angeles home, August, 1890, Dan appears to have been taken in tow by a Dr. A. S. Shorb and wife who are said to have influenced him in his investments and to have aided him in lavish spending.

At the time of his death Harris' estate was estimated at $70,000 not including sums alleged to have been annexed by the Shorbs.

Benjamin Franklin Harris, nephew and sole heir named in Dan Harris' will, brought suit in Los Angeles courts against the Shorbs for an accounting and recovery of the Dan Harris property. Among other charges, he alleged that in July, 1890, one month before his uncle's death, Dan Harris had deposited $25,000 in a Washington bank at 5%; and that this sum speedily found its way into Dr. Shorb's Los Angeles bank account. After a trial, given much publicity, the jury decided in favor of the Shorbs, thus young Harris not only failed to recover the money and property he claimed, but also was required to pay costs of the lawsuit. All the defendants ever turned over to the public administrator was $45 in currency, some household furniture, and a watch; the whole valued at about $335.

In the Bellingham Bay area five lots remained in Dan Harris' name. Appraised at $23,000 in 1892, they were sold at public auction in 1895 after the crash, for $900, less than the cost of probating.

Officially, Daniel J. Harris had died practically penniless.

Long since vanished is the Northern Hotel with his polished marble-topped furniture, pride of "Dirty Dan" Harris. Gone also is his Ocean Dock. But, near the Pacific American Cannery building (today, 1951) there is a rotting stump—the stump of Dan's great flagpole; sole reminder of a very real historical figure—a colorful and appealing character who might well have stepped straight out of the covers of a Robert Louis Stevenson novel.

Chapter XVI.

THE TELEGRAPH TRAIL

THE GRANDIOSE PLAN of joining London and New York by an overland telegraph line spanning the continents of Europe, Asia, and North America originated in the fertile brain of Perry McDonough Collins after early attempts to lay an Atlantic cable had proved futile. He did not learn of the first failure until later. At the time, 1857, he was in Asia for the purpose of developing the commerce of the Amur River.

Perry McDonough Collins, born about 1813, probably at Hyde Park, New York, was named for two naval heroes of the war of 1812, Commodore Perry and Macdonough. (He changed his last to McDonough.) In 1849 he joined the California gold rush. At San Francisco he organized the firm of Collins and Dent, bankers and dealers in gold dust. (Dent was father-in-law of U. S. Grant.)

When the Russians took possession of the Amur River district, Collins, a promoter by nature, interested himself in that area. With the approval of President Pierce, Secretary of State Marcy and the Russian Ambassador, on March 25, 1856, he was appointed Commercial Agent of the United States for the Amur River.

Important friendships were developed by Collins during a six months' delay at St. Petersburg. Then in December, 1856, he began his journey across Europe and Asia over the thousands of wintery miles to Irkutsk. In the spring and early summer he barged down the Ingoda, Shilka, and Amur rivers, reaching the mouth of the latter in July. There he was encouraged by finding a number of American business houses, as well as several American vessels.

Discovery of gutta-percha as an insulating material in 1848 made possible the submarine telegraph cable. In 1851 the first effective cable was laid between Dover and Calais. Five years later the Atlantic Telegraph Company was formed, and, in 1857, attempted laying the Atlantic cable. The line, no thicker than a man's thumb parted after 300 miles. The following year Cyrus W. Fields and his cable company achieved momentary success. The underwater line was completed and for a month messages passed along the ocean floor. Then it failed. Subsequent attempts, costing in all some ten million dollars, were futile.

Then it was that Collins began promoting his overland telegraph plan.

From his own experience he knew there were no insurmountable obstacles in Asia, while Bering Strait would require no more than 40 miles of cable.

Collins memorialized Congress and began efforts to secure authorization to cross Russian Asia, Russian America and British Columbia. Singularly the State Department, Congress and telegraph officials approved the project but no appropriations were forthcoming. Congressman John Cochrane, of the Committee on Commerce, in the committee's report of February 18, 1861, referring to the failure of the Atlantic cable stated: ". . . without some new plan by which a telegraph can be constructed . . . Europe and America must remain as far asunder as if electricity had never been discovered, or Morse, Wheatstone, Amphere, and Siemens never had lived."

With the advent of the Civil War, Congress, while favorable to the Collins project, made no appropriation. The Russians meantime had planned to extend their telegraph line from the Urals to the mouth of the Amur. In the United States the transcontinental telegraph was completed to San Francisco in October, 1861. Senator Miltons S. Latham of California, member of the Committee on Military Affairs, in presenting a favorable report on the Collins project noted this diminishing gap and added: "We hold the ball of the earth in our hand and wind upon it a network of living and thinking wire, till the whole is held together and bound with the same wishes, projects, and interests."

At St. Petersburg, on May 23, 1864, the Russians approved the construction, and operation of Collins' overland telegraph for thirty-three years. A parallel agreement covering British Columbia was signed in London, February 9, 1864.

About the same time, on recommendation of Secretary of State Seward, Congress approved the project, appropriated $50,000 and granted other requested aid. For the sum of $100,000 cash, $100,000 in stock, and the right to buy an additional $100,000 of stock Collins assigned his interest to the Western Union Telegraph Company. The agreement was reached with the company March 16, 1864. To finance the overland line the Western Union Extension Company was organized with a capital stock of $10,000,000. Western Union Telegraph Company share holders were given the preference and they promptly subscribed for practically the entire stock. At the time it was estimated that the two wires of the line could handle a thousand messages per day, which, at twenty-five dollars per message, would bring in $750,000 per month or nine million dollars per year. Because it was thought the plan would improve discipline and give the Company's officers more prestige when dealing with foreign and native peoples, the Western Union Extension Company's service was organized on a quasi-military basis. Camp guards were posted, reports submitted, and accounts kept, more or less in army style. Civilian officials were given appropriate military rank.

Colonel Charles S. Bulkley, then on military leave, who had been head of the Army's military telegraph system in the Department of the Gulf, was selected as the Company's Engineer-in-Chief. This was in August, 1864. Under Bulkley, Franklin L. Pope, well known telegraphic engineer of New York, who later was to become the partner of Thomas A. Edison, was given the rank of major and appointed Chief-of-Explorations in British America. Robert Kennicott, thirty-year-old naturalist and explorer who had proved that the Yukon flowed into Bering sea, not the Arctic, headed the Russian America (Alaska) project. Major Serge Abasa, a Russian, took charge of the 2500 mile sector from Bering Straits to the mouth of the Amur.

Bulkley opened headquarters in San Francisco in January, 1865. Hundreds of men were engaged, supplies and equipment purchased, and a shipping department under Captain Scammon of the United States Revenue Service was organized to transport men and equipment to British Columbia, Alaska, and Asia. Several vessels were purchased, while the United States Government made the U. S. *Shubrick* available to the expedition. Across the Pacific the Russian government placed the steam corvette *Variog* at the disposition of the Western Union Extension Company. At the same time vessels were en route from New York with 1,200 miles of iron telegraph wire, several tons of green glass insulators, brackets, and other telegraphic supplies.

CALIFORNIA STATE TELEGRAPH COMPANY

Meantime the terminus of the Collins Overland Line had been advanced from San Francisco to New Westminster, because of northward extensions by the California State Telegraph Company, later taken over by the Western Union. The wires of this company reached Olympia, Sunday, September 4. Next day the following message, first from the Territory of Washington to the National Capital, was dispatched by the governor:

"Washington Territory, Executive Office,
Olympia, Sept. 5, 1864.

To His Excellency, Abraham Lincoln, President of the United States:

Washington Territory this day sends her first telegraphic dispatch greeting yourself, Washington City and the whole United States, with our sincere prayers to Almighty God that His richest blessings, both spiritual and temporal, may rest upon and perpetuate the Union of our beloved country, of the United States, our brave army and gallant navy, our Congress, and every department of the National Government.

For and on behalf of Washington Territory.

WILLIAM PICKERING,
Governor."

(Reply)

"Washington, D. C., Sept. 6, 1864.

Governor Pickering, Olympia, W. T.:

Your patriotic dispatch of yesterday received and will be published.

A. LINCOLN."

From Olympia the new wires followed the eastern shores of Puget Sound past Seattle, La Conner, Mukilteo, Bellingham Bay,* Marietta, west of Lake Terrell, around the shores of Birch Bay and Semiahmoo to the Fraser River.

In 1864 the British Columbia Legislature Council had granted to the President of the California State Telegraph Company the right to construct a telegraph line connecting British Columbia with the lines of the United States. The final link was the cable across the Fraser River to New Westminster.**

With Governor Seymour at the helm of the little *Leviathan*, the cable was laid successfully, March 21, 1865, but for some weeks communication with the southern cities was unsatisfactory.***

The first news over the new wires, received April 18, 1865, told of the assassination of President Lincoln on April 14.

On June 17, the schooner *Milton Badger* out of New York, arrived at New Westminster with her cargo of wire, insulators and other materials. Ten days later the steamer *Lillooet* laid the Overland Telegraph's own cable across the river a short distance below the California State Telegraph Company's cable. Stringing the wires up the south bank of the river**** was begun at once.

While Major Pope was exploring the country north of Quesnel, the construction work was in the hands of Captain Edmund Conway, an exceptional administrator and organizer. From the first he rushed his crews along the established route such as the Cariboo road.

Conway was honored by the gift of a bottle of champagne when the wires reached Hope, on August 17. Four days later he learned that the

---

*According to the diary of Sheriff James Kavanaugh the telegraph office at Sehome was opened March 16, 1865, in the coal mine store.

**Victoria was linked to the mainland in 1866 when cables were laid between Saanich Peninsula and San Juan Island, between San Juan and Lopez Island and between Lopez Island and Washington Mainland. Communication was established between New Westminster and Victoria, April 24, 1866.

***Communication between Sehome and New Westminster was established April 4, 1865.

****From The COLLINS OVERLAND TELEGRAPH by Corday Mackay in the British Columbia Historical Quarterly—July, 1946.

latest attempt to lay an Atlantic cable had failed. On September 14, 1865, he completed the line to Quesnel, 435 miles from New Westminster. Major Pope erected Bulkley House, winter headquarters at the north end of Takla Lake, while Conway later explored to that point, then returned to New Westminster for the winter.

Because of transportation and supply difficulties Bulkley had not been able to land Kennicott's Alaska party before September. From St. Michael they moved to Nulato and went into winter quarters.

Similar difficulties beset the Siberian party. Fortunately the Brig *Olga*, bound for Kamchatka happened into San Francisco. With Major Abasa and three assistants aboard, the *Olga* sailed July 3, 1865. This little party during the seven winter months, in the face of intense cold, covered the entire distance from the Amur to the Anadyr river and, as Abasa reported next spring: "the route of the telegraph-line (had been) located on the whole distance."

To take advantage of water transportation on the Fraser, Conway, during the winter, had five large bateaux constructed at Quesnel. Work was resumed May 14. On June 1, Conway had eighty-six men in construction work, twenty-six packers with 160 animals, and thirty-eight men transporting supplies in the bateau. The clearing for the wire he reported was twenty-five feet wide on each side of the line, in standing timber and twelve feet in fallen timber. The right-of-way was cleared to make a road fit for a horse. In his final report Conway stated that the road and telegraph line ended at Latitude 55°-42' North and 128°-15' West Longitude which would have been near the Skeena river; or as he put it, 440 miles by road and 378 miles by wire from Quesnel. Telegraph Creek on the Stikine, the intended crossing, and site of the present telegraph station of that name, was not reached by the Overland Telegraph, which fell short, in fact, by a matter of about 200 miles. Conway closed operations in October and sent his crews to New Westminster for the winter via the Skeena River.

With the last of the fortune of Cyrus W. Field riding on her nose, the *Great Eastern* steamed into Heart's Content Harbour, Newfoundland, July 27, 1866, successfully completing the Atlantic cable. Reports by Conway and Bulkley do not mention the cable. Perhaps they felt that this last would fail as had the others and so justify the Overland Telegraph. Small reconnaissance parties remained in the field through the winter.

Progress of the line in Russian-America lagged seriously partly because of the death of Kennicott in May, 1866. Weeks elapsed before the arrival of W. H. Dall, Kennicott's successor. Again the party wintered at Nulato. On May 26, 1867, they started up the river. At Fort Yukon, they heard for the first time that the Atlantic Cable had been successfully laid. Returning to St. Michael in July they decked the telegraph poles with black by way of mourning the abandonment of the Collins enterprise.

Major Abasa in Siberia was having his trouble also. Right-of-ways had been cleared, thousands of telegraph poles had been cut, but the company ships with insulators, brackets and supplies did not arrive until mid-August and as late as September 19, 1866. June 1867 brought word of the Atlantic cable. With July came the order to abandon the project. The summer was spent in assembling construction parties for the return to San Francisco.

Directors of the great work have commented on the cheerfulness and endurance of their men. Reconnaissance parties suffered greatly during intense winter cold. Construction habitually was performed in the summer months. Hence some popular writers seem to have let their fancy roam when they told of workers standing in the snow to their waists while thawing holes and erecting line. Conway's crews working in the summer, did nothing of the kind. In Alaska Kennicott's men holed up each winter at Nulato. It is true, that in the Yukon where the ground beneath the moss is eternally frozen, wood fires would have been necessary to thaw the holes. And any old Klondiker will agree with Artist Wymper that six holes or thaws would be a day's work. But this thawing was done in the summer months. In the sparsely timbered portions of the Yukon, telegraph poles necessarily would be freighted by dog teams. Here again the work would be undertaken, not in the dead of winter, but after the spring thaw and before the "break-up" of the rivers.

Many thousands of miles of iron telegraph wire,* tons of green glass insulators and untold numbers of telegraph poles were left behind for the natives of two continents to marvel at and use. The poles made firewood, insulators could be used as drinking glasses, and the wire was useful for making nails and numerous other things such as constructing the famous Indian suspension bridge at Hagwilget.

Seward, who was negotiating for the purchase of Alaska at the time was disappointed. Information gained from Kennicott's earlier survey undoubtedly influenced him in acquisition of "Seward's Folly," the United States' largest real estate deal—five hundred and eighty-six thousand square miles for seven million two hundred thousand dollars, or at the rate of two cents per acre.

In 1871 the British Columbia government secured a perpetual lease on the Western Union property and grants. The portion to the Cariboo was repaired, that above Quesnel abandoned. Finally in September, 1880, the

---

*According to Donald McNicol, British Columbia Historical Quarterly, July, '46, 8-gauge wire. Copper-covered wire was used first in 1872. Single strand copper wire in 1877.

Government purchased all the Western Union's property and privileges for $24,000.

Peter MacDonough Collins spent his later years in lower Manhattan, handling his investments so well that when he died in January, 1900, at the age of eighty-seven years, he left a considerable sum to his niece. Seventeen years later she bequeathed $550,000 to New York University.

While the Collins Overland Telegraph was building North, the line also was extended south along the old Fort Hope-Whatcom Trail, which thereafter became known as the Telegraph Road. With the failure of the Collins project this line was abandoned in 1867. When it was thought Jay Cooke would make Bellingham Bay his railroad terminus, the telegraph line was rebuilt in 1870. Closing of the Sehome coal mine caused its abandonment a second time, after which it was not rebuilt until the Fairhaven boom in the late '80's at which time the Postal Telegraph also had entered the field.

Much of the construction and reconstruction of the lines was handled by John Fravel, who had come north at the time of the Fraser River Gold Rush.

John Henry Fravel was born at Woodstock, West Virginia, May 3, 1832; moved to Ohio with his parents; thence west in 1850, when he assisted in a cattle drive from Cincinnati to California.

After several years spent in mining in Northern California, he moved first to Portland, then to the Fraser river. For a time after returning to Bellingham Bay he was busied getting out timbers for the Sehome Coal Mine, then joined the California State Telegraph Company's force in 1864 to become one of the most trusted and efficient field men. With the completion of the first line to New Westminster, Fravel joined the Collins Overland telegraph venture and helped push their wires north to the Skeena river.

In 1870 he was assigned the task of restringing the wires along the Telegraph Road. The following extracts from his diary give some highlights on this job and later ones:

"7/8/70 Began building—Put up mile and a half of poles. Made as far as Squalicum.

"7/31/70 I went out to Sumas Lake and returned to camp about 1 P. M. and paid the Indians $38.00 for canoeing wire up Nootsack.

"8/5/70 Worked hanging wire between Sumas and Matsqui. Brush very thick. Have to cut our way through, and most of poles to erect. Most of the old wire down and have to hang it over. Made about two miles.

"8/11/70 Letter from F. H. Lamb, Yale, to John Fravel, Sumas, B. C. 'Telegraph Whatcom to see if you can get Dirty Dan to go as a packer with you—and instructions—reline.'

"Working east from Matsqui. 8/15/70. Reset twenty poles—Shifted half mile of line this forenoon. Moved camp from the lake (Sumas) to Vedders. Worked about four miles. Rood party camped with us.

"8/24/70. Moved camp up five miles from Hope and worked up to camp. Had some very rough country to travel over. Think the man that laid the line out that we came over today must have been drunk or crazy.

"Cash book entries. 4/19/71—Geo. Warbass—to packing three days from Whatcom to Sumas_____$3.00

To use three horses three days_____$9.00

"4/27/71 to canoe and Indians transporting men and materials $6.00 from New Westminster to Chilliwack—Sam and Thomas.

"10/26/74—Engaged to go up country and take charge of line construction between Cache Creek and Kamloops. Wages $100 per month and food and traveling expenses up and down.

"Time book Sept. 1881. V. Roeder, 26 days_____$39.00"

This last entry applies to the time that Fravel was engaged in taking down the telegraph line from Whatcom north, and that to Victoria via Samish Peninsula and the Islands. Victor Roeder reported that this line did not use the green glass insulators.

Today portions of the old Gold Trail are still known as the Telegraph Road. Such a portion lies in Cornwall Park, Bellingham, where there has been placed a two ton boulder from the late Mrs. C. X. Larrabee's estate. On November 11, 1941, the Daughters of the American Revolution unveiled a marker set in this stone which reads:

"Here passed the old Telegraph Road which followed the telegraph line planned to connect America with Europe by telegraph; a project abandoned with the completion of the Atlantic cable. Over this pioneer outlet to the north, thousands of prospectors filed into the Fraser River gold fields in 1858-'59."

LEFT—John Bennett, the first Horticulturist of the Northwest, with the first heather that he found in the Mt. Baker area, and which was similar to the heather in his beloved Scotland.—Photo courtesy of his niece, Miss Belle McAlpine.

RIGHT—County Superintendent William Henry Fouts and his wife in 1881. Picture taken by the Floating Sunbeam Gallery, Puget Sound, Washington Territory, while moored at the west bank of Whatcom Creek across from the Colony Mill site.—Photo courtesy of Mrs. Grace Fouts Hughes.

Chapter XVII

FIRST ASCENT OF MOUNT BAKER

(1868)

M OUNT BAKER, the symmetrical volcanic cone that lifts its snowy head some fifteen and one-half air miles south of the International Boundary, was named for Third Lieutenant Joseph Baker, who first sighted and reported the peak to his commander, Captain George Vancouver. This was on April 30, 1792, when the British vessels, *Discovery* and *Chatham* of the Vancouver expedition were in the Juan de Fuca Strait near Dungeness.

Early settlers have asserted that Mount Baker and other so-called extinct volcanoes of the Northwest have been active at intervals since the arrival of the whites.

No less an authority than Captain Roeder declared that he had seen the mountain throwing off smoke on more than one occasion. Roeder further reported, that, while repairing the bark *Glimpse* at Port Ludlow, he also witnessed an eruption of Mount Olympus.

Settlers of the Ten Mile district variously claimed to have seen Mount Baker belching fire and smoke. John Bennett, early horticulturist of Whatcom county, said he had witnessed several such eruptions. On December 28, 1860, the PIONEER AND DEMOCRAT of Olympia carried the following item: "Mt. Baker is in a state of eruption, throwing off clouds of steam and smoke." The WASHINGTON SENTINEL of August 1, 1863, asserted: "Mt. Baker is reported in a state of eruption."

When the Coleman party made the first ascent of the peak five years later, they stated that the first climber to reach the summit, while waiting for the others to arrive, "had been nauseated by sulphurous exhalations."

UPPER LEFT—Mrs. Nellie Coupe, taken in the '60's.—Picture courtesy of her son, Russ Coupe.

UPPER RIGHT—Isabelle Eldridge-Edens, born in California. The first baby to arrive at Bellingham Bay—May, 1853. She was one of the early Sehome school teachers.—Photo courtesy of her daughter, Mrs. Maud Edens Henderson.

LOWER—Sehome school in 1873. Built in 1861, it stood where Maple street is today near Cornwall Avenue. The teacher, Isabelle Eldridge, stands in the doorway; in front of her is Joe Lanktree, son of the mine superintendent. Alice Jarman is the girl to the right.—Photo courtesy of Mrs. Margaret Gage Roth.

Many years later, this also was the experience of H. J. Dakin of Ferndale, who was member of a party that made the climb in 1897.

To Edmund T. Coleman, artist and Alpine mountain climber, Mount Baker's shapely cone, as seen from his Victoria home, was such a challenge, that he made three attempts to scale the peak. His third and successful effort, he covered in an article, MOUNTAINEERING ON THE PACIFIC, published in HARPER's NEW MONTHLY MAGAZINE, November, 1869.

Coleman's first try was made in 1865, when he was accompanied by Doctor Robert Brown of Edinburgh and Judge Charles B. Darwin of the United States District Court. After they had traveled fifty miles up the Skagit and Baker rivers, unfriendly Indians halted the Whites and turned them back.

Next year, the party which included John Bennett, John Tennant, and two Indian guides, approached the mountain through the Nooksack valley. Near the summit, the climbers were barred by an overhanging cornice of ice. Undaunted, they passed a painful night in ten above zero temperature. In the morning, after another futile attempt to by-pass the barrier, the party returned.

The year 1868 saw Coleman make his third assault, and gain the summit. The party included Thomas Stratton, Customs Inspector at Port Townsend; John Tennant from near Ferndale; and David Ogilvy of Victoria. Again the Nooksack river route was chosen, and once more the mountaineers were to find the approach to Mount Baker as difficult as the climb itself.

George McKenny, Superintendent of Indian Affairs for Washington Territory, had assigned four trustworthy Indians to the Coleman command. These were selected by C. C. Finkbonner, who was in charge of the Lummi Reservation. In his magazine article Coleman said: "To the official sanction thus given and the fitness of our dusky companions, were we indebted for our security in ascending the river. We cannot forget the expertness displayed in many difficulties by Squock and Talum. Squock is the son-in-law of Umptlalum, the principal chief of the Nootsak Indians. Though a Flathead, Squock is very handsome, and with his swarthy face and long limbs, he resembles an Arab."

Coleman and Ogilvy left Victoria, August 4, 1868, in the canoe of some Bellingham Bay Indians, previously engaged. In coming for them, these canoe-men, fearful of the Northern Indians, had taken the southern channel around the San Juan islands. Referring to these Northern Raiders, the mountain climber wrote:

"Of late they have boldly attempted higher game, and have attacked schooners and trading vessels . . . Apart from such casualties, travel is very enjoyable in these waters. The bottom of the canoe is spread with small branches and twigs, and then covered with matting of native manufacture. One's blankets are placed against the thwarts and form a soft cushion, against which he can recline and be as comfortable as in a first class railway carriage. While camping on shore at night, the mats are spread out on the beach, and with one's blankets make a soft bed." . . .

"Having passed San Juan, and steering through a narrow passage near to Orcas Island, we observed a long pole with a crosspiece to it at the top. It is the native arrangement for catching wild-fowl. A net is spread on the cross-poles, fires are lighted at night, the wild-fowl seeking at this time their food, and not seeing the net, fly against it with such force that they drop down, and are seized by the Indians. Vancouver gives a plate of similar poles in his work, but was unable to discover the use of them."

At the Squalicum Creek home of Edward Eldridge on Bellingham Bay, Ogilvy and Coleman found Thomas Stratton of Port Townsend awaiting them, as well as a crowd of well wishers.

The expedition left the Eldridge home, August 10. Before entering the Nooksack, additional Indians were hired, and the salt chuck canoe was exchanged for two shovel noses. Half a mile from the mouth of the river, the mountain climbers passed beneath the wire of the telegraph line, erected four years earlier between Sehome and New Westminster. Five miles up stream the party encountered the big jam. While the Indians made the portage, the three white men visited the ranch of John Tennant, who joined the undertaking as geographer and interpreter. Camp was made the first night at Devil's Bend, where it was discovered that the company of twelve possessed but one spoon and one plate. The bill of fare was bread, tea and bacon.

Next morning the ranch of Colonel Patterson* on the present site of Lynden was reached at 7 A. M. Here the leaders met Indian Jim—Chief Yallakanum Seclamatum, and consulted him about the route.

Above Patterson's, there was another heavy portage. At the forks of the Nooksack, the expedition met Umptlalum, Chief of the Nooksacks, whom Coleman described as a venerable looking man, with white hair, a white tuft on his chin, somewhat short in stature, but looking every inch the Chief.

Upon advice of Squock and Talum, the Middle Fork was selected as the approach to the mountain. After fifteen miles, in which three heavy portages and twenty-seven riffles or rapids were negotiated, the party quit the river.

---

*Colonel Patterson settled on the river after the Fraser River gold rush. In 1870, he assigned his squatter's claim to Holden A. Judson and wife, Phoebe, in return for their rearing his two small daughters—Dollie and Nellie.

"Here we prepared for land travel," said Coleman. "Having taken out provisions for ten days, we stowed the canoes and their contents in a 'cache.' Cutting down some young alders, we fastened them across the trees to form a framework. On this the provisions and other 'iktas' were laid and covered with matting, while the canoes were thrust underneath. Care must be taken that the frame-work is fastened upon young trees that will not sustain the weight of a bear. Having made our packs as light as possible, we plunged into the forest along the bank of the river in order to reach a ford some twelve miles up. With difficulty we made about a mile an hour, over fallen trees, under old logs, down steep ravines, over rough rocks, and through close-set jungle. After reeling under our packs, knocking our feet against stones, and twisting our limbs against opposing obstacles, we came at last to a spot on the bank which we called 'Camp Fatigue.' "

For two days the mountaineers advanced in the river gorge, then began the climb from the 1916-foot level to 5,175 feet, during which they passed through the temperate zone vegetation. Included was a magnificent forest of fir stretching as far as the eye could see; great trees 100 feet to the first branch, all bedecked with moss on the north side of the trunk.

An excellent camping place was found in an open space covered with grass and small clumps of balsam firs. In one of these, where they found traces of elk and bear, there was a snug nook, well sheltered. This was named Camp Hope. The fog which had descended upon them, lifted briefly and they saw two magnificent peaks, which they named "Lincoln" and "Colfax." Large patches of Scotch heather, blue-bells, and lupines were in bloom. Through the fifteenth of August, they remained at Camp Hope because of the fog.

"Ogilvy, Tennant and three Indians went out shooting," according to Coleman, "while Stratton and myself kept camp, doing sundry repairs, posting our diaries, etc. About five o'clock they returned, with four marmots, known in these parts as ground-hogs or wood-chucks. They are grayish in color, about one and a half feet long, and have two long incisors in the front of each jaw. The largest weighed twenty pounds. They had also shot a species of rabbit. Stratton managed to get up a stew, which was christened 'Oudar de pocar.' It was made all the more palatable by half a bottle of sauce, which, with marvelous foresight, he had pounced upon in Mrs. Eldridge's larder at Whatcom and produced in triumph upon this occasion."

On the morning of the sixteenth, the fog cleared, and the summit was seen for the first time; lying to the north of the two peaks already mentioned. In less than two hours the climbers arrived at their last encampment, 7,054 feet above the sea, where the stunted balsam firs, formed a semi-circle round a small volcanic rock.

"Next morning," Coleman continues, "we started at five, and about half past six came to the end of the ridge (about two miles). Here we put on our creepers (crampons) which had been made for the occasion, and spiked boots, made several packs, and took provisions for twenty-four hours. We then roped ourselves together, and left the ridge, keeping twenty-five feet apart. We went up an elevated valley, possibly an extinct crater—filled with 'neve,' (or granular snow), and terminated in two glaciers. The route lay through more than five miles of neve. This was intersected by twenty-seven 'great crevasses.' . . . We crossed them by the bridges formed by avalanches which had fallen in the spring and summer. We did not dare to trust them entirely, but as a precautionary measure, kept firmly attached to each other by the ropes."

The party kept on through the middle of this vast tract of neve. Meantime Stratton had gone ahead without rope or pack and his companions became worried when they saw him make a leap and disappear behind a projecting mass of ice. Later they learned that he had found the tracks of a grizzly bear and decided to trust any icy bridge which had held the weight of the animal.

At an elevation of 9,265, they rested for an hour, then dropping all superfluous clothing, they roped themselves together once more for the next climb. Stratton was waiting on top of the ridge at the foot of the main peak. In the final ascent, which required two hours, they cut 350 steps in the icy slope. The summit was reached at four o'clock August 17.

"The plateau on which we stood," Coleman continues, "was about a quarter of a mile in diameter. The scene was grand in the nakedness of its desolation. The white surface of the snow was unrelieved by a single rock. The forest had been on fire for weeks, and a dense pall of smoke veiled the surrounding scenery from our view. It lay like a reddish cloud beneath us. We felt cut off from the world we had left. Overhead the world poured down his bright beams from a sky which formed a dome of purplish blue, unsullied by a cloud. My companions, to whom for the first time this wonderful scenery unfolded, were deeply impressed. The remembrances of the dangers they had escaped, the spectacle of the overwhelming desolation around, effects of the terrible forces of nature which had been at work, these combined evidences of Almighty Power filled their hearts with deep emotion and awe. The spirit of the 'Gloria in Excelsis' burned within us. With one accord we sang the familiar Doxology: 'Praise God From Whom All Blessings Flow'."

An American flag was erected near the center of the plateau on what they called "General Grant Peak"; also upon an adjacent elevation which they named "General Sherman." Elevations were found to be the same for both heights, 10,613 feet according to the aneroid barometer, a figure that agreed substantially with those American and British topographers had obtained by trigonometric surveys.

While Coleman was making observations, his companions investigated the crater which was about three hundred yards wide and extended under Grant Peak. Walls of the crater were of black rock, streaked with sulphur yellow, red, and green. On the Baker River side, 300 feet of the lip had been torn away where successive layers of lava had flowed out and cooled. Coleman reported: "No traces of fire were visible by daylight but smoke was plainly observed. Fire must be slumbering beneath as there is no snow on the lava."

On their descent, the mountain climbers reached the spot where they had dropped superfluous clothing just as the sun was sinking. Fear that they might have to spend the night on the mountain, caused the group to plunge down slopes and across snow bridges as if pursued by fiends. In the twilight they lost their way and had to retrace their steps. They stumbled on in the darkness, calling to the Indians below. The latter lighted a great campfire beacon. This was reached at 11 P. M. During the night a storm arose, which would have made the ascent of the mountain impossible had it been delayed another day.

"The next morning," Coleman records, "was devoted to botanizing and sketching. The return trip was started the following morning at four o'clock. After some little time we came upon one of Squock's country shooting-boxes. It may be mentioned that when the Indians kill an elk they dispatch a messenger to summon their wives and relatives to assist in dressing and drying the meat, and to pack it down to their lodges. This is quite necessary as there are often 600 pounds of an elk. In cooking the meat, they first dig a hole in the ground, then build a wood-fire, placing stones on top of it As it burns, the stones become hot and fall down. Moss and leaves are then placed on top of the hot stones, the meat is then placed on these, and another layer of moss and leaves laid about it. Water is poured in, which is speedily converted into steam. This is retained by mats carefully placed over the heap. When left in this way over night the meat is found tender and well cooked in the morning."

At length they came to the Forks, opposite Chief Umptlalum's home. Bellingham Bay was reached August 22, 1868. There Coleman telegraphed his account of the climb to the NEW YORK HERALD and other papers. (Opposite page 183).

THE FOREST FIRE OF 1868

Of the many forest fires that swept Whatcom County in the memory of the whites, that of 1868 was the king holocaust of all—more extensive, more fiercely destructive, even, than the terrifying fires of 1885 or 1894.

Thirty years afterward, during the March winds, the monster fir snags regularly crashed to the ground with the thudding roar of siege artillery. Forty years afterward the shingle mills yet were feeding on the fire-killed cedar. Eighty-three years afterward, remnants of stumps and a few logs, left by the great fire, are still visible in several sections of the county.

Old timers from Ferndale declare that the conflagration was driven by a northwest gale. Brands and flaming cedar bark were carried far ahead on the wind, causing the blaze to leap forward like a demon in seven-league-boots.

According to an article in the AMERICAN REVEILLE of June 14, 1908, the 1868 fire originated in British Columbia and traveled almost to the Columbia River. Value of the timber destroyed was beyond estimate. "The fire," so the paper reports, "was so terrible that Whites, Indians, domestic animals, deer, bears, cougars all gathered on the bay shores, common peril making each utterly indifferent to the others."

In later years, speaking of the disaster, Hugh Eldridge said: "It came with a heavy north wind during the night. Next morning we could hear trees falling every few seconds—it sounded like a battle. Gus Julian told me that while he was pulling down the fence to keep the flames from our house, the rabbits were running around his feet like kittens. The fires of 1885 and 1894 were nothing by comparison. This one left such a pall of smoke, that it was impossible to travel by water for days."

In the diary of Sheriff James Kavanaugh there is this entry: "September 23, 1868—I find Unionville coal works, houses, etc. all laid in ashes. Whatcom and Sehome were saved by force of numbers and great exertion. The whole country is afire; such a continuation of dense fogs the oldest inhabitants had not seen before."

The fire also destroyed the largest bridge on the Military road, that erected by Pickett's men across Chinook Ravine, on Astor Street.

Original stands of timber had little underbrush. Afterward, travel through the woods became difficult. Bushes and slash growth all combined with jack straw piles of half burned logs to hamper the clearing of land or cutting of roads.

While the forest fire of 1868 was greatest of all, settlers were so few that actual property loss was less than in the 1885 or 1894 conflagrations. The following vivid picture of the latter, as it swept around her father's home, west of the Guide Meridan Road, has been given by Mrs. Minnie Hagler Huston:

"The big forest fire of 1894—We awoke at midnight and saw the heavens ablaze in the north as the fire came down from Canada. We filled every container we had with water and dug pits into which we put our clothing and bedding and food for fear it would burn. The apples and fruit were baked on the trees, the heat was so intense. The pigs squealed, the cows bellowed, and the horses were frantic as it seemed as though the whole world had come to an end. The smoke was so thick at times one could barely see ten feet. We lost a large barn filled with our harvest of hay, and 2,000 cords of shingle bolts all cut and ready to haul to the mill.

"When the fire calmed down, my brother and I had to go to Whatcom for medicine. We were all sick from heat and smoke and overwork, as we had not had our clothes off for five days and nights, and had had no sleep. . . . We started for town in a two-wheeled cart drawn by a pony and we carried two sharp axes. When we came to a tree across the road, we would chop off the branches, lift the cart over the log, and the pony would jump over. How many times we did this I do not remember, but at least twenty times in the eleven miles. . . ."

JOHN BENNETT

1818 - 1901

The Midwest has its legendary Johnny Appleseed. California honors Luther Burbank. But the Northwest has its John Bennett, who embodies something of each.

Johnny Appleseed allegedly traversed the Ohio Valley, planting seeds of native orchard trees. John Bennett was an even greater traveler, a purveyor of even wider bounties.

Born in Glasgow, Scotland, in 1818, he became a well educated man, trained in the sciences, including botany and geology. To the scientist's mind was added the itching foot of young manhood. After moving to America with his parents, he roamed the seven seas and the land thereof—Asia, Africa, Australia, New Zealand, Europe and America. From each he extracted treasure in the shape of carefully preserved seeds, bulbs, and cuttings—of grasses, grains, flowers and fruits; which treasure he finally heaped upon his chosen northwest land. And there he displayed the patient skill and imagination of a Burbank in the development and improvement of the species and varieties.

Temporary tasks occupied the young scientist between travels. At one time he landscaped the grounds of a polytechnic institute with which a Mrs. Bradley endowed the city of Peoria, Illinois. Such jobs did not satisfy. He needed lands and funds for his experiments.

The California gold strike found him restless, dissatisfied. Fired with thoughts of wealth, he headed west in 1850, like the others. But, with this difference. Across the continent he carried a chest containing the seeds, bulbs and cuttings, he had collected in many lands.

For eight years, Bennett worked as a laborer, mined, or prospected up and down the Mother Lode country, ever trying to cash-in on his knowledge of geology. Wealth eluded him; the early placers were worked out. He was ready to travel again when word of the Fraser River gold strike electrified California. Here was another chance for fortune. Accordingly he joined the stampede which almost depopulated San Francisco and the Mother Lode. John Bennett's precious chest of seeds was carried aboard the schooner for the voyage north.

Like thousands of others, he elected to try the short-cut route from Bellingham Bay to the diggings. Like the others he reeled back, empty handed, broke.

John Bennett was forty years old. If ever he were to take root, the time must be now. Here on Puget Sound was the soil he wanted, the ideal climate for his experiments. He needed land. But that would require money.

The Sehome Coal Mine was short handed. He went to work there. Two years later, in 1860, he had the money to buy Enoch Compton's Donation Claim, which lay northwest of Eldridge's claim. (See page 278). In the clearing on this claim, dwarfed by the great trees surrounding it, was a little cabin. The floor was of split cedar puncheons, the walls of split cedar boards, the roof of split cedar shakes. But this clearing was home—home for John Bennett for the next forty-one years. (Today the cement plant occupies the site.) With title in his name, he hired Indians to help with the clearing of his land. The growth of his garden kept pace with this.

According to the records of the Washington State Society for the Conservation of Wild Flowers and Tree Planting, the first holly tree in the state was set out by John Bennett soon after he secured his claim. The tree was almost destroyed by the great forest fire of 1868.

At that time, John Bennett's clearing was no more than a large hole in the woods. Great fir trees, one hundred feet to the first branch, leaned menacingly close to his garden.

The season had been very dry; a smoke pall obscured the sun at times; rumors of the great fire grew more alarming. Then it was at hand; the crackle and roar of flames was audible. Smoke was stifling; and here and there a great fir suddenly would flare to the top like a giant candle. Brands, charred twigs, and leaves were falling. Patches of dried grass and weeds in the clearing, burst into flames for no reason at all. The fences crackled, flared and burned fiercely. But John Bennett had no time for these. He was fighting doggedly to save his buildings.

Out in the garden, close to the forest edge, the bright hard leaves of the young holly, dried slowly, curled, then burst into flames. To complete the wreck, a dead forest snag toppled suddenly, a branch all but demolishing the shrub.

When the danger was past, John Bennett mournfully surveyed the damage. His holly tree was not only burned, but the main fork was split and broken not far from the ground. Carefully he pruned away the scorched portions cemented and bound the fork. With pioneer hardihood the tree survived to become parent to several hollies growing in Bellingham today.

The beautiful variegated holly was originated by John Bennett and long associated with Bellingham Bay. However it was in the line of fruit trees that he gained his first recognition as a horticulturist. He originated several varieties of apples, the Bennett pear, the Bennett Champion plum, the Challenge plum. He gained further notice by grafting a pear on a mountain ash, and by planting the first cherry tree in Whatcom County—a Knight's Early Black.

To this day there are men past middle age who think gratefully of the Bennett plum; this in connection with the terrific labor of clearing land solely by hand labor in early decades. They recall how, tired and charcoal blackened, father would pause and say: "Son, run over to the Bennett tree for some plums. We'll take a breather." And then the refreshing rest in the shade of some tall stump, while the delicious plum juice made white watery streaks on charcoal blackened hands and chins.

Bennett early imported, and later distributed, non-native trees, such as Sequoia, linden, tamarack, European larch, beech, sycamore, box-elder, Eastern birch, and black and English walnuts, Scotch broom and other shrubs.

His nursery soon began shipping fruit trees and in time distributing throughout Oregon, Washington and British Columbia. Gnarled and forsaken remnants of trees that came from Bennett's nursery, may even now be found near abandoned cabins and on lonely shores.

In 1872, a niece of John Bennett's came west on a visit, but remained to keep house and help with the garden. Later she married and became Mrs. John McAlpine. Through her, many of the anecdotes giving an insight into the real Uncle John Bennett, as he was called, were preserved.

Mrs. McAlpine, to illustrate her uncle's love for plants, once told of a strange seed which he received from China, and carefully planted in a pot. For years he tended it, then transplanted to the garden. One day a mother, walking through the garden, found sudden need to chastise her naughty daughter. She looked for a stick, saw the four foot shoot of the Chinese plant, snapped off the top and switched the little girl. Uncle John Bennett was heart-broken over the destruction of his beloved tree, even shed tears, so the niece reported, and grieved about it for days.

Customarily Bennett used all care possible to prevent injury to his precious plants. His garden was completely fenced and without benefit of gates. All access was via stiles, lest dogs or other animals enter and damage nursery stock.

Scotch heather, the first Bennett had found outside his native land, was noted and identified by him on the slopes of Mount Baker, when the Coleman party made the second unsuccessful climb in 1866. The discovery so pleased him that he potted the plant on his return and had his picture taken with it. Thereafter the botonist became so interested, that he climbed the mountain on more than one occasion to study the flora of the higher altitude. (Opposite page 150).

Before his passing, the pioneer nurseryman was honored by having a street, an addition and school named for him. The latter was located on what is now Marine Drive.

Two generations of adults, who, as children, had absorbed by example some of the lessons of the soil taught by John Bennett, walked behind his casket when he died in 1901. To many, the picture of the Scotchman seen in his prime, was yet vivid. They remembered the folded gunny sacks which padded his knees when he was at work, the close reddish brown curls that fringed his tightly pulled cap, also the accent with that strange Scotch burr under the tongue; a burr, that was deliberately increased, perhaps, and made more unintelligible because the children delighted in listening to it.

On John Bennett's death, Mrs. McAlpine was forced to sell the garden tract portion of his acreage. The cement plant stands on what was once known as the show place of the northwest. Even so, the present owners have been able to save a number of the trees planted by the famous horticulturist.

When the fruit trees of the Ohio valley are heavy with bloom, it is claimed that the spirit of Johnny Appleseed roams through the fragrant spring nights, seeking traces of apple trees, the seeds of which he planted so long ago.

But, if the spirit of John Bennett walks at any time, it is unlikely that his quest will be the same. Even should he pause, where ferns and alders are smothering the gnarled trunks of fruit trees that once came from the Bennett nursery; even while his scientist's ear absently notes the small noises of the Little Folk, going about their business beneath the leaves; his smiling contented glance surely will range far beyond, resting upon the improved shrubs, fruits, and flowers now crowding the lush fields of his well-loved land.

Chapter XVIII

EARLY SCHOOLS

No SOONER had Whatcom County come into existence than the citizens formulated plans for future schools. The first act of the Commissioners, was the levy of a two-mill school tax. This was in accord with the recently enacted school laws, which had been adopted in part at least, because the Federal Government made the Territorial status conditional upon a school system. (Under the Organic Act of 1853 two sections in each township were reserved for school purposes.)

On July 17, 1858, the Northern Light newspaper reported:

"A PUBLIC SCHOOL: Old residents of Bellingham Bay inform us that a public school fund has been accumulating in Whatcom County for four years. The precise amount on hand we are not prepared to say; but it is deemed sufficient to commence with; and the services of a teacher will be required when there are a few more children to add to the nucleus already formed of a school."

Edward Eldridge was the first Whatcom school teacher—not of children but of adults. In the '50's, he organized a night school for the Sehome coal miners, who wished to learn to read and write. The mine management soon closed the school on the grounds that thirst for knowledge would interfere with thirst for liquor and thus curtailed patronage of the company-owned saloon.

To a Mrs. Smith, initials unknown, who afterward removed to California, goes the distinction of teaching the first school for children, in Whatcom County. This was a private school. Mrs. Smith held her short school term in the A. M. Poe* real estate office on E street, nearly across from the brick building; the structure erected the previous year to house the Northern Light.

THE FIRST PUBLIC SCHOOL

The first public school house in the Bellingham Bay country was erected in 1861, on the bluff near the Sehome Coal Mine. This stood near Cornwall

---

*When the Fraser River gold rush folded and William Bausman returned to San Francisco, his Northern Light property reverted to Roeder and Peabody. They conveyed this to A. M. Poe in payment for his survey of their townsite. This chain of ownership is confirmed by the pioneer, James H. Taylor in an interview given to Frank C. Teck in the late '90's. Poe unsuccessfully tried operating a real estate office in 1859, after which Mrs. Smith took over the building with the school. In the '60's this Northern Light office housed the county fair; while in 1878 it was the scene of the first county teachers' institute.

Avenue almost in the middle of what is now Maple Street. Except for a roof of split cedar shakes, the building, which was sixteen by twenty-four feet in dimension, was made of rough lumber from the Roeder mill. The carpenters, William Utter, John Plaster and John H. Fravel framed the structure without studding; setting the twelve inch boards vertically and weather-stripping them. Five windows were provided; two on each side and one in the rear overlooking the Bay. (Opposite page 151). From the wooded hillside in front of the school, sprinkled with flowers in the spring, two rivulets trickled past on either side, on their way to salt water. At the rear of the building ran the "ditch" as it was called, carrying water from above Whatcom Creek falls for use at the coal mine. The stream in this canal was two or three feet deep and four to six feet wide.

Rough homemade double desks lined both walls. These were huge affairs under cover of which mischief was planned. The smoking stove stood in the center of the room, together with a box of fuel from the nearby coal mine. Benches for the little children also crowded the stove. Near the door stood the water pail and common drinking dipper, providing restless pupils with recurring excuses to leave their seats. Until Isabelle Eldridge, a babe in arms when she reached Whatcom, had become teacher at age of sixteen, there was no teacher's desk. In the '80's when Mrs. A. H. Pratt was teaching, a large homemade desk was provided; this with a hinged cover so heavy she usually required help in lifting it.

The first teacher of the Sehome school was George Hall, grandfather of the one time county auditor, Sam Barrett, and of the Fravel Sisters. He was a well educated Englishman, who with three others deserted the British Man-of-War, *Satellite,* at Victoria and escaped across the Sound. On American soil, he dropped his last name, Richardson, and was known by his given names—a common practice among sailors fleeing the rugged life in the Queen's Navy. Later George Hall's children resumed the family name of Richardson.

He successfully conducted the first school term. Available funds would allow no more than three months of schooling. Other teachers, other terms followed at irregular intervals. Pupils, mischievous as always, frequently had their teachers on tenter hooks. Joe Lanktree, son of the mine superintendent, occupied a corner desk during early terms and there engineered various pranks. Handsome and good natured he was the pet of all the girls and popular with everyone but the teachers. Fred Padden of the same period, often had the school in an uproar over the antics of his pet chipmunk, which would explore the school during periods of quiet, then scurry in fright to Fred and whisk into his shirt pocket.

Other practical jokes later pupils perpetrated against unpopular teachers including the nailing fast of door and windows; or the rounding up of the wild wood-hogs and locking them in the school house.

The children's playground included the woods, also the beach where a huge boulder extended from the bank to the tideflats. Here they romped even during high tides. Some of the games were: Stick-Base, Run-Sheep-Run, King William, and Hide-and-Seek. The woods furnished excellent hiding places. There young saplings, when pulled to the ground, also made spirited horses on which to ride.

As the population increased, the settlers from both the West End of the Bay and from the South sent their children to the Sehome school. Fred Allen walked about five miles each way from Marietta. Later the Connelly, Clark, and Padden children came from the South Side. Whatcom children returning from the Sehome school followed a trail, cut tunnel-like through the dense woods above the shore line, to Whatcom Falls. Here they plunged down a flight of stairs to Captain Roeder's mill; then darted through the noisy building, and over the stream to the Whatcom side.

Attendance at the Sehome school varied with the population, fluctuating during good times and bad. Sometimes there would be as many as thirty or forty pupils ranging from the tots in the ABC class to young men and women. At first the teacher was paid forty dollars per month in greenbacks. Later this was cut to thirty dollars. And there were times when the school funds were exhausted, that the teacher had to wait months before being paid.

Teachers who followed George Hall, included John M. Anderson, Mrs. John T. Griffin in 1864, the first woman Public School teacher in Whatcom County; a Mr. Cushany, who was also telegraph operator, and Edward Eldridge. One of his pupils was his daughter, Isabelle, who later was to become teacher of the same school. In April, 1875, a Mr. Setzer was replaced by Mrs. William Griffin from Fidalgo. At one time Mrs. Lottie Roeder Roth stated: "Very vividly I recall a school teacher of refinement, Mrs. William Griffin, who boarded with mother, and her companionship was very pleasing to us." Other outstanding women who taught there in later years included Mrs. Nellie Coupe and Mrs. A. H. Pratt.

As was the custom of the period, the school house became the community social center. There Judge George A. Kellogg organized and superintended a Sunday School in 1871. Later preaching services were conducted regularly. Entertainments and socials gravitated to the school room, as did political rallies. In 1868, Selucious Garfielde, delegate to Congress from Washington Territory, delivered a famous address therein.

Mrs. J. C. Cunningham, wife of a physician and surgeon next appeared in the educational picture in 1866-'67, when she opened the second private school of the Whatcom settlement. This was housed in a small building on Division Street.

The name W. H. Fouts first appears in Whatcom county school records in 1873, the same year the Marietta district Number 13 was created. He had come to Seattle from Iowa in 1871 and the following year taught school in Thurston County. At Marietta the school was held in a small shack where the schoolmaster instructed Fred, John and David Allen, the sons of Solomon Allen during a three month term. His salary was forty dollars per month and board.

Sehome school district up to the year 1874, included Sehome, Whatcom, Lummi Island, Bellingham and what later was Fairhaven. Fouts now started the agitation to divide the Sehome district and open a public school in the town of Whatcom. Superintendent F. F. Lane and the County Commissioners approved the petition. Whatcom School District Number 15 was formed, with H. Roeder, William Utter, H. Hofercamp, directors; and George A. Kellogg, clerk. W. H. Fouts was hired as the first public school teacher of Whatcom. (Opposite page 150). The directors purchased a small building down on Division Street, and moved it to the corner of D and Sixteen streets (Clinton), adjoining the old stockade. Previously the blockhouse had been razed by Jacob Matz (who later lived above Ferndale), the lumber being used to repair the E street wharf. The stockade, however, was untouched, and this enclosure made a fine playground for the pupils. One of their amusements, it is reported, was croquet, the set belonging to Miss Olive Smith.

Some of the children who attended the D Street school of 1874 were: Emma Cootes (whose father, Charles Cootes, was one of the early sheriffs of Whatcom County), Louis Hofercamp, Henry Roeder, Jr., Victor Roeder, Hugh Eldridge, Mary Stevens-Dale, Clara Fouts-Stenger, Rilla Fouts-Stenger, Cecilia Hofercamp-Connell, Laura Cunningham-Pine, Lottie Roeder-Roth and Maud Kellogg-Welbon.

Being unable to live on the salary from one three-month term of public school, W. H. Fouts, in January 1875 announced the opening of a private school in Whatcom, the tuition for the twelve weeks' course to be five dollars.

Three schools were in operation around the Bay in the spring of 1876: Fouts was teaching at Whatcom, Mrs. W. H. Griffin at Sehome, and Alice Eldridge-Gilligan at Bellingham. But all was not harmonious. The division of the school district in 1874 had brought many protests. Apportionment of school funds gave Sehome District Number 1, $128, and Whatcom District Number 15, the sum of $46. It was apparent that neither community alone could support an adequate school. Protest meetings were held in the fall of

1876 and the agitation for the reunion of the districts grew more vehement. In February 1878, the consolidation was effected.

W. H. Fouts protested the reunion, but John A. Tennant, the county superintendent, turned an unsympathetic ear. Fouts then appealed to the territorial superintendent. His protest was dropped however and he appeared satisfied with the situation when W. A. Utter, Harry West and himself were appointed directors of the consolidated district with W. L. Steinweg as clerk. In April twelve teachers applied for the Whatcom-Sehome position. Of these the board selected Miss Cooper of Tumwater.

In June, 1879—after the mine had closed—there were but sixteen pupils in the Sehome school. These represented nine families: Lottie and Victor Roeder; Clara, Rilla, Clay and Grace Fouts; Edward, Anthony and Mary E. Padden; Susie and Thomas Jenkins; Olive Smith; Hanorah Callahan; Maggie and Katie Connelly; and Jane Clark.

For a few years, during the hard times, the school was closed completely, and families that could do so, sent their children away to school. Captain Roeder's boys went to Port Townsend, his daughter to San Francisco. The Kellogg family moved East; the Fouts girls to Nebraska. A few pupils attended the University in Seattle, while some of the younger girls went to a convent in Victoria. One of these was Alice Eldridge. Her father, Edward Eldridge, it is recorded, provided canoe transportation twice a year for pupils attending at Victoria and other points as far south as Olympia.

With the recurrence of "good times" and with increasing population the need for a larger school building became evident. Therefore a special election was held in August, 1883, but the electors seemingly forgot to vote and the proposition calling for a new school house was defeated six to two. However, P. B. Cornwall offered a site on the line between Sehome and Whatcom, thus keeping the project alive.

WHATCOM COUNTY DIVIDED

The year 1883 brought two important changes: Whatcom County was divided into Whatcom and Skagit Counties; and the City of Whatcom was incorporated. Previously, in 1877, the separation movement had been stopped by an agreement that the district courts would go to La Conner, while the county officials would remain at Whatcom.

The separation of the counties became effective November 30, 1883. The change meant a complete rearrangement of school districts. This task

LEFT—Ruins of the Roeder water powered mill, to the right of Whatcom Creek Falls. It burned in 1873.—Photo courtesy Bellingham Herald.

RIGHT—Equipment used in making shakes and shingles.—Drawn by H. C. Jackson.

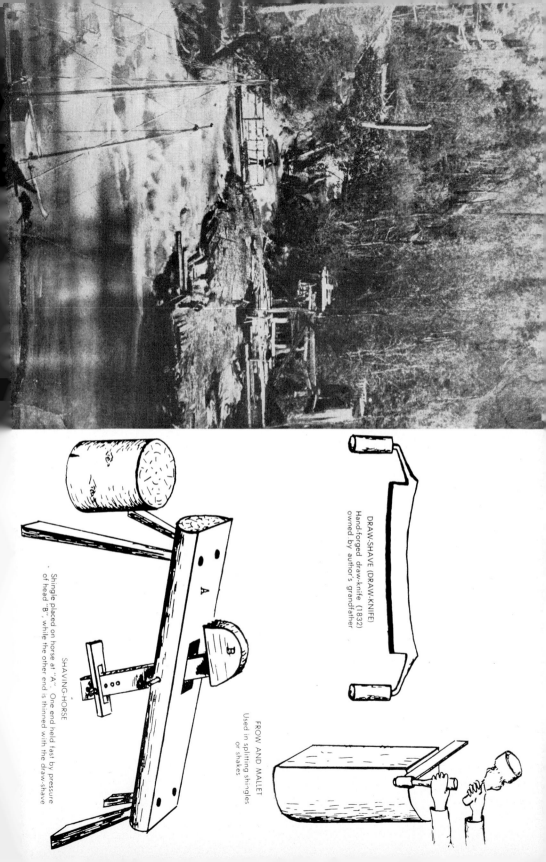

DRAW-SHAVE (DRAW-KNIFE)
Hand-forged draw-knife (1832)
owned by author's grandfather

FROW AND MALLET
Used in splitting shingles
or shakes

SHAVING-HORSE
Shingle placed on horse at "A". One end held fast by pressure
of head "B", while the other end is thinned with the draw-shave

fell on Mrs. Nellie S. Coupe, county superintendent. Old records carry the following:

"City of Whatcom, W. T.
Incorporated November 25, 1883.
Passed by the Common Council of the City of Whatcom,
the 27th day of December, A. D. 1883."

The following May by action of the County Commissioners, Mrs. Nellie Coupe, County Superintendent, approving, the City of Whatcom became School District Number 1.

Prior to the construction of a school building in the new District Number One, the children on the Whatcom side crowded into a little house on H Street. Some of these pupils—the Patchins and Belfords, adults of today—have told that they attended school here, in the spring of 1884, with a Mr. Green as their teacher.

The new district proceeded at once to erect a two story frame school building on the corner of I and Seventeenth (Dupont) streets, present site of the Roeder School. This two-room elementary school was opened in January, 1885, by Professor Swim and Mrs. D. R. Coldwell. School funds being low* the city council donated a large fir log lying on I street, to provide fuel. Whatcom voted a special school tax in 1886, thereby assuring a nine months' term. Miss Kate C. Smith was principal, with Luella Austin primary teacher.

The first Whatcom school library was begun in 1887, when pupils undertook to do janitor work at six dollars per month, the salary to apply to the purchase of books. With an eighteen dollar advance, students purchased Chamber's Encyclopedia, sixteen volumes; Macauley's History of England, five volumes; Bancroft's History of the United States, six volumes, and Walter's Tours in the East, six volumes. Lacking twenty dollars they made a plea for donations through the REVEILLE. At this time 117 pupils were enrolled and the building was so crowded that recitations were held in the ante-room and in the residence of the principal, G. M. SoRelle.

In the meantime, a school house had been erected in Bellingham, District Number 4 (between Sehome and Fairhaven). Maud Kellogg had been suc-

*Shortage due in part to destruction of records by fire, thus delayed collection of taxes.

UPPER—Central School buildings on Seventeenth street (Dupont) between I and J streets. The structure to the right was started in 1884, the second one in 1889 for grade schools. Later they became the Whatcom High School buildings. Roeder grade school is on the site today, 1951.—Photo courtesy of Cecil A. Morse.

LOWER—Teaching staff of New Whatcom High School, November, 1900. Left, Prof. A. P. Romine; Principal J. A. Lee; Miss Ina Pratt-Gnagey; Miss Anna Graham and Mrs. Alice M. Biggs.—Photo by the author.

ceeded as teacher by Mrs. Wilson, who was in charge when the building burned in January, 1889. E. Bartlett, thereupon offered the Bellingham District lots on Sixth and Douglas for a school, to cost not less than $7,000. At the same time bids were being asked for a six-room school house at Fairhaven. The Bellingham children found temporary school rooms in the basement of a Fairhaven church.

A second two-story building was completed at the Seventeenth (Dupont)* street site in 1889. Here the Whatcom school opened in August with a teaching staff consisting of Professor G. B. Johnston, Mrs. Munro, Rose E. Dobbs and Kate Isensee. By February, 1890, the enrollment totaled 243, while Feronia Y. Johnson and Hattie S. Vinton had been added to the teachers, one of them replacing Mrs. Munro.

FIRST HIGH SCHOOL IN THE NORTHWEST

This same year of 1890, the first High School in the Northwest was organized in one of these white frame buildings. Thirty-three pupils enrolled. The BELLINGHAM BAY EXPRESS in its Saturday issue of August 2, 1890, stated: "Principal Johnston of the Whatcom schools complains of the crowded condition and suggests that a number of pupils are getting too far advanced for the present course; that a high school course be organized consisting of those subjects which are necessary for a good business training."

The faculty of this high school consisted of Principal George B. Johnston, who also acted as superintendent; Miss Anna Graham and Miss Delisca J. Bowers (later Mrs. Hugh Eldridge).

When one of the Central Buildings was taken for the High School, it naturally displaced several of the lower grades. One of these pupils, Eva Reasoner-Siemons, has said, that in the fall of 1890, her class attended school in a house on Seventeenth Street (Dupont), directly across from the two frame ones. They were soon shifted to the basement of the Methodist Church on I Street. Some time later, they were marched to a frame structure on Williams Street—across from the present St. Francis Hospital— and attended school there until the Washington and Columbia buildings were finished. Some primary classes were held also in the Congregational Church on F and Astor Streets until the brick buildings were completed.

The BELLINGHAM BAY EXPRESS of August 16, 1890 reported: "The Whatcom schools will be opened September first for a fourteen week term, by which time it is hoped the new buildings will be ready. The following staff of teachers were appointed at a meeting of the directors this morning,

*Old Whatcom and Fairhaven had numbered streets. After consolidation, Whatcom changed its numbered streets to names, in 1904.

viz: Professor Johnston, Miss Anna Graham, Miss D. J. Bowers, Miss Rose Dobbs, Miss Laura Korthauer, Miss Rosa Carew."

Professor Johnston became the first superintendent of the united district comprising Whatcom and New Whatcom (Sehome). He had served for a short time as county superintendent, but resigned that office when the districts consolidated.

With the completion of the new brick buildings after the first of the year—1891—the lower grades were removed to the Washington school on Logan street and the Columbia on Utter. The high school then occupied both of the white frame structures. (Opposite page 167).

The class of 1892 was the first to graduate from the New Whatcom High School. There were three members—George Austin, Josie Gawley-Patch, and Ray Packer. Commencement exercises were held in the Purdy Opera House—corner of C and Thirteenth Streets (West Holly).

In February, 1893, Miss Bowers resigned to be married, and Professor E. E. White was appointed in her place. The next year, City Superintendent Johnston died. Professor Pattison from the Sehome school, became City Superintendent and Professor White was placed in charge of the High School.

There were nine pupils in the second graduating class—1893—Mae Atkins—(Livesey) Valedictorian, Hattie Underwood—(Collier), Jennie Strand—(Robin), Pearl Coleman—(Briggs), Nettie Coleman—(White), Kate Duffner, Ross Chestnut, Richard Burrows, and Burwell Atkins. Their graduating exercises were held in the Methodist Church on I Street.

By 1897, the New Whatcom High School enrollment had increased to 135. The teaching staff comprised: Professors White, Selby, Peringer and Miss Anna Graham.

With the death of City Superintendent Pattison in 1898, Professor White was chosen to fill the vacancy. Professor John Lee was removed from the Washington School to replace Professor White in the High School, and Feronia Y. Johnson took his place as principal of the Washington School. By fall Professor Selby resigned and Mrs. A. M. Biggs was given his position.

Both High School buildings were heated by large wood-burning stoves. In those earlier days the students bought their own books. The library consisted of less than 100 volumes—a Chamber's Encyclopedia; one Webster's dictionary, and about forty or fifty volumes of the Congressional Records. The science laboratory had a Leyden jar, a machine for creating an electric spark, and three or four bottles of acid. (How the boys enjoyed making the girls jump with this electric spark!) There was no such course as vocational training, nor were there any foreign languages taught, except Latin. Baseball and football were played in Elizabeth Park.

These two buildings were used as the High School through the fall of 1903, when the school moved to a brick structure on Halleck Street the first unit of the present Junior High School.

SEHOME SCHOOL

At Sehome, where the small pioneer building was badly outgrown in the late '80's, school was held for a time on the second floor of the R. I. Morse Hardware Store* on Elk Street (State). In the summer of 1887, Sehome advertised for a teacher at $33.33 per month. Anna C. Pence was hired. Her school had an enrollment of thirty-one pupils. Need for a larger structure being obvious, P. B. Cornwall donated a site on High Street, where the present Sehome school building was erected. During the interval, or in 1889, the grade school moved bodily to the basement of the newly completed Presbyterian Church. Sadie McAllister-Gibson, a pupil of that date, has stated that the four higher grades were seated facing in the direction of the Bay, while the other four grades recited and studied facing the opposite basement wall. (The structure today, 1951, is the First Lutheran Church, corner of High and Maple Streets.)

The BELLINGHAM BAY EXPRESS reported in its issue of June 21, 1890, that: "Mr. H. C. Wells, and his crew composing about forty men, engaged in clearing the New Whatcom (Sehome) townsite, a few days ago made a pool and purchased a large American flag and presented it to the school board to be placed over the magnificent school house just erected."

The June 28, 1890, edition stated: "The New Whatcom school directors have ordered a whole complement of the most approved automatic closing school desks and seats for the new school building, to cost about $1,500. No school in the state will be better equipped."

The Sehome school, costing $11,200, was ready for the fall term of 1890. It was a frame structure consisting of six large class rooms and a recreational room. A small elevator was installed for the janitor's use.

Under date of August 16, 1890, The BELLINGHAM BAY EXPRESS an-

---

*ROBERT I. MORSE—founder of the oldest business house on Bellingham Bay, arrived at Sehome on the Steamship *Queen* in 1884, accompanied by his wife, his infant son, Cecil, and a $3,000 stock of hardware and paints. The R. I. Morse hardware store was opened on Elk Street and thereafter carried on at the same address but in four different towns: Sehome, New Whatcom, Whatcom, and Bellingham.

Robert I. Morse was born at Sydney, Maine, June 8, 1858. In 1875, he moved to San Francisco. After several jobs he went to work in his uncle's hardware and paint store. P. B. Cornwall first interested the young man in Washington Territory. With Cornwall, he later built the Sehome wharf and the first water system. Always prominently identified with civic, religious, and fraternal activities, R. I. Morse will be remembered by old timers for his skill with a paint brush, for his energy in distributing his signs along every road and path. R. I. Morse died April 12, 1920, leaving the Morse Hardware Company in the hands of his sons.

nounced: "New Whatcom's (Sehome) fine new school house will be opened on September first. The teaching staff will be, Principal J. M. Hitt, E. N. Livermore, C. H. Brown, Miss Anna Odell, Miss Elsie Morgan, and Miss Lizzie Barrett."

The author attended this school the fall it opened, with her Aunt, Elsie Morgan as her second grade teacher. One day in December, while workmen were clearing and grading the street in front of the building, their reckless blasting hurled rocks through the windows of Miss Morgan's room—the one to the right on the first floor. Several children were cut about the head.

By October, the directors of District Number Two (Sehome), gave a contract for $112 to finish a room in the basement of the new school house, to care for the congestion of the primary department. Miss Rose Morgan was given this grade.

According to the BELLINGHAM BAY EXPRESS of June 6, 1891, the following were selected as teachers of the Sehome school for the ensuing year: "Harry Pattison, Principal; E. N. Livermore, assistant; Miss Anna Odell, Miss Elsie Morgan, Miss Hodges, Miss Lizzie Barrett, and Miss Lillian Butters."

For the proposed Lincoln school Miss Nellie Lee, Miss Jessie Calvert, Miss Carrie Bingham and Miss Burns were named.

The same paper of June 11, 1891, announced that the Whatcom school teachers for the following term would be:

"G. B. Johnston, Superintendent; Dilly J. Bowers and Anna Graham, High School; and J. N. Selby, Rosie J. Carew, Laura C. Korthauer—(Ireland), Rose E. Dobbs, Anna A. Farr, Clara Smith, Emma Campbell, Feronia Y. Johnson, Ida J. Johnson, Nellie H. Abbott, Wm. Levinge, Fannie E. Lees, Beambe E. Campbell, grade schools." The last variously assigned to the Columbia and Washington schools.

By 1892, there were six school buildings and five schools in New Whatcom (Whatcom and Sehome), three of brick and stone, and three frame. The Sehome and the two High School buildings were the frame; and the Washington, Columbia and Lincoln were the brick and stone. The Washington was ready shortly after the first of 1891, the Columbia by the middle of February, and the Lincoln completed in 1892. This boasted of eight rooms, although only five were in use in 1897. There was no large school bell, thus school time was indicated by the raising of a flag, presented by the Junior Order of United American Mechanics.

The school election of 1892 for the trustees of New Whatcom was hotly contested and brought out a record vote of 1,432. C. W. Carter, who had been chairman of the Board of Trustees for the town of Sehome in 1888, commented on this election and said: "When I was on the school board during six years, all the money we handled amounted to about $100 a year. R. I. Morse donated all the hardware the school needed, and I donated all the brooms. Not much rush to get to the polls then!"

FAIRHAVEN SCHOOLS

The first school in Fairhaven was a private one held in the "Tabernacle," an edifice for the use of all religious denominations, on the corner of Gambier and Thirteenth Streets. Miss Goff was the first teacher here. Later a public school was held therein. The second private school was conducted in the basement of the Lathrop building on Eleventh and Fillmore Streets; the fee was one dollar per month. This soon opened as a public school with two teachers.

The Fourteenth Street School, on the site of the present Lowell Building, opened in June, 1890, with an attendance of 350, which had increased to 500 in December. In addition there were more than 100 pupils attending classes in rented rooms, two of which were the Montezuma, corner of McKenzie Avenue and Fourteenth Street, and the J. M. Warriner building, corner of Harris Avenue and Fourteenth Street. This situation was later corrected by the erection of the Larrabee School on Larrabee Avenue (named for the president of the Fairhaven Land Company). Judge Samuel Curry, G. M. SoRelle, and D. R. Huntoon were the first school directors, while Professor C. W. Albright was superintendent. Nine teachers were employed. A successful night school also was featured.

On Saturday, May 30, 1891, the FAIRHAVEN WEEKLY WORLD published the list of elected teachers:

"F. P. Schisler was elected principal of the Larrabee Avenue school and Miss Jennie E. Alexander was re-elected principal of the Fourteenth Street school. Ellen A. Prentice was re-elected vice-principal of the primary department. Mina A. Woodin, Dora Wellman, Mildred Myers, Lydia Whited, and Olive E. Charroin were re-elected. The following new teachers were elected: Helen R. Gleason, Kathryn T. North, Hattie M. Sweet, Addie Jones, and Myrtle Day."

The fall term of 1892 opened with David G. Fenton, city superintendent; and W. J. Hughes, principal of the Larrabee school. Hughes also organized the first Fairhaven High School that same year with an enrollment of twenty-one. This was in the Larrabee building. Teachers were—the Misses Charroin, Foster, Helen Gleason, and Myrtle Day. At this time Miss Jennie E. Alexander was principal of the Fourteenth Street School; the other teachers being the Misses Hattie Kellogg, Sweet, Mina Woodin, Addie Jones and Dora E. Wellman.

First graduates of Fairhaven High School were Clifford McMillin, and Nettie Lehman of the class of 1894. The following year there were five graduates: Frank W. Smith, William Heberdeen, Pearl Day, Margaret Day, and Emma B. Roll.

Graduating exercises were held in the "Pavilion" erected in 1889 on Donovan Avenue between Twelfth and Fourteenth Streets. This was a great heavy-timbered barn-like building that became a community center, where were held club meetings, prize fights, political rallies, and elections, while children skated there in off moments. It also served as a school gymnasium. By the end of 1903, a new brick high school building had been completed on the present site of the Fairhaven Junior High School on Cowgill Street. At first, some grade classes also were held in this structure, which burned New Year's night, 1936.

NORTHWEST NORMAL SCHOOL

First institution of higher learning on United States soil north of the Territorial University at Seattle was the Northwest Normal School which opened its doors at Lynden, October 5, 1886. This was the result of a campaign by J. R. Bradley of Missouri, called "Professor Bradley," which so impressed the citizens that at a meeting in August the community of seven hundred souls subscribed the needed funds, and Contractor E. J. Robinson quickly completed the five-room structure.* The site was a block of ground donated by Holden A. Judson between Sixth and Seventh and Grover and Liberty Streets.

Tuition was eight dollars for a ten weeks' course. Four such terms completed the school year. At the time there were no secondary schools in the county, while elementary schools were sketchy. Accordingly a preparatory course was provided, covering grade school subjects. The curriculum of the Normal School proper included the courses handled by the average liberal arts college, with certain additional professional subjects in each of the four college years.

Board and room were available to students at from three to four dollars per week. Entrance requirements at the Normal were low, girls being admitted at age of fourteen and boys at sixteen. At that time a person of sixteen years, could secure a teacher's certificate by passing an examination in the common branches. Two years later this age requirement was lifted to eighteen years.

Despite inducements offered, the opening enrollment was but sixteen. The following July, attendance reached nearly a hundred. The Principal

---

*Later this building was moved to the corner of Fifth and Grover Streets, and is the I. O. O. F. Hall.

was encouraged enough to add a department of music.

The Wednesday issue of the WHATCOM COUNTY DEMOCRAT on September 12, 1888, stated: "A bell landed at the Sehome wharf Saturday evening for the Lynden Normal School. We understand that institution has also a large consignment of school furniture on the road."

Clearing of the school grounds continued and public spirited citizens donated more funds for further improvement and additions to the building. These were completed November 20, 1889. The next year the Whatcom County Teachers' Institute was held at the Lynden Normal in August. (Opposite page 182). Meantime enrollment had dropped alarmingly. It rose again to a new high of 120 during the spring term of 1891. From the first the school was unprofitable. Accordingly Professor Bradley sold to Professor W. M. Heiney who conducted an eight weeks' summer school in 1892, then closed the Normal permanently.

The faculty of the Northwest Normal School, over its six years of existence, included besides Professor J. R. Bradley, Associate Principal W. H. Heiney, Vice-Principal F. G. Franklin, Professor A. Griffin, Mrs. Griffin, Miss Frances Cleveland-Axtell, Miss Delisca J. Bowers-Eldridge, Mrs. Lillian Heiney, Miss Maude B. McFarland, and Mrs. Clara B. DeCan.

Before the closing of the school, and afterward, there was much agitation and pressure to have the state take control. Later Blaine, and New Whatcom, as well as Lynden offered inducements to have the state establish a Normal in the respective communities. The Panic of 1893, and the hard times following the collapse of the boom prevented any appropriations; but political campaigning and legislative log-rolling continued unabated. Governor McGraw signed a bill in 1893 providing for a Normal School Location Commission but vetoed an appropriation for a normal school.

NEW WHATCOM NORMAL SCHOOL

The Location Commission selected a ten acre site near Sehome Hill offered by the Bellingham Bay Improvement Company and the Fairhaven Land Company, after considering sites at Lynden, Blaine, Ferndale and Lake Whatcom. Here the New Whatcom Normal School, now the Western Washington College of Education, was erected.

Construction began in 1895, after a legislative appropriation of $40,000. No funds were forthcoming in 1897, and it was not until 1899 that needed money was provided and the building completed in time for the fall term starting September 6, 1899.

During the first school year of 1899-1900, 264 students enrolled. The faculty consisted of the Principal, Doctor Edward T. Mathes, John T.

Forrest, Sarah J. Rogers, Ida A. Baker, Francis W. Epley, Catherine Montgomery, Avadana Millett, Robert T. Vaile, and Jane Connell.

. . .

The one-room Sehome School of 1861—primitive beginning of a modern educational system, was outgrown in the '80's. The clatter of slates and the squeak of slate-pencils came to an end and the building became a dwelling place. Presumably it received its first coat of whitewash at this time. For some years longer it remained in the middle of Maple Street near Cornwall Avenue, obstructing "progress." It was razed in 1893—physically that is. To various aging citizens who learned their ABC's in that humble building on Sehome shores, it lingers in nostalgic memories.

EARLY COUNTY SUPERINTENDENTS
1860 — 1904

Before there were any school children, schools, or school districts, Whatcom County, then comprising San Juan and Skagit Counties, boasted a duly elected county school superintendent. The pioneer newspaper, the NORTHERN LIGHT on July 17, 1858, reported the selection of R. V. Peabody at the regular election.

Sehome school, near the coal mines was opened in 1861, at which time George Slater held the office (1860-'61), the first school superintendent with anything to superintend. Slater, who had come to Sehome in 1858 to supervise drilling operations in the coal fields, drew the munificent salary of twenty-five dollars per annum. He resigned the same year and next appears in the public records in 1872, when he preempted 160 acres of land two miles south of Ferndale.

Slater was followed in quick succession by J. L. Wiley, R. V. Peabody, and Patrick Padden, 1862-'63. Eugene Jasper was appointed superintendent when Padden removed from the territory. Public records of the period are meager, lists of public officials sometimes missing. Salaries were small, the duties light and there were many resignations and vacancies.

San Juan County was established October 31, 1873, leaving Whatcom and Skagit county as one political subdivision. W. Y. Deree was superintendent of schools prior to this date, receiving a salary of $100 per annum. He resigned and left Whatcom. William R. Griffin of Fidalgo was then appointed in his stead for the remaining term. In 1874, he vacated his office by leaving the county; thus F. F. Lane became his successor by appointment.

Frederick F. Lane, originally came by wagon train to California and thence reached Bellingham Bay in 1856. Lane, a graduate of an eastern college, possessed a brilliant mind. Said to be a natural educator, he seems to have taken his office seriously. He had some money and this he expended freely in developing the school system. Certain public papers were filed at Olympia at his own expense. The superintendent admitted that some of the fees he received for visiting distant schools did not cover the cost of shoe leather. For one visit to a school below LaConner, he hired an Indian and a canoe, thirty dollars; the fee, five dollars.

In 1875, F. F. Lane was reelected county superintendent, but soon resigned. W. H. Fouts was appointed to the unexpired term. At that time there was no salary provided. The official was dependent on fees: five dollars for each visit to a school; ten cents per mile travel expense; and two dollars for the issuance of each temporary teacher's certificate. There was no limitation as to the number of visits during a school term, nor was there any requirement that the superintendent make any visit at all.

Early schools were sometimes fifty miles apart and could be reached only by strenuous effort. During the '70's and early '80's, county superintendents never saw all the schools under their jurisdiction. As late as 1883, Whatcom County remained a wilderness, with no roads but the Military Road to Fort Bellingham and the Nooksack; and the Telegraph Road to the Nooksack Crossing. The rest of the county was penetrated by trails.

Therefore it is recorded that in 1875, W. H. Fouts walked thirty-two miles in one day, visiting three schools, thus earning eighteen dollars and twenty cents. Two of the schools were in the present Skagit County. School districts in 1875 were fifteen in number. The first seven included Sehome, Number 1; Fidalgo, Number 2; Skagit City, Number 3; LaConner, Number 4; Semiahmoo, Number 5; Ferndale, Number 6; and Samish, Number 7.

D. E. Gage and John A. Tennant in turn succeeded Fouts. Tennant, in 1878 convened the first county teachers' institute on E Street, Whatcom, in a building almost across from the brick courthouse (in the NORTHERN LIGHT building). (Opposite page 198). A dozen teachers participated. The annual teachers' examination was held in the courthouse the preceding day, according to old school records:

"May 1, 1878: The Board of Examiners of Whatcom County, Washington Territory, was Superintendent John A. Tennant, Miss Isabelle M. Eldridge, and W. H. Fouts, assistants, met at the Courthouse on Wednesday, May 1st, 1878."

When W. H. Fouts was elected in 1881, the law had been changed to provide a salary of fifty dollars per month for the county superintendent. A fee of three dollars was allowed for each visit to a school, with the number of visits limited to two per term. The travel fee remained at ten cents a mile.

The last superintendent of the combined territory of the present

Skagit and Whatcom counties was G. E. Hartson, January, 1883-January 17, 1884. By the end of 1883, when Whatcom was divided, the records listed thirty-nine districts in the area.

The first county superintendent of the present Whatcom County was Mrs. Nellie S. Coupe, January, 1884-January, 1885. She was followed by H. J. Swim, January, 1885-March 22, 1887; J. F. Griffin, March 22, 1887-January, 1889; H. J. Swim, January, 1889-March, 1890; G. B. Johnston, March, 1890-December, 1891; J. M. Hitt, December, 1891-January, 1897. During Superintendent Hitt's term in 1895, the school districts in Whatcom County numbered seventy-five. J. W. Tanner followed Hitt in January, 1897-January, 1899; then R. S. Simpson, January, 1899-September, 1903; and R. J. Schusman, September, 1903-September, 1907.

MRS. NELLIE S. COUPE
"MISS NELLIE"
January 25, 1845 — March 26, 1936

Nellie Moore, "Miss Nellie" (Mrs. Nellie Coupe), first teacher on Whidbey Island, pioneer wife and mother in the Lynden District, first Whatcom County school superintendent (after Whatcom and Skagit were separated), was a niece of Colonel Granville O. Haller. And this soldier, so prominent as a major in the Indian wars and the San Juan Island incident, must be credited with launching his relative on her career as an educator—a career that left a definite mark in the Northwest, and an impression that endures to the present in the minds of the older citizens.

Haller, like thousands of soldiers in later wars, became enamored of the Pacific Coast and acquired several pieces of property on Whidbey Island while yet in uniform, with the idea of settling there after his discharge. He returned to Whidbey Island late in 1863. Before leaving the East, he arranged to educate his niece, Miss Nellie Moore, of York, Pennsylvania, with the stipulation that when her studies were completed she would go West as private tutor for his children. The course which the young woman followed in a Baltimore seminary was much more rounded than that customarily given to females of the period, since it included the arts, practical sciences, piano tuning, and general academic subjects.

Mrs. Coupe has stated that she completed her studies in 1865, and left her eastern home; journeying by way of the Isthmus of Panama, and arriving at Whidbey Island in January, 1866, where she assumed her duties as tutor and governess. (Opposite page 151). Vital statistics for this remarkable educator may be taken from her statements in an interview given the AMERICAN REVEILLE of Bellingham, Washington, January 21,

1917, at which time she said, "I am seventy-two years old and sorry to admit it. Now ask ahead." She added that she came to Puget Sound in 1866, and had been a resident of Whatcom County since 1871. At the time of the interview, Mrs. Coupe was said to be an authority on astronomy, was coaching high school students, and had many private pupils which she explained made it necessary to use her bicycle instead of trying to make the calls by use of street cars.

Nellie Moore's success as tutor and governess of Colonel Haller's children on Whidbey Island was such, that offspring of other families were admitted to the private school. These included children of the Ebey, Crockett, Judson, and Roeder families, with all of whom the teacher became a close friend. Two years after her arrival, or in 1868, she made a trip to Whatcom aboard the steamer *Mary Woodruff*, Captain John Cosgrove,* at which time, in company with John Roeder, she descended into the workings of the Sehome Coal mine.

In December, 1870, Nellie Moore married William T. Coupe—"Tommie" —son of Thomas Coupe, founder of Coupeville. The next year, 1871, the young couple squatted on a homestead at Lynden, where she became the second white woman settler north of Whatcom, Mrs. Phoebe Judson being the first. The first white child to be born along the Nooksack was the Coupe's son, Thomas Louis, nicknamed "Russett." This was in 1875.

W. T. Coupe was elected county treasurer in 1881, whereupon the family moved to Whatcom. Almost at once Nellie Coupe was asked to teach the Sehome school that same year with twelve pupils.

After Whatcom and Skagit counties were separated (1883), Nellie Coupe became County Superintendent of the smaller Whatcom county in

---

*After the gold rush, or a short time prior to 1860, Bellingham Bay had no communication with the outside world. Then Captain John Cosgrove—known as "Humboldt Jack"— secured the mail contract and for two years operated the Sloop *Marie* in the North Sound trade. During this period the steamer *Mary Woodruff* also secured a mail contract and soon entered the same territory.

The *Mary Woodruff* built at Port Madison by John Swan, a logger, and Jay E. Smith of Steilacoom, was sixty-three feet overall length with a beam of fourteen feet and a six foot hold. Although a side-wheeler she was propelled by a single engine operating on a cogwheel drive. Her machinery was secured from the old *Ranger,* then on the beach.

Captain Swan disposed of his steamer to Meiggs, the mill-man, who in turn sold to "Humboldt Jack" Cosgrove. Under Captain Cosgrove the *Mary Woodruff* provided an all-around freight and passenger service to every inlet and hamlet until her name was a household word throughout Puget Sound. After other steamers cut into his business, Captain Cosgrove sold to Captain Harry Smith in 1870. That same year Captain Williamson bought the vessel from Smith and operated her for several seasons, then abandoned the sidewheeler on the beach at Freeport, where machinery and furniture were salvaged. The hull burned in 1881. (Data from Lewis and Dryden's MARINE HISTORY OF THE PACIFIC NORTHWEST.)

Blanket Bill Jarman reported that the *Mary Woodruff* had to stop her engine to blow her whistle.

1884. For many years she continued her profession, mostly handling private pupils in her later years, when she found herself teaching children and grandchildren of earlier students. Some of these she instructed in Latin, others in botany or geology, some on the piano, guitar, or cello; others perhaps in painting.

There are men and women in the Northwest today, who received their early education from Nellie Coupe. They yet carry memories of the brilliant and outstanding little teacher, who, in the experimental days of the "safety-bicycle" daringly rode her wheel over the rough streets of Whatcom as she went about her serious business of education.

Chapter XIX.

THE WATER-POWER MILL BURNS

1873

SUPERSTITION has it that Evils travel in threes.
Bellingham Bay communities might well subscribe to this belief after their
bitter experiences in the 70's. The first of the evil triad appeared in August,
1873, when the Roeder sawmill, first in the Northwest, burned. Constructed
in 1853 by Captain Henry Roeder and R. V. Peabody, the mill was one
of the principal sources of income and employment for the district. (Opposite
page 166).

The fire which started in the evening illuminated the sky for miles
around. Settlers at Lake Samish viewed the glow with alarm, as did others
in the opposite direction fifteen miles up the Nooksack. Word spread that
all of Whatcom was burning. Afoot and by canoe volunteer fire-fighters
hurried toward town.

The mill was an inferno but a bucket brigade was formed to save
Auditor George A. Kellogg's home which stood sixty feet distant, up the
hillside. Rhythmically, as fast as the pails came forward, the head of the
line darted into the searing heat to dash a bucket of water on the sides of
the steaming building. Other fire-fighters extinguished sparks and brands
on the roof.

Down on the mill-dock another bucket brigade was fighting to save
100,000 feet of piled lumber. This line was composed mostly of Lummi
Indians who happened to be in town that day. The tide was high. Standing waist deep in water, and clad only in woolen shirts, the Indians passed
up buckets of water all along the dock. On top others dashed the water
on the smoking lumber or stamped out large sparks and brands with their
bare feet.

At the height of the excitement the Jones Hotel on Division Street was
ignited by flaming brands. This was controlled speedily.

The fire was reported at some length by the BELLINGHAM BAY MAIL,*
established one month earlier by James Power, formerly of the OHIO STATE

*The first issue of the BELLINGHAM BAY MAIL was dated July 5, 1873. In the August
issue, Owner-Editor James Power thanked William A. Utter for a set of iron side sticks for
printing forms, and for a large font of pica type, which had been in the possession of the

JOURNAL, who had been drawn to the Northwest by the reported prosperity of the Bellingham Bay communities.

Said the MAIL: "The sawmill was the property of Whatcom Milling Company which consists of John E. Peabody of San Francisco, and Henry Roeder of this place; Mr. Peabody owning two-thirds and Captain Roeder the other third. Captain Utter had no share in the mill as generally supposed but simply acted as agent for the Company. In May, 1853, it was taken in charge by Captain William Utter who has successfully operated it since, with the exception of a few months in the summer season when the water was too low to afford power."

The mill was uninsured. Captain Roeder wished to rebuild. But the West Coast was feeling the effect of an incident on the other side of the Continent—Black Friday on the New York Stock Market, Sept. 18, 1873. Affected by this Panic of 1873, John E. Peabody vetoed Captain Roeder's suggestion and Whatcom Creek water power was not utilized again until after the arrival of the Washington Colony in the '80's.

The second of the portentous evils was caused by the Panic of 1873. In September, a month after the mill burned, the telegraph wires brought word that Jay Cooke and Company of New York had failed and that Bellingham Bay would not be the railroad terminus.

The third of the Triad of Evils delayed five years. Then Sehome Coal Mine closed, the telegraph company shut its Sehome office, and the Bay communities were deep in the doldrums.

HOME-MADE SHINGLES

When periods of hard times oppressed the district, when there was no employment to be had, when there was no market for the farmer's produce, he nevertheless had one salable article—the home made cedar shingle, which year by year passed in exchange at five dollars per thousand.

During the winter months the shaving horse and draw-knife or draw-shave were brought into the house and the kitchen became a shingle factory. And good shingles they were, in many cases protecting the settler's home for half a century before being replaced. (Opposite page 166).

In early days when roads were lacking the shingles often were packed out a bundle at a time, on the shoulders of the maker who traded them

latter's father for ten years past. These undoubtedly had belonged to the NORTHERN LIGHT plant.

The MAIL was published in the brick courthouse, until August 30, 1879. The following week it moved to LaConner. From September, 1879, the publication has been known as the PUGET SOUND MAIL.

for necessities which in turn he carried home on his back. As Roth has stated: "It may almost be said that the County was clothed with shingles."

GUS JULIAN

"SINBAD, THE SAILOR"

Various settlers on Bellingham Bay, during the period when Whatcom lacked a wharf, reached the shore dryshod, only because carried there on the broad shoulders of Gus Julian, sturdy French boatman. Sometimes called Sinbad, the Sailor, Julian had the job of meeting steamers at the Sehome wharf, or off the Whatcom tideflats and transporting passengers and mail to Whatcom in his large fishing boat.

The Frenchman had lived among the Indians and spoke little English, yet by signs and grunts could make himself understood. Thus when his loaded craft grounded far from the beach, while following up the meandering Whatcom creek channel across the tideflats, he could enforce his will on mystified and frightened arrivals from the prairie states, and compel them, men and women alike, to mount his back and ride ashore in turn.

Mrs. Lottie Roeder Roth has described Julian as a sturdy Frenchman with short legs which were out of proportion to his long heavy body. His fat pleasant face was almost hidden by a long flowing beard. In fact when staggering across the flooded tideflats with freight or baggage on his shoulders he made a picture not unlike that of Santa Claus and his pack.

The arrival of a mail steamer was a big event in those days. Thus Mrs. Roth has told of the excitement among the girls at the Sehome school when the *J. B. Libby* appeared in the offing on Friday afternoon; of how the twittering pupils gathered on the beach. And always Gus Julian and his boat were there in advance waiting at the Sehome wharf for the steamer to dock.

The Frenchman's inseparable companion on these trips was little Walter Fouts, who, in checkered apron and sunbonnet, occupied the stern seat, seriously intent on receiving the mail intended for the City of Whatcom. This companionship with a small boy seems to have been a characteristic of Gus Julian who appeared to delight in teaching other youngsters

UPPER—Whatcom County Teachers' Institute at Lynden Normal School, August, 1890. Front row, third from right, Professor J. M. Hitt, Superintendent of Sehome School; fourth, Professor C. W. Albright, Fairhaven City Superintendent; next, G. B. Johnston, Whatcom City Superintendent; County Superintendent H. J. Swim, and Professor J. R. Bradley of the Northwest Normal School in Lynden. Potato patch at their feet.—Photo courtesy of Mrs. Ina Pratt Gnagey.

LOWER—Building the plank sidewalks on Harris Avenue in Fairhaven, Washington. Wardner Castle on the hill, left center (Hilltop House today—1951). Note mud.—Photo taken in early '90's—courtesy Cecil Morse.

MOUNTAINEERING ON THE PACIFIC. 795

SEAHOME.

to fish, and in otherwise entertaining them. The boys, on their part, lured by his occupation, appearance, and strange speech, flocked about him like flies around a honey pot.

Charles I. Roth who reached Bellingham Bay in 1883 was one of Julian's customers on his arrival. The Frenchman's boat met the Seattle steamer about 3,000 feet offshore from the village of Whatcom. Twelve or fifteen passengers boarded Julian's craft. When the boat grounded on the flats, the skipper pulled up the tops of his long rubber boots and stepped overside. Roth and the others were startled as they thought the Frenchman was abandoning ship—leaving the passengers to their fate out on the waters. By signs and grunts Julian made himself understood, and soon each traveler rode ashore piggyback. For each fare, Gus collected fifty cents.

CHARLES DONOVAN
1849 — 1936
1873

No persons can peruse files of old Bellingham Bay newspapers without being impressed by the frequency with which the name of Charles Donovan appears in print. For several decades, whether it was as a public official, the organizer of a baseball team, the head of a committee to wait on the legislature, or to raise funds for a railroad, the man was involved seemingly in every public activity.

His parents, John Donovan and wife, with six children were enroute from England to New Orleans, aboard the ship *Sailor Prince,* when he was born on the high seas, September 27, 1849. The appellation of the ship was perpetuated in his middle name, *Sailor Prince,* which cognomen he soon dropped as being too fancy and causing too many boyhood fights.

After about ten years in St. Louis, during which the father disappeared, the mother in 1862, moved her brood to Salt Lake by ox-drawn wagon; this despite Indian activity that thrilled the boys greatly.

Young Donovan tried his hand as a cow puncher, packer, placer miner, member of a Northern Pacific survey gang. He quit the survey at Lewiston

UPPER—Coal bunkers in Sehome, Washington Territory, drawn by Edmund T. Coleman in 1868, after making the first ascent of Mt. Baker.—Photo courtesy Harper's Magazine.

LOWER—Sehome in 1885, looking northeast up Elk Street (State). Center building in foreground was erected for the Sehome Coal Co. To the left of this building near the beach are the remains of the coal dump, and the first entrance to the Sehome Coal Mine. The Bellingham Bay & British Columbia railroad ran through the left center to Whatcom Creek, then later to Squalicum Creek. The white building, left, middle distance above shore, is the first school building. Second building on left side of Elk street is A. H. Pratt's; near the end of the street is Morse's Hardware Store. The Old Orchard Tract is middle right, "Orchard Terrace" today—1951.—Photo courtesy Cecil A. Morse.

in 1870 and drifted to the Cariboo country, British Columbia, with the gold stampeders. There he hired out as linesman, restringing wire on the old Telegraph line. Having learned the Morse code, he next became operator at Clinton, then at Abbottsford, British Columbia.

South of the Border, the Sehome telegraph office was in the store of the Bellingham Coal Company on Elk Street. The homesick English operator effected an exchange of stations with Charles Donovan, who arrived on Bellingham Bay, June 26, 1873. (Opposite page 199).

A telegrapher's duties of the period included riding the line, removing fallen trees, and making repairs. On these inspection trips, Donovan's sure footed pony would pick its way, ten miles north and return, along the succession of chuck holes, fallen trees, exposed roots, floating puncheon that passed for a road, the Telegraph Road so called. The following day in a hired Indian canoe, he would ride south to Wildcat Cove and follow the wires to the Sehome mine.

When Donovan reached the Bay, Whatcom citizens were clamoring because the postoffice had been moved from the county seat to Sehome with Sutcliffe Baxter as postmaster. This outcry caused the reestablishment of the postoffice in Whatcom in 1874 with James Power, editor of the BELLINGHAM BAY MAIL, the Postmaster. Thereupon, Charles Donovan was appointed Postmaster at Sehome.

Because eligible women were few, the young bloods of the period organized dancing parties that might travel fifty miles by canoe, as far perhaps, as Port Townsend. Thus William Steinweg, clerk at the Sehome Coal Mine, and kindred spirit, met Sue Engle of Whidbey Island, who later succeeded Isabelle Eldridge as teacher of the Sehome school. In 1876, the couple were wed at the school house in a widely-heralded ceremony. Two years later the bride's friend, the comely Sarah Crockett from Whidbey Island, married Charley Donovan.

The two couples took up residence in cottages that later were found to be located in the middle of Elk Street. Here their children were born and here they struggled during the dark days following the closing of the mine. When this occurred in 1878, the telegraph office was closed, but an instrument was left with Charles Donovan, who installed it in his home and thereby was able to keep the community informed on outside news.

Displaying characteristic acumen, Charles Donovan was elected treasurer in 1876. Thereafter until his retirement in 1913, he was almost continuously in public service. Other offices he held were those of auditor, clerk, deputy sheriff, deputy assessor, county commissioner and mayor of Whatcom.

After six years of married life, and after being elected auditor, Donovan

moved his family to Whatcom where he purchased the George A. Kellogg*
house from his predecessor, Ex-Auditor Smith. This stood on the hill near
E and Clinton Streets, close to the site of the pioneers' blockhouse.

Late in the '80's the first Democratic newspaper on the Bay was started
with Charles Donovan as owner and manager, and S. C. Kenny, the editor—
a venture that was unprofitable.

Another unprofitable business was the drug store which he started with
the stock from Doctor A. W. Thornton.*

Charles Donovan was a slender man, a skilled horseman, nervously
active all his life. In old age he still possessed a luxuriant mustache, bushy
eyebrows, and a virile looking, thick mane of grey hair; while his glance
was as fearless and piercing as during his adventuresome youth. As might
be expected of a politician and an Irishman, he had at his command a winning smile and a quick wit.

In times of worry and in private, it is said of the man, that he often
became dour and short tempered. Some who experienced these moods
declared he lacked tact. This charge brought an emphatic "No" from Hugh
Eldridge. "No person lacking in tact," declared Eldridge, "could have held
office so long." The record is the more remarkable when it is considered that
Donovan, a staunch Democrat, was an elected official in a strong Republican county. Nor was his tenure of office due to lack of opposition. Voters
of the day, in fact, took their politics more seriously than in later decades.
Papers of the time referred continually to "Boss Donovan," or "Silk Stocking
Charley," (this last a reference to his meticulous dress). Nevertheless, the
Republican electorate, confident in his known honesty, and his proven
efficiency, returned him to office with monotonous regularity. So well
informed was Charles Donovan, that he could recite the history and chain
of ownership of almost every piece of property in Whatcom county.

He died at Bellingham, September 17, 1936, in his eighty-seventh year.

---

*Judge George A. Kellogg came to Whatcom in 1871, taking residence on the hillside
above the Roeder mill. Here a son, John Kellogg, was born, and here the family resided
when the mill burned in 1873, threatening their possessions. Thereafter Kellogg built a house
on the west side of the creek. This he sold to Auditor Smith in 1874.

*Doctor A. W. Thornton, holder of a degree from the Royal College of Surgeons of
Dublin arrived at Whatcom in 1877 with a stock of drugs. During the ensuing hard times,
he removed to Ferndale, where he practiced medicine until his hearing failed. Then he
turned to the soil. His experiments and contributions to the horticultural, dairying and
flax raising industries, justify ranking his name with those of John Bennett and John Tennant.

In 1913, following the death of his first wife, Donovan married Mrs. deFremery,
widowed daughter of Doctor Thornton.

Chapter XX.

EARLY COAL MINES

SEHOME COAL MINE

W HEN THE DISAPPOINTED GOLD SEEKERS reeled back from the Fraser River stampede that hectic year of 1858, the Sehome Coal Mine, discovered five years earlier, was producing at the rate of 500 tons per annum. Departing argonauts and gloomy citizens alike were unimpressed. To them it was incomprehensible that coal, not gold, would lift the residents from their depression; that the "black diamonds" of the coal measures, would carry them through two decades of comparative prosperity.

While the coal seam at Sehome was uncovered the fall of 1853, it was not the first such find on Bellingham Bay. The first discovery, occurring in 1852, as recorded elsewhere in this history, was at Pattle's Point between Sehome and Fairhaven. This was by William R. Pattle,* the second white man known to have visited Bellingham Bay, and the first to settle thereon.

Two of Captain Roeder's employees, Brown and Hewitt, discovered the Sehome coal vein when they noted a mass of black appearing rock in a hole left by the roots of a giant upturned cedar. This was near the shore line, west of the present State Street and south of Laurel Street, on the Roeder donation claim. The "rock" was found to be a good grade of lignite coal.

The Sehome vein proved to be seventeen feet thick, although containing several streaks of slate. Edward Eldridge wrote that the dip of the seam was forty-five degrees westerly, the angle decreasing with depth. Another authority mentions that the strike was found to be north or slightly west of north. The dip and strike definitely carried the seam under the waters of the Bay. Just as definitely, therefore, according to the records of the Washington State Division of Mines and Geology, coal was mined beneath the tidewaters.

---

*The Pattle coal seam, according to one historian, stood nearly vertical, having a westerly dip from the horizontal of about 75 degrees. The strike, or horizontal extension, was nearly North and South. The coal seam in Pattle's property, called the "Ma-Mo-Sea Mine" was said to be eight feet thick with a three foot parting of shale. It was drifted upon for 175 feet, and 150 tons of fuel were mined and shipped to San Francisco. J Ross Browne in RESOURCES OF THE PACIFIC SLOPE, 1869, mentions an eleven foot vein in this or an adjacent claim, but no attempt was made at development except on the exposure where Pattle mined a small quantity of coal by hand.

THE BELLINGHAM BAY COAL COMPANY

On a Pacific slope so lacking in developed coal measures, any deposit of the kind was important. The canny Captain Roeder was quite aware of this. Hence he promptly employed one Perry Dunfield to mine an experimental shipment of sixty tons. This was freighted to coal hungry San Francisco in the schooner *William Allen* and the surveying steamer *Active*. Brown, one of the discoverers, accompanied the shipment, carrying Captain Roeder's power of attorney to sell the mine.

On the California market, the coal brought sixteen dollars per ton, and Brown promptly sold the mine for $18,000 to Fauntleroy, Calhoun and Benham.* The San Francisco purchasers organized the Bellingham Bay Coal Company, which was to operate the mine for many years. Brown, so Captain Roeder reported, absconded to Colorado with the mine purchase price. Perhaps as discoverer, he felt he was entitled to the major portion of the money, despite Roeder's interest. In Denver, he is said to have built up a fortune with the acquired capital; erecting and owning the famous Brown's Palace Hotel of Denver. It was not until twenty-two years later, according to Roeder, that he secured any sort of settlement from Brown. In 1877, Mrs. Roeder, while enroute east, called on Brown as the Captain's agent and collected the sum of $1,200.

After the sale, Captain Roeder relinquished his donation claim covering the coal property and promptly filed on a better timbered piece of land between West Street and G Street. Captain Fauntleroy, one of the San Francisco owners of the mine, thereupon filed a donation claim covering the mine. This he quit-claimed to Edmund C. Fitzhugh, resident agent of the owners, who at once began development work.

A steam hoist undoubtedly was installed to lift the coal up an incline or shaft, dropped down the dip or pitch of the seam. Operations must have been sketchy and wasteful. For several years production remained low. Then in 1859, the dissatisfied stockholders of the Bellingham Bay Coal Company, meeting in San Francisco, voted to raise and expend $100,000 in the sinking of an adequate incline or slope on the vein; and in the construction of a wharf, coal bunkers, and a tramway from the slope to the bunkers. Fitzhugh remained as resident agent, but the actual construction work was done under the supervision of one Tompkins, an experienced coal man from Pennsylvania.

With the reconstruction work complete, stockholders of the company voted to lease the property for a five year period to two of their number—Sinclair and Moody, each an experienced coal man.

---

*Captain Fauntleroy was master of the United States Steamer *Massachusetts*, used in 1853 as a supply ship during preliminary surveys.

Moody remained on Bellingham Bay in charge of operations while Sinclair became the partnership's San Francisco representative. In order to save on freight bills and to keep their bunkers emptied, one of the first steps of the lessees was to purchase three ocean-going freighters, the *Lookout*, Captain Ackerson (later lost at sea with all on board), the *Amethyst*, Captain S. P. Bates and Captain Hatfield; the *Germania*, pride of the fleet, Captain J. W. Baker.

According to Edward Eldridge, the lessees, Sinclair and Moody, developed the coal property by first dropping an incline for several hundred feet down the dip of the coal seam. This was crosscut at various levels (the first at 100 feet), by lateral tunnels or galleries. Each gallery was given just enough gradient to permit water to flow toward the main slope and for easy movement of loaded coal cars. A series of sixty foot rooms were opened parallel to and just above each gallery. To support the roof, twenty-foot walls of coal were left along the main slope and between each sixty-foot room. A ten foot wall was allowed to stand just above each gallery and below the sixty-foot rooms. In mining operations, the workers dropped their waste against this lower wall while chutting the coal down to the corners, where gallery openings permitted the loading of the coal cars.

Operation plans called for the operation of coal cars, and horse or mule power both above and below ground. Captain James W. Tarte, who in 1869, as a young man, was head teamster for the mine, has written that the company at that time, maintained a stable of four horses and eight mules. Three mules were used constantly below ground while one mule and three horses moved the string of coal cars from hoist to coal chutes. Each string or train consisted of from seven to nine cars of one and one-half tons capacity. Nine trips per day were made when the mine was in full operation. (Opposite page 183).

The first year Sinclair and Moody operated their lease, they reportedly grossed $300,000. More money was in circulation around the Bay than in any other part of the Territory, for men were paid in gold and silver—a practice that was continued even after greenbacks became legal tender and flooded the country.

THE UNION COAL COMPANY

The success of these lessees caused Charles Richards to decide on coal mining as a possible means of recouping his losses on the "brick" building. Knowing that the coal seams on the Pattle and Morrison Donation Claims had not been fairly tested, and wishing to remain unknown in the transaction, he engaged Seth N. Doty to make the deal. Morrison sold his claim to Doty for $3,000, and thereafter on March 2, 1861, according to county records, Doty conveyed a three-fourths interest in the property to Charles E. Richards for $3,750.

The Union Coal Company was next organized with Richards as president. The sum of $40,000 was then raised by the company and expended in opening the mine and in constructing a wharf, store-house, and other buildings. A small community known as Unionville came into being on the coal property adjacent to the Pattle claim, between Fairhaven and Sehome. The seam of the Union Coal Company mine was opened by a 100 foot shaft, (probably an incline). The vein worked was but two feet thick, although thicker beds occurred on the claim. About 2,500 tons of coal were shipped to San Francisco, when the work stopped, never to be resumed.

COAL MINE ON FIRE

Much sulphur occurred in the coal of the Bellingham Bay Coal Mine—Sehome; a constant threat of spontaneous combustion, should moisture reach the mass. This happened on the waste dump, where an evil smelling fire burned for years—a fire useful to mariners making landfall. In the mine the danger increased with the approach of the workings to the surface and with the greater flow of seepage. On one occasion Moody's brother prevented an underground conflagration by hurriedly removing a mass of waste in one chamber just before the debris burst into flame.

When they saw the success Sinclair and Moody were making during their first years of operation, some of the stockholders of the Bellingham Bay Coal Company regretted giving the lease and sought to regain control of the property. The lessees, realizing the increasing threat of fire, wisely sold the balance of their lease back to the company. Then began a series of fires and floods. Incompetent managers and superintendents, untrained labor, petty jealousies, internal dissension, further hampered the mine operations.

In 1863, Michael Padden,* superintendent of the Talbot Coal Mine at Talbot—Renton—former Pennsylvania coal miner, was hired to operate the Bellingham Bay Coal Mine, at Sehome.

Mrs. Nellie Coupe, pioneer school teacher has reported:

"The opening to the mine was on the beach . . . Later the shaft was sunk up on the bluff. During my memorable visit to Whatcom in 1868 with John Roeder, I went down into the mine 500 feet deep, and 500 feet out under the Bay. For some time the old mine was worked to advantage. Then it caught fire and they were obliged to flood it with water. It cost enormously

*When the Sehome mine closed, Michael Padden homesteaded in Happy Valley. He discovered and named Lake Padden. In 1880, a neighbor shot and killed him following a disagreement over a line fence.

to pump it dry. This occurred several times, the fire, the flooding, and the subsequent pumping. The expense was too great, so the mine was shut down and abandoned."

Working in a mine as gas filled, as the chambers and galleries of the Sehome property undoubtedly were, must have been a severe strain on human flesh. B. H. Bruns, later of Birch Bay, entered the mine with his friend, Newhouse, and brother-in-law, Priester, on May 21, 1870. Priester's diary of that date reads:

"May 21, 1870—Mr. Meyers took us through the coal mines. Changed our clothes to overalls and shirts, and with lamp in hand went through the tunnel. Very close with gas, and blasting sounded loud and terrible. We were ready to get out. Headed for steps. Got up our nerve again and tried another tunnel. Went down 700 feet, found lots of gas. Went on to 900 feet and stayed half an hour. The new mines in operation have an underground train. Came out in a carriage driven by steam. Was good to see the top again and get fresh air."

Another interesting picture of the mine operations is found in the following extracts from the diary of Sheriff James Kavanaugh:

"Bellingham Bay, May 23, 1863—A fire broke out today in the coal mine in this place and several persons injured, some very seriously.

"June 23, 1863—Mr. Lovejoy came in this evening with his sloop from Victoria via Port Townsend. He brings five coal miners who came to dig out the coal, the fire and want of air to the contrary notwithstanding. Although this is a small, quiet, dull place it appears to be extensively known. I begin to think that no matter how bad miners are treated here (and they are used very ill under the governorship of Bill Moody) that there will always be a sufficient supply of that material on hand. Indeed their comings and goings remind me very forceably of an endless chain pump. English and Welsh largely predominate. They are very dissipated and ignorant.

"August 28, 1863—C. E. Richards has sold the remains of everything in his store. Barrington carries everything away in his schooner this evening. Morrison comes from San Juan and will prevent if possible the tearing down of the houses and the taking away of the engine. (Richard's store and coal mine at Unionville.)

"October 28, 1863—Removed my residence to Unionville.

"April 9, 1866—Sinclair and Moody have sold out their interest in the Bellingham Bay Coal Mine.

"August 8, 1866—Came to Sehome with the intentions of working the coal mines.

"August 9, 1866—Coal mine on fire.

"August 15, 1866—Did my first day's work below in the mine at loading—find it very hard and disagreeable sort of work.

"August 16, 1866—Worked today on the chute. Chinaman killed on the railroad bridge on the fourteenth.

"October 26, 1866—Fire in the coal mine, can't be put out in the ordinary way in such cases. It is smothered-up for a few days in order to get out a shipment of coal after which the waters of the Bay will be let in. In the meantime I am at work below since the twentieth.

"November 29, 1866—The salt water will be let into the mine this evening. Engineer Harris has just left. I have watched the engine for the past three nights.

"July 8, 1867—Dominick Padden killed in the coal mine.

"February 29, 1868—(Living at Fidalgo Island) Came back from Whatcom. Coal mines again inundated with salt water to put out the fires in the upper gangway."

When in full operation, the mine at Sehome required a force of 100 men. Most of these were transients. Some forty Chinese were required to work on the chutes and in cleaning the coal. According to Captain Tarte, the company kept a force of sixty Chinese at the mine, because they were generally unreliable and could not be depended upon to report for work every day, preferring to sit up all night gambling.

In January, 1875, sailing of the *Germania* was delayed because the Chinese refused to handle coal in weather five degrees below zero—so cold that ice formed on the Nooksack River. A month later, work was at a standstill while the Celestials celebrated one of their religious festivals with displays of banners, flags, and sky-rockets. Again operations were halted so they might go through the ceremony of feeding their dead. Roast pig, chicken, and other delicacies were placed on the graves. Tapers were lighted to the spirits of the departed. Then the Chinese returned—to their cabins—not to the bunkers.

In March, 1875, the company sank a new shaft near the present site of the Chicago, Milwaukee Railroad roundhouse between Laurel and Myrtle Streets on Railroad Avenue. Coal was struck at a depth of seventy-seven feet, being of the same quality as in other workings. A tunnel extended northeast under the present Railroad Avenue, and this was responsible for much trouble in later years through the settling of streets and buildings in the business district. It was not until 1888, when P. B. Cornwall, president of the Bellingham Bay Coal Company, with a gang of twenty men, finally filled the cavein at the corner of Holly Street and Railroad Avenue, that this trouble ended. Nevertheless, Craft's Shoe Store, "The Famous," which stood for so many years on this spot, had trouble with wavy floor and unstable foundations.

THE COAL MINE CLOSES IN 1878

Improvement in the surface workings was made in 1875, but accidents and hardships dogged the company through that year. Finally a new gangway 150 feet above the flooded part of the mine was opened and the lower levels abandoned.

Production and quality of the coal was improved through 1876, but continued prospecting by the company made the settlers feel that all was not well.

The next year, President P. B. Cornwall arrived from San Francisco with Geologist W. A. Goodyear and B. B. Jones, a coal mine expert. Evidently their reports on the mine were not favorable. Goodyear returned in September, after which the mine took a "two weeks'" holiday. In December, came the report that the mine was closed indefinitely. The bunkers held 4,000 tons or more of coal and this kept one steamer busy for some time. In January, 1878, the company held a closing out sale of everything but real estate; and the following month the *Amethyst* sailed out of the harbor with the last of the coal and the salvaged machinery, iron, lumber, and other junk.

Five families alone remained on the Sehome side after the mine closing. All told, there were no more than a dozen families around the Bay. In commenting on the closing of the mine, Edward Eldridge said: "Then followed the gloomiest period that Bellingham Bay had seen from its first settlement by whites. The sawmill that was built at Whatcom in 1853, was burned down in 1873, and had not been rebuilt, and when work stopped at the mine, there was nothing going on in Bellingham Bay whereby a laborer or mechanic could earn a dollar, and for a short time the Bay was virtually deserted by all except the settlers on the donation claims; and the population, that in 1858 exceeded 10,000, in 1879-1880, dwindled to about twenty persons. I remember one day in 1880, going from my home at Squalicum Creek to Dan Harris', now Fairhaven, and returned without seeing a human being either way."

The closing of the mine, likewise, was a tragedy for the settlers on the islands and in the back country. Heretofore, they had been able to dispose of their produce and services for cash, since the miners were paid in hard money. Now their market was closed.

The Gold Rush of 1858 had caused a demand for the surveys of land around Bellingham Bay and north. As soon as the Willamette Meridian could be extended to this latitude, Surveyor General Tilton gave a contract for the surveying of all fractional townships on the waterfront from Chuckanut Bay to the Canadian Border. The rush of gold seekers ebbed, and there was no demand for the acreage. Over the years the Coal Company acquired large tracts of this land at $1.25 per acre, payable in greenbacks when these were worth only fifty cents on the dollar. Much of this property was purchased with the belief that it was underlain with coal. The closing of the mine, therefore, found the Company possessed of 3,000 acres of timbered land. These lands later, were the nucleus of the holdings, sold and administered during boom days and later by the Bellingham Bay Improvement Company of which P. B. Cornwall was president.

In December, 1888, the Cornwall interests acquired 880 acres of land north of Squalicum creek, at ten dollars per acre. Prospecting with a diamond drill was begun three years later. In the tenth hole, sunk September 1892, a fifteen and one-half foot coal seam was encountered at a depth of 410 feet. Although tested by five more holes, no development work was undertaken on this property prior to 1900.

This coal bed now mined by the Bellingham Coal Mines is considered part of the same coal measures as the old Sehome Mine. Like the latter, it uses a slope or incline in following the coal seam, and is headed seaward. Present operations reportedly are 1,500 feet north of the Bay, with the tunnels 1,200 feet below sea level. Daily, 150,000 gallons of water are pumped from this mine, which is the deepest coal mine in the United States.

BLUE CANYON COAL MINE

Before the coal mine was abandoned at Sehome, the existence of coal outcroppings on the shores of Lake Whatcom was common knowledge. No important development work was done prior to the acquisition of some of the prospects, and to the organization of the Blue Canyon Coal Company by James F. Wardner, J. H. Bloedel, and others. This was in 1890. Wardner, who was to acquire a fortune at the Wardner, Idaho, mines, was a real estate plunger, banker, financier, lumberman. He was in the public eye because of his Wardner Castle—(Hilltop House today)—erected at Fairhaven; also because of his reported black cat fur farm to be started at Eliza Island.

Development work on the Blue Canyon seam, situated near the upper end of Lake Whatcom, called for barges to Silver Beach, and wagon transportation thence to Bellingham Bay. A railroad was to follow. With much fanfare J. H. Bloedel moved the first two four-horse wagon loads of coal to New Whatcom in March, 1891.

Further development work reportedly disclosed a twenty-two foot coal seam that pitched into the hill at a twenty-two degree angle. The Blue Canyon coal measures lay about 800 feet above the lake level. Construction of an 800 foot trestle and 400 feet of track provided gravity transportation to the coal barges on the lake.

Late in 1891, Montana capitalists headed by Peter Larson acquired

Wardner's interest in the mine. Under the management of J. J. Donovan, connection was made from Lake Whatcom to the street car system, bunkers were erected, and the first rail shipment of Blue Canyon coal reached tidewater in July, 1892.

Quality of the fuel was such that the Navy and the Coast Guard contracted for it, but numerous faults and swelling rock formations made operations costly. New development work was required frequently.

A mine explosion in 1895 killed twenty-three persons. At that time the first coal seam had "run out," and a new vein at lower level and closer to the Lake shore had been developed.

In later years J. J. Donovan reported that the company had spent $500,000 in the development of the Blue Canyon, "but it was not yet a mine." The owners accordingly abandoned the project in favor of lumbering.

Others unsuccessfully tried operating the mine. For some years Andrew Ecklund dug coal on a royalty basis. The property was abandoned in 1920.

FAIRHAVEN COAL MINE

The Fairhaven Coal mine, at Cokedale in Skagit county, a Larrabee property, and one goal of the Fairhaven and Southern Railroad, began operating in 1891. Work continued for several years. At one time, it supplied fuel for the Northern Pacific Railroad. When the mine was at full capacity, Superintendent Richard Jennings employed thirty men and operated four coke ovens.

J. H. BLOEDEL

J. H. Bloedel, who, as some one has said, used a coal mine for a vaulting pole, to land as a lumber magnate, was born March 4, 1864, at Fond du Lac, Wisconsin.

Stories are told of his early business astuteness and enterprise; of how he gave riding lessons on his high wheel bicycle, or became agent for the wheels. He entered the University of Michigan in 1881; worked on railroad construction; then became a real estate dealer.

When the western fever struck, he visited Puget Sound in 1889; met J. J. Donovan at Fairhaven; and the next year moved to that boom town. Soon he became manager of the Samish Lake Logging Company controlled by J. F. Wardner, who reportedly, had made $60,000 in Fairhaven real estate in sixty days.

In 1890, J. H. Bloedel also helped organize the Fairhaven National Bank, which he served in turn as director, vice president, and president.

While the bank survived the panic of 1893, and the depositors were paid in full, the stockholders lost their entire investments.

Wardner and Bloedel acquired the Blue Canyon Coal Mine in 1890. In 1891, Wardner, who was to amass a great fortune in the lead-silver mines of Idaho, sold his interests in the Blue Canyon to the "Helena" or "Montana" syndicate headed by Peter Larson.

Under the new management, with J. J. Donovan as engineer the coal mine was developed, and a railroad constructed to carry the fuel from Lake Whatcom to the Bellingham Bay bunkers. Several stories are told of the courage and resourcefulness of J. H. Bloedel when the coal seam pinched out, or during hard times when there was no market for coal. At one time, he exchanged a train load of fuel for merchandise, that in turn, was traded to another merchant for food and clothing needed by his employees.

In October, 1898, J. H. Bloedel and Miss Mina Prentice of Saginaw, Michigan were married in the town of Fairhaven.

Meantime, the coal mine, being unprofitable, Larson, Bloedel, and Donovan were utilizing the Bellingham Bay and Eastern Railroad to haul saw logs from Lake Whatcom. This led naturally to the organization of the Lake Whatcom Logging Company, August 11, 1898; capital $6,000, of sixty shares; par value $100 each. Peter Larson, J. H. Bloedel, and J. J. Donovan, the incorporators, purchased standing timber near the lake shore, put their crews into the woods, and began marketing their own logs.

Next, in 1901, the Larson sawmill was constructed on Lake Whatcom to mill the Company's own timber. A second mill was completed in 1906. Peter Larson died the following year. In 1913, the company acquired the Bellingham Bay Lumber Mill, known as the Cornwall mill, in Bellingham, and holdings were consolidated in Bloedel Donovan Lumber Mills. The corporation showed assets of $3,889,875. In fifteen years, therefore, the sixty shares of the Lake Whatcom Logging Company had grown from $100, to $50,000 each.

Prior to this, or in 1911, the anticipated scarcity of timber in Washington State caused J. H. Bloedel to organize Bloedel, Stewart & Welch, Ltd., a corporation that entered the lumbering field in British Columbia.

Through the first World War, J. H. Bloedel served as a "dollar-a-year-man" in charge of the Fir Production Board, under Bernard Baruch, the head of the War Industries Board. He freed car loading and distribution blocks, and soon entire trains of lumber were rolling to the shipyards and cantonments.

Over the years, Bloedel Donovan Lumber Mills acquired and lumbered great tracts of timber in the Lake Whatcom, Skykomish, Nooksack, and

Clallam County areas. With timber reserves, much depleted, Bloedel Donovan holdings were liquidated in 1945 and 1946. The "Cargo Mill" site on Bellingham Bay was sold to the Port of Bellingham in 1947 for $75,000.

Fifty years after the founding of the Lake Whatcom Logging Company or on August 11, 1948, in the name of J. H. Bloedel and Mina Prentice Bloedel, the Bloedel Donovan Park, on the shores of Lake Whatcom, was dedicated to the City of Bellingham. The sum of $150,000 was set aside by the donors for its operation. This twelve and one-half acre park tract was first used in 1891 as terminal for the Blue Canyon Coal scows; and later by the Whatcom Logging Company, and by the Larson Lumber Company.

On the bottom of the plaque, affixed to the principal park building are the words, "Lest We Forget." In his dedicatory speech, J. H. Bloedel explained that these words were intended to remind the citizens of the value of free enterprise. Most appropriate! Who should know better? For as friends in the audience explained, the speaker was the man who had parlayed a bet on a coal mine, into a coal road, a logging road, a saw mill, and a lumber empire.

Chapter XXI.

THE STEAMER ELIZA ANDERSON

1858 — 1897

EARLY ONE MORNING, in the month of May, 1890, a small boy and girl aboard the *Eliza Anderson*, very excitedly watched her being warped up to the Sehome wharf at Bellingham Bay.

Their father had come to Whatcom the year before. Now—just the preceding day, he had boarded the Northern Pacific train at Puyallup, to meet his family and escort them North.

The train trip ended in Tacoma. Then a wait in the parlor of a hotel until sailing time of the *City of Kingston* for Seattle. The boy and girl amused themselves in the parlor, by sliding off the horsehair-covered chairs and sofa. The steamer was finally boarded—such gorgeousness!—in their eyes—the bright red plush covered seats and benches, especially the "ring-around-the-rosy" circular seat enclosing the big smoke-stack. As the children's father strode up the gangplank carrying the great rectangular tin-lunch-box, that had served the family on the overland trip, a hasp slipped free. Dishes, lunch cloths, and edibles plunged into the Bay, while gulls screamed and shrilled-voiced newsboys shouted about "food coming down."

Another wait in Seattle—in the parlor of another hotel—until sailing time for Bellingham Bay. Here the boy and girl amused themselves by trying out the water system they had discovered in a bath room—something they had never seen before.

That evening the old *Eliza Anderson* was boarded. The steamer was resting very low in the water, loaded with cattle and freight below deck, and with more passengers above than could find seats—to say nothing of sleeping quarters. The children's grandmother, aunts, uncle and parents sat up through the long night, while the ship chugged and rolled up the Coast from Seattle to Bellingham Bay. On account of her overload, the *"Lize" Anderson* took the outside passage, instead of the inside—through Deception Pass. The boy and girl and baby brother were put to bed in blankets spread on the zinc floor, (no such splendor here as on the *City of Kingston*). The roar of the big side-wheels, as they revolved, stepping along through the water, soon put them to sleep. The next morning found them watching the *Eliza Anderson* being tied up to the Sehome dock. This was

197

the author's childhood introduction to the famous old vessel.

Among early settlers along the Mississippi River, the steamboat captain was regarded as a really big man; his boat a most important economic force; its arrival a social and mercantile event. And so it was in Puget Sound and British Columbia waters.

Railways and passable roads were slow in arriving, particularly in the Olympic Peninsula and along the upper Sound and Gulf of Georgia shores. Therefore the residents made it their business to know the captain and the crew; their ability to bring the vessel through the island maze in darkness, fog, and storm. They knew the master's skill in navigating by means of echoes of his whistle-blast, hurled back through the night from hidden shores. Likewise these dwellers along tidewaters knew each boat, its capacity, its capability, and its personality—for boats have personality, according to all "salts."

Of the vessels important in Northwest chronicles—sloops, schooners, brigs, steamboats, and steamships; none had a longer or more colorful history than did the *Eliza Anderson*. None crushed competition more ruthlessly. None made more money for its owners than did this side-wheeler. For the *Eliza Anderson* came on the stage at the height of one gold rush, not to bow off the scene for thirty-eight years until wrecked in hostile waters during an even greater gold stampede.

Built by Samuel Farnam at Portland, Oregon, for the Columbia River Navigation Company, this steamer was launched November 27, 1858. Her trial trip took place January 2, 1859. The last word in steamers of that day, she was a side-wheeler, 140 feet long, of 279 tons registry, and was driven by a low pressure walking-beam engine. Although capable of 12 knots per hour, she customarily ran at about 9. A wood-burner* originally, she was converted to coal in later years. (Opposite page 199).

John T. Wright and the Bradford Brothers purchased the *Anderson*

---

*One of the early wood contracts made by the *Anderson* was with the Territorial University in Seattle which had reopened with sixty pupils as a private school, in October, 1862. According to Roberta Frye Watt in STORY OF SEATTLE the University supplied the *Anderson* with wood at $2.50 per cord. Students cut the fuel from land in front of the old downtown university site, being paid $1.50 per cord for their labors.

Whatcom, Washington Territory, 1873. Extreme left, remains of the E street wharf built in 1858; long white structure to the left of the wharf is the Northern Light building, erected in 1858 and used in 1859 for a private school; in the '60's it housed the pioneer county fair; in 1878 it was the scene of the first county teachers' institute under County Superintendent John Tennant. Across the street is the first brick building erected in Washington Territory in 1858 and standing today—1951. In the left center of the picture on Peabody Hill, the roof of the Pickett House is visible through the trees on Bancroft street. To the right is Division street, running parallel to the faces of the buildings. Upper houses are along D street.—Photo courtesy Bellingham Herald.

from the Navigation Company and sent her to Puget Sound under Captain J. G. Husted. There Captain John Fleming took command and fixed fares and rates about as high as the traffic would bear. Thus the fare from Olympia to Seattle was $6.50; to Port Townsend, $12.50; to Victoria, $20.00. Freight rates ranged from $5.00 to $10.00 per ton, by measurement, not weight. A box of feathers cost as much to move as the same box filled with iron. A wagon, if not knocked down, was measured from rear wheels to tip of the tongue. Horses and cattle were carried for $15.00 per head. Sheep and hogs were moved at $2.50 each.

The *Eliza Anderson* reached the Sound in time to skim some of the cream from the Fraser River Gold Rush. After trying her side wheels against the swift waters of the river, she went on the run from Victoria to the lower reaches of the stream, where cargo was transhipped to stern-wheelers. A side-wheeler, it was found, could navigate rough open waters while a stern-wheeler, trying to ride heavy swells would find its wheel revolving in empty air, with engines racing and wracking the craft.*

On May 3, 1862, reporting the boom in the Cariboo country, the WASHINGTON STANDARD stated: "Steamer *Eliza Anderson* takes up run from Olympia to Cariboo mines." The Cariboo strike, following the lower Fraser River gold discoveries, furnished the *Anderson* with a continuing and profitable haul to the mouth of the stream. Mail contracts to various Sound ports added to the fat income from freight and passengers.

Profits made by this steamer were the envy of other boat owners. Some of the rash ones would underbid the side-wheeler on mail contracts. Thereupon the *Eliza's* owners would start a rate war, carrying freight and passengers for almost nothing until the interlopers were bankrupt. The *Anderson's* owners then would buy the other boat, put it on another Sound run or ship it to the Columbia or Sacramento rivers. Two of the many vanquished boats were the *Wilson G. Hunt* and the *Enterprise*.

Because this cut-throat competition was so costly the Starrs who obtained the mail contract in 1872, bought off the *Eliza Anderson's* owners

---

*At the time of the Klondike rush, thirty-nine years later, an attempt was made again to put stern-wheelers on salt water runs. The SCIENTIFIC AMERICAN of October, 1898, stated that an average of five out of eight stern-wheelers that tried open water were wrecked or disabled.

UPPER RIGHT—Charles Donovan—picture taken in 1914 in Dublin by the King's photographer.—
Photo courtesy of his daughter, Mrs. Mabel Donovan Bacon.

UPPER LEFT—Trees were originally cut leaving stumps ten and twelve feet in height, which were cut later into shingle bolts. Hop vines are overrunning this stump. The small boy is Harold Dakin.—Photo by the author in 1901.

LOWER—The side-wheeler, "Eliza Anderson."

for $18,000 per year. Thereafter, for four years, the steamer was tied up at a dock in Olympia. The *Anderson's* agent, John B. Allen, later U. S. Senator collected $1,500 per month and deposited it to the credit of the boat's master, Captain Finch.

In 1882, the *Anderson* sprang a leak and sank at a Seattle wharf. On being raised and refitted, it was found that her timbers were sound. This fact, thereafter was used as an argument for the use of fir timber in ship construction.

Captain Tom Wright was the next owner. This colorful mariner put the vessel on the Seattle-Westminster run, but fell afoul of the law in 1855 when the craft was seized on the charge of smuggling Chinese across the Border. The delays and expense of the trial put Captain Tom and the *Eliza* out of business.

In 1886 the Wright Brothers and Captain Finch sold the side-wheeler to the Washington Steamboat Company.

Through the boom days the *Eliza Anderson* was welcomed everywhere as an old, if provoking, acquaintance. Her record as a training school for pilots and captains was nearly as remarkable as that of her earnings. Captain James W. Tarte was mate and pilot with Captain Tom Wright on the New Westminster run, and afterwards established the route from Seattle to Port Moody, British Columbia. Among others, Captain John (Red Jacks) Elmore—so called because of his red hair, was master on the Seattle, Bellingham Bay, Blaine run at one time. George A. Jenkins, a Whatcom County pioneer, served on the steamer in various capacities. Orion O. Denny, son of Arthur A. Denny of Seattle served as an engineer in the '80's.

An item in the BELLINGHAM BAY EXPRESS, June 14, 1890 reads:

"A horse jumped overboard off the *Eliza Anderson* this morning as she was lying at the Whatcom wharf. The animal at once started to swim ashore, while a boat was lowered and started in pursuit, coming up with it among the piles on the flat. The horse was captured and led ashore none the worse for the swim."

Next the Puget Sound and Alaska Steamship Company became owners of the *Eliza Anderson*. In idle decrepitude the old vessel swung at the Company moorings that June afternoon of 1897, when the *Portland* carrying $800,000, in placer gold, steamed into Seattle harbor, and the electrifying cry, "Gold in the Klondike," swept the continent. Immediately the *Eliza* and almost all other bottoms that would float were fitted to carry the army of frenzied stampeders.

The Yukon route was selected by the promoters of the *Eliza Anderson* expedition. But the side-wheeler was of deep draft and unsuitable for the 1,700 mile journey up that great river to Dawson. Accordingly the shallow, flat-bottomed, Skagit River stern-wheeler, the *W. K. Merwin*, 102 feet overall, 22 feet beam, and 4 foot draft, Captain Lyle Master, was secured to transport passengers from St. Michael to the Klondike. Her wheel and stack were removed and lashed above her ballast cargo of canned goods. To protect her from the crushing Pacific seas, she was covered from stem to stern with a strongly fashioned wooden box, beneath which her sixteen passengers were imprisoned as under a coffin lid.

On the voyage to the Bering Sea, the *Anderson* would need to be coaled several times. Therefore the former Russian Man-of-War, *Politofsky*, was purchased. This one time four-gun ship, built at Sitka in 1866, when she was fitted with shining hand-mined, hand-fashioned copper boilers and pipes, was pulled from the beach sands of Port Blakely and converted to a collier.

The deep-sea tug, *Richard Holyoke*, Captain Harper, was engaged to handle the tow, to which was added the pleasure yacht *Bryant*, of Seattle, with four passengers. This vessel also was battened down, masts and rigging stowed above the cargo of canned goods, and all lashed securely under a heavy tarpaulin.

As the sailing date approached, the clamor of wildeyed stampeders for passage increased. Large bonuses were offered for tickets. There were fights over berths that had been sold twice. Incensed miners tried to throw the purser overboard. Mostly the passengers slept on the floor of the dining room or social hall.

A motley lot, these argonauts—from every social level and occupation —a few competents included with the inept—all ignorant of the life ahead. And the cargo offered by the stampeders was just as motley, weird and fantastic. Much of it was useless equipment foisted on the ignorant chee-chakos by the unscrupulous outfitters.

According to Thomas Wiedemann, Senior, a member of the historic *Eliza Anderson* expedition (ALASKA LIFE, March, 1947), the old vessel left Seattle, August 10, 1897, with 116 gold seekers aboard. She was preceded out of Elliott Bay by the tug *Richard Holyoke* and her strange tow—the *Politofsky*, the *Merwin*, and the *Bryant*.

After several accidents and delays the *Anderson* reached Kodiak, and there coaled for the last time from the *Politofsky*. Five of the passengers abandoned the voyage at Kodiak.

In the face of storm warnings the flotilla pushed to sea to encounter equinoctial gales. For many hours Captain Powers used oil to flatten the waves; resorted to a sea anchor. All of his lifeboats but one were smashed. Flares and rockets calling for aid from the *Holyoke* were perforce ignored. That vessel was making an heroic fight to get a line to the helpless *Merwin* and save the craft after the towing hawser had parted. Then the convoy disappeared in the spume.

The *Eliza Anderson* ran out of fuel after battling the storm for more than sixty hours. Desperately struggling to keep off the murderous lee shore—to keep his wheels turning, Captain Powers ordered the wooden bulkheads of the coal bunkers torn out for fuel. Later portions of the social hall, partitions of the dining salon and some of the staterooms were fed to the hungry firebox.

With steam low, miraculously it seemed to the hopeless passengers, the battered *Eliza* staggered into a sheltered cove of the iron bound coast. There an abandoned salmon cannery was found together with several tons of coal. Much of the cannery lumber was torn down and cut into firewood; then loaded on the steamer together with the coal.

After the storm the voyage was continued. Unalaska was reached just as the fuel again was exhausted. With pressure down and little steerage way, a gust of wind crashed the *Eliza Anderson* into the dock, further damaging her.

No coal was available. The convoy, reporting that the *Anderson* had been lost with all on board, had gone on to St. Michael the week before. The frustrated Captain Powers declared he would take the side-wheeler on to the Yukon mouth, despite Hell and Highwater, if they would give him coal. Both the Alaska Commercial Company and the U. S. Revenue Cutter Service refused his request because of their own needs.

Calling crew and passengers of the *Eliza* "Landlubbers," Captain Powers reluctantly agreed to the chartering of the 57-ton schooner, *Baranoff*, Captain Johnson, Master, for the last leg of the St. Michael voyage, while he remained with his steamer. According to John Quincy Barnum, one of the passengers, the latter raised $1,000, while Captain Powers put up the remaining $500 of the charter price.

Wiedemann has written that twenty-eight of the *Eliza Anderson's* passengers quit the expedition at Unalaska to return south. Barnum has reported that the *Baranoff* carried 107 persons on the voyage to St. Michael. This would include, of course, most of the crew members of the *Anderson*. There was little more than standing room on the *Baranoff* and since it was a wet ship, much hardship resulted. The schooner had no dining salon so meals were served on the deck, where, frequently, dishes and food were swept overboard by the waves. Adverse winds drove the vessel in sight of the Siberian coast, where a Russian vessel fired a warning shot. Hence several days elapsed before the *Baranoff* sighted the convoy at St. Michael.

There the *Anderson* crowd found the *Merwin* with coffin box removed, wheel and stack in place, and steam up, ready for the Yukon voyage. Great was the excitement, when the stampeders, given up as dead, pulled into the anchorage. Wiedemann had written that all of the passengers elected to continue upriver. Barnum, however, has stated that the turmoil at St. Michael, and adverse reports from the Klondike, so affected the miserable and soaked passengers that several of them, including himself, returned to Seattle on the first boat, the *Sailor Boy*.

It was October. The *W. K. Merwin* started for the Klondike, but was caught by the freeze-up a hundred miles from the mouth of the Yukon. Thus the *Eliza Anderson* crowd did not reach Dawson until late in July, 1898, almost a year after leaving Seattle. Two years later the steamer *Merwin* was blown ashore and wrecked near the mouth of the Yukon. The coal barge, *Politofsky,* met the same fate the first winter in the north. That first winter also, the storms put the *Eliza Anderson* on the rocks at Unalaska. There her machinery was salvaged.

Under date of 1899, the NEW WHATCOM DAILY REVEILLE reported that the sturdy *Anderson* had not broken up yet. A Seattle reporter who visited her stated that her tough timbers were resisting the northern storms, although the tides sloshed through her hull as she lay "sore and weak upon the beach rocks." Also he found that "people who write in public places," had lined her cabin wall and ladies' room with names and comments done in pencil or old paint dregs.

According to C. T. Conover writing in the SEATTLE TIMES of August 9, 1948, the remains of the sturdy old *Eliza Anderson* still reposed near Dutch Harbor more than fifty years after the wreck.

To the last the *Eliza Anderson* kept clear her record of never having lost a passenger. Like the old frontiersmen, who elected to die with their boots on, she went out in full stride, in one last burst of heroic effort. Thus she was spared the ignominy of rotting away at some Seattle boneyard.

Chapter XXII.

THE KANSAS — OR WASHINGTON COLONY

ONE OF THE TRAGEDIES in the story of Whatcom—the failure of grandiose plans for a great mercantile and industrial metropolis on Bellingham shores, is brought to light in the history of the Kansas or Washington Colony.

It is a story that had its beginnings in the poor judgment of two founding fathers—Captain Henry Roeder and Russell V. Peabody who complicated townsite matters by conveying to each other a one-third interest in their respective donation claims. Had Peabody lived all would have been well.

The story reaches its climax at a time when the prospects for a transcontinental railroad were bright; when eastern and western capitalists were eager to invest; when immigrants were clamoring to buy lots—only to be defeated by the short sighted covetousness of the various Peabody heirs; their rival claims and lawsuits; and by downright violence. In the end the bubble burst leaving the oldsters with little more than the melancholy thought, "It might have been."

The period from the closing of the Sehome mine in 1878 to the coming of the Kansas, or Washington Colony in 1881, was one of the blackest endured by the settlers of the Northwest. Previously the mill had burned and the newspaper had moved to LaConner. From Fort Bellingham around the Bay to Poe's Point there were perhaps no more than twenty white persons left. These comprised the donation claim owners and the few individuals connected with the meager business of Whatcom as the County Seat.

However, new hope blossomed in the spring of 1881 when Captain Roeder learned from an old newspaper that a colony had been organized in Kansas with the intention of locating somewhere on Puget Sound. Hurriedly he communicated with the president of the organization—General Marquis Alexander McPherson, who had received his honorary rank as member of some governor's staff.

McPherson came west and an agreement was outlined whereby the townsite owners were to give the Colony a millsite on Whatcom creek and a one-half interest in the lots or land of the townsite. In return the Colony was to construct a sawmill, build a wharf out to deep water; erect a church and fifty dwellings; and to bring not less than 100 families to Whatcom.

During the interviews the visitor gave the impression to Roeder, Utter and Eldridge that the proposed Colony was fully able to carry out its part of the agreement. The townsite owners' part of the agreement was more in doubt. Unfortunately a large portion of the Whatcom townsite was owned by the Peabody heirs in Wisconsin. Captain Roeder promptly telegraphed these heirs outlining the proposition, and asking their consent to complete the negotiations. The reply directed Roeder to proceed with the tentative plans, and stated the Peabody heirs would agree to whatever he deemed best. Thereupon a preliminary agreement was made and McPherson hurried back to Kansas, little dreaming how the Colony would be throttled in a maze of tangled titles. Perhaps Captain Roeder himself should not have been so sanguine, having been involved previously with an earlier administrator of the Peabody estate.

Originally Captain Henry Roeder and Russell V. Peabody each staked a donation claim and a homestead. Each conveyed a one-third interest in his donation claim to the other. Peabody died at Indian Wells, California, in August, 1868, leaving his donation claim to his brother, John E. Peabody. Russell Peabody also left, in Whatcom, two half-Indian children, who had a natural interest with other heirs, not in the donation claim, but in his homestead. In turn, John E. Peabody, the brother, died of typhoid fever at San Francisco, in October, 1873, leaving his right in the donation claim to the three Peabody sisters—two of them married to the Pettibone Brothers and one of them to H. B. Williams, all residents of the Midwest.

Following the death of John E. Peabody, Major Granville O. Haller* of

---

*Granville O. Haller, soldier and pioneer was born at York, Pennsylvania, January 31, 1819. He served through the Seminole War in Florida in 1841-'42, and under General Taylor in the Mexican War in '46. He fought in every battle up to the capture of the City of Mexico. Haller was breveted captain and then major for gallant and meritorious conduct on the field.

In 1853 Major Haller was sent to Washington Territory; later to Fort Dalles, Oregon, and during the Indian War fought many engagements. He established and built Fort Townsend in Puget Sound in 1857 and participated in the San Juan embroglio in 1859. In 1860 he was assigned to the command of the military post of Fort Mojave, Arizona; in early 1861 was ordered to San Diego, California, then on to New York to join the army then being organized by General McClellan. Here he was promoted commandant of the general headquarters on General McClellan's staff, and the 93rd New York Volunteers were placed under his command as general headquarters guard.

Major Haller returned to Puget Sound in 1863. In 1879 he returned to the regular army as colonel of the 23rd Infantry and served with his regiment until his retirement. He died in Seattle, May 2, 1897. (From the NATIONAL CYCLOPAEDIA OF AMERICAN BIOGRAPHY.)

In July, 1863, Major Haller was accused of making certain inappropriate remarks in an after-dinner speech and was dismissed from the Army by Secretary Stanton. After his discharge he came back to the Pacific Coast and settled on Whidbey Island. Over the years, he fought for reinstatement and vindication of his honor. Through a special act of Congress his case was reopened; he was vindicated and restored to rank. After retiring from the Army, Haller entered into partnership with A. W. Engle, an attorney, who at one time had been an employee of the Bellingham Bay Coal Company. The two opened an office in LaConner but did an extensive business in Whatcom County.

Coupeville, soldier of the Indian Wars and of the San Juan Incident, was appointed administrator. He qualified at Whatcom in July, 1874. The inventory filed in August recited that: "The estate covers the mouth of the celebrated and well known Whatcom Creek, including the millsite . . . The J. E. Peabody estate is valued at $7,000." Because of involved claims and exaggerated ideas on the part of the heirs as to values, the estate dragged through the courts for more than three years, not being settled until July, 1877, while Major Haller was not discharged as administrator until January, 1878.

The sawmill, erected in 1853, had burned in 1873. Two months before his death, John E. Peabody had disapproved Captain Roeder's recommendation that the mill be rebuilt. (Captain Roeder had a one-third interest in the mill site.) Because of the importance of the mill to the community Roeder held to his idea and in 1876 was instrumental in bringing two capitalists west for the purpose of buying the mill-site. Roeder took the two men to Coupeville to interview Administrator Haller. Because the Peabody estate was as yet unsettled no title to the mill-site could be given and the matter was dropped. The next year, however, when Major Haller sold a portion of the property to pay debts and administration expenses, Captain Roeder purchased the two-thirds interest of the Peabody heirs in the mill-site for the sum of $2,000. This five-acre tract covered the mouth and falls of Whatcom creek.

In the meantime also, the estate of Minnie Peabody, deceased, the half Indian daughter of Russell V. Peabody, was settled by public sale of eight acres of wild land originally given her by her late father. Having previously expressed the wish to buy some land "just for the fun of it," Martha (Mrs. W. H.) Fouts, was advised by her friend, Captain Roeder of the prospective administrator's sale. For the sum of $175, she bid in the acreage, which when surveyed was found to measure almost eleven acres. Year by year Mrs. Fouts held the property as it grew in value, finally selling for $28,000. In 1890 one block of this tract, 200 feet square, was sold for $4,000 to Whatcom county for the court house*

The townsite of Whatcom comprised all that part of Bellingham north and west of Champion street to the Eldridge claim. It included the Roeder donation claim from West Street to G; the Peabody donation claim from G to Champion and north to H; the Peabody homestead; and forty acres of the Roeder homestead.

In 1881, exclusive of lots and lands sold privately and under court

---

*Under the law creating Whatcom county in 1854, it is specifically stipulated that the county seat shall be located, not merely in the town of Whatcom, but on the R. V. Peabody land claim, of which Champion street is the south line.

order, the Peabody sisters owned a two-thirds interest in the Peabody donation claim; and a one-third interest in the Roeder donation claim. They also claimed an interest in the Peabody homestead, as did William G. Utter and Frank Peabody, the half-Indian son of Russell V. Peabody. Captain Roeder owned a two-thirds interest in the Roeder donation claim; a one-third interest in the Peabody donation claim; sole title to his own homestead, and to the five-acre sawmill site.

The Washington Colony was incorporated under the laws of Kansas: capital, $75,000; par value per share, $100. First members of the Colony arrived at the Bay in the fall of 1881 when Roeder and Utter soon realized that General McPherson had been too optimistic. Instead of 100 families, about twenty-five arrived. Not many of them had any money and only a few thousand dollars of the capital stock had been subscribed. Members of the Colony were obligated to subscribe to $100 worth of stock, but were given the privilege of working out this amount. They at once began the construction of residences, the mill, and the wharf, all in good faith.

Early in 1882 the rest of the Colonists arrived. These included the families of William Penfield, Delander, Austin, Cudworth, Frank, Wampler, Schrimsher, Shumusk, Felmley, Spangenburger, Jeff Stewart, Jim Inks, Jim Vernon, Mayhew, Doctor Euclid Van Zandt and wife, and John Y. Collins and wife.

The hopes of the settlers at this time were raised again in the belief that Bellingham Bay would be the terminus of the Northern Pacific Railroad. In August, 1882, the LaConner Mail stated that the Colony was succeeding and that visits by the railroad magnates showed their interest in Bellingham Bay. It may be that these two facts—the apparent success of the Colony, and the possibility that Whatcom might become a great railway terminus caused the Peabody heirs to regret their preliminary agreement, and to refuse its ratification.

Through McPherson's advertising of Bellingham Bay new settlers began arriving from the East. Shortly, Roeder, Utter and the Peabody estate started selling lots. Edward Eldridge dropped out of the scheme thereby avoiding a lot of the later Colony trouble.

The logway of the mill was complete and a small wharf was being erected late in August, 1882. Part of the mill machinery arrived by October. By the end of that month the Colony mill was making 40,000 cedar shingles per day. The new sawmill was ready for operation by December, 1882. (Opposite page 214).

In writing of these days Edward Eldridge said: "We had another vertible boom on Bellingham Bay, and to General McPherson more than to any other man, are we indebted therefor. How he succeeded in doing so, is hard to tell, but he certainly succeeded in inducing a great many people to believe that Bellingham Bay and not Tacoma, was to be the terminus of the Northern Pacific. The advertising of the Northern Pacific brought an immense immigration into the Territory that year, and many found their way to Bellingham Bay, eager and willing to buy town lots. But alas for Whatcom! Old Dan Harris was quite right—'Whatcom was an *ignus fat-you-wus-wus*, always coming and never come'."

At the annual meeting of the Colony early in January, 1883, Doctor Van Zandt was elected president, defeating M. A. McPherson, the first Colony leader, who soon left Whatcom and started a logging camp at Birch Bay.

H. B. Williams arrived early in 1883, holding power of attorney from C. J. Pettibone, trustee of the Peabody estate, authorized to enter into any agreement with the Colony. After weeks of negotiations, a compromise was effected and the Colony secured its contract June 25, 1883, from the townsite owners: Roeder, Utter and the Peabody heirs. This settlement, more than two years after the Peabody heirs had given telegraphic approval to the Colony plan caused great rejoicing as the settlers all felt that their future was assured.

Meantime, although land titles were not secure the Colony mill had been hard at work. A million feet were cut the first six months of the year, all of which had been used in Whatcom. There were orders on file for another 250,000 feet. The first lumber had gone into the Colony wharf now three-fourths of a mile out in the Bay opposite Sehome.

In the spring of 1883, John H. Stenger of Canyonville, Oregon, after being sold on the future of Whatcom by Dr. Van Zandt, bought $25,000 worth of stock in the Colony project, the first real money so invested. Stenger's money came from a $30,000 sale of cattle; his people having successfully engaged in the cattle business since his parents crossed the plains from Peoria, Illinois, in 1852, when they settled at Canyonville. Prior to Stenger's investment outstanding stock amounted to less than $4,000. Most Colony members held one share. A few had two, John Y. Collins had seven. Stenger now learned that under the Washington Colony by-laws each member had but one vote regardless of the number of shares possessed. Faced with possible loss in this situation young Stenger sought the advice of his father, Leonard Stenger, Judge J. F. Gazley and others who came north to investigate, in June. Possibly to forestall over-extended credit Judge Gazley advertised in Seattle papers warning against purchase of drafts issued by the Washington Colony. This caused much bitterness around the Bay. Charges and counter-charges were hurled. However the Stenger party was powerful enough to have the by-laws amended from a membership to a capital basis. This was in August when J. H. Stenger was made superintendent of the Colony mill thereby incurring further ill will.

The year 1883 brought further complications when Frank Peabody,* half-Indian son of Russell V. Peabody, through his friend George Dorffell of Seattle, with G. Haller as attorney, brought suit against the Peabody estate to recover an interest in the Peabody homestead.

The Frank Peabody petition set forth that the collateral heirs, exclusive of the petitioner, had deeded an undivided one-half of the homestead claim to the administrator, William Utter, who resided upon the land and held it adversely to the interests of said petitioner. Before his action came to trial Frank Peabody died in Vancouver. It then was claimed that he had sold his interest in the estate to George Dorffell for a few hundred dollars. William Utter was notified to vacate the premises which order he failed to obey. The REVEILLE of February 13, 1885, stated: "We understand that the Utters have compromised the Dorffell suit by giving fifty lots. This leaves the Colony and the Pettibones yet to make their peace with the successors to the half Indian Peabody heirs."

Scarcely had the ink dried on the June 25th contract or agreement with the Colony before dissatisfied Peabody heirs hurried westward. First came A. W. and W. C. Pettibone, followed a month later by the trustee of the Peabody estate, C. J. Pettibone. The heirs claimed that H. B. Williams in approving the agreement as written, had exceeded his authority. To worried citizens it now was evident that the heirs would attempt to abrogate the contract.

Offers of the Colony to accept a lesser number of lots than the number agreed upon, were declined. The REVEILLE declared that the Peabody heirs "wanted to eat their cake and have it too."

About this time Yesler and Anderson of Seattle offered to buy the Colony holdings. The deal was dropped when Major Haller informed them the title was defective. Under the circumstances real estate sales were halted. Citizens fulminated against the rival parties because of the effect the quarrel had upon the whole community.

Next, the Peabody heirs brought suit to have the agreement of June 25, 1883, set aside, "on account of fraudulent representations." The case was

---

*The Russell V. Peabody house was built on the long sand bar on the west bank of Whatcom creek, next door to the first home of Henry Roeder. Here Frank Peabody was born. Here he lived with his father until the latter went to work for the British Columbia Boundary Commission. Peabody, Sr., then placed his son with a family near Olympia paying for his board and schooling. When Frank was about twelve years old his father died. His uncle, John Peabody, then took charge of the estate. For some time he lived with the Captain Roeder family since it was claimed he was left destitute. Later he removed to British Columbia.

presented before Judge Green in the Seattle courts where it was proved that H. B. Williams had, in fact, exceeded his authority in entering into the agreement of June 25, 1883.

During this period public meetings were held at Whatcom wherein the citizens expressed their opinions about the controversy, while the REVEILLE burned with the heat of partisanship. In the end a settlement was reached out of court under which the Peabody heirs gave the Colony a few lots although they owned the greater part of the townsite. Roeder and Utter made the heaviest grants, the former losing his mill site at the Falls as well as the lots donated by him.

In May, 1884, the Colony was reincorporated under the management of John Stenger. This did not halt the quarrels among the Colonists, nor did it restore the credit ruined by delays and lawsuits. Feeling against John Stenger increased, as was shown when his newly completed residence, the finest in town, erected on the hillside above the mill, was blown up in February, 1885. Stenger was at C. I. Roth's office at the time. When he and City Marshal Badger had extinguished the fire in the debris of the house, they learned from the evidence that two men had entered through a window, had deposited a giant-powder cartridge in a five gallon oil can, had ignited it by means of a fuse, and then had escaped through the woods to the Telegraph Road near the Pickett bridge. The city council offered a reward of $800 for the arrest and conviction of the dynamiters, but the evidence was not conclusive. Stenger finally rebuilt his house and two years later married Clara Fouts, eldest daughter of W. H. Fouts. (Opposite page 214).

The credit of the Colony being ruined, Stenger was obliged to borrow large sums of money from his father and brother in order to operate. Finally, the father, Leonard Stenger, Sr., obtained judgment as the largest creditor, and purchased the Colony at a creditor's sale. This ended the Washington Colony as an organization. Many of its members drifted into the Nooksack country and took up homesteads. Once more times were hard around Whatcom. The bonanza spending expected through an influx of Eastern settlers had been lost due to the long controversy and faulty titles.

Later John Stenger acquired practically the sole ownership of the sawmill and ran it intermittently. It was the only place on the Bay where a day's work could be obtained. But demand for lumber was slow and collections poor, so Stenger, a friend of his men, paid them as he could.

In December, 1888, Nelson Bennett and the corporation he represented bought the Colony mill site, the water power, and the wharf for $42,000. Whatcom had missed the boat completely, or, more properly speaking the train ride, for the Northern Pacific had gone elsewhere with its terminus.

Chapter XXIII.

HURRAH FOR THE FOURTH OF JULY!

1883

GROWING CIVIC CONSCIOUSNESS, created perhaps by the Washington, or Kansas Colony project, early in the summer of 1883 caused the citizens of Whatcom to plan a monster Fourth of July celebration, intended to be the most elaborate patriotic demonstration ever held in the Northwest.

Accordingly Charles Donovan was appointed master of ceremonies, with Hugh Eldridge as chairman of the entertainment committee and Doctor E. Van Zandt as president of the day. Money was subscribed, and a program outlined which included footraces on the beach, a tug-of-war, Indian canoe races, speeches and music. However, one thing was missing—Whatcom had no brass band.

Sometime earlier the old Hyack fire brigade of New Westminster had organized a brass band with twenty-five members. The fame of these music-makers had spread across the Border and therefore the ways-and-means committee for the Whatcom celebration rode up to the Royal City and invited the Hyacks to participate. To protect the easily dented brass instruments it was decided to send these on a haywagon by the roundabout route up the old Yale road, through the Sumas prairie, and thence southwest down the old Telegraph road to Whatcom. The bandsmen on horseback would take the short-cut south, forty-five miles or more, via the Semiahmoo Trail.

In the abandoned stockade on Peabody Hill, there remained the old Farragut cannon, placed there during the Indian war of the '50's, and used through the years to salute distinguished guests, or to celebrate holidays. On July third, Bartender Ad Spangenburger, Jim Inks, George Merriam, Andy Lawrence and three or four others went to the stockade with oxen, placed the muzzle-loader on a sled and dragged it downhill to a point on the beach at the mouth of Chinook Ravine near the intersection of the present West Holly and F Streets.

Henry Morey writing for the VANCOUVER SUNDAY PROVINCE, has described the Hyack Band's trip to Whatcom for the celebration of July 4th, 1883, as follows:

211

"In the year 1883 Dominion Day fell on a Sunday. The Royal City of New Westminster celebrated this sixteenth birthday of the Dominion on the following Monday. The Hyack band supplied the music for the day and also for the dance at night. For this reason the band instruments could not be started on their hay-wagon trip to Whatcom until Tuesday morning, July 3. They had just twenty-four hours in which to make the distance. This meant traveling day and night with a relay of horses at Sumas and much quenching of thirst on the way by quadrupeds and bipeds alike. Dances didn't end an hour or so after midnight . . . Broad daylight only was the signal for breaking up. The bandsmen themselves would have to start on their forty-five mile horseback ride after being up all night.

"The boys were to assemble at Brownsville (now South Westminster) on the south bank of the Fraser. To do this it was necessary to board the old ferryboat K. de K., the first ferry on the river, at New Westminster." (Named for Mr. K. deKnevett.)

Morey has given a vivid description of the nightmarish ride by the bandsmen. Few had a speaking acquaintance with any horse. The animals themselves were a motley lot. It seemed that the fattest musician with the shortest legs, would be found on the plow-horse of broadest beam, bouncing up and down like a grain of poping corn as the animal trotted. The smallest cayuses drew the longest riders whose dangling feet dragged through the ferns of the wayside.

A few miles south of the river, and the fifty year old bandmaster, on the jouncing deck of a heavy trotting draft animal, called in anguish that he was dying. A younger bandsman traded horses with him.

For a time the American guide, Deputy Sheriff Stewart Leckie rode herd on stragglers. Then the route narrowed until tree branches clawed at the riders. Fallen trees, heat, and mosquitoes added to the discomfort.

At noon a halt was made near the present site of Blaine. A full hour elapsed before the last weary steed and battered rider staggered into camp.

A half dozen of the better riders reached Ferndale at 6 P. M. and after supper at a hospitable farm house, elected to continue to Bellingham Bay. The other suffering musicians who arrived through the night eased their protesting bodies into a hayloft. The route to Whatcom lay down river, past Marietta and along the old Military Road. Sheriff Leckie told his charges that the horses could see in the dark and advised them to hug the necks of the animals to protect their faces from tree branches.

Just before midnight, the gallant six found beds in Whatcom but they were too tired to sleep. Before they could compose themselves, or about 3 A. M. on the Glorious Fourth, the eagle began to scream. They were almost shaken from their beds by tremendous explosions just under their windows.

As the Fourth dawned, Spangenburger and Frank Jackson (later a house mover) appeared with a box of gunpowder. They loaded the cannon, using blue clay from the creek bed for wadding. The first volley echoed and re-echoed along the hillside and shore line and aroused the 300 or more Indians who were camped on the beach. These swarmed from their tents. Spangenburger warned them to keep back, but they paid no heed to his shouts. The second shot was fired. Then the bartender dumped the remaining powder into the gun for a grand finale, and wadded the stocky smooth-bore to the muzzle with blue clay.

When the smoke cleared away, fragments of the old cannon could be seen scattered around for hundreds of feet. One Indian lay dead beside a log, and another was mortally wounded by a 100 pound chunk of metal that slashed through his tent. Spangenburger rushed through the woods to the Far West saloon, it is said, seized his six-shooter and belt, and took refuge in the timber. Jackson also retreated to the town, but remained there to spread the alarm.

The Indians were very angry, but Captain Roeder waded in, and quieted them for the time being.

When young Emmett Hawley arrived, Old Sally, who was a neighbor of the Hawleys in Lynden, reported the accident. The man killed was her brother, Dock, an old medicine man. Emmett told her to follow him with a basket, for he was sure the whites would express their sympathy with a silver offering. At the Hayes and Merriam saloon, the first place visited, Hayes tossed in a ten dollar gold piece, while some of the patrons contributed a dollar each. The pair soon covered the business houses along the beach and on Division Street, collecting more than forty dollars. The Indians' ire subsided, for this sum would cover the burial expenses. Previously Chief Henry Kwina of the Lummis had counseled a peaceful settlement. (Opposite page 230).

When the excitement had lessened, the Fourth of July committee realized that not all of the New Westminster band had arrived. The guide, Stewart Leckie, with a fresh horse, left Whatcom at 5 A. M. for Ferndale to round up the rest of the Hyacks.

Morey goes on to say: "They were not all riding, however, when they dragged themselves into Whatcom just in time for the opening of the official programme. Some were leading their horses, hobbling along the road, with smarting bodies and aching limbs, ankle-deep in dust. The bandmaster was amongst these few, and the very last in the sorry procession. The poor fellow was raw and bleeding."

The procession was formed on Division Street at ten o'clock by Marshal Charles Donovan. Headed by the brass band it moved down to 13th Street —(West Holly)—turned west and marched to E Street, then up E Street past the brick courthouse and on up the hill to the cleared square between E and F and 16th and 17th—(Clinton and Dupont)—Streets.

A few minutes later the woods were ringing with the strains of "God Save the Queen." This was satisfactory to the celebrants, since it was their tune of "America." All joined in and sang lustily.

President Van Zandt welcomed the assembly. There was music by the choir; the Declaration of Independence was read; Senator Eugene Canfield of Illinois, the railroad organizer, gave the oration of the day. E. H. Marcy responded to the toast "Our Flag." Although the only piece of bunting at the gathering was a ten cent flag on the table, that did not mar the ardor of the speaker, who retired amid a round of applause. Judge de Mattos spoke on "Washington Territory"; Honorable E. Eldridge responded to "Old Settlers"; C. I. Roth made his maiden address and talked on "Newcomers"; J. J. Weisenburger spoke on "Whatcom, Old and New"; T. C. Austin had the toast "Single Cussedness"; and Judge Gazley, "The Press."

The VANCOUVER SUNDAY PROVINCE stated in regard to all this oratory:

"Patriotic speeches followed; wonderful examples of oratory, some of them. The professional spouter was there and a group of local blow-hards as well. Lively selections from the Hyacks and a fusillade of firecrackers filled in between extravaganzas. Lunch that followed was a barbecue, from a quantity standpoint. The tables were fairly swamped with meat and drink; free for all, too. It took well over an hour to stow it way. Then the athletic sports began. No records were broken—too much lunch."

The tug-of-war was staged in the square; then to the beach for the pony races, foot races, by both boys and girls, and the jumping contests. The big event of the afternoon was the Indian canoe race by twelve entries. The King George team won over Uncle Sam.

After the fireworks in the evening, a grand ball was held in the upper story of a frame building. (Probably in the Washington Hotel on Division Street.) Long before this the celebrants realized that their hired band

---

UPPER—The Washington Colony mill on Whatcom Creek in the early '80's with the mill office to the left; the latter built on the site of the Roeder mill which was destroyed by fire in 1873. The white house, upper center, was the original home of Judge George A. Kellogg and family.—Photo courtesy of Mrs. Cecil Stenger Rinehart.

LOWER—C street viaduct runs through the picture. Seventeenth street (Dupont) crosses C street at the right end of the bridge, where the Reveille building stood. The site of the present day, 1951, disposal plant is under the right end of the viaduct. The square white house, lower right center, is John Stenger's—the one blown up. Colony mill is back of the trees in the center of the photo.—Photo courtesy Cecil A. Morse.

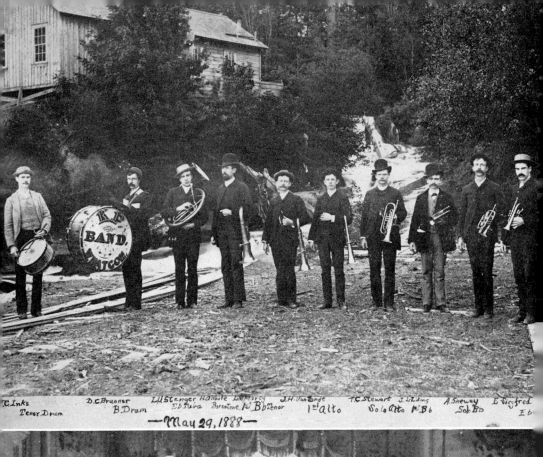

C.Inks   D.C.Brunner   L.U.Stenger   H.White   L.W.Mirey   J.H.VanZandt   T.C.Stewart   J.U.Likins   A.Sneway   E.Seigfred
Tenor Drum   B.Drum   Eb Tuba   Baritone   1st Bb Tenor   1st Alto   Solo Alto   1st Bb   Solo Bb   Eb

—May 29, 1888—

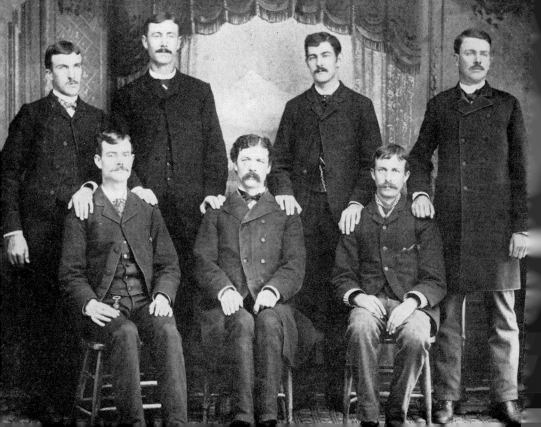

could play just two pieces—"God Save The Queen" and "Wait 'Till The Clouds Roll Bye, Nellie." However, by changing the time it was possible to do the square and the round dances.

The chairman of the entertainment committee, Hugh Eldridge, next asked Emmett Hawley if he would play for the Indians, who wanted to dance also. A violin was found and with the help of Indian Charley (later known as Blind Charley), the two young men fiddled away in another hall, to the delight of the Indians.

Henry Morey's account of the celebration continues: "The rhythmic invitation of the call man to 'balance to partners, s-w-i-n-g!' was too much for some of them. They got in and s-w-u-n-g! There was no break for refreshments at midnight; oh, no, not in those days! The jolly well-behaved crowd just danced and ate and drank, drank and ate and danced until his majesty the sun announced that July the fifth was several hours old. Then with the usual finales—there was a rush for beds. These were scarce and the Hyacks had to be content with being tucked up in trios and quartettes. Four in a three-quarter bed sounds impossible for sleep, yet in five minutes there was not a bandsman awake, except perhaps the band-master. All were aroused at 7 A. M. and preparations for the return ride began." . . . "The bandmaster said: 'Boys, I'm poor and you all know it, but a thousand dollars wouldn't tempt me to straddle anything with four legs again! I'm going home in the hay wagon!'

"The hay wagon with the instruments carefully packed, was ready. The bandmaster was helped to a place alongside the slide trombone. With a drawn-out sigh of relief and a contented grin he measured his bruised body on the billows of soft new-mown hay. He waved a farewell as the clumsy wagon rattled, creaked and disappeared in a cloud of road dust.

"The twenty-four remaining bandsmen made the return trip as they had come, except that horses and horsemen knew each other better and were able to cut down the hours of travel considerably. It was a racking ride just the same. They reached Brownsville in time to catch the 6 P. M. *K. de K.*, and that rickety old ferryboat looked good to them."

Outside of the tragic accident of the day, the Fourth of July Committees were well satisfied with the day's results. They estimated that over 1,500 people had arrived at Whatcom by three o'clock in the afternoon. Enough money had been collected to pay the New Westminster band $300, as well

UPPER—Early brass band at Whatcom Creek on the site of the ruins of Captain Roeder's mill. H. A. White, fourth from the left was the leader. Whatcom Falls in the center of picture, are the ones that flow under the present day (1951) Pickett Bridge.—Photo courtesy of Mrs. Cecil Stenger Rinehart.

LOWER—Sunflower Minstrels—1884. Seated, left to right: Jim Inks, Will Leach, Allen Shewey; standing, Len Stenger, Ed Edson, W. L. Wheeler and D. R. Coldwell.

as taking care of all the prizes of the day. When all expenses were settled the committees found they had $109.85 left. This was voted for the use of the new fire company—Washington Hook and Ladder Company, number one—the apparatus of which had newly arrived.

After this celebration, some of the settlers decided they would organize their own brass band. Henry A. White, the druggist, (who bought out Charley Donovan's drug stock, which he in turn had bought from Doctor Thornton) said, "You just wait until my brother-in-law, Ed Edson, gets here in October; he plays a darn good tuba."

In October the band was organized with E. Shepard as leader, other members being William Reilley, E. C. Pentland, E. C. King, W. L. Asher, James H. Hill, L. Ludwig, J. P. Perry, and Ed Edson. The organization's first public appearance was in November at the Washington Hotel on Division Street where a "grand masquerade ball" was given for the benefit of the fire company. (Opposite page 215).

FIRST MEMORIAL DAY CELEBRATION

Memorial Day, 1884, was the next big occasion for the band. At the time the tuba player was working for Charles Donovan who had a surveying contract in the town of Lynden. Not daunted by the prospect of a twenty-five mile walk, he worked late the previous afternoon, then tackled the river trail. It was almost dark when he arrived at Nooksack Crossing. By the aid of a lantern borrowed from the ferry man, he stumbled over the floating corduroy and exposed tree roots characteristic of that forest tunnel otherwise called the Telegraph Road. Night wore away finally and the lantern was extinguished, but the tuba player, Ed Edson, arrived in time to join the band at the head of the parade.

In the '80's the block on the hill between F and G Streets—16th and 17th (Clinton and Dupont), was used for a cemetery. Thirteen little girls representing the thirteen original states followed the band on the march to the cemetery. Next came veterans of the Civil War, then twenty-five young ladies representing States later admitted to the Union, while last in line were city officials and civic societies.

After the grave of J. C. Elkins, the only veteran of the Civil War, then buried at Whatcom, had been decorated, I. M. Kallock, railroad promoter, delivered the oration of the day. The speaker's stand was on land that had formerly belonged to General Pickett, while the grave which was decorated was on a lot that had been owned by Lieutenant J. W. Forsythe—later General Forsythe of the United States Army.

The first observance of Memorial Day in Whatcom County, also marked the first effort toward the establishment of a G.A.R. post.

SUNFLOWER MINSTRELS
1884

When the band proved to be a success, the organization of "The Sunflower Minstrel Show" followed naturally enough in the year 1884, and, like the band, the troupe was received enthusiastically by an amusement-starved public. The name "Sunflower," was adopted because of the Kansas Colony.

Although in existence for thirty years, Whatcom and Sehome as yet were nothing more than two forest clearings connected by the rutted Military Road and the winding shore trails. To such communities, distantly removed from Seattle, the vocalizing of the minstrels helped to brighten a rather drab existence. (Opposite page 215).

Finding their efforts well received in town, the Minstrels, some months after organization, tried their act on the suburbs, Ferndale being the guinea pig selected. The REVEILLE of January 30, 1885, carries this advertisement:

"SUNFLOWER MINSTRELS

D. R. Coldwell_____Business Manager

W. M. Leach_____Stage Manager

FERNDALE

First Appearance of Sunflower Minstrels and Jubilee Singers.

At the Hall, in Ferndale on Thursday even'g—Feb. 5, 1885,

Consisting of

Plantation Songs, Negro Sketches, Original Jokes and Local Hits"

On the advertised date a river steamboat carried the troupe to the Nooksack metropolis. A steamer at a later date also transported the Minstrels to Lynden where they performed in the Judson's Opera house, situated over the H. A. Judson store, corner of Front and Fifth Streets.

Most renowned performance by the troupe occurred July 4, 1885, when Captain Tarte of the Steamer *Brick,* with two large fishing barges in tow, carried all the footloose patriots of the Bay to a monster celebration at Semiahmoo.

Display of histrionic talent at this period required more than a good voice and stage presence—it called for strong muscles as well, since the performers were required to provide firewood for the steamboat's furnace. Ed Edson has told how he and the other young men felled trees on the site of the Mount Baker Apartments, Bellingham; how they sawed and split the logs to fit the fire box; then sledded the fuel by forest trail around the shoreline to the Sehome wharf. Several trips with horse-drawn sled were necessary to supply enough wood for one roundtrip by the steamer. However, the young minstrel singers felt that the concerts and shows were worth the effort. Years of popularity proved that the public felt the same.

DIVISION STREET FIRE OF 1885

History shows that business centers of towns tend to move, step by step, away from the point of lowly beginnings. Whatcom's first move of the kind followed the disastrous fire of May, 1885, when the principal business district along Division Street* was destroyed. Seventeen buildings with stock, office equipment, and personal belongings were burned at a loss of $35,000. City records were saved, but some of the school records apparently were burned or lost at this time.

The story of the conflagration is reminiscent of a minor scene from Dante. Through the night shadowy figures toiled away from the leaping flames from the saloons with bottles and barrels of intoxicants. Gnome-like they circled their treasure, imbibed deeply, then leaped back to rescue more whiskey. Or perhaps they lurched to the bucket-line. The tide was high and salt water came forward steadily only to be dashed futily toward the crackling walls. One by one the flimsy wooden structures, twenty and twenty-five years old, flared like oily rags, the searing heat then driving the fire fighters back to the next building. And then, after nearly three hours, the finale, when the Pardon O'Brien building was dynamited ahead of the fire and the flames died for lack of fuel.

Next came a mystery—the fire buckets and equipment used so valiantly through the night, all disappeared.

Also charges and counter charges of arson circulated freely. The finger of suspicion pointed at two or three, but an investigating committee could uncover no evidence justifying an arrest.

Judge William H. Harris, in an article written years later from California has described the Division Street fire quite vividly. Harris said, in part:

"The fire started in the Washington Hotel** early in the night, and before the inmates had gone to bed. It was a large two story wooden building that burned fiercely and was soon consumed. The occupants of the second floor had barely time to get out, and could not remove their

---

*Division Street is between C and D and Astor and Dupont Streets

**There is a difference of opinion on the source of this fire. Roth's history states that it originated in the rear of the Steinweg store.

baggage. Harry Fairchild was a roomer and lost his trunk and all his belongings. The hotel contained the usual bar-room, well stocked with a variety of liquors, and the probable reason why so little of the useful property was saved, was the number who soon energetically worked to save the intoxicants.

"The barrels were rolled out: the jugs, demijohns and bottles carried out—all to a place of safety from the fire but not from the multitude. The fire spread to the buildings across the way, one being the Steinweg store, on the second floor of which J. P. deMattos had his law office. The stairs went up on the outside, and the little lawyer was frantically striving to bring his law books downstairs in his arms. Barnes and I, seeing his situation, hurried to his help, and both being accustomed to physical effort, soon had the Judge's law library in a safe place, close to the aforesaid barrels, jugs, and demijohns. There were vacant lots between most of the vacant buildings which helped to check the fire, and before midnight it was out. Water was handy and buckets were used to stop the fire. (Opposite page 230).

". . . Many of the fire fighters made frequent trips to the vicinity of the barrels, and after the fire was subdued a 'cheer-up' meeting was held there, and every motion to adjourn was declared out of order. It was a strange co-incidence that nearly every attendant at the fire had a cup and a cork-screw with him—rescued from a burning store . . . As the night wore on the meeting dwindled to the last man, who remained in the capacity of watchman."

While the destruction of the business district was a great blow to the community, recovery was rapid. The great boom of 1889 was in the offing. However, new buildings as erected all faced C Street. Division Street thereafter was nothing more than an alley.

Chapter XXIV.

ELLA HIGGINSON

POET LAUREATE OF WASHINGTON

WHEN ELLA HIGGINSON, the poet laureate-to-be of Washington, first arrived at Whatcom, she waded in mud over her high-topped button shoes while walking up Thirteenth Street (West Holly), in search of a hotel. Having found one, she spent the night in terror, her bureau pushed against the unlocked door, while listening to cries, screams, and groans, during a fatal stabbing affray in the saloon below. Accompanying her on the hectic journey was her husband, Russell Carden Higginson, who had come North to open a drug store in Sehome.

Writing of the incident twenty years later in the AMERICAN REVEILLE of June 14, 1908, Mrs. Higginson said:

"It was a cold and stormy night in October, 1888, that we boarded the old *Idaho*—even then rheumatic and short of breath—bound f o r Sehome and Whatcom. A handful of lights flickered on the hills where now is one of the marvels of the country—Seattle.

"Seattle claimed only 20,000 people in 1888; and neither Seattle nor Bellingham was ever known to claim less than it deserved.

"There were two people on the *Idaho* that night whom I shall never forget. One was a girl from LaConner; the other was a deck hand. From the latter I received the first genuine, spontaneous kindness that cheered my heart on Puget Sound.

"We had brought all the way from Eastern Oregon, a big black curly dog, named Jeff, who was precious. He was chained to the lower deck directly under our cabin, and his sobs and moans of loneliness made sleep impossible for me. I could hear the deck hands swearing and throwing things at him but now and then a kind tenor voice consoled and comforted him.

"But the sobs and moans continued. At 2 o'clock in the morning, I arose, dressed, and went down to the lower deck. The deckhands were all lying around on the floor sleeping. I was compelled to walk between and around them, and almost over them to get to the dog. Finally one sat up.

" 'Can I do anything for you, lady?' said he; and it was the kind tenor voice that spoke—low not to arouse the other men.

"I asked him if I might not stay down there with my dog.

" 'It wouldn't be just the thing,' said he, politely. 'But I'll tell you what. You kind of introduce me to your dog, and I'll lay down by him and pet him now and then.'

"So I told Jeff that this man, whose face I couldn't see in the darkness, was a friend who would take care of him; and there was no further sound of grief from the dog that night.

"I never saw the man, and I never heard his voice again; but he is unforgotten. He belonged to the great Order of Kind Hearts, whose members may be found the world over in high places and low.

"The girl from LaConner I remember for another reason. We had read the most brilliant stories of Whatcom's 'booming' prosperity, and our hopes were high. I sat on deck talking to this girl.

" 'Whatcom is having a boom, isn't it?' said I, innocently; I used the word almost with awe, not knowing exactly what it meant, being from Oregon.

" 'Yes,' said the girl, yawning. 'Whatcom is always having booms.' "The words gave me a quick cold shock of apprehension, and in the years that followed they became a kind of household motto. We left Seattle at 8 o'clock on a Tuesday night and we did not reach Whatcom until midnight Wednesday. Where we were in the meantime, I neither know nor care; but like the wandering Jew, we 'kept going' all the time.

"It was raining, and the night was black. We landed at the old Colony Wharf, nearly a mile out over the tide-flats. There was one man on the wharf, with a smoky lantern and a wheel-barrow, in which to carry the mail.

" 'You'd better follow this lantern pretty close,' said he cheerfully. 'There's some plumb terrible holes in this wharf. If you happen to step into one, you're a goner from Goneville, sure.'

"We were exhausted from a long journey and loss of sleep; and our hearts were low as we stumbled along behind that smoky lantern, expecting with every step to go plunging to the bottom of the Bay.

"At Thirteenth and C Streets the wheelbarrow and the lantern stopped and we were left in inky darkness.

" 'There's two good hotels,' a man told us. 'One's over on Fourteenth (Astor); the other's the nearest. It's straight up Thirteenth (West Holly), about two blocks. You'll have to walk careful. They're just raising the grade. Some's raised, and some ain't and you're liable to pitch down fifty feet onto the tideflats, or into the Bay. You'd best put down your umberell and jab along ahead of you with it.'

"As we started on our dismal procession, he called after us, 'Say, lady! Hold up your dress! It's soft, oozy mud, clean to your knees that you've got to wade through.'

"There were no sidewalks; nothing but soft mud. We toiled painfully and silently through it. We could not see one another, we could not see the earth, nor the heavens. But at last we did see the 'hotel,' and when we had fully seen it, we turned about and retraced our steps, in search of the other 'good one.' The one to which we had 'jabbed our way with our umberell' was a low saloon with three or four rooms above it. The saloon was full of men, smoking, drinking, gambling and clog-dancing. One 'fiddle' squeaked out a pitiful discord, the player beating time with his foot.

"At 2 o'clock in the morning we reached the 'other.'* There was a saloon on one side of the hall, and parlor on the other side. Mud dripped and oozed from our clothing and from the tip of every hair on the dog. . . .

"We were assigned the Chamber of Honor over the saloon; and scarcely had we fallen asleep when we were awakened by the most terrifying and blood-curdling sounds beneath us. Oaths, scuffles, groans of mortal agony, and pitiful calls for help, stupefied us with horror.

"There was no key to our door and I had fortified it with a chair under the knob. I now arose and wheeled the bureau against the chair; and if I could have budged the bed, I should have had it against the bureau— notwithstanding the scorn of the other occupant of the room.

"In the morning we learned that a man had really been stabbed to death, and that it was his dying groans we had heard. Desperate, then, became our search for a place to live, and in our daily increasing anguish of body and mind, we even nerved ourselves to approach private residences and ask for rooms. Had it not been for the kindness of the late Mr. H. E. Waity, we could not have remained on the Bay.

"We settled down to live, at last, in Sehome, which at that time consisted of Morse's Hardware Store, Carter's Dry Goods Store, an eating house where one could do everything on earth save eat, a drug store, a livery stable, one cow—with her milk all engaged, yea to the last drop— and a saloon for every ten men, and mud.

"Between Sehome and Whatcom was solid forest. A wagon road wound between, but was impassable, so we went down to town on the beach— when the tide was out. When the tide was not out, we stayed at home.

---

*This was the old Whatcom Hotel, at the corner of Fourteenth (Astor) and E Street, just north of the brick courthouse

"There were no sidewalks at Sehome, and women waded about in rubber boots. But ah! the joy of those first years! All was 'boom,' rush, and excitement. Each day was better than the one that went before. Fortunes were made over night on corner lots and every frog on Sehome Hill said, 'Struck it—struck it'!"

One poem alone, FOUR LEAF CLOVER, would have sufficed to bring lasting fame to Ella Higginson; yet for decades, prose and verse evoking highest praise from world critics, flowed from her fertile pen. FOUR LEAF CLOVER is the official song of the National Federation of Women's Clubs. Many composers have set the poem to music. Best known arrangements are those composed by Leila Brownwell and by C. Whitney Coombs. Oley Speaks composed the music for the poem THE LAMP OUT WEST, and Charley Willeby, the English composer, that for FAIRY LULLABY and WHEN THE BIRDS GO NORTH AGAIN.

Ella Higginson was born Ella Rhoads at Council Grove, Kansas, in the '60's, the daughter of Charles Reeves Rhoads and Mary A. Rhoads. While she was yet an infant her family crossed the plains to Oregon. Her father and brother drove an ox-drawn covered wagon, while her mother and sister handled the reins of a horse-drawn two-seated carriage in which Ella rode. To her end, although biographers made various guesses, Mrs. Higginson declined to give the date of her birth. "It was," she said, "in the '60's . . . It is part of my religion that if we did not celebrate birthdays there would be no old age." And yet in later years the author enjoyed celebrating her birthday which occurred January 28. (Opposite page 231).

Another unusual trait of this author was her refusal to be lionized. Catherine Montgomery, who accompanied her to Alaska on two of the three trips made when she was gathering material for her book, ALASKA, THE GREAT COUNTRY, has written: "No president of the Bellingham Normal College (she preferred the old name) was successful in having her appear on the platform. In Alaska, where celebrities were uncommon, she, through sheer shyness, refused to be the object of those who came to 'see and admire.' Her regrets were expressed in polished little notes."

Ella Higginson's sister, Carrie Blake Morgan, whom she adored, was a poetess in her own right, with published verse. Her father was the story teller of the family, with a relish for the dramatic. But her mother, she declared, was the real poet of them all, "and often would call me to see or hear something beautiful in nature—a falling star, a rainbow, a mourning dove, a new red rose; and from her I inherited a passionate love for old china, antique furniture, and Georgian silver."

In Oregon the Rhoads family lived at many places; in LaGrande, in the Grand Ronde Valley, Portland, on the Willamette river farm, Oregon

City, and again in Portland. Mrs. Higginson's warmest memory was of the Willamette farm. Possesed of an older brother and sister, she was indulged in idleness and never punished. For her there was no farm drudgery.

Chief feature of the farm house was a large fireplace, hung with cranes used in cooking. This was flanked with book cupboards filled with standard literature (a fine library for that day).

Mrs. Higginson's recollection is of a farm house constantly filled with visitors. While the Rhoads were poor, all these guests (even the undeserving) were fed. "It was a fine place" she stated, "to eat." Culinary triumphs, descriptions of meals, found in some of her stories, undoubtedly had their origin in remembered gastronomic delights, down on the farm.

The schooling of the future poetess was a bit sketchy. She spent some time in public schools. Also, in Oregon City she attended the Seminary of Doctor S. D. Pope, who, she reported, often made her stand in the corner, face to the wall, so she could not make the other children laugh.

According to this author, a consuming desire to write drove her on from her earliest days. Thus, despite any gaps in her education she learned to write by writing until she became known for her command of English, her facility of expression, her polished lines. As she put it, "I was blessed with 'faith and hope, and love'" (the triad of her poem) "and blessed God to give me good luck, all of which is another name for hard work."

The first poem of Ella Rhoads Higginson, one concerning a little girl and a terrifying thunder storm, was written when she was eight years old. The consequent teasing by her eighteen year old brother deterred her from further effort until she was fourteen. Then the OREGON CITY ENTERPRISE published a poem, written in the first person, and telling of a passionate but blighted love affair occurring ten years in the past. A too literal editor commented dryly that the author must have been about four years old at the time of the love passage.

Another OREGON CITY editor, more tolerant of the Muse and of poetic license, gave her a job on his paper when she was sixteen. There she learned to set type, was responsible for the editorial page into which she slipped an occasional poem; and, in fact, ran the paper when the editor was absent. At that time, an observer has reported, she had become a good looking and attractive young lady. Her poems began to appear in other Oregon publications about this date, all contributed without pay.

Ella Rhoads and Russell Carden Higginson of New York were married in Portland three years before the couple reached Bellingham Bay. The husband has been described as a very courteous young man, of New England antecedants, possessed of a quick temper but never given to swearing. His wife reportedly felt that he did not understand nor appreciate her literary efforts. Russell Higginson died in 1909 at the height of his wife's fame.

In the shacktown that was Sehome in 1888, the Higginsons opened a drug store on Elk Street, across from the Orchard Tract. Catherine Montgomery has reported that the couple at first lived in rooms above and at the rear of the establishment; also that the wife tended store as necessary. However, she found time for her writing. Russell Higginson soon opened a second drug store in booming Fairhaven on Eleventh Street. The FAIRHAVEN WEEKLY WORLD in 1891 stated:

"Higginson and Hardy started Fairhaven's first drug store on or about July 1, 1889, in a small wood building on Eleventh Street, in that part of Fairhaven formerly known as Bellingham. Later they moved into the Fairhaven Mason Block. In addition to their Fairhaven store the firm owns two more handsome stores in Whatcom and New Whatcom."

Later these stores were combined in a new location at Dock (Cornwall) and Holly Streets.

While in Grande Ronde Valley, Oregon, Ella Higginson had ridden horseback. In Sehome she continued this recreation. On her side-saddle, with flowing habit she explored the hills and country side, observing workmen while they hewed the town from the woods or opened and graded streets.

The young writer also took part in various civic activities, particularly the establishment of the first public library which opened in a room shack on Forest Street. With some gusto Mrs. Higginson has described her part in a public dinner given for the benefit of the library. She had been asked to donate and bake a dollar's worth of beans. These were put to soak in every available pot and pan. In the morning the swollen beans covered the table and the floor. All her husband said was "You and your beans!"

With prosperity the Higginsons erected a large house on High Street, close to the present Western Washington College. There under one roof-tree, the author, in turn, was citizen of four municipalities: Sehome, New Whatcom, Whatcom and Bellingham.

It was with some awe, during the first winter on the Bay, that this author received the first pay for any of her writings. This was a ten dollar check from COLLIER'S (then called ONCE-A-WEEK), for a sonnet entitled, WINTER IN PUGET SOUND.

Mrs. Higginson's earlier short stories appeared in the OREGON LITERARY VIDETTE of Salem. In 1890, from her Sehome residence, she conducted a woman's page in the WEST SHORE MAGAZINE of Portland. In 1890 also, her poem, FOUR LEAF CLOVER, published in this same magazine, first brought her general public recognition.

Later this writer handled the literary department of the SEATTLE SUNDAY TIMES. Meantime her fiction appeared in McCLURE'S MAGAZINE, LIPPINCOTT'S, LESLIE'S WEEKLY, SHORT STORIES, THE NEW PETERSON. Early in the '90's, she won a $500 first prize in the McCLURE'S MAGAZINE contest with her story, THE TAKIN' IN OF OLD MISS LANE. In 1914, a similar prize was hers in the COLLIER'S contest, her story being entitled, THE MESSAGE OF ANNIE LAURA SWEET.

Over the decades books of poems, volumes of short stories, a novel, MARIELLA OF OUT WEST, a travel book, ALASKA, THE GREAT COUNTRY, flowed from her pen, most of them being issued by the Macmillian Company Press of New York.

Her novel, MARIELLA OF OUT WEST caused the greatest furor locally, because of its characterizations. The matter was played up in a SAN FRANCISCO EXAMINER Sunday feature entitled, SEVEN WOMEN ON THE WARPATH. This told how Bellingham women were threatening the author with violence because they claimed they were portrayed as the character, Mrs. Flush, of the novel. One neighbor later said: "Mrs. Higginson used her friends in her stories, often making them recognizable, but putting strange dialect forms of speech in her characterizations of them, which turned them into enemies." The author of course always denied having any one character in mind.

The house on Sehome Hill with its Rose Heart Room lined with purple heart wood from the Amazon; with its Rosary Room containing a frieze of rosaries collected the world over; with all its treasures; with its windows commanding the wide sweep of waters, islands and mountains, was very dear to Ella Higginson. She remarked, more than once, "I don't mind dying, but I can't leave my home."

Her trees also were greatly treasured. With prescience of the forthcoming leave taking, just a year before her death, she completed these verses:

"I cannot take my hemlocks,
    Nor my tall fir-trees;
Nor my sweetly scented locusts,
    Set with honey-seeking bees,
When I drift out the narrow straits
    Into the midnight seas.

Nor can I take my birches,
    That delicately reach
To lure the Balm-of-Gilead;
    Nor my one lovely beech,
That every night at sunset
    With God Himself hath speech.

Nor can I take my elm tree
  Where, on a June night,
A passion shaken hermit thrush,
  Pausing on northward flight,
Poured from its pale green silences
  His lyrical delight.

I'll miss them, when I've left them,
  When I have said goodbye
To all their wistful loveliness
  Trembling against the sky—
When I have turned and left them
  And said my last goodbye!"

Physically, Ella Higginson was five feet, five and a half inches in height, of medium complexion, with clear blue eyes, large nose, large mouth, and possessed of a sad, strong face. (Some have described the face as 'sober, neither sad nor glad'). In listing characteristics her friends have used the following words and phrases: "brave, honest, generous, friendly, proud of her tiny feet and hands; a person who would not take a dare, one given to playing jokes on friends, over-worked and given to sudden quick-silver moods."

Despite a lively sense of humor and a capacity for sustained cheerfulness, photographs from childhood to age reveal a serious face. This is in accord with her religious nature and the melanchony touch found in some of her poems such as THE LAMP IN THE WEST, the last stanza of which reads:

"When I sail out the narrow straits,
  Where unknown dangers be,
And cross the troubled moaning bar
  To the mysterious sea;
Dear God, wilt Thou not set a lamp
  Low in the West for me."

Deeply moved when the United States was forced into World War I, in the spring of 1918, Ella Higginson wrote the poem: GOD HAS NOT SPOKEN YET!, the last stanza of which reads:

"God has not spoken yet!
  But Courage must not fail, nor faith grow weak;
    To work!—for Freedom's sun must never set.
  God has not spoken yet—but God will speak."

Shortly before her death, the poet, greatly disturbed by the opening shock of World War II cataclysm, took up her pen once more. A stanza written in anguish runs:

"I hear the hoofs of a mighty steed,
    They pierce my heart like a knell;
And who is this in the saddle seat,
    Who rides so wild and well?
Oh God, my God, 'tis the World I love,
    Galloping on to Hell!"

Death came to Ella Higginson December 27, 1940, in her hillside home, where for half a century she had looked out upon Nature's panorama, receiving inspiration therefrom for her writings. Her passing prompted the following editorial from the BELLINGHAM HERALD:

ELLA HIGGINSON

"One day in the spring of 1890 Ella Higginson was walking through the Old Orchard tract on Elk (State) Street when she spied a four-leaf clover. On her return home she wrote for her department in the PORTLAND WEST SHORE MAGAZINE a poetic gem that has, in the past fifty years, been sung by tens of thousands of voices, FOUR LEAF CLOVER.

"The beautiful poem breathed, 'faith and hope and love'—qualities which gave Ella Higginson a personal hold on her reading public and on her devoted friends.

"Of the emblematic clover she said: 'If you step on it, it goes down flat, but just glance over your shoulder and you will see it lifting its head serenely, and you will fairly hear it say—"just you wait"!'

"Ella Higginson, Bellingham's most distinguished citizen, has completed her work, but the record of her literary talent lives on. To the thousands of residents not so fortunate as to have listened to the flash of her wit and enjoyed the spontaneity of her humor, her poems and her prose works themselves remain a source of continuing appreciation and delight.

"Washington's poet laureate was a pioneer of the second generation. When she came to Bellingham Bay from Oregon in 1888, she already had won a place in Oregon literature. She had indeed, become known as one of the West's leading literary figures. The beauty of the Puget Sound country and the relative rawness of the spread-eagled towns then struggling for supremacy on Bellingham Bay combined to give her background for her best verses and stories. During the '90's, when short stories, poems and novels flowed from her pen in profusion she became a national figure in the world of letters. Imparting the flavor of the Northwest, they remain a lasting monument to her genius.

"But Ella Higginson was more than a gifted author, more than a woman of rare charm and personality; she was withal an influential citizen. For many years she was on the library board, and she was long active in numerous organizations for the advancement of the social, civic and cultural life of the city.

"Internationally famous, for half a century she wrote and lived her 'faith and hope and love' for the Bellingham country. Like the clover she immortalized, her memory endures."

FOUR LEAF CLOVER

"I know a place where the sun is like gold,
    And the cherry blooms burst with snow,
And down underneath is the loveliest nook
    Where the four-leaf clovers grow.

One leaf is for hope, and one is for faith,
    And one is for love, you know,
And God put another in for luck—
    If you search, you will find where they grow.

But you must have hope, and you must have faith,
    You must love and be strong—and so—
If you work, if you wait, you will find the place
    Where the four-leaf clovers grow."

—ELLA HIGGINSON.

Some of the works of Ella Higginson:

THE FLOWER THAT GREW IN THE SAND, AND OTHER STORIES; FROM THE LAND OF THE SNOW PEARLS; THE MESSAGE OF ANNE LAURA SWEET; A FOREST ORCHID; WHEN THE BIRDS GO NORTH AGAIN; MARIELLA, OF OUT-WEST; THE VOICE OF APRIL-LAND; ALASKA, THE GREAT COUNTRY; and THE VANISHING RACE, AND OTHER POEMS.

Chapter XXV.

AROUND THE WORLD IN SIXTY DAYS—?

FUTILE ATTEMPT BY GEORGE FRANCIS TRAIN

1891

"NELLIE BLY" (Elizabeth Cochrane Seaman), newspaper woman of York and Pittsburg, who gained national fame in 1888 by entering the Rockwell Island Insane Ward and exposing the brutal treatment then prevalent, further achieved world wide notoriety one year later when she raced around the world in seventy-two days, six hours, eleven minutes. The wide acclaim given Nellie Bly, so irked or challenged that great egotist, George Francis Train, writer, lecturer, and "World Citizen" that he proclaimed he would duplicate the feat in sixty days. This idea he sold to the TACOMA LEDGER which backed the attempt. Train left Tacoma March 18, 1890. Unavoidable delays boosted his time to sixty-seven days, thirteen hours.

Undaunted, Train sought a backer for another attempt. Always plausible he convinced the people of New Whatcom that great advertising benefits would accrue, should he make the sixty-day journey under the auspices of the Northwest metropolis. Citizens raised $1,000 to finance the effort.

Under date of May 7, 1891, The BELLINGHAM BAY EXPRESS reported: "Citizen Train arrived this morning—at 6:00 A. M. aboard the *City of Seattle*. He regards himself as an old citizen of Whatcom, (he objects to New Whatcom.) 'I was here the guest of the Oregon Navigation Company in July, 1869, with Captain Ainsworth, Sam Wilkinson, Jay Cooke's son, Captain Roberts and other officials to establish the Northern Pacific Railroad.' He said there was not much on the Bay at the time but the coal

UPPER—Division street, Whatcom, Washington Territory, 1884. It runs in front of buildings 1-2-5-6 and 7, and includes stores, hotels and saloons. No. 8 is Phelps & Van Wyck structure on C and Thirteenth streets (West Holly). Sehome is across the Bay; Sehome Hill upper right. The little white school house is near the shore, extreme left. There is no viaduct between the towns.

LOWER—Division street after the fire of 1885, runs from the lower right across the picture. Colony mill, upper right, is on the other side of Whatcom Creek, which flows between the mill and Smith & Parson's store. Whatcom Falls is in the upper center. The building to the left had previously been the W. H. Fout's boarding house and home, with the smoke house for curing hams and slabs of bacon, at the side.

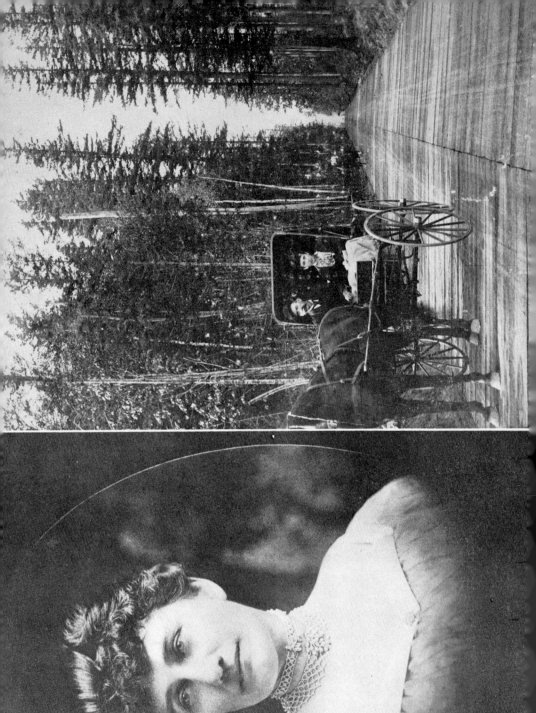

mine. The Company had tried to pump out the mine for several months. Train asked if he could visit the workings. When underground he tasted the water and found it salty, then told officials they were trying to pump out the Pacific Ocean.

The WHATCOM REVEILLE of May 8, 1891 reported that Train had been holding an informal levee at the Bellingham Hotel (John Stenger's) the previous day. The reporter described Train as: "a man of medium height, solidly built and sixty-two years of age.—Swarthy face, shock of white hair, gray mustache, and a restless steel blue eye. Perpetual motion, (never still) talks a dozen languages, Bostonian but lives in New York. Has the culture of a Harvard professor, and slang of a Chicago stock jobber; intensely egotistical, knows something about everything, and a great conversationalist . . ."

Under the spell of the man's personality the reporter naively wrote:

"The problem to be solved for Whatcom is whether or not its geographical position gives it the advantage over all other Pacific ports . . . By a port is meant a land-locked harbor without a bar where 10,000 vessels may ride at anchor . . . Such is the harbor at Whatcom and opposite the Strait of Fuca, there can be no doubt at the result. Citizen Train has volunteered to solve this problem for us and he is just the man to do it."

That same Friday afternoon, the schools being dismissed in his honor, Train greeted the children, their teachers, and others gathered on Holly Street in front of the Oakland block.* That evening he spoke to the citizens assembled in Lighthouse Hall** at one dollar per head.

Train began his world girdling effort the morning of May 9, 1891, on the Steamer *Premier*. (Opposite page 238). To give him a fitting send-off, enthusiastic excursionists crowded the vessel for the trip to Victoria. Some 300 persons came aboard at the G Street wharf. Train, with 200 more admirers, the Carpenters' Band, and the Wardner No. 2 Band came up the gang plank at Sehome. And then Fairhaven had the last laugh. Despite

---

*P. B. Cornwall's elder brother Doctor Ambrose Cornwall was the builder and owner of the Oakland block—West Holly and Champion Streets—which he named in honor of his home town, Oakland, California.

**The BELLINGHAM BAY EXPRESS in May, 1890, reported that Mr. J. C. Lighthouse from Rochester, New York, had purchased the corner lots at Holly and Dock Streets—Cornwall— and was having the trees cleared off. "He will build a large structure of brick and stone to cost $35,000, the contract for doors and windows being $2,873.75." (This is the Seattle-First National Bank Building—1951.)

LEFT—Ella Higginson—Poet Laureate of Washington. She came to Bellingham Bay in 1888.—Photo courtesy of the Herald.

RIGHT—Plank road on the Guide Meridian in the late '90's. George Dellinger and his daughter, Edna, in the carriage; to the rear, at the left, is Harriet Dellinger Browne on her famous pony.—Photo courtesy of the Herald.

the previous pontifical announcements by the World Tour committee that New Whatcom would be the last American port that Train would touch before returning via New York, the *Premier* pulled in to the Fairhaven wharf before swinging to Victoria.

Just off Victoria, amidst the cheers of the passengers, Train boarded the *Empress of India* and that beautiful and graceful ship swung out through the Strait at high speed. The excursionists, after a full day in the British port, returned to New Whatcom at 11 P. M.

Inspired by Train and the challenge of a race with time, the *Empress of India* cut two days and six hours from all previous records to Yokohama.

Luck failed the world traveler at Hong Kong, where he lost three days when he arrived twenty minutes too late to catch the English mail. A monsoon caused a four-day delay, and some one's stupidity, so said Train, cost another three days at London.

Once more the World Citizen had failed in his sixty day goal, although his lapsed time of sixty-four days had bettered Nellie Bly's record and also his previous effort.

Train arrived in New Whatcom from his world girdling tour, wearing a huge white tourist's helmet circled by a small American flag, the only one he saw on the trip, so he said. Around his waist was a bright red silk sash.

During the trip Train had kept the committee advised of his journey and of how he was advertising New Whatcom. On his return he spread clippings, newspapers, menus, and pictures about his hotel rooms to show further how well he had done his work.

The night of his return, Train lectured at the Purdy Opera House, (C and Thirteenth—West Holly), admission twenty-five cents. His reception was not at all cordial. During his absence a story had been repeated that he had registered at times as being from Tacoma. This Train hotly denied and professed to be greatly hurt by the lack of friendliness. Nevertheless hard-headed citizens were heard to declare that they had not received a thousand dollars' worth of advertising; that the town had been "done in" by a smooth talker.

Chapter XXVI.

EARLY ROADS

BECAUSE OF GREAT TREES shouldering each other in close ranked forests; because of a heavy rainfall that turned each unballasted road into a chain of watery chuckholes, few places outside the tropics presented the early road builder with more obstacles than did the Northwest coast.

Lacking money, manpower, powder, or the power machinery of later years, the early builder could do little more than whittle through fallen trees, while following a snake-like track around stumps, much too large to be disturbed.

First step in road building was a trail wide enough for pack animals, a great improvement over the footpath followed by the Indian, or later by packers. Such a trail was visioned by the Whatcom County commissioners the spring of the Fraser River gold rush, 1858, when they ordered that the Nooksack road should be cut suitable for a pack trail not less than six feet wide with fallen timber cut not less than eight feet in width.

Thirty years after the first settlement on Bellingham Bay there were as yet no passable roads into the back country. Newswriters of the day urged the establishment of flour mills, canneries, and the like so that money expended for these products would circulate at home, but there were no roads on which to move raw materials to a processing plant. The papers also pointed out that staples could be landed by water from the Atlantic seaboard more cheaply than by pack horse from the Whatcom County hinterland.

In July, 1854, the county commissioners appointed W. R. Pattle, H. Roeder, and Ellis Barnes as "viewers" to locate a road from Poe's Point, (near the present P.A.F.) to the "Lumma" River. This road, which was no more than a trail was established that same year from Poe's Point to the mouth of Whatcom creek. The following year a road, or rather a trail, was opened from Whatcom to the Roberts donation claim where Fort Bellingham was to be erected the following year. Over this general route the Military Road from the Fort to Sehome was to be constructed during the years 1857-'58.

The Fraser River Gold Trail or the Telegraph Road, was for many years little more than a shaded, undrained trail often laid with floating corduroy, just wide enough for pack stock, or, at best, the passage of an ox-drawn sled. The citizens at this period and later, worked out their poll tax on the roads, chiefly in cutting drainage ditches and filling chuck holes.

In the year 1883, the Northeast Diagonal and the Northwest Diagonal roads were established on paper by the County Commissioners but it was two years later before the first wagon from Ferndale rolled into Whatcom over the Northwest Diagonal. The Guide Meridian, and the Fairhaven-Lake Samish roads were established in 1884, the Chuckanut Drive road in 1891. Several different persons have claimed the distinction of bringing the first wagons over the routes. Certainly these first teamsters carried planks which were laid against logs and up which they pushed the vehicles, while the horses were led around the obstacles.

Road construction progress is indicated by the following items from the REVEILLE:

September 26, 1884—"The Telegraph Road is said to be in an almost impassable condition.

"The REVEILLE is informed that funds are again being raised to complete the Diagonal Road between this city and Ferndale. Less than three miles remain to be cleared. The appropriation of $300 made by the County Commissioners cannot be used until the road is completed . . . The greater portion of this appropriation will be required for corduroying."

FIRST WAGON

On October 22, 1884, the first team and wagon passed over the road from Whatcom to Ferndale via Lummi. The following year the REVEILLE of April 10, 1885, reported:

"J. R. Jenkins and wife came in over the Ferndale road on horseback this week, and found it open with the exception of a few hundred feet along the south bank of Squalicum between the end of the Roeder clearing and the bridge."

April 10, 1885: "Will Senor, J. W. Hardin, John Little, S. W. Hardin, and S. L. Willard came down over the Diagonal Road from Ferndale with a wagon last Wednesday. This is the first time a wagon has ever come over the road, and is an item that deserves to go on record. Contractors Willard and Lamphear are now entitled to their money."

July 3, 1885: "The Guide Meridian road leading from Lynden to Whatcom should be completed. It would open a country now as thoroughly isolated from us as if hemmed in by the Wall of China."

July 31, 1885: "The Lake Whatcom road is again open and the bridge is ready for wagon travel."

December, 1885: "The Nooksack road from Whatcom to the Crossing is almost impassable; the corduroy portions simply serve as resting places and the spaces intervening are deep, bottomless, unfathomable mudholes. This is particularly true of all the first two miles out of Whatcom. Nothing but continuous corduroy will afford relief."

The formal opening of the Northwest Diagonal does not seem to have smoothed the thoroughfare. Complaint was made that, no drainage ditches having been provided, corduroy, with a few inches of earth on top, was afloat in the road, endangering the legs of horses. The prize story was told in December when it was reported a large salmon was seen swimming across the road.

Timber was plentiful, hence the problem, it was thought, was solved during the '90's when the main roads were planked. The relief was but temporary. Under the hammering by the iron-rimmed wagon wheels, and horseshoe calks, the planks quickly wore away, leaving chuck holes even more spine jarring than those of the dirt roads. Soon the planks were replaced with gravel, a surfacing used on most roads until after the arrival of the automobile age and pavements. (Opposite page 231).

How the citizens themselves assisted in road building during the days of meager appropriations is told by George H. Bacon* in his manuscript entitled BOOMING AND PANIC-ING ON PUGET SOUND.

"Small tax receipts," writes Bacon, "meant very small road funds, so we had to turn in on volunteer road work and pass around the hat vigorously for donations. The first wagon road connection between Whatcom and Skagit counties was built entirely of donations. We first collected what we could in small donations of cash in Whatcom. Then a friend and I went to Skagit. None of them had any money but nearly all we saw contributed a few tons of hay and oats apiece. The freight boat hauled this produce to Whatcom for half price, and the feed men handled it for nothing, and the road workers took half pay. So by everybody helping we got a passable highway that we could drive over, and even bicycle upon very comfortably. As the very cheapest method of getting about, bicycles had become a popular mode of travel by that time."

BOOM DAYS OF 1889

TIDE FLAT CONTROVERSIES

The hectic boom days of 1889-'90, when lots and lands changed hands like magic, when flimsy structures mushroomed over night, when hotels and wharves blossomed on every inlet, when, now long forgotten, townsites were platted throughout the timbered wilderness; are illustrated by the

---

*Mrs. George H. Bacon gave the author permission to quote from this.

following extracts from the manuscript, Booming and Panic-ing on Puget Sound by George H. Bacon as he continues:

"The tide flats in Whatcom were claimed by the upland shore owners as lying adjacent to and a part of their property, but on account of line disputes these owners were beginning to quarrel vigorously among themselves as to their rights. Just then a rumor arrived that the Territory was intending to claim them all. One night about dusk and at low tide, as I was returning to my hotel, I noticed lanterns out on the flats and I heard sounds of stake driving, loud protests and general quarreling and confusion. A man in rubber boots whom I accosted in the street, to find out what it was all about, said, 'They are jumping the tide flats.' I made a quick decision—good-bye to my Illinois job. I got hold of some rubber boots, picked up a friend who was a heavy weight, and looked like a fighter, and together we staked out, and put our claim notices on 100 by 85 feet.

"The next day we let a contract for piling a part of this tract, and on its completion built a frame shack for an office with a sidewalk out over the water to connect with the nearest street and moved in. This took several weeks' time during which a couple of University of Illinois friends arrived, also to locate. We had a big sleeping room with several beds in it behind the office and some bunks in the basement, so we had plenty of accommodation for our friends and soon picked up several more newly-arrived youngsters who became part of our 'gang.'

"I was served with the usual protest notice by a shore owner claimant but there were so many of us by this time that it was thought best to let us alone, although there were many fist fights elsewhere and one shooting scrap in which no one was injured. Later on, sure enough, the State surveyed and claimed the whole area but allowed titles to squatters who had built, and actually lived on, their tracts, so we got our 100 by 85 feet. Fifteen years after, we sold that same piece of water to the Great Northern Railway for $3,000 cash.

During the day our crowd would scatter out to various occupations of surveying, carpentering, pile contracting, and water front work, but all met at night to go to the same restaurant together and then adjourn to the office for the night.

"Two of our pick-up members were taking up homesteads out in the timber and we all had to go and see their claims and one or more spent a night at their cabins. The density of the timber and the matted tangle of underbrush everywhere made it impossible to go fifty feet from the trail without a compass to guide us back. In fact one of the Illinois boys got lost in town not 400 feet back from the bay in a deep cedar jungle where now stands a fifteen story hotel.

"By that time we had added to our crowd:

Item No. 1—A spoiled youngster from Connecticut sent out here by rich relatives to keep him out of mischief. Item No. 2—a hard-bitten, very radical surveyor from Kansas. Item No. 3—A long-mustached ex-sheriff from Idaho, twice our age who seemed to like to be with us so much that we gave him a bunk downstairs, and adopted him.

"Other buildings had sprung up around us, all being over the water, so we soon had a miniature Venice made of board shacks, with firewood, boxes of apples, etc., delivered to us by canoe.

"Frequently a south-eastern would kick up a big storm with heavy rollers and in the middle of the night bring in a log to bump our pile foundation. This would wake up the ex-sheriff whose job it became to climb out in his night shirt and fish around with a pike pole until he got that log loose and headed toward some other man's shack. It was no trouble at all to the rest of us for we were too sound asleep to know anything that was happening.

"Within a few months of my arrival in Whatcom, the town lot boom in Whatcom was on in full blast. There were several 'professionals' wandering up and down the Sound, who had been following the booms all over the West and most of whom had just come in from California. They were experienced, quick in their decisions, had ample cash to operate with and generally got out with a profit in three or six months' time. One of them, I remember particularly, was a cheerful rosy-faced man with both legs off at the knees, who stumped around on knee-pads, carrying an umbrella to use as a cane. It took him double time to walk a mile, but he asked no odds of anyone and got there just the same. He bought and owned for six months a lot, with a ledge of rock on it now almost the exact center of the city of Bellingham. He made two or three thousand dollars on it and let it go—in fact this traveling fraternity of good sports were generally much more successful operators than we locals who over-stayed the market.

"For several months during 1889, values—or what we called values— were changing so fast that property owners were actually afraid to sell or quote a price. Money was at a discount—apparently everyone had worlds of it, but property was at a premium. One real estate man sold the same lot three times in one day, making for himself three commissions and for the different owners $1,000 apiece. Everything was sold by the map, and anyone asking to be shown the actual property was laughed at. For a short time you could have safely bought anything that had a good title anywhere and have been sure of making a good profit.

"The Fairhaven boom was typical of that which was going on in half a dozen other places on the Sound, so a description of its technique will fit them all.

"Imagine first a sloping side hill with timber all cleared off and the stumps remaining. The initial construction was always a roomy shed made of rough lumber for the Company offices, with a large windowed addition for the engineer's map and drafting table. Next. Out went a wharf where supplies and visitors could land and a clearing crew started to work on the street selected to be the main business thoroughfare. Before the powder men could get away from the first block, the engineers were upon them putting in the permanent corners for the business lots, for these would sell ahead of everything. Next. Tent or very temporary shack restaurants, real estate offices and bunk houses went up.

"Meanwhile, a large grading outfit would be at work on the transcontinental railroad line, which always started from the waterfront inland to meet and make connection with the one from New York, Boston, Philadelphia or Chicago and was anxious to get through to the Coast. Haste was so imperative that after a mile or two was graded the ties and rails were laid and an engine and a few flat cars made their appearance. These were presumably sent out by the higher-ups to expedite progress, as shown by the initials newly painted on the engine, and whenever a boat of visitors arrived this train was busy switching and whistling down at the waterfront end, so as to be both seen and heard.

"By this time some timber man would have been induced to start a saw mill. This saw mill also had a good loud whistle and as the boat landed the engineer found occasion to turn it loose. If the pile drivers could possibly raise a squeal they joined in. Maps and plats of town lots and additions had been blueprinted by the scores and the real estate men were en masse at the wharf. The scene was set. At last, Oh Visitor, your long search for the El Dorado of your dreams has ended! Here was the place, the only place, to invest your money! You could either stay with it and

UPPER—Sehome, Washington Territory in 1889. Railroad Avenue crosses the picture in the foreground. Elk street (State) crosses in the center. The Grand Central Hotel (later called the "Baker"), is in the upper center and stood on the southeast corner of Holly and Forest streets. The housing shortage in 1890, put the author's family in the little white house to the right of the empty hotel building. Thus the lot, with its stumps next door, the big porch of the hotel and the vacant block between Forest and Elk street (State), became the playgrounds of the author and her brother. This building with its twin and the Roger's Hall just south, still stand today—1951. The buildings to the left are on East Holly street. Jenkins' Apartment House, under construction, is on Forest street, left of Holly street.— Photo by courtesy of Miss Belle McAlpine.

LOWER—George Francis Train, in the center foreground at the Sehome wharf, is about to board the steamer, "Premier" on May 9, 1891. She was to carry him and these excursionists to Victoria, where he would board the steamer "Empress of India" for Yokohama. He was endeavoring to circumnavigate the globe in sixty days and advertise New Whatcom, Washington.

help it grow, or you could leave it and go away confident, happy and fully assured that your fortune was made."

THE CROSS-ROAD SHINGLE MILL

When the monuments to the Winning of the Northwest are erected, one shaft should be dedicated to the little Cross-road Shingle Mill, since this provided the hard dollar needed so desperately by the frightened settler after the boom had collapsed—after the Panic of 1893 had placed the black grip of hard times on the land—a grip that was not eased until the Spanish and the Philippine wars; and the Klondike and Nome gold rushes, had breathed new life into trade channels. (See opposite page).

The completion of the Northern Pacific Railway to Puget Sound started a movement of settlers westward that dwarfed the earlier covered-wagon migrations. Through the late '80's this flood increased. The immigrants arrived by the thousand, traveling by day coach, by Pullman, by freight train. Whole families, sometimes entire communities, occupied long strings of freight cars, together with their livestock, farm implements, and household goods; eating and sleeping in these cars as they rolled toward the promised land.

Whatcom County settlers on reaching the rail-head moved north by boat, for the most part. Nevertheless the Northern towns mushroomed no less amazingly than those farther south. From dawn to dark hundreds of carpenters' hammers, near and far, rattled against the rising buildings like machine gun chatter. New houses and stores were completed as if by magic.

Promoters platted new townsites, sold lots; perhaps optimistically erected hotels or docks—this in town, the very names of which are now forgotten.

Hopeful settlers splashed over muddy, rutted roads and trails, or followed the river, and bought tracts of almost impenetrable woodland.

The crash found these worried immigrants overflowing their unfinished houses, which stood in narrow stump-filled clearings where dripping forest trees leaned oppressively close.

UPPER—Ten oxen pulling a big log over a skid road. These roads were constructed, after a right-of-way had been cleared through the timber, by partly sinking peeled logs at regular intervals across the road. Then these were greased well, with dogfish oil, thus making it easier for the logs to slide over the skids.

LOWER—The cross road shingle mill came to the rescue of hundreds of settlers after the hard times of 1893. It made it possible for him to cut down the tall cedar stumps standing on his farm, and to hunt out the burned over cedar logs, then saw them into shingle bolts which were hauled to the cross-road shingle mills, thus supplying the settler with a few necessary large, round silver dollars. This was the Ed Brown shingle mill at Custer, Washington.—Photo courtesy of P. M. Behme.

Weaklings that could do so returned East. The others, their money gone, no crops or produce in sight, no jobs at hand, waited grimly. And then they found the shingle mill!

The Great Northern Railway began building to the Coast in 1889, but it missed the traffic of the land boom, since the 1893 panic had arrived before the rails reached tidewater and the last spike was driven in the summer of 1893. Meantime this railroad had constructed a line along the coast into British Columbia. Thus the Northwest was provided with rail transportation and a method of moving its mill products. Providentially the East demanded these, particularly cedar shingles, even during hard times.

In the early '50's and '68 and again in 1885, a great fire swept large sections of Whatcom county, leaving dead cedar trees standing everywhere, as well as tall, partly burned snags and stumps; also much down timber; all mingled with rotting fir logs. But the cedar was sound—sound as the day it was fire killed. This the settler found on his land, screened by birch and alder, and by second growth fir.

Doubtfully the newcomer, fresh from the prairie states, fingered the edge of a double-bitted ax. Or he watched neighbors standing on spring boards, high above the ground, dragging a long heavy cross-cut saw through the butt of a dead cedar being felled for shingle bolts. (Opposite page 199). To his pleased surprise he learned that a strong man, by working ten hours a day, might cut and split a cord of shingle bolts and swamp out a path, so that these might be dragged by stone-boat out to the road. For this labor he would receive one round silver dollar. He learned also that if he owned the timber he might exact additional pay for each cord cut; that if he possessed a team he might earn another dollar per cord by hauling the bolts to the mill.

The black cloud had disclosed its silver lining. Here were the bare necessities—flour, lard, salt pork, and beans; or shoes, overalls, and calico— (the flour sacks would provide the underwear).

Living meagerly, dressed poorly (yet fully as well as his neighbors), the late immigrant settled grimly to his task. In spare time he chiseled ever wider his hole in the woods, sinking the family roots deeper and deeper into the land. If he faltered at times, a shrill and challenging voice reached him from the cross-roads where the little wheezy, rickety, one-block* shingle mill flaunted its black smoke plume as bravely as ever floated the white plume of Navarre.

---

*One-Block: A one-block mill was one generally using a manually operated shingle machine, with one saw, cutting on one cedar block, and producing one shingle at each forward motion. There were mechanical two-block or ten-block machines that would cut on two blocks or ten blocks at one time.

In a cattle country the small boy is going to be a top rider when he grows up; in a railroad town an engineer's job is his aim. So in this new land the boy decided he would be a knot-sawyer when he was old enough. The mill engineer's job did not tempt him, nor that of the shingle weavers whose swift moving hands packed the shingles into bundles. The shingle-sawyer up on his platform, busily shoving his single cedar block back and forth through his screaming horizontal saw, admittedly had an important task, one that produced a satisfying noise. Yet he was not tops. No, the knot sawyers were the aristocrats, the big money earners, the free spenders of the community. Up on the hurricane deck they stood in the black, wide-bottomed trousers characteristic of the trade. Covered with red cedar dust these slim men moved with catlike surety. "Zing, Zing"; the flying fingers had edged a shingle, "Zing, zing"; a knot had been split away; and ever the vicious little saw was reaching for those fingers. Few sawyers indeed, long retained as much as one whole finger. And this was one of the charms of the job for the small boy. Here was a position calling for courage, for the shedding of blood, as well as being one of high pay.

In 1894 another great fire swept over much of Whatcom county, leaving vast areas of dead fir to the grubs and the rot; but also adding more tracts of dead cedar.

For a full generation longer the cedars that had died in early fires continued to provide the needed extra dollar to the growing families. Many a pair of school shoes; many an extra term at school or college came from shingle bolts hewed from stumps or snags that earlier cutters had discarded. And many an ambitious youth developed his muscles this hard way, swinging a great iron-bound wooden maul against crab-apple tree wedges, or dragging his seven-foot cross-cut saw down through a half buried cedar log.

And then, finally, the last stump had been cut into bolts. The voice of the last Cross-road Shingle Mill was stilled. The mill had vanished. In all likelihood, gone also was the little country store and postoffice that had gravitated originally to the one-time communal center. The very mill site, perhaps, was forgotten, unmarked as it was, even by a pile of moldy sawdust.

THE IRON BOLT

In hundreds of American communities the phrase, "From across the tracks," evokes a picture of social inequality and of gang warfare. With the Bellingham Bay municipalities there was no, "Across the tracks." The rails came late and followed the shore line. However, there was a line of demarcation for these towns; not of social distinction—but of a jealously regarded tribal boundary. This was marked by the Iron Bolt.

The Iron Bolt is the bench mark of the original surveys of Sehome and Whatcom, made in 1858. It is the initial point of the common boundary. The bolt was driven into solid rock, near the shoreline of the sandstone ridge at the corner of Champion and West Holly Streets.

Sehome was surveyed May 8, 1858, by W. W. DeLacy. The plat of the Whatcom townsite, surveyed by A. M. Poe, is dated July 24, 1858. During this same month of July, 1858, public records first mention the Iron Bolt. This is in a lease by Peabody to Latson, covering the mill property at Whatcom Falls. When Eugene Canfield had the first survey made for a proposed railroad to extend along the shore line as far as Squalicum Creek, the initial bench-mark used was the Iron Bolt.

The present survey and plat of that portion of Bellingham originally known as Sehome, was made in 1883 by E. C. Prather, and was filed that same year by P. B. Cornwall of the Bellingham Bay Improvement Company. Description therein of the common boundary between Whatcom and Sehome or New Whatcom, contains the following reference: "The initial point of the survey of New Whatcom is an iron bolt driven in the solid rock on the side of the bluff." (Opposite page 87).

From earliest days Whatcom and Sehome were active rivals. Consolidation was urged frequently but neither side would concede much. Each faction was suspicious and jealous of the other. Near the end of the agitation, the Iron Bolt boundary-line in fact had become a sort of a Watch on the Rhine.

Inflamed by charges and counter charges, the Whatcomites decided to make the Sehomites eat their words. With much clamor, a crowd led by Robert Knox, so the story goes, formed in Old Town and marched up the Viaduct. They crossed the boundary, below the Oakland Block, and halted uncertainly. Meantime some unknown Sehome Paul Revere had carried word of the coming invasion. A Sehome force, reportedly led by Ed Cosgrove, marched down Holly, whereupon the Whatcomites retreated to the line and stood their ground. The Sehomites rushed up, then halted at the boundary just as suddenly. Threats were exchanged, but each side seemed disinclined "to put the issue to the touch of battle." With tempers cooling, the warriors finally marched away, each side claiming victory. However, small boys later carried on the warfare, raiding across the line, well knowing they would be beaten if caught.

The contest was settled December 27, 1890, when the citizens voted 620 to 94 for the union* of the two towns. Reporting on the election the newspapers appeared with the headlines: "Good-bye Iron Bolt."

---

*November 25, 1883—Whatcom incorporated
December 27, 1883—Passed by the Common Council of the City of Whatcom
July 17, 1888—Sehome incorporated. (Continued on page 243).

Chapter XXVII.

EARLY RAILROADS

FOR YEARS Northwest settlers talked railroads. Then, suddenly the rails came—mostly during the hectic decade ending in 1893. Many an individual recalls how, as a child, he crouched behind a stump, to stare in terrified delight at the first noisy, smoking locomotive rocketing down a forest aisle.

The insulting blat of the present day diesel leaves this person cold—evoking no dream of travel in far places such as thrilled him when the scream of the first locomotive shrilled through the moonlit nights. His memory is of that decade when each wild rumor stimulated land speculation; when each community dreamed of some special railroad that would trail cities and prosperity in its wake; when paper railways blossomed by the score.

This chapter primarily is an outline of coastal railroad building from the Fraser River to Seattle, covering the period ending about 1904. A partial sketch of overland roads for the same period has been included. In some few instances and particularly in biographies, it has been necessary to continue the story beyond the year 1904.

After years of agitation, Congress in 1853 appropriated $150,000 for the survey of four rail routes to the Pacific coast. This sum was to be expended under Secretary of War Jefferson Davis, who believed that a southern line alone would be practicable and would result in the extension of slave territory.

Major Isaac I. Stevens was placed in charge of the Northern survey, at the same time being appointed Governor of the newly created Territory of Washington, and named Superintendent of Indian Affairs.

Stevens assembled his force of engineers, scientists and helpers at St. Paul, at the same time asking that Captain George B. McClellan be given command of the survey at the western end of the line.

(Continued from page 242).

May 8, 1890—Sehome reincorporated as New Whatcom
May 6, 1890—Fairhaven incorporated
February 16, 1891—Whatcom and New Whatcom consolidated as New Whatcom
February 19, 1901—New Whatcom name changed to Whatcom by Legislative Act
October 27, 1903—Citizens of Fairhaven and Whatcom voted to consolidate under the name of Bellingham
July 12, 1904—New charter adopted
July 29, 1904—"City of Bellingham" held its first official meeting

The new Governor completed his portion of the work and reached Olympia in December, 1853. In the meantime, McClellan seems to have displayed the timidity and dilatory tactics that eight or nine years later, when he commanded the Union armies, threatened the very life of the nation. His report filed February, 1854, tended to discredit the entire rail- · road project. Accordingly Stevens disregarded his subordinate's findings and forwarded a comprehensive report of his own in the spring of 1854. For years this was the recognized authority on Puget Sound.

Urged as a war measure, the railroad to San Francisco was authorized in 1862 when Congress granted charters to the Union Pacific and the Central Pacific railways, each company being given substantial land and government bond subsidies.

Two years later, 1864, President Lincoln signed the Northern Pacific bill providing for a road from Lake Superior to Puget Sound with a line down the Columbia to Portland. The measure carried no monetary bonus but did grant the company twenty sections of land per mile of track in the states of Oregon and Minnesota and forty sections per mile in the territories. Also the law carried a clause forbidding the bonding of company property; this last a proviso that delayed construction and altered railroad history.

After several futile attempts, Jay Cooke and Company were asked to finance the road. Several agents of the great banking firm were sent over the proposed route, the western agent, after visiting Puget Sound, submitting the following report:

"What can't be got out of the soil which sustains the growth of sawing firs and cedars 200 feet high? Salmon are not caught here, they are pitch-forked out of the streams. Jay, we have the biggest thing on earth. Our enterprise is an inexhaustible gold mine."

Before Cooke and Company could finance the road it became necessary to amend the charter so bonds might be issued. According to Edward Eldridge, the Congressman from Oregon prepared to block the proposal unless the Northern Pacific would agree to build the Columbia line first, with the branch extending from Portland to Puget Sound. It was believed that Portland would become the terminus and the line across the Cascade would not be constructed. The road agreed to these terms and Congress approved the amendment to the Charter.

Accordingly the road was bonded for $100,000,000, the banking firm agreeing to sell the bonds at par and to allow the railroad company eighty-eight cents of each dollar received. In addition to this commission, the bank was to receive $200 in stock with each $1,000 bond sold. A pool was formed and within thirty days Cooke and Company sold $5,000,000 worth of bonds. Despite a monster advertising campaign, the funds thus raised were inadequate. Shortly after the rails of the Union Pacific and Central Pacific had been joined at Promontory Point, Utah, in May, 1869, Jay Cooke and Company negotiated a $50,000,000 loan from a syndicate of German bankers. Edward Eldridge, about 1890, wrote: "All arrangements were made for the signing of the papers when the French and German War took place, which broke up the matter . . . But for the war the Northern Pacific would have been finished by the Centennial and there would have been a city on Bellingham Bay of 100,000 inhabitants today."

Bitter controversy raged as to the location of the northern terminus of the Portland-Puget Sound branch line. In 1869, Thomas Canfield, managing agent of the Company, inspected various lands and water frontage offered by rival towns. Later, at his request, Edward Eldridge met two company agents, General Sprague and E. S. Smith, and using a large canoe, the three inspected all the shoreline and all sites from Seattle to Bellingham Bay.

The railroad plat showed a line from Portland to Bellingham Bay with the usual withdrawal of forty sections of public lands per mile. This the Secretary of Interior declined to approve on the grounds that such road would be in competition with water transportation along the Sound and therefore unneeded, hence would not justify such extensive land bonuses. Railroad lands were returned to public entry as far south as Seattle, which act created the belief that Seattle would be the Northern Pacific terminus. Wild land speculation followed which did not abate, according to Eldridge, until it was announced, July 14, 1873, that Tacoma would be the end of the line.

Prior to this, in July, 1870, the Northern Pacific began building west from Thompson's Junction, Minnesota. The line from Kalama on the Columbia River to Tacoma was started the same year, and was completed in December, 1873. Construction work halted when Jay Cooke and Company failed in September during the panic of 1873.

A year later, or in 1874, Henry Villard, Bavarian born correspondent entered the railroad picture, when, on behalf of various German bond holders, he opened negotiations with Ben Holladay, transportation mogul of the Northwest. In 1879, Villard organized the Oregon Railway and Navigation Company to control the Holladay and other properties, thereby acquiring a monopoly of Columbia valley traffic. To protect this monopoly and prevent the Northern Pacific from building in his territory, he persuaded Wall Street financiers to subscribe $8,000,000 to a blind pool, which he used to purchase control of that railroad in 1881. Villard completed the Oregon Railway and Navigation Company line up the south bank of the Columbia to Ainsworth at the mouth of the Snake River during the year 1883. That same year as president of the Northern Pacific he pushed to completion the segment of that road extending eastward from Ainsworth.

In his capacity as president of the Northern Pacific, Villard, on September 8, 1883, at Gold Creek, Montana, presided over elaborate gold spike ceremonies, attended by Ex-President Grant and other dignitaries. Immediately thereafter, the first through train to Portland rolled west over the combined trackage of Villard's two systems.

Judge William H. Harris, one time probate judge of Whatcom county, who with his family was moving west from the Yellowstone valley, has left the following account of the journey by the first Northern Pacific overland train:

"In August, 1883, the N. P. R. R. was not completed, but the day of its completion and the celebration thereof by the driving of the golden spike, was fixed at a time some thirty days later, and we made a race with the officials of the road to be ready to travel when it should be opened. And we were passengers ticketed to Portland, Oregon, on the first through train.

"We were obliged to wait two days in Portland for further transportation . . . We took a steamer from Portland down the Willamette and the Columbia Rivers to Kalama on the Washington side of the Columbia, from where the railroad extended to Tacoma . . . On reaching Tacoma our travel by rail ended, and we were literally hauled onto a small wheezy, asthmatic, overloaded steamer that reached Seattle in about six hours . . . We remained two days in Seattle, awaiting the semi-service to Whatcom by the steamer *Washington*, which put us into Bellingham Bay early in the afternoon, after an eighteen-hour trip from Seattle."

Railroading on the Tacoma-Kalama branch was decidedly primitive according to W. A. Fairweather who drove one of the first locomotives. Tenino was the only telegraph station between terminals, cars were left on the main line for unloading. These were picked up by the next train, pushed to the nearest switch and cut-in. Despite these primitive methods, no wrecks occurred. Rolling stock, through 1874-'76 included two passenger coaches, two baggage cars, four thirty-ton and two five-ton locomotives. The latter had water tanks on top of the boilers, but the capacity of these

---

UPPER—Number 1 engine at Bellingham Bay in 1889. It was built by H. J. Booth & Company (later Union Iron Works) of San Francisco in 1868 as "D. O. Mills" for the Black Diamond Coal Company, and shipped to P. B. Cornwall in Sehome, Washington Territory, along with the "Black Diamond" to be used on his line, the Bellingham Bay and British Columbia Railroad. Billy Mann, the first engineer on the B. B. & B. C., is in the cab. This picture was taken by Fred Jukes at the B. B. I. Co.'s mill in 1902.—Photo courtesy of Fred Jukes.

LOWER—The Fairhaven & Southern Railroad train leaving Fairhaven, February 14, 1891 to meet the New Westminster Southern Railway at the international border at Blaine.

was insufficient for the run between supply points. Therefore wooden water tanks were built on flat cars and coupled directly to the engines by means of bent crowbars. These wooden tanks were higher than the engines, and much heavier when full, so there was danger of the locomotive being run over in case of an abrupt stop.

Although the Kalama branch of the Northern Pacific was completed in 1873, that road did not have the distinction of operating the first locomotive to Puget Sound. That honor was claimed by the Seattle Coal and Transportation Company, (the Dinsmore road) which by barge and tram was bringing coal from Newcastle through Lake Washington-Lake Union to bunkers at the foot of Pike Street in Seattle. The SEATTLE POST-INTELLIGENCER of March 25, 1872, thus records the event:

"Friday last was decidedly a holiday in this city owing to the opportunity afforded everyone to indulge in the novelty of a free ride behind the first locomotive that ever whistled, and snorted and dashed through the dense forests surrounding the waters of Puget Sound. Business in town was not exactly suspended, but it might very near as well have been, as an excursion on Dinsmore's Railroad, connecting Union Lake with the Sound, with its constantly departing and returning train of cars during the day, seemed uppermost in the minds of all, and pretty much monopolized every other consideration."

NORTHERN PACIFIC REACHES TACOMA

Construction of the Northern Pacific Main Line continued from the Columbia up the Yakima river toward Tacoma, the route from Ellensburg to Stampede Pass being closely paralleled decades later by the Chicago, Milwaukee and St. Paul line on its way to Snoqualmie Pass. Contract for the tunnel was let in 1886. Work on the switchback was begun the following March and completed June 1, 1887. The first train over the new route arrived June 6. On July 4, Tacoma staged a monster celebration attended by notables from both sides of the Border.

Meantime Nelson Bennett, later the owner of the Colony Mill at Whatcom, and one of the developers of the Fairhaven townsite, completed

UPPER—Great Northern trestle across the Bay to the left. A drawbridge is in the span; just beyond is the Whatcom depot, and between the drawbridge and the depot is the Colony wharf, or "B" street wharf, and on maps of later date, called the "Fairhaven Land Company's Wharf," which extended out to deep water. The G street wharf is the one beyond.—Photo courtesy Cecil A. Morse.

LOWER—New Whatcom, Washington in 1892. Prospect, Champion and Bay streets are in the foreground. The B. B. Furniture store stands on the triangle today—1951. The Reveille building was moved and Prospect street cut through the triangle thus joining Holly street. The Lighthouse building is in the center (Seattle-First National Bank Building). Large building, upper left, is the Grand Central Hotel, corner of Holly and Forest streets.—Photo courtesy Cecil A. Morse.

the tunnel under adverse conditions of weather and topography. The great bore costing $1,100,000 brought him a profit variously estimated at from $100,000 to $250,000. When the final shot broke through May 3, 1888, rival crews from the east and west each struggled to shove a representative into the other workings. Mrs. S. J. Bennett, sister-in-law of Nelson Bennett, was the first woman to traverse the tunnel. After being stuck in the first narrow opening, she was dragged triumphantly through to the damage of dress and epidermis.

The first vestibuled train rolled westward through the tunnel June 25, 1888. Again Tacoma celebrated.

And again the emigrant trains also rolled; not trains of covered wagons, but trains of box cars in which most of the emigrants cooked and slept while traveling with their livestock, farm machinery, and household effects. Attached to these trains were coaches, called Emigrant or Tourist Sleepers. These cars were provided with upper berths and with slatted uncushioned seats that might be folded together and covered with a board so as to support a mattress. The tourist provided his own mattress and bedding. In one corner of the car was a flat topped wood stove for the warming of food or the making of coffee.

Selection of Tacoma as the Northern Pacific terminus in 1873, did not settle the railroad question. Additional routes were advocated, paper lines were created by the score, and railway talk raged for years. In the Bellingham Bay area, overland railroad proponents severally urged a route through the Skagit passes, one to the North of Mount Baker, and third, a connection with the Canadian Pacific Railway.

Local roads northward from Seattle eventually fell into two systems. One of these, lying from ten to fifteen miles inland, formed the Seattle-Sedro-Woolley-Sumas branch of the Northern Pacific Railway. The other group, closely paralleling the shore, became the Seattle-Bellingham-Vancouver division of the Great Northern Railway.

BELLINGHAM BAY AND BRITISH COLUMBIA RAILROAD

P. B. Cornwall, president of the Bellingham Bay Coal Company electrified Whatcom County citizens in 1883 with the announcement that the Bellingham Bay and British Columbia Railroad had been formed to build a line from Whatcom to Burrard Inlet, British Columbia (site of Vancouver) where it would connect with the Canadian Pacific Railway. Included in the board of directors of the ten million dollar corporation were D. O. Mills, New York financier, P. B. Cornwall, Louis McLane and other capitalists. The company owned the Sehome townsite and 4,000 acres in surrounding areas. Cornwall further stated that both the Canadian Pacific and the Northern Pacific had arranged to connect with the new line. Platting of a new townsite and preliminary surveys for the road were begun at once.

According to the WHATCOM REVEILLE the first sod on the new railroad grade was turned April 7, 1884, by Mrs. H. Hofercamp. The paper dwelt at length on this "important niche in the chronology of historical events . . ." Through several depression years work stagnated. The Canadian Pacific refused to make connection with the Cornwall road. Hope revived in 1888 when the Canadian government voted to pay the Canadian Pacific $14,000,000 to surrender its monopoly clause, thus making possible the building of connecting lines.

Two locomotives, the "D. O. Mills" and the "Black Diamond," the first to operate on the Bay, were delivered to the Cornwall road in October, 1888. (Opposite page 246). Thirty flat cars and 400 tons of rails also were landed. T. G. Nicklin and wife, who rode the engine "D. O. Mills" from the machine shop to the Whatcom creek bridge and return, claimed the distinction of being the first railroad passengers in Whatcom county. With no construction work under way, the locomotives had no duties. Old settlers declared its sole purpose was the impressing of visitors—hence it was run back and forth on the track with much whistling and flowing off of steam whenever a boat arrived with prospective settlers or lot buyers.

L. M. Stangroom an experienced engineer, next was placed in charge of construction and under his direction the Bellingham Bay and British Columbia Railroad, twenty-three miles in length, was completed to Sumas, March 1, 1891. Several weeks later the Canadian Pacific made connections at the Border.

THE GREAT WATER FIGHT

To welcome the first overland Canadian Pacific train, due June 22, 1891, New Whatcom staged an elaborate celebration. This mis-fired so badly it became almost an international incident. Two bands, patriotic organizations, and firemen, all in uniform, awaited the visitors at Holly Street and Railroad Avenue where a great arch had been erected, carrying the British and American colors on separate pillars.

The Donald Farquharson family, arriving that day from Michigan, have told how the fire companies of Sehome and Whatcom lined up on opposite sides of the tracks, it being planned that the train should arrive beneath an arch of water. Unfortunately the rival companies started a water fight, and the train rolled in between opposing columns of water delivered with force sufficient to break the coach windows and drench the guests. Roth reports that, after abject apologies had been accepted, the distinguished guests sat down to a banquet at the Purdy Opera House—C and Thirteenth Street (West Holly).

During the interval certain excitable youths noted that the British flag on the arch, was a few inches higher than the American. In attempting to equalize the height of the two flags the British emblem was dropped, trampled under foot and left, as the prime movers of the act fled. The Canadians naturally were highly incensed and the insult was discussed in the Chancelleries of Canada, Great Britain and the United States, but responsibility was not fixed.

J. J. Donovan whose first railroad experience was with the Northern Pacific in Montana, in 1898, became general superintendent and chief engineer of the Bellingham Bay and British Columbia Railroad. Under his direction the survey of an extension to Spokane was undertaken. Construction work on a branch line from Sumas up the Nooksack River was pushed in 1900 and 1901, but the road was completed no farther than Glacier. A branch line was constructed to Lynden in 1903.

Later, in 1911, the Bellingham Bay and British Columbia passed to the Chicago, Milwaukee and St. Paul Railroad. The REVEILLE reported on October 18, 1912: "The Milwaukee will formally absorb local road today." Thus ended the B. B. & B. C.

PIERRE BARLOW CORNWALL
November 23, 1821 — September 25, 1904

Pierre Barlow Cornwall, born November 23, 1821, in Delaware County, New York, early graduated from a country school to a commission and shipping house in Buffalo. The report on Fremont's expedition to the Pacific Coast (1845-'46) so fired his imagination that in 1848 he headed a party of five, bound for the Northwest. Word of the California gold discovery, received enroute, caused him to turn south. He reached California late in August. After a brief mining experience he established himself in the trading and real estate business at Sutter's Fort, Sacramento.

Cornwall was a member of the first California territorial legislature. Moving to San Francisco he became widely identified with shipping, merchandising, and manufacturing interests. For years he headed the Bellingham Bay Coal Company. He became manager and president of the Black Diamond Coal Company, successfully mining coal deposits at Mt. Diablo near San Francisco, also working the very profitable Black Diamond coal mine southeast of Seattle.

As head of the company owning the Sehome townsite and large acreage surrounding the Bay, Cornwall platted and developed the town of New

Whatcom. Besides the Bellingham Bay and British Columbia Railroad Company, he acquired and operated the street railway system, the water-works, and light system. He also constructed the largest sawmill, which he replaced, after it burned, at the cost of $300,000.

While leading citizens of the Bay communities frequently disagreed and clashed with Cornwall, none could doubt his sincerity. Bruce Cornwall, son of the man whose life was so closely interwoven with that of Belling-ham, has reported that his father was characterized by a knightly courtesy; an effect heightened, perhaps, by a snow white moustache and imperial. The son attributes to his father a buoyant hopefulness in the face of adversity, and also an inflexible determination. This was illustrated by a law suit that Cornwall continued for thirty years because he felt he was right. He won his case in 1895.

P. B. Cornwall died September 25, 1904. In 1908, his daughter, Mrs. Bertha James Cornwall Fischer, gave the City of Bellingham, Cornwall Memorial Park. Dock Street was renamed Cornwall Avenue in his honor.

CANFIELD ROAD

No sooner had P. B. Cornwall announced the organization of the Bell-ingham Bay and British Columbia Railroad than Senator Eugene Canfield, of Illinois, in August, 1883, informed the delighted citizens of the Bay that a second road was to be constructed.

Canfield had visited the district a few weeks earlier. In fact, he had delivered the Fourth of July oration. Like Cornwall, he stated that a con-nection would be made with the Canadian Pacific. The new venture designated as the Bellingham Bay Railroad and Navigation Company was capitalized at $1,000,000 with Eugene Canfield as president—the purpose: to build a railroad north from Fairhaven to the Boundary along the old Telegraph Road—a duplication of the Cornwall project.

Jay Cooke and Company reportedly were backing Canfield. At least Cooke's attorney bought for the promoter large tracts of land behind the Cornwall holdings. Friends of the new road seized tidelands outside the donation claims for depots, switches, etc. Thereupon Captain Roeder secured an injunction to halt this tide-land jumping. An amicable settlement was effected and the Company purchased all available lots fronting the waterway. In the meantime this activity had started a wave of tideland jumping similar to that of 1858. The AMERICAN REVEILLE of August 17, 1883, reported: "As high as ten trade dollars per day are planked down for the braves who were willing to rush into the briny surf up to the belt and build board fences around the watery waste, and drive piles they never owned, on ground they never possessed, only to be washed down again and floated out to the wide, wide sea."

Canfield engineers ran lines to Lake Whatcom and to Samish valley. They reported an easy grade through the Chuckanut Range. At the same time a number of buildings were erected on the tide flats fronting Whatcom.

From the first, inadequate financing hampered the Bellingham Bay Railroad and Navigation Company, which made frequent public appeals for cash bonuses. Surveys were made east of Sehome. Next, Canfield abandoned his first proposed route to Sumas and selected one instead to serve Blaine and New Westminster. In accord with this plan the city council of Whatcom eventually granted the road a right-of-way across the waterfront, vacating all streets but C and F (required for public wharves) but stipulating that any railroad thirty miles long might use Canfield's tracks at a fair rental. It was planned that the proposed line along Twelfth street (Roeder Avenue) would connect with the rails of the Bellingham Bay and British Columbia at the Sehome wharf. Broadway was the wharf site.

SEATTLE LAKESHORE AND EASTERN RAILWAY COMPANY

Hoping to secure a transcontinental route, either through the Cascades or through Canadian territory, citizens of Seattle in 1885 organized the Seattle Lake Shore and Eastern Railway Company.* Following a route from Lake Washington, generally ten or fifteen miles inland from the coast, the road was completed to Sumas on the Canadian Border in 1891, at which time it passed to control of the Northern Pacific Railroad. In the meantime it had experienced trouble with Senator Canfield.

SEATTLE AND WEST COAST RAILWAY COMPANY

Apparently with the blessing of Northern Pacific officials, the Seattle and West Coast Railway Company was incorporated in 1887 for the purpose of constructing a railroad from Seattle to the Border. Terminal rights were secured in Seattle and that same year 14.4 miles were constructed from Woodinville to Snohomish. Thereupon it sold out to the Seattle Lake Shore and Eastern, to become eventually part of the Northern Pacific system.

CITIZENS OFFER BONUS

Delays in the completion of both the Cornwall and the Canfield railroads became a matter of great concern to the citizens of Bellingham Bay. Dan Harris, owner of the Fairhaven townsite, hoping to speed construction,

*Variously operated under traffic agreement, receivers' sale, lease, and sale; by the Northern Pacific, Seattle and International, Canadian Pacific, and Northern Pacific railways.

visited railroad magnates of San Francisco in 1887 at which time he offered one-half of his lands to the first railroad to reach Fairhaven.

Citizens of the four rival towns on the Bay, forgot their differences for the moment, and called a joint meeting at which it was urged that each real estate holder donate twenty-five per cent of the asssesed value of his property to the first railroad to cross the Cascade Mountains. Captain Roeder, William Utter and Dan Harris went farther, offering to make the donation fifty per cent.

NELSON BENNETT ROAD

The railroad situation was enlivened in 1888 by the arrival of Nelson Bennett for the avowed purpose of constructing a railroad to the Skagit river coal fields. Rumor had it that he represented the Hill roads which were expected to drive a transcontinental line through the Skagit Passes. Bennett acquired the Colony Mill holdings in Whatcom and extensive portions of the Fairhaven townsite. On December 22, 1888, Nelson Bennett, E. M. Wilson, E. L. Cowgill, S. E. Larrabee and C. X. Larrabee, incorporated the Fairhaven and Southern Railway for the purpose of constructing a railroad from the International Boundary to the Columbia River.

Meantime in 1886 the Canadian Pacific Railroad completed its branch from New Westminster to Vancouver. First lots in the newly platted town-site were sold in May, 1886. Fred Bloomquist of Whatcom, much impressed by Vancouver, spoke of it as: "the young giant city of forty hotels, fifty saloons, five churches and miles of sidewalks."

NEW WESTMINSTER AND SOUTHERN RAILWAY

At New Westminster there was much clamor for a rail outlet to the south. Accordingly Canfield organized the New Westminster and Southern Railway in 1888 for the purpose of connecting with the American Railway systems at Seattle. Benjamin Douglas was president. By agreement the pro-moter was to build the road to Whatcom in one year and to Seattle in two years. John Leamy, contractor, began work at once and was progressing nicely when it was discovered that Canfield would be unable to keep his agreement. Thereupon the New Westminster and Southern bought out his interest, paying $20,000 for work completed. Next, they entered into a new contract with Nelson Bennett for the completion of the road.

South of the Border, Canfield, also was hampered financially and had done very little construction work. Accordingly he sold the Bellingham Bay Railroad and Navigation Company to Bennett in July, 1889.

SENATOR EUGENE CANFIELD

John J. Cryderman, last of the railroad engineers of the boom days, has stated that Eugene Canfield entertained the hope of being elected one of the first United States Senators from the new State of Washington. Loss of his hearing blasted that dream.

Cryderman, who was Canfield's chief engineer on the Bellingham Bay Railroad and Navigation Company surveys in 1889, reports that Canfield, then fifty-two years old, was a man of remarkable memory, wide acquaintance, of considerable charm and ability as an organizer. When he started his railway project thirty of his eastern friends put up $1,000 each to be expended by him as he saw fit, without accounting, and without date of repayment.

EXCLUSIVE RIVER CROSSINGS

Canfield had been a senator in Illinois. As a young man he had known Abraham Lincoln when the latter was riding the court circuits. He knew General Grant well enough to call him by his first name. Thomas Canfield of the Southern Pacific was his cousin. Senator Hoare was his friend. In the United States Senate and House were friends, cousins, and relatives by marriage. Certainly the man had great influence or he would not have been able to induce Congress to grant him a charter giving his road the exclusive right to bridge all the rivers north from Seattle to the Border, including the Nooksack. Congress had the right to legislate for the territories but such a monopoly probably was unconstitutional. Judge Thomas Burke representing the Seattle Lake Shore and Eastern thought so, but did not wait for legal tests. Through subterfuge, collusion with the Sheriff, and some fast construction work, his line threw its rails across the Snohomish river before Canfield's injunction could be served. The constitutionality of Canfield's injunction was not tested owing to the collapse of his road, and to the admission of Washington to statehood.

However, the Northern Pacific had different views about the value of Canfield's charter with its exclusive river crossing provisions. About the time that Judge Burke's fast foot-work gave the Seattle Lake Shore and Eastern the opportunity to bridge the Snohomish River before Canfield's injunction could be served, N. P. officials tried to buy the Senator's property.

According to John J. Cryderman who was Senator Canfield's chief engineer in 1889, the Northern Pacific offered Canfield $175,000 for his charter and railroad, plus all money expended to that date by the Bellingham Bay Railroad and Navigation Company project, together with six per cent interest thereon; plus, also, the exclusive townsite rights and lot sales for all towns on the line from Seattle to the Border. Still obsessed with the idea of constructing his own railroad, Canfield declined the offer. In the end, the sale of his bankrupt company brought him very little.

THE CANFIELD SURVEY

Cryderman, who ran location for Canfield from Whatcom to the Border has reported that the proposed route differed from that of Bennett's Fairhaven and Southern and was not used by the latter.

The Bellingham Bay Railroad and Navigation survey, after leaving the Whatcom waterfront, extended up Squalicum creek, past one of the Canfield additions, thence generally along the route of the Northwest Diagonal highway and on to Ferndale. Not receiving the land grants he expected at Ferndale, Canfield had Cryderman shift the proposed line. Under the new survey, the Nooksack river was crossed near the Matz ranch. Some distance north of Ferndale, Canfield set up the townsite of Kingsboro on land donations from H. Cowden, A. W. Tiffany, William J. Malloy, D. R. Henderson and James Lynch. Ferndale citizens were furious. The line was surveyed through Cloverdale above the Border rather than through Blaine.

North of the International Line the grade was almost completed at the time Bennett took over the New Westminster and Southern. South of the Border there was practically no clearing or grading. As Bennett's survey did not follow that of Canfield, the former acquired very little of value except the Broadway street wharf site and the right of way along the Whatcom waterfront.

FAIRHAVEN BOOM

Arrival of Nelson Bennett and the announcement of his railroad project touched off Fairhaven's greatest boom. Dan Harris sold his townsite property to the promoters for $70,000. The Fairhaven Land Company capitalized at $250,000, was incorporated November 26, 1888, by E. M. Wilson, E. L. Cowgill, Nelson Bennett, Charles X. Larrabee, and Samuel E. Larrabee.

J. J. Donovan, Bennett's engineer, reached Bellingham Bay in January, 1889, a pack on his back, after having made a preliminary trip of inspection over the proposed route of the Fairhaven and Southern Railroad.

To Donovan was assigned the task of resurveying and platting the Fairhaven townsite. Lot prices soared. Clearing and grading operations were pushed, while streets along the hillsides were bulkheaded with logs, then planked. The rattle of carpenters' hammers became continuous, as dwellings and business houses seemed to spring from the earth in all directions.

· FAIRHAVEN AND SOUTHERN

Work on the Fairhaven and Southern was pushed vigorously during 1889. The Padden estate donated land for round-house and shops in Happy Valley. Surveys were run behind Sehome hill toward Lake Whatcom, and a grade extended toward the lake past York addition to Sehome. The route to the Skagit coal mines led from Fairhaven up Padden creek, through Chuckanut valley, past Samish lake and up a steep grade to Jarman's Prairie, where the road ended in a bridge. In December townsite officials made a hand-car excursion to the end of the line.

This division of the Fairhaven and Southern reached Sedro-Woolley in July 1890. The following year, near Burlington, connection was made with the Seattle Montana Railway Company to complete the Great Northern Shore route.

With the acquisition of the Canfield lines and shore right-of-ways the Fairhaven Southern abandoned its earlier surveys and began its extension toward New Westminster.

Both Bennett and Donovan were known as "big powder" men. Experience through years of rock work on the mountain divisions of the Northern Pacific had taught them how extra charges of giant powder saved time, labor, and money. Soon heavy explosions were shaking Fairhaven and Bellingham, sometimes breaking windows, while the contractors were blasting great boulders far into the waters of the Bay. Later through the timbered belt north it was the same. Mostly, the huge stumps were split with powder and dragged away by donkey engines. But occasionally, on a slope, a whole stump or an entire tree would be lifted clear of the right-of-way by an extra charge of "giant."

Nelson Bennett, who had declared the Whatcom right-of-way to be the equivalent of a $50,000 bonus to the road, did not choose to make use of the shore line rights acquired with the purchase of Canfield's Bellingham Bay Railroad and Navigation Company. Instead, he elected to swing his road far out from the beach line, and in one long sweeping curve, throw a high railway trestle from the foot of the bluff south of Squalicum creek, to the vicinity of Sehome wharf. (Opposite page 247).

The long planked viaduct leading to the Whatcom wharf; variously called the B Street, the Colony wharf, or on maps of later date, termed the Fairhaven Land Company wharf; crossed the railroad trestle line. South of the Whatcom wharf a drawbridge was provided. North of the long wharf, a pile-supported platform was constructed on which was placed the Whatcom city railway depot, a small frame building. The Sehome depot, of similar proportions, was erected near the Sehome wharf.

Over the long trestle soon would roll the Great Northern trains with sonorous rumble, audible for miles, most satisfying to townsmen who had waited so many years for that sound.

In March, 1890, it was reported that James J. Hill of the Great Northern Railway had acquired controlling stock interests in the Fairhaven and Southern railroad and the New Westminster and Southern Railway. The management, it was announced, would remain unchanged until the roads were completed.

Driving of the piling for the trestle was begun at the Sehome end of the span. Week by week progress on the road to the Border may be followed in excerpts from some of the papers of the day.

In referring to the extension of Bennett's Fairhaven and Southern toward New Westminster, the WHATCOM REVEILLE refers to the northern division as the "Fairhaven and Southern." The BELLINGHAM BAY EXPRESS of Whatcom just as persistently calls the northern branch the "Fairhaven and Northern."

From the REVEILLE of May 16, 1890: "Contract for the drawbridge between Sehome and Whatcom was let yesterday to the San Francisco Bridge Company. It is to be placed in front of the saw mill between the two towns and is to be a 182 foot span."

The BELLINGHAM BAY EXPRESS of Whatcom on June 3, 1890 reported: "Yesterday papers were signed by representatives of the Bellingham Bay and British Columbia Railroad granting the Fairhaven and Northern Railroad right-of-way through and across their property along the waterfront . . . One stipulation in the right-of-way agreement insisted upon by the B. B. & B. C. R. R., was that a first class depot should be erected somewhere between the Sehome Dock and Broadway . . ."

"June 21, 1890: The piles are driven on the Fairhaven and Northern nearly across the New Whatcom water front. Yesterday the road was cut through the long wharf and now pile drivers are hard at work at it pushing the work in front of Whatcom."

"August 8, 1890: The last pile has been driven in the railway along the waterfront. The engines' whistles will soon be heard."

"August 23, 1890: The track layers on the Great Northern have now got across Squalicum Creek and are advancing on Blaine at the rate of one and one-half miles per day."

"Saturday, October 11, 1890: The first train on the Great Northern steamed into Ferndale, on Thursday afternoon."

From the FAIRHAVEN WEEKLY WORLD: "Saturday, October 11, 1890— The first shipment of freight by rail from here to Ferndale went out over the Fairhaven and Southern Thursday. There is now a regular daily train to the Nooksack, leaving here at 11:30 A. M."

From Ferndale a horse-drawn stage carried passengers north to Blaine and New Westminster. This was the stage line operated in the early '90's between Whatcom and New Westminster by Ed Brown, Custer farmer, store-keeper, mill owner and legislator. Horses were changed at the Ben Ferguson ranch three miles north of Ferndale.

The BELLINGHAM BAY EXPRESS: "Thursday, October 23, 1890—HEAVY RAINS: Yesterday the log jam in the Nooksack started and carried away two warehouses and the bridge of the Great Northern Railroad at Ferndale. Three hundred pounds of powder were used to break the jam, the concussion breaking nearly every pane of glass in Ferndale."

Mrs. Maria Oxford, wife of the homesteader, Thomas Oxford, living near Ferndale, was much impressed by the speed with which the one hundred-man track crew advanced the rails on the way toward Blaine. In an interview published July, 1936, in the FERNDALE RECORD, Mrs. Oxford stated that ties were carried forward to the crew by an endless belt suspended from the engine. As soon as these were laid, she said separate groups of six men each came forward with the rails and aligned them over the ties to be spiked in place by the waiting "hammer men." The whole process was completed so fast, she reported, that the train kept up an almost steady creeping pace and moved out of sight in less than two days.

With change of ownership, the Canfield townsite of Kingsboro, north of Ferndale was abandoned. The present depot site, nearer the river was donated by Augustus Griffin, together with a right-of-way 300 feet wide and half a mile long across his homestead. This was approved by E. H. Beckler and J. J. Donovan, chief engineers, respectively, for the Great Northern and the Fairhaven Southern railroads.

While grades generally were easy north of Ferndale, the engineers nevertheless had their troubles with some stream crossings and marshes. North of Enterprise was one morass that absorbed many train loads of ballast. Nearby, according to Peter Harkness, old time telegrapher at Blaine, was a stretch of swelling or rising ground which exasperated graders called the "Devil's Bread Pan." Each evening the crews would leave the tracks level. During the night, the yellow brown earth would swell like rising bread, and lift the rails well above grade. Curious sightseers, according to Harkness, made trips by handcar from Blaine to view the phenomenon.

North of the Border other troublesome spots were encountered. These are mentioned in the FAIRHAVEN WEEKLY WORLD of April 23, 1891, which reported an official inspection of the New Westminster and Southern Railway, made by British Columbia officials.

Referring to one of the soft spots on the new road the WORLD reporter mentioned the Nikomekl River, where the bridge supports required a double tier of piling, the upper ones resting on lower ones forty feet in length.

THE LOST TRAIN

Soft grades continued to harass the road years later, in one instance costing the Great Northern an entire train and locomotive. According to John J. Cryderman of Seattle, Canfield's former engineer, this occurred in 1910 between Burnaby Lake and the summit of the Fraser River—Vancouver extension. Under date of September 27, 1949, Mr. Cryderman has written as follows:

"The Grant Smith Company—one of the best of the big R. R. Contracting firms—had a construction camp there—the site of the accident—and when the crew brought a train load of gravel to use in raising the constantly sinking track, they left it on the side track and went in to dinner.

"When they came back the track, train, and all had vanished and there was simply a sheet of water where it had been. The train consisted of the locomotive and twelve gravel cars.

"Later they tried driving piles there and by fastening one on another —doweling we call it—they went down over two hundred feet but no bottom —SO! that was that. No, they never located either locomotive or cars.

"This is by the courtesy of Mr. N. A. Peltier, who was Great Northern trainman, conductor for many years, and was on much construction work in those early days."

No sooner had the Fairhaven Southern rails reached the Boundary December 1, 1890, than President C. X. Larrabee celebrated with an excursion to Blaine. Unfortunately the locomotive, No. 199, knocked its smokestack off on the frame work of the Nooksack river bridge. Ferndale, equal to the occasion, produced an empty cider barrel in lieu of the stack. With the substitute lashed in place, the train proceeded north, but the misadventure caused many slurring remarks, since Larrabee's excursionists were the Good Templars of Fairhaven.

According to a Seattle reporter the gathering at Blaine, February 14, 1891, to celebrate the junction of the New Westminster and Southern and the Fairhaven and Southern railways was a veritable international love feast attended by high officials and citizens of both nations. (Opposite page 246).

Gaily decorated trains from North and South reached the Boundary almost simultaneously, about 10:45 A. M. As part of the ceremony four highly polished spikes, were brought forward to bind the last rail and were pounded into the ties by Vice-President John Hendry of the Westminster and Southern and by President C. X. Larrabee of the Fairhaven and

Southern. Governor Nelson of British Columbia and Acting Governor Laughton of Washington hammered the spikes deeper. Then the wives of the two governors, Mrs. Nelson and Mrs. Laughton, wielding two solid silver hammers, struck the finishing blows.

During the succeeding celebration at the Blaine opera house, a long and flowery telegram felicitating the representatives of Canada and the United States on the union by rail, and commenting on the significance thereof, purportedly sent by Secretary of State James G. Blaine, was received by the mayor and read with much enthusiasm. (The town of Blaine had been named for the statesman.)

When a copy of the telegram was sought, Peter Harkness, telegraph operator at Blaine denied any knowledge of such a message. Secretary Blaine disavowed sending the telegram. One writer stated that the telegrapher was dismissed because of the fraud, but Peter Harkness in later years declared that his friends rallied to him and prevented such an injustice.

Henry Villard's associates of the Oregon Improvement Company in 1888 organized the Seattle and Northern Railway Company for the purpose of building a railroad from Seattle to the Border. First a branch line intended to lead over the Cascade Mountains was started at Ship Harbor (Anacortes) and extended eastward past Burlington, toward the Skagit River. Late in 1890, a junction was made at Sedro Woolley with the Seattle Lake Shore and Eastern then building toward Sumas.

By coincidence the Seattle Lake Shore and Eastern while extending its grades northward; the Seattle Northern while building eastward; and the Fairhaven and Southern while pushing its line southeast, closely intersected at the newly created townsite of Woolley thereby forming a fifty foot triangle. Townsite-owner Woolley requested Engineer Cryderman of the Seattle Northern to move his line slightly north to form a hundred foot triangle which he felt would be large enough for a depot site. This was done.

Grades of the Seattle Lake Shore and the Seattle Northern were completed at the crossing and although no trackage was near, each road planned to put down a few lengths of rails to preempt the crossing. The Seattle Northern had a hundred feet or more of standard weight steel; the Lake Shore a few twenty pound rails.

As a clash between rival crews seemed imminent, Cryderman and Mrs. Woolley climbed on top of a large fir stump that commanded the scene.

"I hate to see these railroad fights," worried Mrs. Woolley.

"I am a peaceful man," Cryderman assured her, "there will be no trouble."

But when the Seattle Northern construction crew came forward with their steel they were confronted with a triple line of husky lumber jacks and mule skinners stretching up and down the north-south grade. Each front rank man had a peavey, jabbed into the ground, and crossed with that of his neighbor, thus forming a solid fence.

Cryderman hopped off the stump and took command of the Seattle Northern crew. He had his men pick up a steel rail and line up as thickly as possible alongside. Eight or ten feet were left exposed at the front. A wedge of men formed at the side and rear. At a word of command they loped forward. The rail-battering-ram crashed into the peavey fence. Peaveys and men flew in all directions. The ram carried on to the railroad grade where it was dropped. With Lake Shore men surrounding the Seattle Northern gang, the free-for-all battle raged for several minutes. Then, honor being satisfied, by mutual agreement it was decided to let the lawyers of the two companies settle the crossing argument. The Seattle Northern laid its east-west lengths of steel on the grade; the Seattle Lake Shore dropped its rails on top.

When Cryderman returned to the stump, Mrs. Woolley sniffed, "You and your peaceful methods."

After higher ups had settled all difficulties and the tracks were in, an excursion over the completed portions of the two roads was arranged for November 23, 1890.

The excursion train left Tacoma at 6:55 A. M. but it was not until 6 P. M. that the thunder of cannon announced the arrival of the excursionists at Anacortes. A reporter of the event stated that the crowd was led through the gaily decorated streets to, "A magnificent banquet spread in the large warehouse of the Oregon Improvement Company. Afterward," he said, "came speechmaking, and wit, wine, and song were intermingled in highly satisfactory proportions for several hours."

The Seattle Northern was completed to Hamilton in 1891. Interest in the Skagit Passes having faded with the selection of Stevens Pass by the Great Northern, road building was discontinued for a decade. In 1900 after the Great Northern acquired the line, it was extended to Sauk and the next year to Rockport, to serve lumbering, mining and power interests.

SEATTLE MONTANA RAILWAY COMPANY

Articles of incorporation for the Seattle Montana Railway Company, a subsidiary of the Great Northern, were filed in Seattle on March 7, 1890. This line was intended, not only to complete Hill's coast system, but to provide ingress to coast towns for the overland line then building in Montana. Seattle granted franchises, whereupon surveyors pushed rapidly northward that year toward a junction with the Fairhaven and Southern and with the Seattle and Northern.

GREAT NORTHERN COAST LINE COMPLETED

The New Westminster and Southern and the Fairhaven and Southern, passed to the control of the Great Northern Railway Company during the year 1891. Including the trackage of the Seattle and Montana from Burlington to Seattle, the Great Northern shore line was complete.

Train service, from St. Paul over the Canadian Pacific via Winnipeg and New Westminster, was established as far as Whatcom in October, 1891. At the latter point passengers for the south were transferred to the Steamer *Premier.**

JAMES J. HILL (1838—1916)

To James J. Hill, great financier and greatest railroad builder of them all, must go much of the credit for the transportation, agricultural, and industrial development of the Northwest. Without Federal land grants or bonuses which made a scandal of earlier railroad building, he created a rail principality over which he ruled beneficently. His was a system noted for easy grades, wide curves and low operating costs. Soundly financed at low interest rates, he was able to plow earnings into road improvements when rivals were going bankrupt.

Hill was distinguished from the Wall street railroad man by his closeness to the people he served. Their problems and welfare were his. In a day before farm advisers were known, the Jim Hill roads became the farm ad-

---

*The screw propeller steamer, the *Premier,* came around the Horn from the Hudson river to enter the Puget Sound run at the height of the Fairhaven boom. George H. Bacon in his BOOMING AND PANIC-ING ON PUGET SOUND, remembers her chiefly because of her three chord whistle, starting at "sol," dropping to "mi" thence to a beautiful rumbling bass "do." Bacon describes the steamer as a "palace of luxury inside," all seats and chairs being cushioned in a heavy green plush, while the central stack was circled by a cushioned bench on which eight or ten men customarily slept, head to toes.

LEFT—Whatcom, Washington Territory, 1883, in foreground. Court House on E street, left foreground was the first brick building in the Territory in 1858. Tide water flowed up to the foundation of this structure, but has receded several blocks now—1951. Phelps & Van Wyck building—left center—on C street and Thirteenth (West Holly). Sehome is in the distance. The little Sehome school house is near the shore line, right center. There is no connection with Sehome across the water.

UPPER RIGHT—The old brick building on E street in 1950, showing the street regrade, and the change in the shape of the roof.—Photo by author.

LOWER RIGHT—Rear of the old brick building in 1950, showing the back doors on the ground floor, making entrance to the structure easier for those coming down Division and D streets. These are the rushes and reeds in which the red-winged black bird makes his home.— Picture by author.

visers of the Northwest, seeking to encourage the use of, and to provide for, better seed, better livestock and improved farm methods.

James J. Hill was born at Guelph, Ontario, September 16, 1838. He settled in St. Paul in 1856 where he became shipping clerk for J. W. Bass & Company, agents of the Dubuque and St. Paul Packet Company. Later he founded the warehouse of Hill, Griggs and Company and in 1870 organized the Red River Transportation Company.

Sir George Stevens and Sir Donald A. Smith furnished the capital for the acquisition of the bankrupt St. Paul and Pacific Railroad with its 496 miles of track. Reorganized as the St. Paul, Minneapolis and Manitoba Railway Company, the road extended its lines over Minnesota, North Dakota, and a portion of Southern Manitoba.

Hill also had become a director of the Canadian Pacific Railroad and as such urged the development of the prairie provinces, rather than the building of the overland route. The latter was needed to tie British Columbia to the rest of the Dominion, hence the overland road was pushed. Hill resigned.

Next, the Empire Builder visioned branch lines serving all the Border country, with roads through the Spokane and Big Bend wheat-fields. All holdings were concentrated in the Great Northern Railway Company, and the march to Puget Sound was begun.

Recording the westward progress of the Great Northern Railway, the FAIRHAVEN WEEKLY WORLD of December 18, 1890, reported that the road was expected to reach the Rockies by Christmas; and that supplies were concentrated in the Flathead Valley for westward extensions.

John F. Stevens,* noted engineer, had discovered Marias Pass across the Rocky Mountains in December, 1889. Hill assigned to him the Cascade problem. After examining the Skagit County passes he selected one farther south, shown him by an Indian, and which now bears his name.

Stevens Pass was first crossed by a switchback. This was not abandoned

---

*John F. Stevens, April 25, 1853 - January 2, 1943. At Marias Pass, Montana, stands a heroic statue of John F. Stevens who in 1889, despite superstitious Blackfeet Indians, located this pass through the Rocky Mountains. Stevens Pass, in the Cascades on the route of the Great Northern Railway, named for its discoverer, was located a year later. Stevens, appointed by President Theodore Roosevelt 1905-07, preceded General George W. Goethals as chief engineer of the Panama Canal.

UPPER—Steamer "Mikado." Eighty foot wood-burner used by the owners, Jenkins and Alton, as a ferry boat on the Fairhaven-Whatcom run in the early nineties. This with the "Success" made a fortune for the owners. Later Captain George A. Jenkins removed the "Mikado" to Lake Whatcom and still later she had a profitable Everett-Snohomish run.—Photo by E. A. Hegg.

LOWER—A street car of the Fairhaven and New Whatcom Electric line in 1892.

until 1900. The route west followed the Skykomish and Snohomish Rivers to Lowell, Washington, which was reached January 6, 1893. That same year the Great Northern began its tunnel under the City of Everett, Washington, to tide water. Franchises secured in the name of the Seattle and Montana Railway Company gave the road access to Seattle. On Elliott Bay, the Great Northern constructed its terminal facilities including the docks for Hill's oriental fleet.

On June 18, 1893, the first Great Northern Overland Train left Seattle. Four days later the first westbound sleeper arrived. Promptly the road cut passenger rates to St. Paul to thirty-five dollars.

More than a decade after the rails arrived at Bellingham Bay or 1902 the Great Northern Railway replaced the Happy Valley-Chuckanut Valley route to the south with a shore road—the Chuckanut Cut-Off. This line about nineteen miles long, was one of heavy rock and tunnel work costing an estimated one million and a half dollars. For the right-of-way into Fairhaven, land owners appear to have asked fabulous prices. Jim Hill was convinced that he was being held up, even by old friends, and threatened to make Fairhaven a mere whistle stop on his road.

That same year the Great Northern abandoned the long and expensive trestle across Bellingham Bay and constructed the shore-trackage down Roeder Avenue—approximately on the one time right-of-way of the Bellingham Bay Railroad and Navigation Company. As part of the improvement, the Company erected a brick depot, at that time said to be the best on its line west of Spokane.

American Railway history is epitomized in the life of James J. Hill. A few short line railroads existed in the east at the time of his birth. His was an active part in the first phase, as the railroads, growing bolder, like mariners on uncharted seas, plunged westward into the wilderness.

And he was in the thick of the second phase when railway princelings, through politics, secret agreements, discriminatory rates and schedules, high financing and monopoly, sought to hold inviolate their exclusive railroad baronies.

Jim Hill lived to see the present phase: the end of railroad building, abandonment of unprofitable feeders, automotive competition, joint track usage, and regulation as a public utility.

Death came to the Empire Builder May 29, 1916.

BELLINGHAM BAY AND EASTERN RAILROAD

Primarily a coal road, intended to move fuel from the Blue Canyon mine on Lake Whatcom to Bellingham Bay, the Bellingham Bay and Eastern Railroad was incorporated in December, 1891. While the road was building, track rights were secured over the line of Fairhaven and New Whatcom Railway Company, a newly completed street railway. J. J. Donovan was given the task of building a line from Lake Whatcom to the street car tracks and another from a convenient point in New Whatcom to the Coal Company's bunkers.

The Great Northern objected violently to the overhead crossing of its line by the track to the bunkers. Old papers of May, 1892, tell of a battle that raged for several hours between rival crews; with the Great Northern spotting engines and trains at the focal point while Donovan's crew rushed their timbers across at the bridge abutments. In the end special officers and police quieted the row. By the first of July, coal trains were rolling over the joint street car-railroad trackage, to the newly completed bunkers.

With the failure of the Blue Canyon mine as a coal producer, Peter Larson, J. H. Bloedel, and J. J. Donovan operated the B. B. & E. as a logging road for a number of years. The line was completed from Bellingham to Wickersham in 1902. Both the Great Northern and the Northern Pacific were interested in the road, but, because Bloedel and Donovan felt their town would benefit by the entrance of a second transcontinental railway, the line was sold to the Northern Pacific on July 1, 1903.

NELSON A. BENNETT
October 14, 1893 — July 20, 1913

Nelson A. Bennett, the noted railroad builder and financier, so closely associated with the development of Bellingham Bay and of Tacoma, was born at Sutton, Canada, October 14, 1843. At the age of seventeen he moved to Orleans County, New York, then to Pennsylvania, where a few years later he had become an oil well contractor.

In 1867, Bennett moved west and engaged in freighting and mining. The year 1882 found him doing construction on the Northern Pacific Railroad under William Dunn. With the death of the latter he took over Dunn's contracts.

Bennett later appeared as contractor on the Northern Pacific, Pasco-Puget Sound division, but his greatest fame was achieved as builder of the tunnel at Stampede Pass. Nor was his courage ever put to a more severe test. Some of the equipment for the big bore had to be dragged forward a distance of 90 miles. Snow six to ten feet deep impeded on the heights. He was out some $125,000 before the first shot was fired.

In Roth's history, Bennett is described as "a man of strong physique, big broad shoulders, wide forehead, strong far-seeing eyes, and like most men of his day, he wore both beard and mustache. Roth adds that he was a man of large affairs and his own general manager.

The Skagit coal fields attracted Bennett and with him in 1888, or following after, came his tried and experienced engineers and associates: J. J. Donovan, E. M. Wilson, E. L. Cowgill, J. F. Wardner, George A. Black, T. W. Gillette, S. E. Larrabee, and C. X. Larrabee. Railroad organization and construction paralleled the coal field development, until the Bennett road became part of the Great Northern Railway system.

At that time the interests of Bennett included land developments in Portland, Tacoma, and Fairhaven; interests in steamboats, hotels, newspapers, banks, sawmills, and coal properties.

In speaking of the transfer of the Fairhaven and Southern Railroad to the Great Northern, Bennett said afterward that he sold just in time. Not so with some of his other interests. The panic of 1893 stripped him of his fortune. He advanced cash and securities to his banks in New Whatcom and Tacoma but failed to save these institutions.

However, like Jay Cooke who went down in the panic of 1873, Bennett made a comeback to a new fortune. On the way up he built the Palmer Cut-off for the Northern Pacific. Nearing his seventieth birthday, the old fighter died July 20, 1913, while he was driving the Northern Pacific Point Defiance tunnel in Tacoma. The tunnel, then almost finished, was completed by his wife.

JOHN JOSEPH DONOVAN
September 8, 1858 — January 27, 1936

For more than fifty years, almost from the day he finished school to become a rodman on the Northern Pacific Railroad survey in Montana, J. J. Donovan played a constant and vital part in the civic and industrial development of the Northwest. His name long was a household word. School boys spoke of him familiarly as "J. J.," just as they spoke of "Teddy" (Roosevelt) the Rough Rider—and for the same reason—his activities, his power and personality captured their imagination.

John Joseph Donovan was born at Rumney, New Hampshire, September 8, 1858. At the age of nineteen he graduated from the New Hampshire State Normal school and thereafter taught school for three years. With his earnings, together with those paid him as janitor and waiter he put himself through the Worcester Polytechnic Institute. In 1882 he graduated at the head of his class and immediately went to work for the Northern Pacific in Montana. Next, he ran surveys, often through deep snows, for the Stampede Pass Switchback and Tunnel; he was chief engineer of the

Cascade division until its completion in June, 1887; then moved to Montana again as construction engineer for some of the Northern Pacific's branch lines.

In April, 1888, Donovan returned to New England long enough to marry Clara Isabel Nichols. The couple at first made their residence at Tacoma. As soon as a house could be erected in the raw boom town of Fairhaven, then lacking in streets, stores or a passable road to Sehome, the couple moved north.

At Fairhaven, Donovan was chief engineer for Nelson A. Bennett's coal mine, railroad, and townsite projects. Finishing his railroad work under Bennett, he became engineer for the Blue Canyon Coal Company, the Bellingham Bay and Eastern Railroad, and for the State Harbor Line Commission. Donovan, in 1898, became a partner with Peter Larson and J. H. Bloedel in the Lake Whatcom Logging Company. That same year he was appointed Chief Engineer and General Superintendent of the Bellingham Bay and British Columbia Railroad.

He resigned this position in 1906, to devote his time to logging and logging-roads of the Lake Whatcom Logging Company. On this subject he became a recognized authority. The Lake Whatcom Logging Company, in 1913, merged with the Larson Lumber Company and the Cargo Mill to form the Bloedel Donovan Lumber Mills. "J. J." was vice president and engineer of this multi-million dollar enterprise.

One of the unfulfilled ambitions of the man was the construction of a railroad from Bellingham over the Cascades. When he took over the management of the B. B. & B. C. in 1898, his surveys and the 1900-'01 railroad construction up the Nooksack River had this in view as one objective. Later in 1913, when John N. Donovan graduated from his father's alma mater, Worcester Polytechnic Institute, J. J. Donovan was there also to receive a delayed civil engineering degree. His thesis: "Proposed Railroad from Bellingham to Spokane."

Physically J. J. Donovan was a man of medium stature, about five feet eight inches in height. Because of his vigor and strong frame he gave the impression of being a larger man.

Friends said that he stood out in most gatherings because of his virility, his Irish wit, and kindly expression. All agree his interest in people was real. Habitually he welcomed the newcomers; sought to make them at home, took many of them on trips through the area; a sort of unofficial welcoming committee "serving a need," as one friend has sadly commented, "that has not been so adequately filled since 'J. J.'s' passing."

This interest is manifested in the numerous boards, commissions, committees on which he served—local, state and national, in extent including such early ones as the State Board of Road Commissions, 1894.

Engineering, mining, railroading, lumbering, all his activities were conducted south of the Border. When his partner J. H. Bloedel in 1911, invited him to join in organizing a British Columbia lumber concern, Donovan stated he preferred to keep his interests at home. J. J. Donovan died January 27, 1936.

JOHN J. CRYDERMAN
March 29, 1860

No civil engineer ran lines and levels for more early north Puget Sound railroads than did John J. Cryderman. Born in Vallonia, Indiana, March 29, 1860, Cryderman as a young men followed engineering and railroad construction until caught by the Washington Territory fever. From Kansas he came west in December 1887, via the Northern Pacific Railroad.

Through the years 1888 and 1889, Cryderman worked for Canfield's Bellingham Bay Railroad and Navigation Company; for Bennett's Fairhaven and Southern Railroad Company; and for the Oregon Improvement Company's road, the Seattle and Northern Railway Company; all later included in the Great Northern Railway Company's system.

At Anacortes, Cryderman and his partner, L. C. Roberts, surveyed the townsite, owned by the Oregon Improvement Company. They finished in December, 1889. After a six weeks' absence Cryderman returned to find that the town had grown meantime from thirty persons to between 2,000 and 3,000.

Money was appropriated in 1893 for the survey of a wagon road from Glacier across the mountains to Marcus on the Columbia River; the purpose, cattle drives from Eastern Washington to Puget Sound markets. Cryderman was appointed survey member of the Commission named to pass on the road. J. J. Donovan became a member of the commission. It was found that there was no grass on the proposed route; that cattle would starve on the long overland drive, hence the project was dropped as impractical, and the unused money was returned to the State treasury. Much criticism followed, both from project boosters and from politicians who could not understand the return of any state money once it was appropriated.

When the Bellingham Bay and British Columbia Railroad Company extended its line up the North Fork of the Nooksack in 1900-'01, Cryderman was one of the location and construction engineers. This was before the advent of great earth moving machinery, hence the engineers had many little subcontractors to check. A half dozen men with wheelbarrows would be moving earth from a barrow pit to a low fill. Nearby a crew with horses and scrapers would be scratching through an earth ridge. Farther along an outfit with hand drills and little hand propelled dump cars would be working in a rock cut.

At the time, both President Cornwall and his engineer, J. J. Donovan, were interested in pushing the line to Spokane. Cryderman made surveys through Hannegan and Whatcom passes to Bridgeport on the Columbia River. Heavy costs and limited financing prevented the overland extension.

When the Bellingham Bay and Eastern Railroad was built around Lake Whatcom to its connection with the Northern Pacific, Cryderman was the engineer; then for some time he served in the same capacity with the State Land Office in Olympia. Also he constructed a number of miles of the City of Seattle railroad extension up the Skagit Valley to the Power-plant at Newhalem.

In later years the aged engineer became interested in oyster culture on the tide flats near Blanchard.

John J. Cryderman, at Lynden, Washington, on October 25, 1894, married Dora May Wellman, early Fairhaven school teacher. Mrs. Cryderman died November 23, 1933.

CHARLES XAVIER LARRABEE
November 19, 1843 — September 16, 1914

C. X. Larrabee whose name is associated with the development of three states, Montana, Oregon, and Washington, became in 1889 associated with Nelson Bennett in the Fairhaven Land Company, the Fairhaven and Southern Railroad Company, as well as in banking, milling, mining and other interests.

Charles Xavier Larrabee was born at Portville, New York, November 19, 1843. The family later moved to Wisconsin, whence young Larrabee, in 1875, followed an older brother to Montana. At Butte City he acquired a fortune in connection with the development of the Anaconda and St. Lawrence mines and the discovery and development of the Mountain View copper mine. Selling his mining interests in 1887, he invested heavily in Portland real estate.

As president of the Fairhaven Land Company, as vice-president and later president, and principal stockholder of the Fairhaven and Southern Railroad Company, which afterwards sold to the Great Northern Railway, he vitally affected the destiny of his adopted town.

Sixteen acres of Fairhaven Park were given jointly to the City by Charles Larrabee and Cyrus Gates of the Pacific Realty Company of which the former was president. Characteristic of the philanthrophy of the man was the donation of the $40,000 Y. W. C. A. building in the name of his wife, Frances Payne Larrabee and their daughter, Mary. This was shortly before his death on September 16, 1914. Larrabee State Park, Larrabee Avenue, and Larrabee Public School perpetuate his name.

. . .

To the pioneer who recalls the first locomotive whistle, shrilling through the forested aisles of the Northwest, the following paragraph from Mrs. Nellie L. McClung's CLEARING IN THE WEST will evoke nostalgic memories:

"When I am old I want to live near the railway where I can hear the long whistle of trains trumpeting through the night, hear them pounding the rails, screaming out signals and ringing their bells. By day I'll see them hauling their heavy loads, with their smoke plumes darkening and thinning, coming back over their shoulders as they sweep across the plain. With their force and strength, their minds set upon the far country, they will vitalize me again and fill me with the joy of living. And in my mind I will go with them as far as I can. Then, one night when I am old and tired I shall not come back, and friends will say, 'Wasn't it a nice way to go?' "

LOCAL NORTH COAST RAILROAD CONSTRUCTION

GREAT NORTHERN RAILWAY COMPANY
(Fraser River-Seattle Coast Line)

> Constructed by:
New Westminster and Southern Railway Company
Bellingham Bay Railroad and Navigation Company
Fairhaven and Southern Railroad Company
Seattle and Montana Railway Company

GREAT NORTHERN RAILWAY COMPANY
(Anacortes-Rockport Line) (Skagit County)

> Constructed by:
Seattle and Northern Railway Company

NORTHERN PACIFIC RAILWAY COMPANY
(Seattle-Sedro-Woolley-Sumas Line)

> Constructed by:
Seattle Lake Shore and Eastern Railway Company
Seattle and West Coast Railway Company

NORTHERN PACIFIC RAILWAY COMPANY
(Bellingham-Wickersham Line)

> Constructed by:
Bellingham Bay and Eastern Railroad Company

CHICAGO, MILWAUKEE ST. PAUL AND PACIFIC RAILROAD COMPANY
(Bellingham-Sumas-Glacier Line)

> Constructed by:
Bellingham Bay and British Columbia Railroad Company

OVERLAND ROUTES OF THE NORTHWEST

(Completion Dates)

Northern Pacific-Oregon Railroad and Navigation Company joint line to Portland	1883
Canadian Pacific Railway	1885
Northern Pacific Line to Tacoma	1887
Great Northern Railway	1893
Chicago, Milwaukee and St. Paul	1909
Canadian Northern Railway	1915

Chapter XXVIII.

THE OLD BRICK BUILDING

A JAUNTY RED-WINGED BLACKBIRD does sentry duty today at the rear of the oldest brick building in the State of Washington. This is in Bellingham, two blocks west of the sewer reduction plant on Whatcom Creek—past the sandspit and the old Division Street business district, where the town of Whatcom had its beginnings in the early '50's. The tired old building, drousing in an atmosphere of decay, faces Northwest on E Street just above Holly, where it was erected by T. G. Richards & Company in 1858, during the Fraser River Gold Rush.

The bricks used in the two-story structure were manufactured in Philadelphia and shipped around the Horn. In San Francisco the merchant transhipped these north, together with iron and glass, hardware and equipment, groceries and clothing required for the prospective establishment.

The store, sturdily erect on the beach line, once brazenly flaunted its brick-red walls—raw as the new town, brazen as the men and women stampeders who crowded its doors. Today (1951), because of a change in sidewalk level, the structure appears to crouch on its knees close to the bluff, awaiting the inevitable dissolution.

At one time the waves of the Bay, with curving white teeth, slashed at its foundations, so that bulkheads were required. (Opposite page 262). Now the baffled waves have retired several blocks. A bit of the old tide-flat, storm flooded and junk strewn, extends from E and West Holly back of this one-time store and courthouse. Nature is trying to hide decay with cattails and willows; and here the red-winged blackbird makes his home.

When the town was new and the NORTHERN LIGHT was published across the street in 1858, a high bridge at Astor and F Streets, on the Military Road from Fort Bellingham, spanned "Chinook Ravine" as Editor Bausman called it. The Road and Bridge have vanished; the very ravine gone—filled, as are other gullies and draws with the waste of a city—fiber and wood, brick and stone, plastic and plaster, porcelain and glass, together with various cunningly fashioned metals of all sorts—the rape of a continent. Through the gullies, also at the foot of the bluff; and on the waste dump at the mouth of Whatcom Creek, the rubbish grows—a city's offscourings that archeologists two thousand years hence will classify as deriving from a city—not of the stone age, not of the bronze age, the iron age, nor yet of the steel age, perhaps, but certainly from an Age of Waste.

Contemporaries of the brick building in the Division Street business area were destroyed in the fire of 1885. Thereafter the Thirteenth or West Holly district enjoyed a boom. In the '90's a wide planked viaduct on C Street led up from Holly to Dupont. (Opposite page 214). On D Street, a steep plank road was bordered with high sidewalks, down which tripped the "fancy ladies" on the rim of the bluff. West Holly, on both sides, was lined almost solidly from the Creek to G Street with business houses—stores, saloons, restaurants, rooming-houses and offices; the majority on piling with the tides sloshing beneath. Most of these contemporaries also have succumbed to age, and vanished.

Concerning the beginnings of the brick building the NORTHERN LIGHT on July 24, 1858 (4th issue) reported:

"T. G. Richards & Company are clearing ground for the erection of a two-story brick store and banking house.

On August 28, 1858, the paper stated:

"NEARLY FINISHED—The fine two-story fire-proof brick building of T. G. Richards & Company on E Street is so far completed as to require only a few finishing touches to render it fit for occupancy, and will be inaugurated by the reception of a stock of groceries and provisions in a few days.

The same issue carried this advertisement:

"T. G. Richards & Company

> Having completed their new fire-proof
> Brick Warehouse, are now prepared to carry on a
> > Storage and Commission Business
>
> Cash advances made on consignments and goods stored in our
> > Warehouse.

Whatcom, Washington Territory.   August 28, 1858."

County records show that Charles E. Richards bought a one-third interest in the property on October 12, 1858, and that on January 12, 1859, he sold half of this interest to John G. Hyatt for $1,000.

Richards and Hyatt continued their mercantile business until May 7, 1863, when C. E. Richards sold their brick building to Whatcom County for a court house. The deed* filed next day, was mislaid and did not reappear until June, 1871. Originally T. G. Richards & Company expended

---

*When Whatcom County was organized in 1854, the R. V. Peabody cabin at the mouth of Whatcom Creek was designated as the courthouse. Later a cheap wooden building was erected for a courthouse on the Square—E to F and Clinton to Dupont Streets on Peabody hill. When this building was flattened in a wind storm, county offices scattered to various residences, and some of the records appear to have been lost at this time.

$8,000 in erecting their store. C. E. Richards disposed of the property to the county for $2,000 payable in county warrants. These he sold to William Moody at a great discount.

When the second newspaper of the Northwest, the BELLINGHAM BAY MAIL made its appearance in 1873, it found quarters in the courthouse. James Power, the publisher, reported later: "There was ample room for my newspaper and county business too, including the jail. I used to work an occasional prisoner on the press . . ." Doctor A. W. Thornton, who arrived from San Franicsco in 1877, found room for his drug store in a corner of the first floor.

The treasurer's safe frequently held more than county funds. Citizens with money habitually labeled a bag and left it with the treasurer, a practice that continued even after the first Bank of Whatcom was established in 1883.

Over the years the brick building required many repairs and alterations. In 1874, Sheriff Upson and T. H. Kruse were ordered by the commissioners to erect a break-water to protect the foundation from the tides. More permanent repairs were required in 1883, when the construction of five new cells and a fire-proof vault, was authorized.

On the vacant southwest corner of West Holly and C Streets, rising from the tideflat below to street level, there stands today—1951—a stone box 12 by 12 by 18 feet in dimension, filled with broken rock and earth, that once was the foundation of a bank vault. The two story and basement bank building completed on this site November, 1884, at a cost of $6,500 by L. C. Phelps and A. Van Wyck—M. C. Latta builder—was considered one of the finest on Puget Sound. It housed the bank, postoffice, Purdy's Opera House and various offices.

Soon after the bank was opened for business, the new-fangled time clock regulating the vault door failed to work. The banker consulted the sheriff, who reported: "I have a prisoner up in the brick building that I haven't been able to keep locked in. He picks the locks and goes in and out as he pleases. I'll go up to the jail and bring him down—if he's still in."

The prisoner, after inspecting the lock admitted he could open it, but insisted he work without spectators. The worried banker perforce agreed, and soon the prisoner had the vault door opened. Next morning the sheriff found his prisoner missing. At the same time the banker reported, so the story goes, that when the vault was opened, an employe found a note therein reading: "I have taken $7.50 to pay me for the work I did yesterday." Whatcom County never saw the lock-picker again.

Because the brick courthouse was regarded as unsafe for large audiences, the 1885 session of the district court was held in the Purdy Opera House of the Phelps, Van Wyck building. Nevertheless the brick structure served as a courthouse and jail until a new courthouse on G Street was completed in 1891.

Various tenants have occupied the brick building over the years. In 1906 it became the home of the Grand Army of the Republic, after the county deeded it to John Edens and others as trustees for that organization. At one time the Junior Order of United American Mechanics owned the property. In 1947, it was sold to The Security Benefit Association, Bellingham Council No. 2414, and in 1950 to a Bellingham church group.

Through the years the structure has been changed somewhat in appearance. The flat roof has been replaced by a gabled one. A coat of stucco covers and preserves the brick walls. The iron shutters are gone. The sidewalk level has been raised to the second story. The wall on the Holly Street side shows scars of former windows, an outside stairway and a door. (Opposite page 262).

Rain drives in from the southwest and the old building patiently humps its shoulders to the storm. The tempest passes, and like an old man busied with his memories, the fading structure seems to drouse in the sun. The blackbird springs his rattle and bravely flashes his red shoulders. A few soft liquid notes follow. In the willows, his lady in rusty, demure black, answers timidly. In her keeping is the future, new life, regeneration. The old building seemingly slumps lower amid the decay—waiting. Death and life—life and death—so the wheel turns.

Chapter XXIX.

AND THEN THERE WAS ONE

FROM THE EARLIEST DAYS civic leaders and
newspaper men urged that the small communities on Bellingham Bay be
consolidated into one city. William Bausman, editor of the first paper, the
NORTHERN LIGHT, as early as 1858 advocated the dropping of rivalries and
the union of the budding towns. At that time there were three settlements:
Whatcom, Sehome, and Pattle's Point, the latter to become in turn, Unionville, and then Bellingham, before being absorbed in 1890 by the incorporated
town of Fairhaven.

As is the fate of most "Do-Gooders" Bausman's words, as well as the
advice of later editors, went unheeded. Rivalries continued to the detriment
of all—continued for forty-five years after Bausman, until the four original
towns of Whatcom, Sehome, Bellingham, and Fairhaven, after several
partial consolidations, became parts of one city, Bellingham.

The charts below give the historic dates in each settlement's progress
toward the final union:

WHATCOM

Located on Roeder's and Peabody's claims

Settled	December 15, 1852
Platted by Alonzo M. Poe, plat filed	July 24, 1858
Incorporated	November 25, 1883
Voted to unite with New Whatcom (Sehome)	December 29, 1890
Consolidated with New Whatcom and became the "City of New Whatcom"	February 16, 1891
Name changed to "Whatcom" by an act of the State Legislature	February 19, 1901
Voted to consolidate with Fairhaven	October 27, 1903
City of Bellingham's new charter adopted	July 12, 1904

SEHOME

Located on claims of Edmund C. Fitzhugh and Charles C. Vail

Settled—Fitzhugh's claim filed_____June 10, 1854
    Vail's claim filed_____October 2, 1855

Platted by W. W. DeLacy, plat filed_____May 8, 1858

Replatted by E. C. Prather

Plat filed by P. B. Cornwall, President of the Bellingham
  Bay Improvement Company as "New Whatcom"_____August 31, 1883

Incorporated as Town of Sehome_____July 17, 1888

Reincorporated under the name of New Whatcom_____May 8, 1890

Consolidated with Whatcom to form New Whatcom_____February 16, 1891

Name changed to "Whatcom" by an act of the
  State Legislature_____February 19, 1901

Voted to consolidate with Fairhaven_____October 27, 1903

City of Bellingham's new charter adopted_____July 12, 1904

OLD BELLINGHAM

Located on parts of William Pattle's and Morrison's claims

Settled _____January, 1853

Plat dedicated and filed for record by A. A. Denny,
  David Phillips, and Dexter Horton of Seattle_____May 16, 1871

Town of Bellingham, (new Plat), comprising William Pattle's
  and Morrison's claims
Dedicated by Erastus Bartlett and Edward Eldridge

Filed for record_____April 24, 1883

Townsite purchased by Nelson Bennett_____1888

Incorporated with Fairhaven_____May 6, 1890

FAIRHAVEN

Located on John Thomas' claim; later that of Daniel J. Harris

Settled _____January, 1853

Plat filed by Dan Harris_____January 2, 1883

Incorporated _____May 6, 1890

Voted to consolidate with Whatcom_____October 27, 1903

Became City of Bellingham, new charter adopted_____July 12, 1904

"Bellingham" became City of First Class, and held its official
  meeting of new officers_____July 29, 1904

For years the rival towns were separated physically as well as spiritually. In 1889, after long agitation construction was begun on a viaduct connecting Whatcom's Thirteenth Street with Sehome's Holly Street. The Nelson Bennett interests objected unless a long draw span be provided at Whatcom creek to permit passage of large vessels to their newly acquired Colony sawmill. When the city fathers refused this proposition, Manager E. L. Cowgill of the Bennett mill had a large boom of logs towed across Thirteenth Street, where he placed a gang of his men as guards. At once the city council ordered Marshal Stimson to swear in deputies and remove the obstruction by force, if necessary. Fifty business men were deputized and within two hours the logs were out of way and the pile drivers were at work joining the principal business streets of the two towns in one thoroughfare.

Between Sehome and Fairhaven the road was as sketchy and rough as the back country roads. Citizens of the two towns traveled back and forth in the Steamer *Mikado* at ten cents per head. (Opposite page 263). During boom days street car systems were chartered and work begun. Under date of November 25, 1890, the BELLINGHAM BAY EXPRESS reported:

"Track laying has commenced at the Fairhaven boundary for the Whatcom and New Whatcom electric street railway. Mr. Cryderman, the engineer, says the road will be in operation by the first of January."

Horse drawn cars began operating March 28, 1891, on the Bellingham Bay Electric Railway Company system. Electric cars were placed on the run in June of the same year. The rails used on this road, which extended to the northwest city limits, were spiked to the plank roads.

In Fairhaven the electric cars of the Fairhaven Street Railway Company were running by October 19, 1891. However, it was necessary to walk or ride by carriage from the end of the Fairhaven trackage to the end of the Whatcom line.

In the meantime, July, 1891, the Lake Whatcom Electric Railway Company was organized to provide service to Lake Whatcom.

Before this line was completed or in September, the concern consolidated with the Fairhaven system to form the Fairhaven and New Whatcom Railway Company. (Opposite page 263). The tracks were connected February 15, 1892. During the same year, through sale and lease, all systems were consolidated, thus providing unified service. The fare from New Whatcom to Fairhaven was fixed at five cents, so reducing the patronage of the *Mikado*, which had cleared as much as $15,000 during one of the boom years; that she was removed to Lake Whatcom.

OPPOSITE—Bellingham Bay in 1890, showing the four towns, Whatcom, Sehome, Bellingham and Fairhaven.—Map drawn by author.

LANDS OF THE

J. Bennett

E. Eldridge
Donation Claim

County Road.

North West diagonal Road

Meridian

WHATCOM

BROADWAY

B.B. & B.C. R.R. Co.

B.B. & B.C. R.R. Co.

CENTRAL
WHATCOM

Whatcom Creek

HOLLY ST.

SEHOME

YORK
ADD.

Whatcom Wharf

Sehome Wharf

ELK ST.

ELDRIDGE &
BARTLETT ADD.

Coal
Bunkers

BELLINGHAM

BAY

BELLINGHAM

FRONT ST.

BELLINGHAM

Bellingham
Wharf

LYSLE'S
1ST.

Dead Man's
Point
Fairhaven
Wharf
Poe's
Point

FAIRHAVEN

Padden Creek

Graveyard
Point

Sixteenth Street Extension

Proposed Plank Road

LAKE
PADDEN

SOUTH FAIRHAVEN

CHUCKANUT

BAY

Sehome was reincorporated as New Whatcom, May 8, 1890. Less than a year later or on February 16, 1891, Whatcom and New Whatcom were united under the name of New Whatcom. Ten years later by act of the legislature the name of the combined town on February 19, 1901, once more became Whatcom.

In the meantime the towns of Whatcom and Fairhaven had become more closely united physically by the street car system, by improved roads, and by the clearing of the lands between the two municipalities; and it became evident to the most partisan of citizens that a union of Whatcom and Fairhaven would give improved public service at reduced costs. By a majority vote in each town the electors approved the union of the municipalities, October 27, 1903, the compromise name of Bellingham being adopted.

Both Old Whatcom and Fairhaven had numbered streets, which the former agreed to relinquish. Thus the northwest-southeast streets through "Old Town" to Broadway were renamed. Thirteenth—the main street—became West Holly.

Following the election, the citizens of Fairhaven and Whatcom thereupon joined in a mass meeting held at Commercial Point to celebrate their new status as citizens of Bellingham, which by the union—at that time—became the fourth largest municipality of the State.

UPPER—Eight oxen pulling a wagon load of logs on wide rimmed wheels, as the inroads began on the forest primeval.

LOWER—A ten horse team pulling a large log over a skid road. At the left is a typical bunkhouse while at the right is one of the early wood-burning donkey engines, which have long since vanished.—Photo courtesy of Mrs. Minnie Hagler Huston.

Chapter XXX.

FINALE

GONE ARE THE FIRST HUNDRED YEARS since
the Migration; and rapid have been the changes in the last half century.
Prairie schooner, pack horse, canoe have vanished before rails, concrete,
and wings. The last merchantman sail has been forgotten.

Great stumps that dotted the landscape fifty years ago are a memory
to the present farmer who plowed among them as a boy. Old world hus-
bandmen have aided in the great dairy industry and the production of
world famous flower bulbs.

Rutted roads have given way in turn to plank roads, gravel, and
concrete.

The long line of yoked oxen that once dragged great logs on skid-roads
greased with dogfish oil, have yielded to mechanical marvels that twirl
giant trunks on high lines across mountain canyons enroute to mills just
as modern.

The little shingle mill that fifty years ago screamed at every crossroads
is gone. So are the local sawmills. But soil conservation and forest restoration move on apace to ensure continuation of land and forest products.

The great traps that once threatened the existence of the salmon hordes
have been replaced by saner methods of fishing which will ensure the per-
petuation of this resource.

Schools have grown, as was to be expected, since the establishment of
that first Normal school at the turn of the century, all part of the American
heritage evidenced by that first little school house on the shores of the Bay,
so long ago.

More and more through the past fifty years has our regard grown for
the friends above the 49th parallel, who have stood shoulder to shoulder
with us through two world wars and whom we proudly hail as, "Neighbor."

What of the next hundred years? Who will write that history? A broad
sketch book and facile pen will be needed. Great have been the changes
of the last hundred years, greater perhaps than all those before, back to
the time when the Mediterranean was a Roman lake, but they will seem
meager compared to changes the next historian must record.

The Great Migration has become prophetic now. All the world in effect faces the Pacific—Millpond?—Cockpit? Down over the curve of the earth lie the teeming millions of the Indies, China—Mass Man on the move. Farther North, through the frost fogs, is seen the portentous shape, the covetous scowl, of "The Bear that walks like a man."

The children of this Fourth Corner of the land face the future with assurance, confident that when the history of the next centennium is written it will show that they have carried forward the torch of American liberty, as effectively, as bravely, as did their courageous ancestors, who dared the terrors of the great rivers, plains, mountains, deserts, and hostile peoples, so long ago.

THE PIONEERS OF THE WEST

"Would God that we, their children, were as they—
Great-souled, brave-hearted, and of dauntless will!
Ready to dare, responsive to the still,
Compelling voice that called them night and day
From that far West, where sleeping Greatness lay
Biding her time. Would God we knew the thrill
That exquisitely tormented them, until
They stood up strong and resolute to obey!

God, make us like them, worthy of them; shake
Our souls with great desires; our dull eyes set
On some high star whose quenchless light will wake
Us from our dreams, and guide us from this fen
Of selfish ease won by our fathers' sweat.
Oh, lift us up—the West has need of Men!"

—ELLA HIGGINSON.

BIBLIOGRAPHY

BANCROFT, H. H. *History of the Northwest.* History Company Publishers, San Francisco, 1886.

BINNES, ARCHIE. *Northwest Gateway.* Doubleday, Doran & Co., Inc., Garden City, New York. 1941.

BOWDEN, ANGIE BURT. *Early Schools of Washington Territory.* Lowman and Hanford Company, Seattle, 1935.

Building a State, Washington, 1889-1939. Washington State Historical Society Publications, Volume III. 1940.

CLARK, DONALD H. *18 Men and a Horse.* The Metropolitan Press, Seattle, 1949.

CORNWALL, BRUCE. *Life Sketch of Pierre Barlow Cornwall.* The Stanley-Taylor Co., San Francisco—1906—publication.

Dictionary of American Biography, Volumes VIII and XIV. Charles Scribner's Sons, New York. 1932.

FULLER, GEORGE W. *A History of the Pacific Northwest.* Alfred A. Knopf, New York. 1931.

HOWAY, F. W. AND SCHOLEFIELD, E. O. S., *British Columbia.* S. J. Clarke Publishing Company, Chicago, Illinois. 1914.

HOWAY, SAGE AND ANGUS. *British Columbia and the United States.* Edited by H. F. Angus, Toronto, The Ryerson Press. 1942.

HUNT, HERBERT AND KAYLOR, FLOYD C. *Washington West of the Cascades.* Volumes I, II, and III. The S. J. Clarke Publishing Co. 1917.

JEFFCOTT, P. R. *Nooksack Tales and Trails.* Sedro-Woolley Courier-Times. 1949.

LAUT, AGNES C. *Conquest of the Great Northwest.* Volume II. The Outing Publishing Company, New York. 1908.

McCLUNG, NELLIE L. *Clearing in the West.* The Fleming H. Revell Company, New York. 1936.

MEANY, EDMUND S. *History of the State of Washington.* New York, Macmillan Company. 1910.

MEEKER, EZRA. *Pioneer Reminiscences of Puget Sound.* Lowman and Hanford, Seattle, Wash. 1905.

PICKETT, LASALLE CORBELL. *Pickett and His Men*. The Foote & Davis Company, Atlanta, Georgia. 1900.

POWERS, ALFRED. *History of Oregon Literature*. Metropolitan Press Publishers, Portland, Oregon. 1935.

PROSSER, COL. WILLIAM FARRAND. *A History of the Puget Sound Country*. Vol. I and II. The Lewis Publishing Co., New York, Chicago. 1903.

ROTH, LOTTIE ROEDER. *History of Whatcom County, Washington*. Volumes I and II. Pioneer Historical Publishing Co. 1926. Chicago, Seattle.

SNOWDEN, CLINTON A. *History of Washington*. Volumes I, II, III, IV. Printed by John C. Rankin Co., for the Century History Company. 1909.

SPLITSTONE, FRED JOHN. *Orcas, Gem of the San Juans*. The Courier-Times Press, Sedro-Woolley, Washington. 1946.

STERN, BERNHARD JOSEPH. *The Lummi Indians of Northwest Washington*. Columbia University Press. 1934.

The Railway Commission of Washington, First Annual Report. 1906. C. W. Gorham Public Printer, Olympia, Washington. 1907.

UNDERHILL, RUTH, PH. D. *Indians of the Pacific Northwest*. Sherman Institute Press, Riverside, California. 1945.

WARREN, SIDNEY. *The Farthest Frontier—The Pacific Northwest*. Macmillan Publishing Company, New York. 1949.

WATT, ROBERTA FRYE. *History of Seattle*. Lowman and Hanford, Seattle, Wash. 1932.

WHITING, J. S. *Forts of the State of Washington*. Privately published. 1946.

WRIGHT, E. W. *Marine History of the Pacific Northwest*. Lewis and Dryden. 1895.

Pacific Northwest Quarterly. Seattle, Washington. July, 1942.

The British Columbia Quarterly. Victoria, British Columbia. July, 1946.

ACKNOWLEDGMENTS

Special thanks go to the following:

The Bellingham Herald—for the privilege of searching their files for clippings and pictures, and the perusal of their bound volumes, particularly the NORTHERN LIGHT; and to W. C. Carver for his patience and great interest and assistance in the never-ending research through these issues.

The Bellingham Public Library—for the help rendered by the employes, who graciously aided in the search for data.

The County Superintendent's Office—to Miss Eklund for her kindness and the interest shown in searching the old records of Whatcom County's teachers and superintendents, and allowing the author to copy therefrom.

The Comptroller's Office in the Bellingham City Hall—to the employes therein for their bringing forth the old records of the first minutes of the towns of Sehome, New Whatcom, and Whatcom, and their assistance rendered.

The Whatcom County Abstract Office—to Mr. H. P. Weber and his office force who patiently searched the large volumes of old records and maps to assist in establishing the legend of the Donation Claims around Bellingham Bay, and the chain of ownership of other properties.

Professor L. A. Kibbe for his kindness and generosity in allowing research through his priceless library.

Professor Bruce Cheever has provided invaluable aid in the preparation of the chapter on the railroads, by permitting perusal of his thesis, THE DEVELOPMENT OF RAILROADS IN THE STATE OF WASHINGTON, 1860-1948.

The author's thanks are extended to:

Willard O. Youngs, Head of the Reference Department, Seattle Public Library;

Archie Shiels in supplying maps and data;

Jessie Knight Grisdale for perusal of the letters, etc., in the Jimmie Pickett trunk and the privilege of photographing the same;

Bruce A. McKelvie, Victoria, British Columbia, for generously supplying factual material on Governor James Douglas and Colonel I. N. Ebey;

Sheldon L. Glover, Supervisor, Division of Mines and Geology in the

State of Washington, Olympia, Washington, for his report on the mines around Bellingham Bay;

Mrs. Mabel Donovan Bacon for the privilege of copying from her Pioneer Grandfather's letters, and from the manuscript BOOMING AND PANICING ON PUGET SOUND written by her husband, George Bacon;

The Ferndale Record for material used from the same;

Colonel Christiancy Pickett for factual information in regard to his Grandfather, General George E. Pickett;

The Department of the Army, Adjutant General's Office, Washington, D. C., for their kindness in replying to inquiries concerning General George E. Pickett;

Mrs. Conner Reed, Clyde Banks, and Depue, Morgan & Company of Seattle, for their efforts in securing certain pictures.

And to the many others who loaned books, clippings and photographs.

Some of the people interviewed through the years:

Captain Henry Roeder, Mrs. Phoebe Judson, Lottie Roeder Roth, Charles Roth, R. E. Hawley, Henry Jukes, Alice Gilligan Jukes, Maud Edens Henderson, Annette Edens, Edna Roth Abbott, Margaret Gage Roth, Hallie Lysle Campbell, Harry Smith, Judge John Kellogg, Roland Gamwell, Cecil Morse, Gladys Lindse Morse, Will Pratt, John V. Padden, Archie Shiels, Peter D. Harkness, Belle McAlpine, Catherine Montgomery, Mabel Donovan Bacon, Eva Reasoner Siemons, Sadie McAllister Gibson, Cecil Stenger Rinehart, L. A. Kibbe, Howard Buswell, Mrs. Russ Coupe, Ben Coupe; Sadie Frank Miller and Willa Frank Farmer, granddaughters of Mr. and Mrs. Charles Roberts; Huldah Hofercamp Stephens, Minnie Hagler Huston, Grace Fouts Hughes, Clara Fouts Stenger, Edwin H. Bruns, Herbert Offerman, J. H. Pascoe, Bruce A. McKelvie, Professor Bruce Cheever, J. J. Cryderman, Chief August Martin, Mr. and Mrs. George Kinley, Mr. and Mrs. James Sullivan, and Mrs. Florence Boone.

INDEX